Encyclopedia
of
DEATH

Encyclopedia
of
DEATH

Edited by
Robert Kastenbaum
and
Beatrice Kastenbaum

ORYX PRESS
1989

The rare Arabian Oryx is believed to have inspired the myth of the unicorn. This desert antelope became virtually extinct in the early 1960s. At that time several groups of international conservationists arranged to have 9 animals sent to the Phoenix Zoo to be the nucleus of a captive breeding herd. Today the Oryx population is nearly 800, and over 400 have been returned to reserves in the Middle East.

Copyright © 1989 by The Oryx Press
2214 North Central at Encanto
Phoenix, Arizona 85004-1483

Published simultaneously in Canada

Printed and Bound in the United States of America

∞ The paper used in this publication meets the minimum requirements of American National Standard for Information Science—Permanence of Paper for Printed Library Materials, ANSI Z39.48, 1984.

Library of Congress Cataloging-in-Publication Data

Encyclopedia of death / by Robert Kastenbaum and Beatrice Kastenbaum.
      p.   cm.
   Bibliography: p.
   Includes index.
   ISBN 0-89774-263-X
   1. Death—Dictionaries. I. Kastenbaum, Robert. II. Kastenbaum, Beatrice.
HQ1073.E54 1989   89-9401
306.9′03—dc20   CIP

Contents

Introduction

Magical thinking and the written word share an ancient history. In spells, incantations, prayers, and curses, words were thought to possess or transmit awesome powers. For many centuries the written word was regarded as particularly impressive—in part because relatively few had mastered the arts of reading and writing. The written word eventually became associated with arcane and dangerous practices that were intended to influence the natural course of events. In one particularly relevant example, a daring but uneasy group of people would gather furtively in a graveyard to follow the expert instructions of their necromancer guide. (See **Necromancy**). A crucial phase of the endeavor involved drawing a magic circle, and reading incantations from a secret book. Here, indeed, magical thinking and the mysterious powers of the written word coalesced.

And what is the encyclopedia? A circle within which knowledge is en-closed, en-compassed, en-cycled. This rather staid and academic sounding term—"encyclopedia"—owes something to its long, partially obscured history. Traces of this distant heritage cling to the encyclopedic volumes of today. Everything one needs to know about a subject is within this or that encyclopedia, that magical circle.

In fact, simply burdening our shelves with an impressive set of frowning and forbidding volumes may itself seem to confer an aura of erudition upon the premises. However, the contented feeling that "all I need to know" is up there on the top shelf may not survive a determined perusal. In our experience, the "most completest" encyclopedia has more than occasionally failed to yield the information we sought. The "up to datest" may have already fallen behind and, perhaps most unsettling, vital issues and controversies may have been glazed over rather than illuminated by bland academic prose. Please make no mistake: we do relish our own household encyclopedias, whether general or specialized, rambling through many volumes or economically concise. But we have learned that the promise of a comprehensive and infallible magic circle of knowledge is unlikely to be fulfilled, regardless of the skill, effort, and devotion given to the enterprise.

You will find that the *Encyclopedia of Death* offers a broad range of information without claiming to be all-inclusive, and a variety of expert contributors without claiming infallibility. Furthermore, the editors and contributors have attempted to convey the questions as well as the answers, the controversies as well as the areas of consensus. We have tried to provide straightforward and definitive information in the most direct way when such information exists. When, however, the facts are in doubt, and the questions themselves in need of re-examination, we have given these problems at least some of the discussion they need. You will also find some topics that, by their very nature, require thoughtful discussion as much as they do a survey of factual information. Accurate knowledge is certainly beneficial as we review our attitudes toward life and death, but deep-rooted values and beliefs remain fundamental as well.

Although a concise one-volume work, the *Encyclopedia of Death* possesses the features one would expect from a work of this genre. There are, for example, internal cross-references throughout the book. The reader who decides to start with **Dying** will discover several other entries for further readings (e.g., **Black Death, Death Fears and Anxiety, Deathbed Scenes**, etc.). Similarly, **Rigor Mortis** will also suggest **Brain**

Death, Cemeteries, and **Funerals;** while **Dance of Death** will share cross-references with **Ars Moriendi, Black Death, Death Themes Through History,** and **Memento Mori.** We think this will (usually) help you find what you are seeking and (sometimes) a little more as well. Selected readings are also listed at the end of each entry for those interested in exploring the varied and extensive literature that is now available on death-related topics. If we succeed in stimulating as well as satisfying your curiosity, you will find a number of useful further sources.

The *Encyclopedia of Death,* then, *is* an encyclopedia. But is it a good encyclopedia? Does it do justice to the challenging subject matter? Is it accurate? Authoritative? Do the contributors have in-depth knowledge of their topics, and are they able to share their knowledge in a clear and accessible manner? These questions will eventually be answered by each reader. The editors have taken a rather basic approach in trying to develop a resource book with the qualities that every reader has the right to expect. We simply asked ourselves: "Who would we want to read? Who knows this topic from the inside? Who has played a major role in developing this part of the field?" And then we invited Myra Bluebond-Langner to draw upon her own major research as well as the work of others to write **Children, Dying.** Similarly, in the area of **Near-Death Experiences,** the research leadership of Kenneth Ring has been dominant. To gain perspective on **Suicide,** we might have needed to invent a Norman Farberow, did he not already exist as a distinguished clinician and researcher. And so it went. Fortunately for us all, many such major contributors to caregiving and knowledge agreed to become contributors to this book. We are grateful to each and every one.

In selecting the topics, we again took a perhaps simplistic approach—what would we expect to find in an *Encyclopedia of Death*? What would our students and colleagues hope to find? What information would be particularly valuable for the general reader? And what neglected or misunderstood topics should be covered? We immediately disabused ourselves of any fantasy that all death-related topics could be covered within a work of reasonable length, or that this was even a desirable goal. Death has been the shadow of life and the hidden subtext of many documents from ancient stiles and runes to this morning's reports of recombinant genes research. Limiting ourselves to one volume of moderate length seemed practical, economical, and reasonable.

Why an Encyclopedia of Death?

A book of this type would have been nearly unthinkable and almost certainly unpublishable not many years ago. Western society in the twentieth century could not countenance the idea of death, nor face the realities of dying, grief, suicide, and other death-related situations. In Great Britain, Geoffrey Gorer (1965) decried "the pornography of death," a prevailing attitude that regards natural death as obscene. In the United States, Herman Feifel observed that death had become a taboo topic—and he had to battle against his publisher's "better judgment" to keep that obscene five-letter word in the title of his breakthrough book, *The Meaning of Death* (1959). Earlier, sensitive physicians such as Alfred Worcester (1935) had called for more effective and compassionate care for the dying person, and a few social scientists such as Thomas D. Eliot (1930) attempted fruitlessly to interest their colleagues in the significance of grief as a human experience.

Fortunately, the situation has changed. Death education, the hospice movement, suicide and crisis centers, and grief counseling are among the clearly identifiable emergents from our society's renewed ability to cope with mortality. This means that there is not only a more receptive attitudinal climate for consideration of death-related topics, but also many new developments that deserve consideration. Accordingly, the *Encyclopedia of Death* offers information in all these areas of recent and ongoing activity. You will find, for example, basic information on a number of organizations that are concerned with death-related issues, and on periodicals that are devoted to these topics.

The contributors have been invited to share some of their own experiences, beliefs, and suggestions, as well as their objective knowledge. These comments generally come at the end of the entries. Although we have all attempted to write well-balanced entries with an objective tone, there is also a place for individual expression and judgment on topics of such piercing concern. "Pure objectivity" would be a strained and unrealistic goal to pursue here, although perhaps appropriate for some other subject matters.

For a little more perspective on this book and our own times, it is interesting to take down from the antiquarian shelf a volume that first blinked at the light of day in 1896. The author was J. R. Francis, and the title: *The Encyclopaedia of Death.* This book, like the one you hold in your hand, was very much a product of its times. Its intent and approach is more accurately conveyed by the subtitle: *Death and the Spirit World Critically Examined.* This sampling of major chapter titles and headings will further convey its preoccupations:

- Apparent Death Critically Examined
- A Young Lady Saved From Burial. The Wonderful Resuscitation of Clara Munce
- The Keen Intuition of Dogs Realize that a Lady had been Buried Alive
- On the Verge of Being Buried Alive
- Horrible Details of Premature Interment. Illustrating the Dense Ignorance of Physicians
- Death by Torture Vividly Portrayed

You get the picture. As a matter of fact, you can still get the picture today by purchasing (or, as I usually do, sneaking a look at) one of the sensationalistic "newspapers" on sale at many supermarket check-out counters. Lurid thrills have been enjoyed through the centuries, especially deliciously warped conjunctions of death and sex. It is probable, however, that these thrills were sharper and more satisfying a century or so ago when the spiritist (or spiritualist) movement had expanded to its degenerative commercial phase. Much of the material that comprises Francis's book was already second-hand at the time, and the naive type of spiritistic approach to death endures today in the shade of old weeping willows, rather than in the glaring sun of a functionalistic, technologically oriented society. Some of the themes and "data" presented in Francis's work have been re-examined in our own time (e.g., Kastenbaum & Aisenberg, 1972), but for the most part we have different concerns that demand priority attention. The first *Encyclopaedia of Death* was not an encyclopedia at all in format or content, but, in its own provocative way, did manage to express one generation's fears and hopes—and not long before the silence of death as "pornography" and "taboo" descended upon society.

We invite you, then, to explore at your leisure what a present generation of caregivers, scholars, and scientists can tell us about death and its place in our lives. It would be reassuring to think that there will be later generations who can smile forgivingly at our quaint assumptions and inadequate knowledge.

—ROBERT KASTENBAUM & BEATRICE KASTENBAUM

References

Eliot, T.D. (1930). "The adjustive behavior of bereaved families: A new field for research." *Social Forces, 8*: 543–49.

Feifel, H. (Ed.) (1959). *The meaning of death.* New York: McGraw-Hill.

Francis, J.R. (1896). *The encyclopaedia of death.* Reprint ed. Amherst, WI: Amherst Press, n.d.

Gorer, G. (1965). *Death, grief, and mourning in contemporary Britain.* London: Cresset.

Kastenbaum, R. & Aisenberg, R.B. (1972). *The psychology of death.* 1st ed. New York: Springer.

Worcester, A. (1935). *The care of the aged, the dying, and the dead.* Springfield, IL: Charles C. Thomas.

Contributors

Kalle Achté, M.D.
Chief of the Clinic and Professor of
Psychiatry
University of Helsinki Central Hospital
Helsinki, Finland

Myra Bluebond-Langner, Ph.D.
Department of Anthropology
Rutgers University
New Brunswick, NJ

Thomas Cattrick
Mercer Mortuary and Chapel
Phoenix, AZ

Joyotpaul Chaudhuri, Ph.D.
Associate Dean
College of Liberal Arts
Arizona State University
Tempe, AZ

Grace H. Christ, A.C.S.W., Director
Department of Social Work
Memorial Sloan-Kettering Cancer Center
New York, NY

Kathleen Cohen, Ph.D.
Chairman, Art Department
San Jose State University
San Jose, CA

Malcolm L. Comeaux, Ph.D.
Professor of Geography
Arizona State University
Tempe, AZ

Charles A. Corr, Ph.D.
Professor of Philosophy
Southern Illinois University at
Edwardsville
Edwardsville, IL

Donna M. Corr, R.N., B.S.N.
St. Louis Community College
St. Louis, MO

Ann Armstrong Dailey, Director
Children's Hospice International
Alexandria, VA

John DeFrain, Ph.D.
Department of Human Development &
The Family
University of Nebraska–Lincoln
Lincoln, NE

Kenneth J. Doka, Ph.D.
Professor of Psychology and Thanatology
Graduate College
College of New Rochelle
New Rochelle, NY

David M. Dush, Ph.D.
Department of Psychology
Central Michigan University
Mount Pleasant, MI

Franz R. Epting, Ph.D., Director
Counseling Psychology Program
University of Florida
Gainsville, FL

Norman L. Farberow, Ph.D.
Board of Directors
The Suicide Prevention Center
Los Angeles, CA

Ellen Gee, Ph.D.
Department of Sociology
Simon Fraser University
Barnaby, British Columbia

Anne J. J. Gilmore, M.D.
Founder and Chief Executive
Prince and Princess of Wales Hospice
Glasgow, Scotland

David S. Greer, M.D.
Dean of Medicine
Brown University
Providence, RI

Bruce Greyson, M.D.
Department of Psychiatry
University of Connecticut Health Center
Farmington, CT

John S. Hatcher, Ph.D.
Professor of English Literature
University of South Florida
Tampa, FL

William L. Hendricks, Th.D.
Southern Baptist Theological Seminary
Louisville, KY

E.J. Hunter, Ph.D.
Hunter Publications
San Diego, CA

Robert M. Johnston, Ph.D.
Seventh-Day Adventist Theological
Seminary
Andrews University
Berrien Springs, MI

Richard A. Kalish, Ph.D. (Deceased)
Dean for External Programs
Antioch University
Yellow Springs, OH

Beatrice K. Kastenbaum, M.S.N., R.N.
College of Nursing
Arizona State University
Tempe, AZ

Robert Kastenbaum, Ph.D.
Department of Communication
Arizona State University
Tempe, AZ

Dennis Klass, Ph.D.
Department of Religion
Webster University
St. Louis, MO

Maurice Lamm, Director
National Institute for Jewish Hospice
Los Angeles, CA

Maxine Lazarus, Administrator
The Foundation of Thanatology
New York, NY

Daniel Leviton, Ph.D., Director
Adult Health and Development Program
University of Maryland
College Park, MD

Richard Lonetto, Ph.D.
Department of Psychology
University of Guelph
Guelph, Ontario

Joan Lowell, M.P.A., Director
Hospice of the Valley
Phoenix, AZ

Leona Martens
Department of Human Development and
the Family
University of Nebraska—Lincoln
Lincoln, NE

Susan Masterson-Allen
Center for Long-Term Gerontology and
Health Research
Brown University
Providence, RI

John L. McIntosh, Ph.D.
Department of Psychology
Indiana University at South Bend
South Bend, IN

Willam A. McKim
Department of Psychology
Memorial University of Newfoundland
St. John's, Newfoundland

Joan N. McNeil, Ph.D.
Department of Human Development &
Family Studies
Kansas State University
Manhattan, KS

Brian L. Mishara, Ph.D.
Department of Psychology
University of Quebec at Montreal
Montreal, Quebec

Vincent Mor, Ph.D., Director
Center for Long-Term Care Gerontology &
Health Research
Brown University
Providence, RI

John D. Morgan, Ph.D.
King's College
University of Western Ontario
London, Ontario

Thomas H. Olbricht, Ph.D.
Chairman of Graduate Studies
College of Biblical Studies
Abilene Christian University
Abilene, TX

Nancy J. Osgood, Ph.D.
Medical College of Virginia
Virginia Commonwealth University
Richmond, VA

Karlis Osis, Ph.D.
American Society for Psychical Research, Inc.
New York, NY

R. Michael Perry
Alcor Life Extension Foundation
Riverside, CA

Beth P. Poppell
Associate Editor
Thanatos
Tallahassee, FL

Therese A. Rando, Ph.D.
Clinical Director
Therese A. Rando Associates, Ltd.
Warwick, RI

Joseph Richman, Ph.D.
Albert Einstein College of Medicine
and the Bronx Municipal Hospital Center
Bronx, NY

Kenneth Ring, Ph.D.
Professor of Psychology
University of Connecticut
Storrs, CT

Rev. Gerald Q. Roseberry, D.Min.
Ecumenical Chaplain for the Homeless
St. Vincent De Paul
Phoenix, AZ

Paul C. Rousseau, M.D.
Chief, Geriatrics Section
Veterans Administration Hospital
Phoenix, AZ

Giles Scofield, Attorney
Concern for Dying
New York, NY

Jane I. Smith, Ph.D.
Vice President and Dean of Academic Affairs
Iliff School of Theology
Denver, CO

Jan Stork
Department of Human Development and the Family
University of Nebraska—Lincoln
Lincoln, NE

Warren Stork
Department of Human Development and the Family
University of Nebraska—Lincoln
Lincoln, NE

Jacque Taylor, M.A., Executive Director
Fremont County Alliance Against
Domestic Violence & Sexual Assault
Riverton, WY

Donald I. Templer, Ph.D.
California School of Professional Psychology–Fresno
Fresno, CA

James I. Warren, Jr., Ph.D.
Department of Christian Education
Scarrit Graduate School (Nashville)
Nashville, TN

Hannelore Wass, Ph.D.
Professor of Education
University of Florida
Gainesville, FL

Penny B. Weingarten
Program Coordinator
Concern for Dying
New York, NY

Julia Willis
Director, Volunteer Services
Hospice of the Valley
Phoenix, AZ

Alphabetical List of Articles

Guide to Related Topics

BIO-MEDICAL ASPECTS OF DEATH

Acquired Immune Deficiency Syndrome (AIDS)
Autopsy
(The) Black Death
Brain Death
Causes of Death
Cryonic Suspension
Death Certificate
Embalming
International Classification of Diseases (ICD)
Mortality Rate
Prolongation of Life
Rigor Mortis
Uniform Anatomical Act

CHILDREN AND YOUTH

Adolescence and Death
Children, Dying
Children and Death
Children's Hospice International
Grief: Death of a Child
Hospice: Children
Lullabies of Death
Make-A-Wish Foundation
Siblings of Dying Children
Stillbirth
Sudden Infant Death Syndrome (SIDS)

THE DEAD

Autopsy
Autopsy, Psychological
Burial: "Going Home"
Cemeteries
Cremation
Cryonic Suspension
Days of the Dead
Death Certificate
Embalming
Epitaphs

Funerals
Necromancy
Necrophilia
Necrophobia
Rigor Mortis
Tombs
Uniform Anatomical Act
Vampire
Zombie

THE DYING

Appropriate Death
Awareness of Dying
Children, Dying
Deathbed Scenes
Dying
Extreme Unction
Hospice: Children
Hospice: Philosophy and Practice
Hospice: Volunteers
Hospice Development in the United Kingdom
National Hospice Study
Siblings of Dying Children
Socrates' Death
Stages of Dying
Tame Death
Trajectories of Dying
See also Organizations

FEARS, HOPES, AND THOUGHTS

Adolescence and Death
Children and Death
"Crossing the Bar"
Death Anxiety: Measures
Death Anxiety: Reduction
Death Education
Death Fears and Anxiety
Death Instinct
Death Threat Index (TI)
Deathbed Scenes
Epitaphs

Humor and the Fear of Death
Old Age and Death
Personifications of Death
Socrates' Death
"Thanatopsis"

THE GRIEVING

Anticipatory Grief
Compassionate Friends
Grief
Grief: Death of a Child
Grief: Missing in Action Families
Grief, Vicarious
Grief Counseling
Kaddish
Psalms of Lament

HISTORICAL EVENTS, MYTHS, AND THEMES

Ars Moriendi
Biathanatos
(The) Black Death
Charon
Dance of Death (*Danse Macabre*)
Death Themes Through History
Funerals
Hades
Memento Mori
Mors
Prolongation of Life
Socrates' Death
Styx
Suttee (*Sati*)
Tame Death
Thanatology
"Thanatopsis"
Tombs
Tuonela
Vampire
Zombie

JOURNALS AND MAGAZINES

Death Studies
Euthanasia Review
(The) Hospice Journal: Physical, Psychosocial, and Pastoral Care of the Dying
Journal of Near-Death Studies (Anabiosis)
(The) Journal of Psychosocial Oncology
Omega, Journal of Death and Dying
Suicide and Life-Threatening Behavior
Thanatos

LEGAL, ETHICAL, AND SOCIO-POLITICAL ASPECTS OF DEATH

Acquired Immune Deficiency Syndrome (AIDS)
Brain Death
Cryonic Suspension
Death Penalty
Death System
Death Themes Through History
Euthanasia
Euthanasia Review
Hemlock Society
Jonestown
(The) Living Will
Murder
Socrates' Death
Suttee (*Sati*)
Uniform Anatomical Act
See also Suicide

ORGANIZATIONS

American Association of Suicidology
Association for Death Education and Counseling
Children's Hospice International
Compassionate Friends
Concern for Dying
Foundation of Thanatology
Hemlock Society
Hospice Association of America
International Association for Near-Death Studies
International Work Group on Death, Dying, and Bereavement
Make-A-Wish Foundation
National Funeral Directors Association
National Hospice Organization
National Institute for Jewish Hospice

RESEARCH AND THEORY

Adolescence and Death
Anticipatory Grief
Autopsy, Psychological
Awareness of Dying
Children and Death
Death Anxiety: Measures
Death Education
Death Fears and Anxiety
Death Instinct
Death Threat Index (TI)
Deathbed Scenes
Grief

National Hospice Study
Near-Death Experience: Scale
Near-Death Experiences
Old Age and Death
Personifications of Death
Stages of Dying
Thanatology

SUICIDE

American Association of Suicidology
Biathanatos
Hemlock Society
Jonestown
Suicide
Suicide: Aged Adults
Suicide: Asian-American
Suicide: Assisted
Suicide: Black
Suicide: Hispanic
Suicide: Indirect
Suicide and Life-Threatening Behavior
Suicide: Native American
Suicide: Youth
Suttee (*Sati*)

SURVIVAL OF DEATH

Evidence For and Against
Life After Death?
Near-Death Experience: Scale
Near-Death Experiences

Mythological
Barzakh
Charon
Hades
Psychopomp
Styx
Tuonela

Religious Beliefs
Survival Beliefs and Practices: Baha'i
Survival Beliefs and Practices: Baptist
Survival Beliefs and Practices: Buddhist
Survival Beliefs and Practices: Church of
    the Latter-Day Saints
Survival Beliefs and Practices: Churches of
    Christ
Survival Beliefs and Practices: Hindu
Survival Beliefs and Practices: Islamic
Survival Beliefs and Practices: Jewish
Survival Beliefs and Practices: Roman
    Catholic
Survival Beliefs and Practices:
    Seventh-Day Adventist
Survival Beliefs and Practices: United
    Methodist

VIOLENT DEATH

Adolescence and Death
Causes of Death
Death System
Grief: Missing in Action Families
Jonestown
Murder
Vampire
See also Suicide

Encyclopedia
of
DEATH

A

ACQUIRED IMMUNE DEFICIENCY SYNDROME (AIDS)

The Disease

Since the acquired immune deficiency syndrome (AIDS) was first described in 1981, it has been recognized around the world and has reached epidemic proportions. The cause is believed to be a virus that has been named the human immunodeficiency virus (HIV). An estimated 1.5 to 2 million Americans already are infected. No cure is presently available for the disease. It is the assured fatality of the disease that leads us to explore its challenges here.

Dr. Robert Gallo, head of the National Cancer Institute's laboratory of tumor cell biology and codiscoverer of the virus, believes:

> Human retroviruses probably existed in man for hundreds if not thousands of years . . . restricted to certain secluded, rural populations. These viruses spread outside of these populations because of societal upheaval that saw huge numbers of Africans leaving their small villages and journeying to the cities. It is these social changes not some sudden mutation of the virus which are at the heart of the spread of AIDS. (Sorelle, 1987)

Like all viruses, HIV cannot reproduce except within a living cell. Unlike other viruses, it contains reverse transcriptase, which is an enzyme that allows the virus to incorporate its own genetic material into the host cell's deoxyribonucleic acid (DNA). The cell is thus programmed to produce more viruses instead of performing normal cell functions. The ability to "retrofit" the cell program leads to the designation "retrovirus." HIV has an affinity for the T4 (also called T-helper) cells in the body's immune system, the system which fights infection and identifies abnormal cells. HIV also attacks various cells in the brain.

The virus is transmitted through contact with blood, semen, and vaginal secretions of an infected person. Low quantities of virus are found in other body secretions, but transmission through contact with them is considered unlikely. Mosquitoes, toilet seats, casual contact, intimate contact in the same household (even sharing the same toothbrush) have not been found to transmit the disease. The modes of transmission are:

- having intimate sexual contact
- sharing needles for drug injection
- receiving contaminated blood or blood products (This mode has been almost eliminated by testing of blood for HIV since 1985.)
- passage from infected mother to fetus or newborn

High-risk behaviors have led to the disproportionate appearance of HIV in homosexuals, bisexual intravenous drug users, heterosexual drug users, and those who have sexual contact with them. A smaller number of cases are seen in persons who received transfusions before screening for the virus was possible and in hemophiliacs. Health care workers are at risk because of contact with blood and the danger of needle-sticks and cuts when working with an infected person. (Because it is not always possible to know who carries HIV, health care workers are advised to use precautions that protect from contact with blood and body fluids of *all* patients).

Once infected, a person's body retains the virus and can transmit it for life. There is a latency period—average 3–5 years, but as long as 15—before development of AIDS itself. It is thought that repeated challenges to the immune system may speed reproduction of the infected T-helper cells, spilling more viruses into the body. As more and more T-helper cells are infected the body becomes less able to resist opportunistic infections and tumors. Death comes quickly when treatment no longer holds the infections at bay.

AIDS is defined as the presence of HIV-1 (demonstrated by tests for antibodies to the virus in the person's blood) and two or more opportunistic infections. Fifty percent of AIDS patients demonstrate symptoms of dementia as the virus or other infections affect the brain. Pneumonia and wasting are common. Kaposi's sarcoma (purplish tumors on the skin) may also be present. The pre-AIDS syndrome, AIDS-related complex (ARC), is characterized by malaise, weight loss, persistent fevers, diarrhea, repeated common infections, and persistent swollen lymph nodes.

Treatment focuses on controlling the infections and tumors. In 1987, Retrovir (zidovudine, formerly known as AZT), a drug that slows HIV replication by suppressing bone marrow (and T-helper) reproduction, was approved for use in the United States. Other drugs and combinations of drugs are presently in experimental trials. Adequate nutrition, prevention of infection, and control of stress may also slow the development of AIDS in an HIV-infected individual. Quackery and false panaceas abound in this "no cure" situation.

A vaccine that will prevent infection by the virus is many years from practical use. Until then, prevention of transmission is the only control available.

Education of the general public has been urged to prevent the further transmission of HIV. In 1988 Surgeon General C. Everett Koop and the U.S. government mailed a pamphlet to every household in the United States explaining AIDS and outlining ways to avoid contracting the disease, such as abstinence, mutual monogamy (not serial monogamy), proper use of a latex, spermicidal condom, and no needle sharing. It is important that parents, young people, and health care workers understand how HIV is transmitted.

Testing for HIV is not considered to be a viable way of controlling the spread of the virus. Doctors fear that programs which mandate testing or lack confidentiality will discourage potential carriers from taking the test and receiving the counseling that accompanies it. Nevertheless, many people are being tested for the virus. Applicants for insurance, some types of employment, and for military service are likely to be tested. Some states test applicants for marriage licenses. In other states drug addicts, known homosexuals, and prostitutes are tested if arrested and jailed.

AIDS is a worldwide epidemic. While it is believed to have first occurred in Africa, almost no country is now free of cases. The World Health Organization estimated in 1988 that as many as 10 million people may already be infected with HIV-1 (Gadsby, 1988). There are differences in the pattern of spread, and in the willingness of various countries to report the disease. The days of easy travel and easy sex have made the spread seem akin to the proverbial wildfire.

This new threat must be understood not only as a disease entity but also for its effects on those who are living and dying with the disease, as illustrated by the following typical examples.

The People

Rick

In September 1979 a 37-year-old fifth grade teacher in the Bronx, New York City, was suffering from some unusual bumps behind his ear. A biopsy showed that the bumps were a rare tumor called Kaposi's sarcoma (KS). Rick's doctor noted the similarities between Rick's case and that of another young man in New York who also was 37 and homosexual.

Later Rick developed such overwhelming fatigue that he quit his job. By December, Rick's lungs were filling with "something." It was clear he was dying. Rick said no to machines that would keep him alive but not cure him. His lover took him home to their brownstone on the Upper West Side of Manhattan. On December 24, 1980, Rick became the fourth American to die of the disease that only later was named AIDS (Shilts, 1987).

Christina

Christina said she was a virgin when she met her man. He said he had "slept around." They agreed to be faithful to each other because Christina was afraid of AIDS. In March 1988 they discovered that he had AIDS and that Christina was positive for HIV, even though she had no symptoms of disease. "I wanted to commit suicide," she says.

Christina, 22 years old, was working two jobs, going to school, and "trying to make it." Within the next few months she had strep throat, bronchitis, unexplained high fevers, diarrhea for weeks at a time, swollen lymph nodes, throbbing back and neck pain, and she was tired, "always so tired." She quit first one job and then the other. She stopped seeing her friends. She did not return to school in the fall. Her boyfriend moved to his mother's home, refused to take any medicine, and died in May 1988.

Christina's mother was "real positive" when told of the AIDS but would not drink out of a glass Christina had used. Her father does not believe she has the disease. One brother encourages her, the other brother doesn't know. She lives with two homosexuals who also are HIV-positive.

Christina is depressed now. "I can never have kids. I can never have an (intimate) relationship with anybody. I wouldn't be able to tell them. . . . I'm so sick of people saying it's a gay disease, because I'm not gay, you know and he's not gay. . . . It's not the faggots and their AIDS, it's me" (Higgs, 1988).

Sarah

Infant Sarah's mother left home when she was 15. She was a drug abuser and sometime prostitute. She contacted her family only when she needed money. Then she came home—pregnant and with AIDS. Shortly after Sarah's birth, her mother left

again. (Infants born of HIV-infected mothers carry their mother's antibodies but nevertheless have a 30–50 percent chance of being infected with the virus. There is a 12–15 month waiting period while the mother's antibodies clear from the baby's body and it begins to make its own antibodies before it is possible to know if infection has occurred.)

Sarah's aunt, a single careerwoman, made a home for Sarah even though her own life changed completely as a result. The hardest part was finding babysitters. The rest of the family could offer little help. A daycare center refused to continue to accept the child when it found out about the AIDS antibodies. "My only life now is taking care of this baby. That, and wondering constantly what the future holds for her."

Later, the pressure became too much for Sarah's aunt. She lost her job because she missed work whenever a baby-sitter would not show up. Eventually she left Sarah to move to another city. Sarah's grandmother is now caring for her. At age 11 months, it has been learned that Sarah is infected with HIV. She already has an enlarged liver, spleen, and lymph glands (Siegel, 1988).

The Issues

AIDS has attracted a fearful, irrational response from the public and, at times, from the media. This reaction may be related to the relatively sudden eruption of the disease, its early association with homosexuals and drug abusers, and the time required to replace ignorance, assumptions, and speculations with hard facts. In a recent poll conducted by the American Association of Blood Banks, it was found that 22 percent of those polled believed that AIDS can be caught from *donating* blood. The fact that this percentage is down from 34 percent in 1985 indicates that efforts at rational education about the virus may be leading to less hysteria and uncertainty. But that one-fifth still hold this belief is certainly disheartening for those who hope to disseminate enough information to rationally control the disease. In the same survey, those polled ranked AIDS as the most serious health problem facing the country today, outranking the foremost killers—cancer and heart disease (AABB, 1988).

Perhaps the public is beginning to realize that AIDS will be with us for a long time to come. Although not many have died yet, there is a tremendous pool of infected individuals. How will we care for these people as they sicken and die? Who will pay the bills? One year of treatment with Retrovir costs approximately $7,000. It is estimated that care for one AIDS patient costs $150,000–$300,000. Costs will increase as we become more successful at prolonging life without finding a cure. Who will care for these critically ill patients in a time of nursing shortages across the nation? Will the care of old people suffer as resources are used for AIDS patients? Will the public be willing to pay health insurance increases or skyrocketing taxes to care for AIDS patients? Can we expect our government to support the research which will find the answers to the puzzles of vaccine development and cure?

Or will the public seek "retribution" as Surgeon General Koop fears (Knutson, 1988)? Will the public feel as one talk show caller expressed it, "They brought the disease on themselves. Let them pay for it"?

Shilts' book, *And the Band Played On,* describes the response of the government and media to the growing menace of AIDS in the early 1980s. It is a story of embarassment and lack of willingness to deal with the sexual nature of the transmission of the virus. It seemed preferable to many officials not to report "too much" about this new disease affecting homosexuals; Gay Liberation was at the time a new phenomenon. The government only reluctantly supported research into this new virus. People with a conservative orientation opposed education of the public, especially children and adolescents, about homosexual practices and prevention through use of condoms. Shilts relates this timidity to the government's awareness that the Moral Majority was a powerful political force. Gradually this attitude has been changing, in part because the public has become aware of well-known public figures, such as actors and politicians, who have died from AIDS—and of people within their own circle of friends and relatives

AIDS brings into question a basic tenet of the sophisticated health care system of the twentieth century. Can we still assume that everyone will be cared for and that no one will be turned away? Can we trust that the best care possible will be given even to those who cannot afford it?

Or will medical ghettos develop? Will only doctors and nurses who cannot find work elsewhere care for AIDS patients? And will the public refuse to accept care in a hospital that also cares for AIDS patients? Will hospice organizations be viewed as tainted if they accept AIDS victims and will this development prove harmful to the still new and vulnerable hospice movement? Even though AIDS patients make up a small percentage of total patients, avoidance behaviors in the professions and public can already be observed.

What about the children who are HIV positive? Some day care centers and schools have refused to care for and educate these children. Will society turn away from the tenet that every child has a right to the best education possible?

What about the individual's right to privacy, especially the protection from invasion of our very bodies? Will mandatory testing for HIV with disclosure to schools, law enforcement officials, landlords, and employers lead to loss of opportunity for many members of society?

Will the fact that AIDS victims come disproportionately from minority groups halt or reverse the progress against social injustices of the past?

The questions proliferate. One positive result of our increasing knowledge of the disease is the light it may shed on other diseases of the immune system. But such benefits come only with adequate funding for research. More important, perhaps as we face the challenges of the disease we will develop a health system that truly does "care" for all who come to it.

The Threat to Our Well-Being

Robert Kastenbaum (1988, p. 12) helps to explain some of the dynamics of our response to AIDS, when he points to the threat of AIDS not only to reality but to fantasy.

AIDS has most of the elements that are necessary for a thoroughly catastrophic vision of death. The death in life appearance of the body. . . confusion and dementia . . . the death-through-sex connection that is even more unacceptable to the general public than was the case with syphilis. . . AIDS is the product of a "dirty" life, and of a tainted spirit who dared to flaunt God's moral laws. Fear and revulsion are further magnified by the fact that AIDS often claims people in the prime of their lives—it is no unobtrusive scavenger that carries off those who society has already half-forgotten.

Furthermore AIDS "does not abide by the rules established for the general model of dying" which has recently become "acceptable" through hospice care of cancer patients.

AIDS is the death toward which our unconscious fantasies surge. It is the death in which a diabolic anti-self, a perverted angel, turns upon the victim with many of the terrors history has witnessed or invented. It is the death that appears among the most dangerous because it is among the most encompassing—the victim's entire life may be stigmatized and destroyed: the past as well as the future.

The blood transmission element in AIDS is also seen as resonating with vampire fantasies that have haunted the human race for many centuries.

Summary

The mist that surrounds AIDS is beginning to dissolve. Gradually we are learning about the virus and there is hope for a vaccine. The people who have AIDS, such as Rick, Christina, and Sarah, do not belong to a race apart; they are people who had the misfortune to be exposed to HIV. They are facing very real problems in affording medical care, avoiding discrimination in jobs, housing, and insurance coverage, and in adjusting to living with a disease that is presently without cure.

AIDS challenges not only our scientific and medical ingenuity but the fiber of worldwide humanity. This modern day Black Death threatens our young, our beliefs, our resources, our sense of security and control. How well we will meet the challenge remains as much a mystery as the disease itself.

See also (The) Black Death; Causes of Death; Death Fears and Anxiety; Hospice: Philosophy and Practice; Vampire.

—BEATRICE K. KASTENBAUM

References

American Association of Blood Banks (1988). Unpublished report of survey findings.

Centers for Disease Control (1987). "Recommendations for prevention of HIV transmission in health-care settings." *Morbidity and Mortality Weekly Report, 36*: 3s–17s.

Gadsby, P. (1988). "Mapping the epidemic: Geography as destiny." *Discover,* April: 28–31.

Higgs, D. (1988). "The face of AIDS: Disease devastates life of young victim." *Tempe Daily News Tribune,* June 19.

Kastenbaum, R. (1988). "'Safe death' in the postmodern world." In A. Gilmore & S. Gilmore, (Eds.) *A safer death: Multidisciplinary aspects of terminal care.* New York: Plenum Press, pp. 3–13.

Koop, C. (1988). *Understanding AIDS.* HHS Publication HHS-88-8404, U.S. Department of Health and Human Services.

Shilts, R. (1987). *And the band played on: Politics, people, and the AIDS epidemic.* New York: St. Martin's Press

Siegel, M. (1988). "The youngest victims: Children with AIDS." *Good Housekeeping,* August: 106, 149–55.

Sorelle, R. (1987). "Role of new African viruses debated at AIDS conference." *Oncology Times, 9*: 15.

ADOLESCENCE AND DEATH

The major theme of adolescence is change. Physical changes are the most apparent and predictable between the ages of about 12 and 20. Intellectual and personality changes are not nearly so obvious but are just as important. Compared with their thought processes in childhood, adolescents have a growing capacity to think abstractly and to solve subtler problems, as well as to conceive of what might occur in the future. This enables them to grasp most adult concepts of death and to explore death's meaning in their own lives. Curiously, most textbooks on adolescence have ignored this special challenge and accomplishment.

Conversations with a variety of individual teenagers reveal that they do have "a heightened sense of futurity (which) allows a glimpse of what one might be—but also the recognition that one might not be" (Kastenbaum, 1986, p. 11). The realization of mortality is among the most significant developments in adolescence, although this sometimes escapes the notice of parents, teachers, and other adults. Adolescents also change greatly in self-awareness and in emotional intensity as they strive to establish a sense of genuine identity. In this task they are "particularly vulnerable to the threat of death" (Rando, 1984, p. 246). Thus, life and death questions, fears, and explorations of ways to handle relationships, losses, and other life events are inevitably part of the adolescent's pattern of growth and change. Meanwhile, contemporary society provides a complex, sometimes violent and impersonal, often death-related and stress-provoking environment in which to grow. Wise support from families, teachers, or peers may not always be available (Gordon, 1986).

As part of normal development, many early adolescents are not inclined to give concentrated attention to such serious matters, preferring more lighthearted give-and-take with friends. Intellectually, they may also be in the grip of a type of adolescent egocentrism that Elkind (1967) has called "the personal fable," a feeling that they can take virtually any risk without danger. Despite warnings from parents and other adults, such teens will appear to go out of their way to drive recklessly, to drink too much, or to experiment with potent drugs (Karsh, 1987), in a form of rebellion that can produce tragic results.

Such egocentrism seems to decline in most teens at about midadolescence, when most young people begin to develop a broader understanding of other people and their motivations. This development has been characterized as a stage of mutual role-taking (Lapsley & Murphy, 1985). Some writers have emphasized the importance of a sense of "belonging" both emotionally and socially within one's family and within the larger world. The fears of death engendered in many (perhaps the brightest) young people by the omnipresent threat of nuclear war may impair their sense of security and trust. The possibility of nuclear catastrophe appears to be of urgent concern to many adolescents (Beardslee & Mack, 1982; Austin & Mack, 1986; Stillion, 1986). Undoubtedly, teenagers' knowledge of violent death can come from their repeated exposure through television to disturbances in the world: the murder or attempted assassination of national leaders, the explosion of a space shuttle, terrorism on a global scale, and war in over a dozen countries, including the lasting effects of the conflict in Vietnam.

Much of their response to social stresses is reflected in adolescent culture, especially in the many forms of popular music: ballads, rhythm and blues, folk, country and western, jazz, and rock (Rice, 1987). Attig (1986) has emphasized the "distorted image of death" as perceived by teenagers and revealed in their music. He observes that death themes in adolescent music include personal encounters in thoughts of old age, time and immortality, loss and grief, suicide, war, hunger, drugs, murder, and nuclear holocaust.

We do not have as yet a clear picture of the thoughts and feelings of a total population of contemporary adolescents, however. The vast majority of normal teenagers, as portrayed in studies of more than 20,000 adolescents by Daniel Offer and his colleagues (1981, 1984), tend to report no major problems in their lives, are hopeful about the future, and believe they can cope with whatever challenges life has to offer. A somewhat different view is provided in autobiographical statements of a number of young people which movingly describe their complex responses to experiences with death and grief (Pendleton, 1980; Sternberg & Sternberg, 1980; Krementz, 1981). Still other writers point out that the common elements of adolescent experience—the lengthiness of this period of life, the myriad changes, the uncertainty about the future, the anxiety over choices—tend to make adolescence a stressful period altogether (Hoffman et al., 1988).

Realities of Stress and Adolescent Responses

Not all behavior of adolescents is disturbed, nor do all youths have emotional problems. But not all the news is good. Some of today's adolescents evidently are more troubled than teenagers of the 1950s. Over the past thirty years there has been a clear rise in some aspects of adolescent disturbance. Those with poor family relationships, vulnerable personalities, and intense pressure from friends seem more likely to become involved in a variety of unhealthy practices. By the end of the tenth grade, 90 percent of all adolescents have used alcoholic beverages. Although most teenagers drink alcohol moderately, more than three of ten can be classified as problem drinkers. In turn, alcohol abuse appears as a major factor in delinquent behaviors, family violence, traffic accident fatalities, and homicide. The trend in drug use and abuse appears to have declined somewhat in the 1980s, with fewer students using illicit drugs such as marijuana, stimulants, hallucinogens, and heroin, but the use of cocaine and inhalants has risen slightly (Johnston et al., 1985).

Some distressed females develop eating disorders such as anorexia nervosa, "the dieter's disease," which affects 1 percent of adolescent girls of all economic classes. Almost all anorectics (95 percent) are between the ages of 12 to 18. The serious risk involved in anorexia is revealed by the fact that an estimated 5–10 percent of the young people afflicted with this condition die because of medical problems associated with their poor nutritional status. We still do not have definitive knowledge on the cause of anorexia, and research continues (Yager, 1982).

Adolescent pregnancies present still other problems. More than one million teen pregnancies occur in the United States each year. When the mother is younger than 16, her risk of dying during pregnancy or childbirth is five times the national average (Bolton, 1980).

Some teenagers appear to be at special risk because of poverty and environmental deprivations that have affected them since birth. Adolescents of low socioeconomic status, sometimes called disadvantaged or culturally deprived, are found with relatively higher frequency among such minority groups as blacks, Mexican Americans, and Native Americans. The latter population has the highest birthrate, the highest death rate, and the shortest life expectancy of any group in the United States. Native Americans also suffer more from hunger and malnutrition. Accidents, liver ailments (attributable to poor nutrition and excessive drinking), and homicide are nearly triple the national rate. Suicide is the leading cause of death among Native American youths from 15 to 19 years of age, with a death rate five times the national average (Farris & Farris, 1976).

Although death rates for all adolescents are very low, when young people do die it is usually through some violent modality. The mortality statistics in 1980 show that 119 persons between the ages of 15 and 24 died for every 100,000 members of this age group in the general population (Papalia & Olds, 1986). Eighty percent of all deaths in this age group stemmed from accidents, homicide, and suicide. This represents a marked increase from the 51 percent who died from these causes in 1950. Death rates are three times higher for adolescent males than females, and 20 percent higher for blacks than whites. The leading cause of death for white youths is motor vehicle accidents, and the leading cause of death for blacks is homicide. The third leading cause for both groups is suicide (Holinger, 1979).

Suicide

The suicide rate among adolescents has increased 300 percent in the last thirty years (U.S. Department of Commerce, 1981). More girls attempt suicide than boys, but more boys actually kill themselves, because they are more likely to use violent methods such as guns (Cantor, 1985). Of the adolescents who attempt suicide, 90 percent are firstborn girls who are unusually close to their mothers. Of the adolescents who actually commit suicide, 75 percent are white middle-class boys. They tend to be later-born children who keep their problems to themselves and find it difficult to accept help from others. Some adolescents are so depressed by the death of a family member or close friend that they may try suicide. Others make a

suicide attempt after they have been isolated for a long time, after they have failed
repeatedly, or when they have been feeling
unworthy, desperate, and hopeless (Tishler
et al., 1981). In discussing many of the
complex factors in adolescent suicide,
Berman (1986) emphasizes that suicidal
behavior among teenagers is most often
not the expression of a wish to be dead,
but, rather, of a wish to escape from a
crisis or stressful life situation.

Many writers have addressed the need
for helpful counsel with suicidal young
people from sympathetic adults such as
teachers, parents, and friends (e.g.,
Klagsbrun, 1976; Giovacchini, 1981; Peck
et al., 1985). Nevertheless, in spite of the
considerable attention that has been given
to this subject in numerous studies of
trends, causes, and strategies for prevention and intervention, there is still much
we need to learn about suicidal behavior
in adolescence.

The Dying Adolescent

Adolescence is basically a healthy time
of life. The most common physical problems usually have their origins in psychological and life-style causes. Cancer is the
most common disease-related cause of adolescent death (Plumb & Holland, 1974),
and the percentage of deaths from malignant neoplasms, diseases of the heart, and
congenital anomalies is small. Of course,
the statistical profile is only part of the
picture, as these deaths are tragic and poignant in a society in which relatively few
young people die. Effects upon families are
profound, for the tasks of coping with a
chronic illness are stressful enough, and
the death of a youthful member may increase the stress level to an almost intolerable level (McCubbin & Patterson, 1981).

Dying adolescents are "forced into a
quandary. Their impending death is a personal devastation of all of life's
goals. . . . It is against the very nature of
adolescents to accept their own death without contention" (Adams & Deveau, 1986,
p. 79). Waechter (1984) reports that the
major concerns of the dying adolescent are
a strong sense of isolation, worries about
body deterioration and the future, as well
as the emotional challenge of coping with
the intense threat of premature death. Life-
threatened teenagers also need to maintain
their sense of identity and remain independent and in control. They still retain a
need for privacy and a concern for living
as fully as possible until death comes.
When death is inevitable, family care of
dying adolescents at home can be a valuable alternative to remaining in the hospital. The increasing availability of hospice
services can help to make this possible in
many instances.

Loss, Grief, and Bereavement

The literature on bereavement contains only a few suggestions toward a theory of grief and mourning in adolescence
(Sugar, 1968; Raphael, 1983), and only a
few studies of bereaved adolescents. Fleming and Adolph (1986) have proposed a
helpful model of adolescent grieving that
relates loss to the tasks and conflicts of
normal adolescent development. These are
seen as occurring in three maturational
phases: at approximately ages 11–14,
14–17, and 17–21. Fleming and Adolph
have also identified five core issues that
bereaved adolescents confront at each of
these age levels: predictability of events,
self-image, belonging, fairness or justice,
and mastery or control. Each of these issues provokes responses of thinking, feeling, and behaving. This theory may stimulate further understanding of the needs of
bereaved teenagers, as well as the design of
more relevant and thoughtful research.

Among the few studies dealing with
bereaved adolescents are those concerning
death of a parent or sibling. According to
Raphael (1983), the death of a parent is
likely to be one of the greatest losses for
the adolescent, especially in the earlier
years, when he or she is still dependent
upon parental authority and guidance. In a
study of 182 college students whose parent
had died, Murphy (1986–87) reported that
60 percent of her sample of 18- to
24-year-olds had been between 12 and 16
years of age at the death of their parent.
She found that the students who reported
fewer "mourning behaviors" soon after the
parent's death were significantly more
lonely and had lower self-esteem than other students in the sample, a possible consequence of unresolved grief.

Grief over sibling death is a relatively unexplored topic. Balk (1983) found that teenagers experienced fewer grief complications in families that encouraged closeness and open communication. However, the emotional impact of a sibling's death tended to be long-lasting and affected the survivor's self-concept, grades, study habits, and relationships with peers. Hogan's work (1986) has confirmed these findings. In their longitudinal study of adolescent sibling bereavement Guerriero and Fleming (1985) found that grief reactions and death anxiety levels tend to fluctuate over time. The most severe reactions were usually observed six to twelve months after a death, and again at eighteen to twenty-four months.

Death of an adolescent peer undoubtedly has a strong impact upon the lives of teenagers, similar in many ways to the effects of a sibling's death, although this area has received little research attention. Many adolescents are deeply affected by a friend's death, yet they are not generally recognized to have suffered a bereavement (Raphael, 1983). Valente and Sellers (1986) offer practical suggestions for interventions and support in such situations. Teachers and counselors can play a useful role in helping young people to deal with their thoughts and feelings after suffering a death-related loss (e.g., Jones, 1977; McHenry et al., 1980; Balk, 1984; Calvin & Smith, 1986). Peer support groups can also be important in a therapeutic process (Riber & Berman, 1987).

Bereaved adolescent parents have rarely been given attention in either professional or popular writings. The plight of such vulnerable young people is addressed with clarity and compassion by Barnickol et al. (1986), who discuss the problems of adolescent pregnancies and infant death from miscarriage, SIDS, premature births, or birth defects. On a related theme, Joralemon (1986, p. 120) has pointed out that "of all the pregnancy-related losses in adolescence, elective abortion is the most common and least often recognized." She maintains that this difficult experience—which affects teenage girls and boys and their families—needs special understanding and concern from all those who work with youth.

Gordon (1986, p. 23) writes convincingly of the challenge to parents and teachers to "educate children and teenagers to face life and life's inevitable end with a sense of mastery, purpose, and dignity." Many other recent writers have emphasized the importance of death education in school systems as helpful preparation for life and loss experiences (e.g., Leviton & Wendt, 1983; Wass et al., 1985; Rosenthal, 1986). Warm, honest and open communication about life and death issues in the home between parents and adolescents is also recommended (McNeil, 1986).

See also Causes of Death; Children and Death; Death Education; Grief; Hospice: Children; Stillbirth; Sudden Infant Death Syndrome (SIDS); Suicide: Native American; Suicide: Youth.

—JOAN N. McNEIL

References

Adams, D.W. & Deveau, E.J. (1986). "Helping dying adolescents: Needs and responses." In C.A. Corr & J.N. McNeil (Eds.) *Adolescence and death*. New York: Springer, pp. 79–96.

Attig, T. (1986). "Death themes in adolescent music: The class years." In C.A. Corr & J.N. McNeil (Eds.) *Adolescence and death*. New York: Springer, pp. 32–56.

Austin, D.A. & Mack, J.E. (1986). "The adolescent philosopher in a nuclear world." In C.A. Corr & J.N. McNeil (Eds.) *Adolescence and death*. New York: Springer, pp. 57–75.

Balk, D. (1983). "Adolescents' grief reactions and self-concept perceptions following sibling death: A study of 33 teenagers." *Journal of Youth and Adolescence, 12*: 219–28.

Balk, D. (1984). "How teenagers cope with sibling death: Some implications for school counselors." *The School Counselor, 32*: 150–58.

Barnickol, C.A., Fuller, H., & Shinners, B. (1986). "Helping bereaved adolescent parents." In C.A. Corr & J.N. McNeil (Eds.) *Adolescence and death*. New York: Springer, pp. 132–47.

Beardslee, W.R. & Mack, J.E. (1982). "The impact on children and adolescents of nuclear developments." In R. Rogers (Ed.) *Psychosocial aspects of nuclear developments*. Task Force Report 20. Washington, DC: American Psychiatric Association, pp. 64–93.

Berman, A.L. (1986). "Helping suicidal adolescents: Needs and responses." In C.A.

Corr & J.N. McNeil (Eds.) *Adolescence and death.* New York: Springer, pp. 215–30.

Bolton, F.G. (1980). *The pregnant adolescent.* Beverly Hills, CA: Sage.

Calvin, S. & Smith, I.M. (1986). "Counseling adolescents in death-related situations." In C.A. Corr & J.N. McNeil (Eds.) *Adolescence and death.* New York: Springer, pp. 132–47.

Cantor, P. (1985). "These teenagers feel that they have no options." *People Weekly,* February 18: 84–87.

Elkind, D. (1967). "Egocentrism in adolescence." *Child Development, 38*:1025–34.

Fleming, S.J. & Adolph, R. (1986). "Helping bereaving adolescents: Needs and responses." In C.A. Corr and J.N. McNeil (Eds.) *Adolescence and death.* New York: Springer, pp. 97–118.

Giovacchini, P. (1981). *The urge to die: Why young people commit suicide.* New York: Macmillan.

Gordon, A.K. (1986). "The tattered cloak of immortality." In C.A. Corr & J.N. McNeil (Eds.) *Adolescence and death.* New York: Springer, pp. 16–31.

Guerriero, A.M. & Fleming, S.J. (1985). "Adolescent bereavement: A longitudinal study." Presented at annual meeting of Canadian Psychological Association, Halifax, Nova Scotia.

Hoffman, L., Paris, S., Hall, E., & Schell, R. (1988). *Developmental psychology today.* 5th ed. New York: Random House.

Hogan, N.S. (1986). "An investigation of the adolescent sibling bereavement process and adaptation." Unpublished Ph.D. Dissertation, Loyola University of Chicago.

Holinger, P.C. (1979). "Violent deaths among the young: Recent trends in suicide, homicide, and accidents." *American Journal of Psychiatry, 136*:1144–47.

Johnston, L.D., O'Malley, P.M., & Bachman, J.G. (1985). *Use of licit and illicit drugs by American high school students, 1975–1984.* Washington, DC: National Institute of Drug Abuse, U.S. Department of Health and Human Services.

Jones, W.H. (1977). "Death-related grief counseling: The school counselor's responsibility." *The School Counselor, 24*:315–20.

Joralemon, B.G. (1986). "Terminating an adolescent pregnancy: Choice and loss." In C.A. Corr & J.N. McNeil (Eds.) *Adolescence and death.* New York: Springer, pp. 119–31.

Karsh, E. (1987). "A teenager is a ton of worry." *New York Times,* January 23.

Kastenbaum, R. (1986). "Death in the world of adolescence." In C.A. Corr & J.N. McNeil (Eds.) *Adolescence and death.* New York: Springer, pp. 4–15.

Klagsbrun, F. (1976). *Too young to die: Youth and suicide.* Boston: Houghton Mifflin.

Krementz, J. (1981). *How it feels when a parent dies.* New York: Knopf.

Lapsley, D.K. & Murphy, M.N. (1985). "Another look at the theoretical assumptions of adolescent egocentrism." *Developmental Review, 5*:201–17.

Leviton, D. & Wendt, W. (1983). "Death education: Toward individual and global well-being." *Death Education, 7*: 369–84.

McCubbin, H.I. & Patterson, J.M. (1981). "Family stress and adaptation to crisis." Presented at annual meeting, National Council on Family Relations, Milwaukee, WI.

McHenry, P.C., Tishler, C.L., & Christman, K.L. (1980). "Adolescent suicide and the classroom teacher." *Journal of School Health, 50*: 130–32.

McNeil, J.N. (1986). "Talking about death: Adolescents, parents, and peers." In C.A. Corr & J.N. McNeil (Eds.) *Adolescence and death.* New York: Springer, pp. 185–201.

Murphy, P.A. (1986–1987). "Parental death in childhood and loneliness in young adults." *Omega, Journal of Death and Dying, 17*: 219–28.

Offer, D., Ostrov, E., & Howard, K.I. (Eds.) (1981). *The adolescent: A psychological self-portrait.* New York: Basic Books.

Offer, D., Ostrov, E., & Howard, K.I. (Eds.) (1984). *Patterns of adolescent self-image.* San Francisco: Jossey-Bass.

Papalia, D.E. & Olds, S.W. (1986). *Human development.* New York: McGraw-Hill.

Peck, M.L., Farberow, N.L., & Litman, R.E. (Eds.) (1985). *Youth suicide.* New York: Springer.

Pendleton, E. (1980). *Too old to cry, too young to die: 35 teenagers talk about cancer.* Nashville: Thomas Nelson.

Plumb, M.M. & Holland, J. (1974). "Cancer in adolescents: The symptom is the thing." In B. Schoenberg, A.C. Carr, A.H. Kutscher, D. Peretz, & I. K. Goldberg (Eds.) *Anticipatory grief.* New York: Columbia University Press, pp. 193–209.

Rando, T.A. (1984). *Grief, dying, and death: Clinical interventions for caregivers.* Champaign, IL: Research Press.

Raphael, B. (1983). *The anatomy of bereavement.* New York: Basic Books.

Ribar, M.C. & Berman, C. (1987). "'Nobody understands': A support group for high school students." In C.A. Corr & R.A. Pacholski (Eds.) *Death: Completion and discovery.* Lakewood, OH: Association for Death Education and Counseling, pp. 189–96.

Rice, F.P. (1987). *The adolescent: Development, relationships, and culture.* 5th ed. Boston: Allyn & Bacon.

Rosenthal, N.R. (1986). "Death education: Developing a course of study for adolescents." In C.A. Corr & J.N. McNeil (Eds.) *Adolescence and death.* New York: Springer, pp. 202–14.

Sternberg, F. & Sternberg, B. (1980). *If I die and when I do: Exploring death with young people.* Englewood Cliffs, NJ: Prentice-Hall.

Stillion, J.M. (1986). "Examining the shadow: Gifted children respond to the nuclear threat." *Death Studies, 10*: 27–41.

Sugar, M. (1968). "Normal adolescent mourning." *American Journal of Psychotherapy, 22*: 258–69.

Tishler, C., McHenry, P.C., & Morgan, K.C. (1981). "Adolescent suicide attempts: Some significant factors." *Suicide and Life-Threatening Behavior, 11*: 86–92.

U.S. Department of Commerce (1981). *Social indicators of suicide.* Vol. 3. Washington, DC.

Valente, S.M. & Sellers, J.F. (1986). "Helping adolescent survivors of suicide." In C.A. Corr & J.N. McNeil (Eds.) *Adolescence and death* New York: Springer, pp. 167–82.

Waechter, E.H. (1984). "Dying children: Patterns of coping." In H. Wass & C.A. Corr (Eds.) *Childhood and death.* Washington, DC: Hemisphere, pp. 51–68.

Wass, H., Corr, C.A., Pacholski, R.A., & Forfar, C.S. (1985). *Death education II: An annotated resource guide.* Washington, DC: Hemisphere.

Yager, J. (1982). "Family issues in the pathogenesis of anorexia nervosa." *Psychosomatic Medicine, 44*: 43–60.

AMERICAN ASSOCIATION OF SUICIDOLOGY

The American Association of Suicidology (AAS) was founded in 1968 by Edwin S. Shneidman, a psychologist who has contributed significantly to theory, research, and prevention of self-destructive behavior. AAS is a not-for-profit, tax-exempt organization whose goals are to contribute to the understanding and prevention of suicide.

AAS serves as a national clearinghouse for information on suicide and promotes a variety of public awareness programs as well as training opportunities for professionals and volunteers. Included in the membership are mental health professionals, researchers, crisis center volunteers, survivors of suicide, and a variety of interested laypeople, as well as organizations such as suicide prevention and crisis intervention centers and school districts. Membership is encouraged both from individuals and organizations; application blanks and further information can be obtained from the address given below.

The first week of May is designated as National Suicide Prevention Week. During this annual effort, local suicide prevention and crisis intervention centers, in conjunction with AAS, work with print and broadcast news media to furnish the public with current information on issues related to suicide and its prevention. AAS also provides consultation throughout the year to those interested in understanding and preventing suicide, participates in the development of legislative initiatives, and provides expert testimony for congressional committees.

AAS has developed standards for the certification of suicide prevention and crisis centers and works closely with many such organizations throughout Canada and the United States to assist in the provision of high-quality services. This project is described in the AAS Certification Standards Manual for Crisis Intervention Programs.

The Annual Conference of AAS is held each spring, rotating throughout all the regions of the country. State and regional groups affiliated with AAS also hold conferences to support local efforts. Other AAS activities include assistance to survivors of suicide and an active Speakers/Writers Bureau.

Further information can be obtained from:

AAS Central Office
Julie Perlman, MSW, Executive Officer
2459 S. Ash Street
Denver, CO 80222
(303) 692-0985

—ROBERT KASTENBAUM

See also Suicide.

ANTICIPATORY GRIEF

With recent advances in medical technology, the quality of terminal illness has changed. The interim between diagnosis and death is lengthening. Termed the "living-dying interval" (Pattison, 1977), this period can offer circumstances that are a blessing, a curse, or both. The "blessing" comes from the time and circumstances provided during the illness for the opportunity to prepare emotionally and practically for the loss, complete unfinished business with the dying person, help the dying person with the dying process, and in other ways to gradually absorb the reality of death and its consequences. The family can direct its coping mechanisms toward the expected end and can be spared the numerous problems associated with a sudden death.

However, the family very well may carry emotional scars long after the death because of problems originating from the chronic nature of most diseases and because of the difficult experiences loved ones must endure as a family member is dying. For example, today's terminal illnesses often bring a progressive decline of the patient, often with numerous remissions and relapses, and many emotional reactions to each. There is the stress of demands for major changes in the family, and from increased financial, social, physical, and emotional pressures. The illness can bring long-term family disruptions, along with psychological conflict, emotional exhaustion, physical debilitation, social isolation, and discord. Along with extended periods of uncertainty, there are often intensive treatment regimens that are burdensome and may have unpleasant side effects. All these factors may produce dilemmas about decision-making and treatment choices.

The Concept

It is within this context of terminal illness that the complex issues of anticipatory grief commonly arise. The concept was first introduced by Erich Lindemann in his important 1944 article, "Symptomatology and management of acute grief."

Here he noted that the threat of death or separation itself could initiate a bereavement reaction. Lindemann observed that one could be so concerned with adjustment after the potential death of a loved one that all the phases of grief are undergone prior to the death. However, as Lindemann also pointed out, such advanced preparation is not without some cost. Although anticipatory grief can serve as a safeguard should the death actually occur, it may inhibit continued involvement if the death does not occur. Lindemann cited the example of a soldier who returned from the battlefront to find that his wife no longer loved him and demanded an immediate divorce. This was interpreted as constituting the effects of grief work that had been done too effectively. Out of fear of his possible death, this woman had emotionally emancipated herself from her husband so completely that she no longer had any emotional investment in him. In effect, he had become "dead" to her, even though he was still alive.

Prompting controversy about anticipatory grief is the concern that this process inevitably leads to premature detachment from the dying patient. However, this need not be the case. The following discussion examines the phenomenon from the loved ones' perspective; the patient's own anticipatory grief is discussed later.

Basic Facts and Some Common Misconceptions

It is important that the nature of anticipatory grief be understood accurately. Anticipatory grief is unique in offering critical opportunities for primary prevention. Interventions at this point can prevent problems in mourning from developing after the death; later intervention can only attempt to remedy difficulties that have already occurred. To the extent that healthy behavior and interaction can be promoted during this "living-dying" interval, the survivor's postdeath mourning can be made relatively less distressing than it would be without the therapeutic benefits of appropriate anticipatory grief.

Several notable researchers have written that anticipatory grief as such is an impossibility (Parkes & Weiss, 1983;

Silverman, 1974). However, their assertions fall victim to at least two major misconceptions. The first derives from an overfocus on the ultimate loss of death, with the consequent neglect of the other losses that are inherent in a terminal illness. The second major misinterpretation is that anticipatory grief necessarily involves a major decathexis (emotional detachment) from the dying individual. Actually, the term "anticipatory grief" is a misnomer because "anticipatory" suggests that one is grieving only for anticipated as opposed to past and current losses, and also because "grief" implies to some the necessity of complete decathexis from the dying person.

There are actually three time foci toward which anticipatory grief directs itself: past, present, and future. Even in the face of a terminal illness, there are losses that have already occurred that must be mourned. For example, in nursing her husband through his final bout with cancer, it is not uncommon for a wife to grieve over the vibrant and healthy man she has already lost to cancer, and to mourn their altered relationship and life-style. It would not be unusual for her to remember the activities they shared when he was well; to grieve over the fact that so many limitations have been placed on their lives; and to mourn for all that has been taken away by the illness. Each of these losses is a fait accompli. Thus even in the shadow of the ultimate loss of death, there are other losses that already have occurred that necessitate grief.

During the terminal illness the patient and family experience conditions stimulating grief for the present. These include the ongoing losses of progressive debilitation, increasing dependence, continual uncertainty, decreasing control, and so forth. A fundamental component is grief for what currently is being lost and for the future that is being eroded. This is different from grief about what will happen in the future. Rather, it pertains to grief over what is slipping away right now—for the sense of the loved one being taken away from those who cherish him or her, and for what the increasing awareness of the impending death means at this very moment in time.

Finally, there is grief for future losses that are yet to come. Not only is the impending death mourned, but also the losses that will arise before death (the vacation that will not be taken or for the loss of mobility that will occur), as well as the losses that might ensue as a consequence of the death (the loneliness, the social discomfort, the absence of the person at future family functions).

Anticipatory grief does not necessarily mean premature detachment. Some individuals feel that grieving the expected loss of a loved one means separating from him or her in the present. This is not necessarily true. There does not have to be detachment from the dying patient prior to the death. Indeed, this is a time for involvement with the patient in the here-and-now. What needs to be separated from is the image of the patient as a living individual who will be physically present in the survivor's future after the death. The griever must begin to relinquish the emotional investment that had been placed in the hopes, dreams, and expectations of a long-term future with and for the dying loved one. Emotional energy gradually must be withdrawn ("decathected") from the notion of this person being available for interaction, from the conception of this person as having an earthly life beyond the terminal illness.

If the griever prematurely detaches from the dying person before death, then anticipatory grief has been misdirected. While this outcome has occurred in far too many cases, it is not inevitable. The future can be grieved without relinquishing the present. Continued involvement with the dying person and maximizing whatever living is possible is not inconsistent with, nor precluded by, anticipatory grief.

Contradictory Demands

A critically important task in anticipatory grief is to balance the mutually contradictory demands of the process. The griever is pulled in three opposing directions. First, the status quo is maintained as one continues to be involved with and attempts to hold onto the dying patient. At the same time, however, the griever is starting to move away from the dying patient in terms of realizing that this person will not be a companion in the future. Furthermore, the griever is also drawn toward the dying patient as a consequence of acting to direct increased attention, energy, and behavior toward the patient during the illness. This process brings the griever even closer to the patient. Because all three processes are operative at the same time, the griever faces the difficult task of managing the incompatible demands of simultaneously holding onto, letting go of, and drawing closer to the dying patient—as well as coping with the stress generated by their incongruity.

Therapeutic Anticipatory Grief

Therapeutic anticipatory grief requires the appropriate engagement of three processes. Specific interventions (Rando, 1986) will facilitate this end, as summarized below:

1. *Individual intrapsychic processes.* In the individual intrapsychic realm, the person experiences four interrelated subprocesses of anticipatory grief: (a) awareness of and gradual accommodation to the threat (four components); (b) affective processes (six components); (c) cognitive processes (eight components); and (d) planning for the future (three components).
2. *Interactional processes with the dying patient.* Anticipatory grief engenders numerous interpersonal processes involving the dying patient. This is critical to the concept and invalidates the belief that anticipatory grief necessarily must lead to premature detachment from the patient, cause the relationship with him or her to deteriorate, or predispose the survivor to guilt after the death. All of the processes here imply continued involvement with the dying patient and can actually intensify the attachment or improve the relationship: (a) directing attention, energy, and behavior toward the dying patient (seven components); (b) resolution of personal relationships with the dying patient (five components); and (c) helping the dying patient (eleven components).
3. *Familial and social processes.* Anticipatory grief stimulates a series of familial and social processes. These illustrate that the dying of the patient takes place in a social context, which itself is affected by the loss (six components).

What Remains to Be Learned

Much still remains to be learned about anticipatory grief. We already know that anticipatory grief can have profound benefits and that the lack of it can be quite harmful. Yet, how much is therapeutic? Recent studies have elucidated what the wise and observant clinician has known for years: there can be too much of a good thing! For example, Rando (1983) found that there can be an "optimum amount" of anticipatory grief. In her study, too much or too little both interfered with appropriate participation in the dying patient's hospitalization and predisposed mourners to greater anger, hostility, and loss of emotional control.

The risks and costs of anticipatory grief need to be determined. Rosenblatt (1983) has offered evidence that anticipatory grief can lead to enhancement of postdeath grief if it increases one's involvement in the care of the dying person. Care then makes the loss hurt even more and leaves one with more memories, emotional involvement, and behavior links from which to disengage after the loss. Also, death's shattering of a daily routine centered on the dying patient mandates the development of a new pattern of life. The changes in routine and role may augment the grief to be experienced following the death. Last, Fulton and Fulton (1971) observed that a period of anticipation may reduce the amount of public mourning displayed by grievers after the death. This in turn can cause guilt or shame stimulated by their own reactions to the disapproval of others. It may also make survivors feel that funeral rituals are unnecessary, depriving them of the opportunity to experience the social confirmation and support afforded by such rituals.

There must be additional research conducted on anticipatory grief not only to further our knowledge of this phenomenon, but also to eliminate the considerable confusion that still exists in the literature. Since Lindemann, numerous writers have articulated the costs and benefits of anticipatory grief (most notably, Fulton & Gottesman, 1980; and Siegel & Weinstein, 1983). There has been an accumulation of seemingly contradictory information regarding the value of having some advanced warning and the opportunity to experience moderate amounts of anticipatory grief prior to a death. Research results have been quite inconsistent, primarily because of the conceptual confusion. For example, anticipatory grief has been confused with forewarning of loss, delivery of diagnosis, or length of illness, and has been assumed incorrectly to be identical with postdeath grief except for its earlier appearance. Also, the study of anticipatory grief has been riddled with invalid premises, confounding variables, the lack of precise definition and measurement, and flawed research designs. These problems must be addressed before the inconsistencies about anticipatory death can be resolved successfully.

Conclusion

Anticipatory grief is a complex and multidimensional set of processes that occur during a time of stress. These processes offer therapeutic potential and provide the opportunity for primary prevention of distress on the part of the survivor, but anticipatory grief itself is not without its own demands and conflicts.

See also Dying; Grief Counseling.

—THERESE A. RANDO

References

Aldrich, C.K. (1974). "Some dynamics of anticipatory grief." In B. Schoenberg, A. Carr, A. Kutscher, D. Peretz, & I. Goldberg (Eds.) *Anticipatory grief.* New York: Columbia University Press, pp. 3–13.

Fulton, R. & Fulton, J. (1971). "A psychosocial aspect of terminal care: Anticipatory grief." *Omega, Journal of Death and Dying, 2*: 91–99.

Fulton, R. & Gottesman, D.J. (1980) "Anticipatory grief: A psychosocial concept reconsidered." *British Journal of Psychiatry, 137*: 45–54.

Lindemann, E. (1944). "Symptomatology and management of acute grief." *American Journal of Psychiatry, 101*: 141–48.

Parkes, C.M. & Weiss, R.S. (1983). *Recovery from bereavement.* New York: Basic Books.

Pattison, E.M. (Ed.) (1977). *The experience of dying.* Englewood Cliffs, NJ: Prentice-Hall.

Rando, T.A. (1983). "An investigation of grief and adaptation in parents whose children have died from cancer." *Journal of Pediatric Psychology, 8*: 3–20.

Rando, T.A. (Ed.) (1986). *Loss and anticipatory grief.* Lexington, MA: Lexington Books.

Rando, T.A. (1988). *Grieving: How to go on living when someone you love dies.* Lexington, MA: Lexington Books.

Rosenblatt, P. (1983). *Bitter, bitter tears: Nineteenth-century diarists and twentieth-century grief theories.* Minneapolis: University of Minnesota Press.

Siegel, K. & Weinstein, L. (1983). "Anticipatory grief reconsidered." *Journal of Psychosocial Oncology, 1*: 61–73.

Silverman, P. (1974). "Anticipatory grief from the perspective of widowhood." In B. Schoenberg, A. Carr, A. Kutscher, D. Peretz, & I. Goldberg (Eds.) *Anticipatory grief.* New York: Columbia University Press, pp. 320–30.

APPROPRIATE DEATH

What Herman Feifel (1959) described as the American "taboo on death" has since been alleviated to some extent by research and teaching, the advent of hospice care, and a somewhat more receptive social climate for discussion. One of the first issues to arise from the new dialogue concerned the nature of a good or desirable death. Previously, the idea of death had been so repellent and unspeakable to many people that it would have been very difficult to explore the possibility that some deaths might be better than others.

A thoughtful answer to this question was offered by Avery D. Weisman (1972, p. 41), one of the few psychiatrists at that time who had both clinical and research experience with terminally ill (and suicidal) individuals. Weisman proposed the concept of appropriate death: "a death that someone might choose for himself—had he a choice."

In Weisman's view, it is critical that the meaning of a death be judged with respect to the person's own personality and values. One should not simply draw up a list of types of death that are "appropriate" or "inappropriate." What really matters is what the timing and manner of a death mean to the person who is most intimately involved. Loving friends and relatives as well as competent caregivers will avoid imposing their own values on the person whose death is in prospect: "Obviously, appropriate death for one person might be unsuitable for another. . . .What might seem appropriate from the outside might be utterly meaningless to the dying person himself. Conversely, deaths that seem unacceptable to an outsider, might be desirable from the inner viewpoint of the patient" (p. 37).

Weisman urged that the dying person be helped to remain relatively free of pain and other forms of suffering, such as social and emotional isolation. There should be an opportunity to continue to exercise whatever abilities one retains, as well as to resolve longstanding problems and satisfy final wishes, whenever possible. Recognizing that the dying person gradually loses much of his or her control over life, Weisman emphasizes the importance of having people available to whom control can be relinquished with a sense of trust and security. Furthermore, the dying person should also have the opportunity to exclude visitors who are not welcome for any reason, while also sending for those whose presence is desired.

Because an appropriate death involves some sense of purpose, it might be argued that suicides should also be considered appropriate. However, Weisman cautions that purpose alone does not necessarily demonstrate that a death was appropriate. Although a person may have rational reasons for choosing self-destruction, the stated reasons may not tell the whole story or even the most important part of it. Weisman suggests that we not come too hastily to the conclusion that a person had "good reason" for a suicide attempt, and, therefore, the choice was entirely appropriate. He notes, as have other researchers and clinicians, that after being rescued from an attempt on their own lives, "few . . . complain. . . . A man who is suicidal at 3 AM may find the idea unthinkable at 9 AM, even though his reasons remain the same." Although recognizing that there are circumstances in which suicide may appear to be the lesser evil, Weisman argues against the assumption that a death by suicide was appropriate simply because that course of action was chosen.

In a later book, Weisman (1974) provides an interesting case example of what might be considered an appropriate death. A man was down and out at age 43, having a history of alcohol abuse, tuberculosis, physical abuse of family members and, by now, unemployability. His hospital records invariably reported "how charming, intelligent, likeable, he is, then how he disrupts the psychiatric ward before checking out" (p. 143). Gazing at a mirror in the window of a Skid Row store, he realized the depths to which he had sunk; he walked up to a police station and asked to be put away someplace. This proved to be a turning point. With the help of Alcoholics Anonymous, he put his drinking days behind him and had five years of much improved life. When he became terminally ill, one of his major fears was that he would revert again to drinking. He was also lonely, with no family members to care for and sympathize with him. Nevertheless, he did succeed in maintaining his new alcohol-free life-style, and received genuine respect and affection both from other AA members and from the hospital staff. In the subsequent psychological autopsy, one participant noted that the patient had seen his frailty very clearly and did not pretend to have attained a false serenity: he died with a "pretty decent" self-image. It was not a "happy" death, nor one in which the man had "accepted" all aspects of his life and fate, nevertheless, "he shows how someone can be hopeless but not helpless, and still muster enough to be responsible."

In commenting on this case, Weisman (1974, p. 151) offered a key insight on the concept of an appropriate death: "Don't confuse the pigeon with our pigeonholes. What is appropriate for me may not be appropriate for you. Operational criteria for an appropriate death are all right, but what can they tell us about how to measure the meaning of death for any individual? The final judge is the patient—whether it feels right to die at that moment."

Two additional points are worth keeping in mind: A death can be regarded as appropriate without necessarily involving a hypothetical final stage of "acceptance," and it is actually the circumstances associated with dying, not death itself, that usually comes to the fore when one asks whether or not a "death" has been "appropriate."

See also Autopsy, Psychological; Stages of Dying; Suicide; Tame Death.

—ROBERT KASTENBAUM

References

Feifel, H. (Ed.) (1959). *The meaning of death.* New York: McGraw-Hill.

Weisman, A.D. (1972). *On dying and denying.* New York: Behavioral Publications.

Weisman, A.D. (1974). *The realization of death.* New York: Jason Aronson.

ARS MORIENDI

There is an art to dying as well as to living. The two, in fact, are intimately related. One should live each day as though it might be the last. Furthermore, this should not lead to immoderate and self-indulgent behavior: the sure prospect of death must surely inspire us to the highest plateau of moral rectitude. And in life's final scene one will face such fear, such agony, and such temptation that it will require all the purity, strength, and faith one can bring to the crisis.

Such was the message conveyed by most of the literature comprising the *Ars moriendi* (also given as *Artes moriendi*) tradition. The first examples of Christian guidebooks for the dying appeared early in the fifteenth century. Jean de Gerson (1363–1429), chancellor of the University of Paris, devoted a section of one of his books to those who were in a position to help others die well. This was essentially a how-to-do-it book, offering a ritualistic framework for priests and laymen who might be called upon in a deathbed scene. In the second decade of the fifteenth century, a block book was commissioned by the Council of Constance to encourage more devout Christian living. This work, *Tractatus,* or *Speculum, artis bene moriendi,* also included a section on Christian dying. Not long afterward, this section

appeared in revised form under the title, *Ars moriendi.* It was a rather simple offering that depicted the temptations faced on the deathbed by Moriens, an Everyman-type character. The work consists of eleven woodcuts and their brief accompanying texts. Most of the pictures showed a swarm of demons attempting to snare the dying man's soul. In some of the pictures they are countered by angels, at times accompanied by the Virgin Mary or the crucified Christ (Beaty, 1970). Much of the material included in this work found its way into later tracts and books. Overall, there is much repetition among the *Ars moriendi* publications until we reach the more original contribution of Jeremy Taylor (1651/1977).

Confession is portrayed as a valuable preparation for those who would die well. From Dominicus Capranica, *De Arte bene moriendi,* Venice, 1490. Reprinted, by permission, from Ernst & Johanna Lehner, *Picture Book of Devils, Demons and Witchcraft,* p. 88. © 1971 by Dover Publications, Inc.

Representative publications from the *Ars moriendi* tradition were later gathered into *The Book of the Craft of Dying and*

Other English Tracts Concerning Death, which passed through a number of editions. It is this work that has been most often consulted by later generations. The intent and scope of the book are well expressed by the opening passages (Comper, 1917/1977):

> Here beginneth the book of the craft of dying.
>
> Forasmuch as the passage of death, of the wretchedness of the exile of this world, for uncunning [ignorance] of dying—not only to lewd men [laymen] but also to religious and devout persons—seemeth wonderfully hard and perilous, and also right fearful and horrible; therefore in this present matter and treatise, that is of the Craft of Dying, is drawn and contained a short manner of exhortation, for teaching and comforting of them that be in the point of death. This manner of exhortation ought subtly to be considered, noted, and understood in the sight of man's soul; for doubtless it is and may be profitable generally, to all true Christian men, to learn and have craft and knowledge to die well.
>
> This matter and treatise containeth six parts of chapters:
>
> The first is of commendation of death; and cunning to die well.
>
> The second containeth the temptations of men that die.
>
> The third containeth the interrogations that should be asked of them in their death bed, while they can speak and understand.
>
> The fourth containeth an instruction to them that all shall die.
>
> The fifth containeth an instruction to them that shall die.
>
> The sixth containeth prayers that should be said to them that be a-dying, of some men that be about them.

Two interesting explanations suggest themselves for the emergence of *Ars moriendi* tracts early in the fifteenth century and their continued popularity for the next two centuries. The first explanation takes note of society's exceptional encounters with death during the catastrophic fourteenth century. Many died in pain and despair, and the shaken survivors were left with horrifying memories (Kastenbaum, In press). Philippe Aries (1981, pp. 131–32) offers another view:

How many of us today would feel the slightest inclination at death to take along a portfolio of stock certificates, a coveted automobile, a magnificent jewel? Medieval man could not bring himself to abandon his riches even at death. He sent for them; he wanted to touch them, to hold them.

The truth is that probably at no time has man so loved life as he did at the end of the Middle Ages. The history of art offers indirect proof. The love of life found expression in a passionate attachment to things, an attachment that resisted the annihilation of death and changed our vision of the world and of nature.

The guides to Christian dying, then, may have had several functions: (1) practical handbooks for those who would come into the presence of the dying person, (2) a model of proper behavior that dying people themselves could try to follow, (3) an assurance that one might pass safely through the dread crisis, and (4) an aid to making the transition from the things of life to the hereafter. The tracts did offer comforting words, along with their depiction of temptations to be overcome. It is clear that the deathbed scene had now become an important theme in Christian thought.

The *Ars moriendi* tradition reached its pinnacle with a book whose complexity of thought and literary quality transcended its predecessors: *The Rules and Exercises of Holy Dying* (short title). Jeremy Taylor (1651/1977), chaplain to King Charles I, informs his dedicatee, Lord Carberry: "My lord, it is a great art to die well, and to be learned by men in health." It is with Taylor that the *Ars moriendi* tradition enriches itself with systematic consideration of the way people live every day of their lives, not simply how they meet their final moments. *Holy Dying* continues to use biblical and classical sources to bolster its arguments, but also includes Taylor's own incisive thoughts. One of the points insisted upon by Taylor is "a daily examination of our actions." It is folly to wait until we are upon our deathbeds to recant our sins of omission and commission—chances are that we won't even remember most of them! The wise person will review the moral errors of each day before retiring for the night, the better to wake up on the morrow as an improved and holier person (or to fly heavenward in a more devout state if no morrow should dawn).

The *Ars moriendi* tradition eventually receded to bookshelves and footnotes as the high-spirited Renaissance, the vigorous Industrial Revolution, and the rise of science transformed the conditions of everyday life. Today, however, as we experience the beginnings of what some call the postmodern world, the idea of dying well has again attracted attention. Such issues as "mercy death" for those on life support systems in persistent vegetative states, the "right to die," and efforts to define the "good death" are among the current concerns that invite a review of the old *Ars moriendi* tradition. It is improbable that many people will find the answers they are seeking in the pages of *Ars moriendi* texts per se, but our sympathies may be deepened and our perspectives broadened through acquaintance with this tradition.

See also (The) Black Death; Euthanasia; *Memento Mori*; Suicide: Assisted.

—ROBERT KASTENBAUM

References

Aries, P. (1981). *The hour of our death.* New York: Alfred A. Knopf.

Beaty, N.L. (1970). *The craft of dying.* New Haven, CT: Yale University Press.

Comper, F.M.M. (Ed.) (1917/Reprint 1977). *The book of the craft of dying.* New York: Arno Press.

Kastenbaum, R. (In press). *The psychology of death.* 2nd ed. New York: Springer.

Taylor, J. (1651/Reprint 1977). *The rules and exercises of holy dying.* New York: Arno Press.

ASSOCIATION FOR DEATH EDUCATION AND COUNSELING

The Forum for Death Education and Counseling was incorporated in 1976 as a nonprofit organization devoted to improving the quality of death education and death-related counseling. In 1987 its name was changed to the Association for Death Education and Counseling (ADEC).

The essential goal of ADEC is to promote and upgrade responsible and effective death education and death-related counseling in a variety of settings while also stimulating research.

ADEC provides to its membership:

1. A newsletter to increase communication between death educators and counselors.
2. National conferences to foster an exchange of knowledge and experience, stimulate research, provide mutual support, and encourage cooperative endeavors among members.
3. Programs to train individuals and representatives of institutions in the theory, methods, and subject matter of death education and/or death-related counseling. The first national training workshop with separate tracks in death education and death-related counseling was conducted in Orlando, Florida, in 1979, and other workshops have subsequently been conducted throughout the United States and Canada. A certification procedure is also available.
4. A directory listing members by name, location, and area of specialization.
5. Discounts on subscriptions to the journal *Death Studies* and to proceedings of conferences.

ADEC encourages a diverse membership of laypersons, students, and individuals with academic and professional credentials. Members may also become affiliated with one of the several regional chapters located throughout the United States. ADEC is governed by an elected board of directors and officers.

Correspondence may be addressed to:

Association for Death Education
 and Counseling
2211 Arthur Avenue
Lakewood, OH 44107

—DANIEL LEVITON

See also Death Education.

References

Corr, C.A. & Pacholski, R.A. (1987). *Death completion and discovery.* Lakewood, OH: Association for Death Education and Counseling.

Crase, D. & Leviton, D. (1987). "The forum for death education and counseling: Its history and future." *Death Studies, 11*: 345–59.

AUTOPSY

Autopsy, which literally means "seeing for one's self," is usually restricted to medical use entailing dissection of a dead body to determine the cause of death, nature of disease, or current status and quality of medical care.

Ancient Origins

The roots of the autopsy can be traced back 5,000 years to the time of Sargon I when the Babylonians practiced the animistic custom of haurispicy (King & Meehan, 1973). Haurispicy, or hepatoscopy, involved foretelling the future through examination of the entrails (usually the liver) of sacrificial animals. The liver, at that time considered the seat of the soul, has been found diagrammatically illustrated in many ancient sites, purportedly for instruction of student diviners. While the Babylonians learned much about gross anatomy, this information was utilized primarily for religious purposes. Nevertheless, their observations contributed significantly to the accumulation of anatomical knowledge.

During the Talmudic epoch, the Jews, to assure that their meat came from beasts free of disease, fostered further awareness of anatomy through examination of slaughtered animals. This practice, initially performed on any creature "dying of itself," was eventually extended to all butchered animals (King & Meehan, 1973).

Subsequently, Hippocrates (468–377 BC) proposed a naturalistic philosophy of disease, advancing the belief that illness resulted from natural rather than supernatural causes. Viewed as the first naturalistic physician, Hippocrates considered the autopsy "an unpleasant, if not cruel, task" (McPhee & Bottles, 1985), and, veritably, 1,800 years passed before autopsy acquired an eminent position in pathology.

The Greeks devoted little study to the anatomy of solid organs, embracing instead the premise that disease resulted from disturbed proportions in the fluid components of the body. Edelstein (1967) believes that no human dissections occurred in the Grecian world prior to the third century BC but holds that dissections were done in Alexandria through 130 AD. Kudlein (1969), another scholar of the history of anatomy, disagrees, asserting that human dissections were performed only during the third century BC.

Meanwhile, the Egyptians were becoming quite proficient in the techniques of embalming and, in Alexandria, permitted human dissection to ascertain normal anatomy as well as the purmutations of disease. Herophilus (335–280 BC), a prominent teacher of the times, wrote an admirable dissertation on human anatomy but failed to stress morphological changes because of his adherence to the humoral theory of disease. Erasistratus (310–250 BC) also performed autopsies in Alexandria, but, contrary to Herophilus, forsook the humoral philosophy in favor of the solidist theory, an hypothesis that surmised illnesses were accompanied by changes in the solid organs. He described an apparent case of cirrhosis, noting "the liver of a man who died from dropsy was hard as stone, but in a man who died of snake bite the liver was soft" (Dorsey, 1978). Autopsies probably continued in Alexandria until approximately 200 AD, during which time Galen (130–200 AD), a proponent of autopsy, dissected animals, viewed wounded men, and examined two skeletons, one washed out of a grave by flooding, the other an unburied brigand picked clean by vultures (King & Meehan, 1973).

Whether or not human dissection was practiced in Rome during the fourth century AD remains a difficult question to answer. An ostensibly ancient portrayal of autopsy was found in a catacomb in Rome dating from the fourth century AD. However, there is disagreement as to the significance of the painting. Some observers view the picture as merely a surgical procedure, others as an autopsy (Proskauer, 1938).

From the Middle Ages to Modern Times

Knowledge of the practice of autopsy is likewise scant for the early Middle Ages. In the year 1111, a human dissection was documented whereby wine was ascertained to be harmful to the liver. A manuscript dated 1290 includes a depiction of what appears to be an autopsy. Dissections were performed in Italy between 1266 and 1275, probably for medicolegal purposes. In 1286 a Franciscan friar detailed an autopsy of a hen and an autopsy of a man, noting that both succumbed to a "vesicular aposteme" of the heart. Another account of human dissection, carried out by court order to investigate the suspicious death of an Italian nobleman in 1302, further indicates that autopsy was known during this period.

The church in early Christianity objected to autopsies, although without any theological basis. The Council of Tours in 1163 states "the church abhors blood," which was taken to mean that no surgery or autopsy could be performed on the living or the dead. The clergy—which at the time included most physicians—thus discouraged autopsies, though stopped short of outright prohibition. In 1410, when Pope Alexander died unexpectedly, an autopsy was permitted to establish the cause of death, and Pope Sixtus IV (1471–1484) issued an edict permitting autopsy by students at Bologna and Padua. Accordingly, by the sixteenth century, the Catholic Church wholly accepted the practice of autopsy.

The Jewish religion forbade autopsy until the eighteenth century, when it was permitted only to save the life of a living person, such as an accused murderer. It was not until the twentieth century that the Knesset (Israeli parliament) broadened the criteria for human dissection, authorizing autopsies under limited, but more liberal conditions.

The Italian physicians Bernard Tornius and Antonio Benivieni advanced the practice of autopsy in the late fifteenth century by detailing and recording autopsies. Their reports, while laconic and lacking in detail, were characteristic of medical thinking of that era. The sixteenth and seventeenth centuries witnessed a surge in the number of autopsies performed and recorded. In 1679, Theophilus Bonetus (1620–1689) published a compendium of more than 3,000 autopsies by 450 physicians, including prominent practitioners such as Galen, Batholin, Fallopius, Malpighi, Vesalius, and Harvey (McPhee & Bottles, 1985). This publication, reissued in a second edition in 1700, was titled *Sepulchretum* and is considered a landmark review of medical practice and autopsy of that era.

Herman Boerhave (1668–1738) championed the art of autopsy in the eighteenth century when he described the first reported case of a ruptured esophagus, a syndrome that bears his name. G.B. Morgagnim (1682–1772) also furthered the cause when he correlated clinical observations with autopsy findings. The Frenchman Xavier Bichat (1771–1802), considered the father of histology, discerned twenty-one different tissues in the body before the development of the microscope. He embodied the image of the "complete physician," blending basic science with bedside care. France subsequently became the medical center of the world in the early nineteenth century under the leadership of physicians such as Laennec, Louis, and Corvisart. Physicians relied heavily on autopsy findings as cell theory emerged after the introduction of the microscope. Karl Rokitansky (1804–1878), considered by some the most capable gross pathologist in medical history, performed 30,000 autopsies but was without the use of the microscope until late in his career (McPhee & Bottles, 1985). Virchow (1821–1902), seventeen years younger, greatly utilized the microscope, contributing significantly to the basic theories of pathology. His 1876 treatise on the technique of performing an autopsy became a valuable and influential guide. Prior to this time, autopsies often were performed by inexperienced surgical assistants in a random fashion, without definite technique (King & Meehan, 1973).

The early twentieth century witnessed continuing growth and importance of the autopsy, bolstered by the Flexner Report (1910), which elevated the standards of medical education, including pathology, and set criteria for the education of medical personnel. Subsequently, hospital accreditation became based in part on the number of autopsies performed. Clinicians of the period believed that good hospitals had high autopsy rates, poor hospitals low rates. It was therefore not surprising that autopsy rates rose to approximately 50 percent by World War II (McPhee & Bottles, 1985). The number of human dissections then began to decline, nurtured by a 1956 editorial in the *Journal of the American Medical Association* that condoned the dwindling autopsy rate by declaring that the present is "characterized by an increased reliance on experiment as a means of acquiring knowledge." Since that time, the autopsy has failed to recover its once dominant status and today its advocates struggle to maintain its presence in medical education.

What has brought about this decline in autopsies? Primarily, physicians were and are ordering fewer necropsies. Technical advances, allowing greater diagnostic confidence, have encouraged clinicians to belittle the value of the autopsy. Furthermore, physicians may be reticent to request an autopsy for fear that pathologic findings will increase malpractice risks. Second, hospital pathologists find very little time to perform autopsies. Clinical laboratory duties, as well as evaluation of surgical pathology specimens, place great demands upon their time. Moreover, professional advancement and recognition are not afforded pathologists performing autopsies, further abating their desirability. Third, in 1971 the Joint Commission on Accreditation of Hospitals (JCAH) altered the requirements for hospital accreditation, eliminating the compulsory 20 percent autopsy rate (McPhee & Bottles, 1985). Fourth, the process of obtaining permission for autopsy is awkward, arising at a time when family members are emotionally vulnerable. They may feel their loved one has suffered enough, and view an autopsy as the final insult. Furthermore, cultural or religious principles may lead family members to refuse autopsy permission. Perception of what an autopsy entails and the supposed appearance of the body afterward, unfamiliar to many, also may lead relatives to take an unfavorable attitude to postmortem examination. Finally, autopsies are expensive and do not generate income for hospitals (Council Report, 1987).

The cost per autopsy averages $900–$1,100, and insurance companies and Medicare do not reimburse this cost. Under the recently established Diagnosis Related Groups (DRG) system, financial constraints on autopsies are expected to become even greater.

Purpose of the Autopsy

Autopsies are usually performed to assess the current status and quality of medical care as well as the discovery or clarification of diseases, diagnoses, or legal issues. Various studies have documented premortem errors in diagnoses ranging from 5 to 40 percent (McPhee & Bottles, 1985). Accordingly, autopsies improve the accuracy of vital statistics. Autopsy also aids in the evaluation of new diagnostic technologies and therapeutics, such as toxic sequelae of chemotherapeutic agents. Postmortem examinations likewise assist in the discovery of new diseases. This is aptly illustrated by Legionnaire's disease, acquired immunodeficiency syndrome (AIDS), and toxic shock syndrome. Postmortem dissection also advances medical research, stimulating the pursuit of the origins of disorders as diverse as carcinogenesis and atherogenesis.

Environmental and occupational maladies may also be assessed, often supporting the financial compensation of surviving family members and the development of preventive measures. Other benefits to surviving family members from autopsy results can be the detection of communicable or hereditary diseases, making treatment or genetic counseling possible. Feelings of guilt may also be allayed by determination of the cause of death, especially in the loss of children.

Forensic autopsies endeavor to establish the cause, manner, and time of death in circumstances where the precipitants of demise are unknown or suspicious. At other times, the forensic examination is used for identification of bodies, insurance claims, or validation of industrial accidents. More recently, autopsies have become a valuable reservoir of transplantable organs and tissues. Surviving family members may therefore be consoled somewhat by the knowledge that others are being helped.

The Postmortem Examination

Misunderstandings and fears regarding autopsies abound. Most people are unfamiliar with the procedure of postmortem dissection and fear that the body is treated disrespectfully, or so disfigured that an open-casket funeral is unfeasible. Neither assessment is correct.

The autopsy is performed in a methodical fashion, and may be complete (involving the whole body), or local (restricted to a specific area). The pathologist begins with an examination of the exterior of the body, observing for wounds, scars, or tumors. A surgical incision is then made, usually a vertical cut from the base of the neck to the lower abdomen. This allows visualization of the internal organs. Each organ is examined, weighed, and measured, then pieces are cut to allow scrutiny of internal structure. Tissue samples may also be obtained for culture, toxicological analysis, or microscopy. The brain and spinal cord are then examined. Care is taken that the removal of the brain does not lead to disfigurement. When the postmortem discussion is complete, the incisions are sutured and the body released to the mortuary. The entire procedure is done in a manner that expresses respect to the body and concern for the family.

Obtaining consent for an autopsy is often emotionally burdensome. The surviving spouse or next of kin must authorize or prohibit the postmortem dissection, although in certain cases the coroner or medical examiner may dictate an autopsy without consent of the next of kin. In California and several other states, a person may authorize an autopsy prior to death by including such instructions in his or her will.

Recommendations

Autopsy serves an educational, scientific, and humanitarian purpose. Knowledge is gained with each dissection and, therefore, autopsy might be recommended for every death. Realistically, however, this is impossible. Financial constraints inhibit an autopsy for each individual, and permission would be unlikely from every family.

What circumstances, then, warrant an autopsy, aside from postmortem procedures ordered by the coroner or medical examiner? Five criteria are proposed, although many more also exist. An autopsy should be performed:

1. When the cause of death is unknown.
2. When a genetic disorder is suspected.
3. When research is involved in the process causing death (e.g., Alzheimer's disease, AIDS).
4. When organs are to be donated for transplantation.
5. When the medical inquiries of professionals and family members would be unanswerable without an autopsy.

See also Autopsy, Psychological; Uniform Anatomical Act.

—PAUL C. ROUSSEAU, M.D.

References

Council Report (1987). "Autopsy: A comprehensive review of current issues." *Journal of the American Medical Association, 258*: 364–69.

Dorsey, D.B. (1978). "A perspective on the autopsy." *American Journal of Clinical Pathology, 69* (suppl): 217–19.

Edelstein, L. (1967). "The history of anatomy in antiquity." In O. Temkin & C.L. Temkin (Eds.) *Ancient medicine: Selected papers.* Baltimore: The Johns Hopkins Press.

Flexner, A. (1910/Reprint 1960). *Medical education in the United States and Canada: A report to the Carnegie Foundation for the Advancement of Teaching.* Bulletin 4. New York: The Carnegie Foundation for the Advancement of Teaching.

King, L.S. & Meehan, M.C. (1973). "A history of the autopsy." *American Journal of Pathology, 73*: 514–44.

Kudlein, F. (1969). "Antike anatomie und menschlicher leichnam." *Hermes, 97*: 78–94.

McPhee, S.J. & Bottles, K. (1985). "Autopsy: Moribund art or vital science?" *American Journal of Medicine, 78*: 10–113.

Proskauer, C. (1938). "The significance to medical history of the newly discovered fourth century Roman fresco." *Bulletin of the New York Academy of Medicine, 34*: 672–88.

AUTOPSY, PSYCHOLOGICAL

Psychological autopsy is the name given by Edwin S. Shneidman to a systematic multi-disciplinary inquiry into deaths of ambiguous or undetermined cause. The first psychological autopsies were conducted by staff of the Los Angeles Suicide Prevention Center in collaboration with Theodore J. Curphey, M.D., then chief medical examiner for Los Angeles County. The psychological autopsy is a supplement, not a substitute for the traditional medical postmortem examination. The team is likely to consist of nurses, physicians, psychologists, psychiatrists, social workers, and others with relevant skills and experience to contribute. As outlined by Shneidman (1976), the psychological autopsy requires attention both to the entire scope of the decedent's life and to many possibly illuminating details. It has been described also as a "reconstruction" of the victim's lifestyle (Wekstein, 1979). Application of the psychological autopsy has resulted in altered classifications of cause of death (Curphey, 1961) and to insights for suicide prevention. The psychological autopsy method has also been praised as a valuable experience in cooperation for experts representing a variety of disciplines. The general method has been modified to serve a variety of related purposes, including the study of the terminal phase of life in geriatric patients (Weisman & Kastenbaum, 1972). In some settings the procedure is now conducted under a different and less dramatic name in an effort to reduce possible tension and reluctance to participate. In general, the psychological autopsy procedure develops and evaluates information on the life of a recently deceased person, including, but not limited to, factors surrounding the death.

See also Causes of Death; Old Age and Death; Suicide.

—ROBERT KASTENBAUM

References

Curphey, T.J. (1961). "The role of the social scientist in medicolegal certification from suicide." In N.L. Farberow & E.S. Shneidman (Eds.) *The cry for help.* New York: McGraw-Hill.

Shneidman, E.S. (1976). "Suicide among the gifted." In E.S. Shneidman (Ed.) *Suicidology: Contemporary developments.* New York: Grune & Stratton.

Weisman A.D. & Kastenbaum, R. (1972). *The psychological autopsy: A study of the terminal phase of life.* New York: Behavioral Publications.

Wekstein, L. (1979). *Handbook of suicidology.* New York: Brunner/Mazel.

AWARENESS OF DYING

"Doctor, don't tell my husband . . . he couldn't take it!" "We'll just go in and act normal, talk about all the little things. That way, she won't know we know." "Tell a patient that he's dying? That would be cruel. It would take away all hope."

Statements such as these were once heard with great frequency. It was assumed by many health care professionals as well as the general public that the terminally ill should be protected from the awareness of dying as long as possible. This attitude sometimes went to such an extreme that it was believed the "good death" was one that came unexpectedly—the person just slipped away without ever realizing his or her terminal condition. Attitudes of this kind are still encountered today. However, research and clinical observation have persuaded many that the attempt to shield people from the awareness of dying is often both difficult and harmful.

Contexts of Awareness

One of the most influential studies was conducted by sociologists Barney G. Glaser and Anselm L. Strauss (1965). Both these researchers had experienced the death of a parent and were concerned about the pattern of communication they observed among the health care providers involved. It had been difficult to speak openly about the situation. They sensed the expectations that one should remain silent, ignoring the central reality. Subsequently, Glaser and Strauss realized that these personal experiences had not been unusual. Avoiding the awareness of dying seemed to be the rule rather than the exception.

Glaser and Strauss decided to study the social contexts within which the dying process unfolds. Some of their work focused on "trajectories of dying," what happens when the process is short or protracted, expected or unexpected (Glaser & Strauss, 1968; See **Trajectories of Dying**). Other observations focused directly on the issue of awareness. These observations were made in the midst of hospital activities. Glaser, Strauss, and their colleagues conducted fieldwork studies in a teaching hospital, two county hospitals, a private Catholic hospital, a state hospital, and a Veterans Administration hospital. Services and wards studied included premature baby service, pediatrics, geriatrics, intensive care, cancer, general medical, neurosurgery, and urology. The investigators spent several weeks in each setting to make direct observations of communication patterns and later conducted interviews with nursing students.

Glaser and Strauss introduced the concept of "awareness contexts" in order to take the entire pattern of communication into account: not only what the doctor thinks the patients knows but also what the patient thinks the doctor thinks he knows. They observed the following types of awareness contexts.

Closed Awareness. In this context of communication, the patient does not recognize that he or she is dying. Physicians and nurses make a point of preventing the patient from realizing that death is in prospect. Information that might lead the patient to suspect the truth is kept hidden and may even be denied. Family members become part of the conspiracy and are expected to help guard the secret. All these precautions are unnecessary, of course, if the patient is considered to be comatose or otherwise unable to comprehend the situation. The closed awareness context is threatened when a patient starts to ask "too many questions," which may lead staff and family to improvise "stories" to explain away alarming developments or distract the patient. These explanations are likely to become ever more strained and

unconvincing as the dying process asserts itself. Staff and family are apt to become even more tense and "on guard" to protect the secret.

Suspected Awareness. In this situation, the patient is attempting to verify his suspicion that he is dying by luring or forcing others to "spill the beans." The dying person's suspicion may be aroused by noticing different behaviors and attitudes from different shifts of personnel, some firmly guarding the secret, others making less effort to do so. The patient may also be receiving strong clues from the nature of his or her ward assignment and treatment—being moved to the intensive care unit, for example, is likely to raise questions and concerns. Staff often assume that the patient knows or at least suspects what is happening even if he or she hasn't been told, reasoning that the patient has observed his or her own deteriorating condition, changes in treatment, etc. And it seems clear that physicians and other caregivers generally prefer that patients draw their own conclusions rather than being told the truth directly. In this awareness context, nurses field patients' questions by saying, "I don't know, you'll have to ask the doctor." The doctor, in turn, attempts to avoid giving a definitive answer.

Mutual Pretense Awareness. This has become perhaps the best known and remarked upon of the awareness contexts since first described by Glaser and Strauss. The patient knows he or she is dying and so does staff and family. However, all continue to speak and act as though the patient were going to recover. Glaser and Strauss report the mutual pretense interactions are the most subtle involved in any of the awareness contexts. Everybody seems to be exercising great care to keep the pretense going. The mutual pretense awareness context is fostered by the habitual avoidance of death-talk by personnel in many health care settings. The patient is implictly instructed to join the conspiracy of silence, even (or especially) if he or she knows better. Often there seems to be a tacit understanding that is reached jointly by patient and staff. For example, the patient may "flash cues to the staff about his own dread knowledge" but discover that they are unwilling to talk openly about it. In consequence, both enter into a "let's pretend" ritual in which each knows that the other knows, but neither will openly admit it. Patients may become very adept in keeping up their side of the pretense, fixing up their rooms to look "like home," for example, and, in the case of women, taking care with their hair and and makeup. This makes it easier for staff members to keep up their side of the pretense as well. If the mutual pretense context is to continue, then everybody involved must play his or her role in this ritual drama in every interaction.

Open Awareness. This awareness context exists when patient and staff not only know that the patient is dying but acknowledge this fact in their actions and conversations. The open awareness context is conducive to a number of necessary activities, such as finishing important tasks, taking leave of loved ones and caregivers, and reflecting upon one's own life and its meanings. It affords more opportunity to cope with regrets, fears, and other psychological problems with the help of a friend, clergyperson, or counselor. It is much harder to "say goodbye," for example, if the person doesn't realize he or she is dying or doesn't feel able to fracture the mutual pretense agreement. The open awareness context is far from simple, however. A person may realize he or she is dying and still not be aware of several other important facets of the situation. Caregivers are still faced with many decisions regarding the amount, type, and timing of information that should be communicated. Glaser and Strauss note that people take on additional responsibilities when they become aware that they are dying. For example, they now might be tempted to commit suicide, but staff and family expect them not to do so. A person who seems to have brought on his or her own plight (e.g., a drunken driver who has suffered critical injuries) may be treated rather coldly by the staff because that person has "broken an implicit pact with society not to die 'this way'". The dying person is also expected to "live correctly." This obligation obviously is not placed fully upon a person who is unaware of his or her terminal status. Part of the price of awareness, then, is to conform with a variety of social expectations that might be placed on the dying person.

Some Cautions and Guidelines

The observations and concepts of Glaser and Strauss have proven illuminating and durable, along with many other contributions to this topic (e.g., Sudnow, 1967; Kastenbaum, 1978; Nimocks et al., 1987; and Weisman, 1972). The subsequent development of the hospice movement has encouraged a shift toward open contexts of awareness. Several cautions and guidelines might be kept in mind, however.

Contexts of awareness are seldom static. Interpersonal dynamics change over time and, of course, the dying process itself introduces significant changes. It remains useful to analyze situations from the standpoint of awareness context, but (as Glaser and Strauss repeatedly note), the situation can change in either abrupt or subtle ways.

Not everybody is prepared to function well in an open awareness context. Some people have a strong characterological tendency toward the use of psychological denial mechanisms. Others fear the exposure involved in the open awareness context because they have limited communication skills or uncontrolled anxiety about their own mortality. Education and counseling are among the techniques that can help to equip caregivers for the open awareness context, but this form of assistance has often been excluded from professional education and in-service training. It is obvious that physicians, nurses, clergy, and others sometimes prefer closed or mutual pretense contexts in order to control their own anxieties.

There may be particular situations in which the open awareness context has serious drawbacks. It might be as unwise to demand that "full and open disclosure" pertain at all times and in all situations as it was in the past to insist on "protecting" the patient from awareness of his or her own condition. Those well experienced in terminal care often emphasize the need for sensitivity and flexibility rather than simply replacing one rigid and inadequate set of procedures with another.

See also Children, Dying; Deathbed Scenes; Dying; Hospice: Philosophy and Practice; Trajectories of Dying.

—ROBERT KASTENBAUM

References

Glaser, B.G. & Strauss, A.L. (1965). *Awareness of dying.* Chicago: Aldine.

Glaser, B.G. & Strauss, A.L. (1968). *Time for dying.* Chicago: Aldine.

Kastenbaum, R. (1978). "In control." In C. Garfield (Ed.) *Psychosocial care of the dying patient.* New York: McGraw-Hill, pp. 227–44.

Nimocks, M.J.A., Webb, L., & Connell, J.R. (1987). "Communication and the terminally ill: A theoretical model." *Death Studies, 11*: 323–44.

Sudnow, D. (1967). *Passing on: The social organization of dying.* Englewood Cliffs, NJ: Prentice-Hall.

Weisman, A.D. (1972). *On dying and denying: A psychiatric study of terminality.* New York: Behavioral Publications.

B

BARZAKH

Belief in a boundary or barrier that separates the dead from the realm of the living is found in a number of cultural and religious systems of thought. For Muslims, the living/dead barrier is known as *barzakh*, although the Qur'an does not describe it in detail. Perhaps the most widely known boundary between the living and the dead is the river Styx across which, in Greek mythology, the ancient boatman Charon transports deceased souls to their new abode.

See also Charon; Styx; Survival Beliefs and Practices: Islamic.

—ROBERT KASTENBAUM

BIATHANATOS

English poet John Donne (1572–1631) took death as a major theme in his writings and lectures. In 1608 he completed a book whose full title was *Biathanatos. A Declaration of that Paradoxe or Thesis, that Selfe-Homicide is not so Naturally Sinne, that it may never be otherwise. Wherein the Nature, and the Extent of all those Lawes which seem to be violated by this Act, are diligently surveyed.*

In the dedication to Lord Phillip Harbert, Donne pleads that protection be given so that this book be not either "utterly lost" or "utterly found." He was concerned that his arguments might lead to reprisals from church authorities on the one hand, and to damaging appropriation by "some of those wild Atheists, who, as if they came into the World by conquest, owne all other mens Wits."

Much of the book is given to review and commentary on suicide in history and scripture. Attention is given to personal circumstances and legal considerations. It is evident that Donne used the subject of *selfe-homicide* as a vehicle for expressing a moral critique of his own times, but *Biathanatos* is also important as one of the earlier extended treatises on suicide and as an effort to steer a balanced course between absolute condemnation and complete withdrawal of sanctions. Although a serious intellectual work, *Biathanatos* also is graced occasionally by the author's literary imagination and sly humor.

The original edition (London: John Dawson) is extremely rare. A 1930 reprint edition was made available by the Facsimile Text Society of New York, and has long been out of print. A more recent edition, also out of print but less difficult to locate, is the 1977 reprint by Arno Press.

See also Suicide.

—ROBERT KASTENBAUM

Reference

Donne, J. (1608/Reprint 1977). *Biathanatos*. New York: Arno Press.

(THE) BLACK DEATH

Two stories are told by historians. In the year 1346 the merchant city of Caffa, an important seaport in the Crimea, was under siege by a Mongol army. A devastating illness broke out in the encampment. Although disease was familiar to the medieval soldier and often more of a threat than the battlefield, the new illness struck in a most alarming manner. A seemingly healthy man would suddenly become incapacitated and, in a few days or even less, perish. The invaders soon retreated. The city had been saved. Actually, however, the terror had just begun. According to some accounts, the invaders used their catapults to hurl the bloated corpses over the walls. By this means or another, the disease soon spread to the inhabitants of the besieged city. As merchant ships put out to sea, they took the lethal illness with

them. Within a short time, Europe was being ravaged by the pestilence known to history as the Black Death. The second story is a variant in which the spread of the disease is attributed to a Genoese fleet that landed in northeast Sicily with its crew deathly ill (an original, perhaps, for the "Flying Dutchman" legends). They were said to have contracted their illness in the Orient. (Central Asia is sometimes mentioned as a more specific locale.) The harbor masters at Messina attempted to halt the pestilence by quarantine, but their efforts failed, and the Black Death ran unleashed. Both versions have been put forth confidently by qualified scholars, and perhaps both have their share of the truth, for the arrival of the dying sailors in Messina occurred some few months after the incident at Caffa.

Two assumptions about the Black Death need to be re-examined. It has long been thought that the disease in question was the bubonic plague. As will be seen

Black Death victims, buried alive in 1347, return from their graves to frighten a pair of gravediggers. From an engraving by A. Aubrey, Germany, 1604. Reprinted, by permission, from Ernst & Johanna Lehner, *Picture Book of Devils, Demons and Witchcraft*, p. 113. © 1971 by Dover Publications, Inc.

below, however, an alternative explanation has recently been advanced and deserves consideration. If it was the plague, however, then the assumption that the disease was "new" also requires modification. There is evidence to suggest that the plague or a disease very similar had appeared previously and also taken great toll of human life. It is probable that plague was the same highly contagious and often fatal disease that attacked most of the known world in the sixth century AD.

The central facts about the Black Death far outweigh the remaining questions. It has been estimated that approximately one of every three Europeans died of this disease (McNeil, 1976). Some villages ceased to exist as all men, women, and children (as well as their household and farm animals) died. The Black Death was also devastating in the congested cities such as London and Paris where the poor lived—and now died—in misery. The Muslim world was not spared this onslaught. In Alexandria a hundred or more perished each day as the Black Death took hold, and within a few months the daily toll had approached a thousand. Cairo was at that time among the largest cities in the world with approximately a half million people residing in the metropolitan area. Here the daily lists of the dead reached into the thousands, with estimates of the peak toll ranging from 7,000 to 20,000 per day. The holy city of Mecca also suffered greatly. It is probable that by 1349 the entire Islamic world had been devastated, with an estimated 40 percent of the population fatally stricken by the Black Death.

Society buckled under the impact of the Black Death. Medical skills and public health responses were almost completely inadequate. Neither cause nor cure were known, and many died without comfort from family or church. Such "remedies" as filling the sick room with smoke often added to the suffering without providing cure or comfort. So-called plague nurses, recruited from the most desperate and disreputable women, became notorious for robbing the dying and dead. Those doctors who would see the stricken at all had little to offer and were themselves frightening apparitions with their beaklike masks intended to reduce the chances of contagion. Many priests and higher church officials proved themselves as susceptible to panic and self-interest as anybody else; for years afterward the religious establishment had to contend with its failure to comfort the dying and carry out their obligations to the dead and bereaved. Cults and bizarre practices flourished as people sought relief from their fear and suffering. The Flagellants, for example, were bands of penitents who flogged themselves as they marched lugubriously from village to village with their message that the Black Death was God's punishment for the sins of mankind. Six hundred years before Hitler, Jews were persecuted and killed in some German-speaking communities because of their imagined role in bringing on the pestilence. Magic and ritual were invoked in the hope of preventing or curing the Black Death. Quackery flourished, as well as remedies put forth in good faith yet possessing no medical value (Tuchman, 1978).

People fled in terror but usually found the Black Death waiting for them somewhere farther along the road. Although all ranks and classes were vulnerable, the privileged sometimes evaded contagion by isolating themselves in remote retreats. One group of affluent refugees was entertained by a storyteller in their midst who sought to divert them from the horrors going on around them. Boccaccio's *Decameron,* a celebrated collection of adventures and bawdy tales, became an enduring part of world literature.

The immediate effect of the Black Death was great loss of life and widespread devastation, along with a shattering blow to the social institutions that provided so little relief. Nevertheless, the human spirit proved resilient. Society rebuilt itself but was never again the same. The Black Death had demonstrated beyond dispute that all people are, in a sense, created equal, for all were equally helpless before virulent death. The first expressions of egalitarianism did not last long, but a theme had been introduced that would contribute to the principles embodied in the Bill of Rights of the United States Constitution and other instruments of individual liberation. The political structure was also affected by the fall of some ruling families and the rise of others. In general, the survivors now had a larger share of land and other resources. This tendency toward centralization of power proved to have long-lasting consequences. Another significant change was in the differential pattern of repopulation. In some decimated areas the population was so rapidly replenished that it soon exceeded the prescourge level. Other areas, however, remained so underpopulated that once-great cities never did regain their former influence and prosperity.

The Black Death exercised a tremendous influence over the human mind. Lacking effective means of preventing or treating the disease, people with the gift of artistic expression generated a creative response to the terror. This response took such forms as the *Ars moriendi* (art of dying) movement, the *Memento mori* (remember your death) tradition, and the Dance of Death (the final procession, led by Death himself). Many of the themes and images created in response to the Black Death have remained part of the world's cultural heritage, and have in turn stimulated subsequent orientations toward death and dying, not excluding current attitudes toward AIDS. Even familiar "innocent" childhood songs and games such as tag ("Dead Man Arise!") and "Ring-around-the-Rosie" have been traced to the Black Death period (Kastenbaum, In press).

What of the disease itself? The traditional view has been that the Black Death was plague, a bacterial (*Yersinia pestis*) infection. This is considered to be one of the most virulent of all human infectious diseases. It is also considered to have its home base in "permanent reservoirs in central Asia, Siberia, the Yunan region of China, parts of Iran and Libya, the Arabian Peninsula, and east Africa" (Gottfried, 1983). The plague may break out for a short period of time and then subside because the conditions in the local rodent and bacteria populations are not favorable for its persistence. The major pandemic eruptions occur in the presence of certain climatic and other environmental conditions.

In the plague transmission cycle, a rodent is afflicted by *Y. pestis* bacteria and, if susceptible, develops severe septicemia (blood poisoning). A flea that feeds on the dying rat itself suffers stomach blockage from the rapidly multiplying bacteria.

When the flea leaves the body of the rat host it carries the highly toxic bacteria to its next victim. A human attacked by a plague-infected flea usually experiences first symptoms in the lymph glands of the armpit, neck, and groin. These parts of the body become swollen and painful. (Known as buboes, from the Greek word for groin, these swellings became dread signs of the Black Death.) Fever often follows in a day or two. The victim may die, or may discharge pus but recover from the primary infection either to survive or to die of exhaustion and other secondary problems. Very rapid death—in a matter of hours—occurs in some forms of the plague. It is also possible for the plague toxin to produce a disorienting effect on the nervous system with a loss of coordination and either wild delirium or stupor.

The rapid and widespread transmission of plague seems to require a more effective intermediary than the diseased flea. This would be the pneumonic or respiratory form that can transmit the disease from person to person through such mechanisms as coughing and sneezing. The extremely contagious nature of the Black Death suggested to many experts that the more highly contagious pneumonic form of the plague had been responsible.

An alternative view has been offered by Graham Twigg (1984). He agrees that many of the symptoms described during the 1346–1349 pandemic are consistent with plague. However, he notes that these symptoms also occur with some other conditions as well and that another disease more accurately fits the profile of the Black Death. A zoologist and authority on rodent biology, Twigg attempts to show that the rat-flea cycle could not have accounted for the Black Death's catastrophic toll. Much of his theory is based upon studies of rat biology and behavior which suggest that rats are unlikely to play a decisive role in such a highly contagious and rapidly disseminating disease. His research base includes field studies of rat populations in more recent outbreaks of the plague, mostly in the Orient. His evidence and reasoning also suggest that rather special conditions are necessary if the pneumonic form of the plague is to become widespread, and that these conditions did not exist during the time of the Black Death.

Twigg's alternative theory is a surprising one on the surface. Anthrax is a disease that is often fatal to sheep, goats, cattle, and pigs. It is also a highly infectious condition that can be borne on the wind. Through a careful and ingenious examination of both historical reports and contemporary studies, Twigg proposes that anthrax had the power and the opportunity to become the pestilence known as the Black Death, and clinical features similar to those observed in plague victims.

Whether one accepts the traditional or the revisionary explanation of the specific nature and transmission of the Black Death, it is obvious that this highly toxic and contagious disease took its toll among people living in unsanitary and unhealthful circumstances and often weakened by malnutrition and other physical conditions. Today, both plague and anthrax are among the conditions that can be controlled with appropriate public health measures. Nevertheless, although we are removed in time and technology from the fourteenth century, the specter of the Black Death has not entirely faded from the collective human experience.

See also Acquired Immune Deficiency Syndrome (AIDS); *Ars Moriendi*; Dance of Death (*Danse Macabre*); *Memento Mori*.

—ROBERT KASTENBAUM

References

Gottfried, R.S. (1983). *The Black Death.* New York: The Free Press.

Kastenbaum, R. (In press). *The psychology of death.* 2nd ed. New York: Springer.

McNeill, W.H. (1976). *Plagues and peoples.* Garden City, NY: Anchor Press/ Doubleday.

Tuchman, B.W. (1978). *A distant mirror.* New York: Alfred A. Knopf.

Twigg, G. (1984). *The Black Death: A biological reappraisal.* London: Batsford.

BRAIN DEATH

Physicians have known for many years that basic physiological functions may continue in the absence of demonstrable mental activity. After a period of time respiration and circulation usually cease, indicating a state of "total death," but occasionally partial or even complete recovery of thought and personality occurs. In the past the possibility of a delayed spontaneous recovery contributed to a fairly widespread fear of being buried alive, even when all detectable vital signs of life had ceased. The practice of holding a "death watch" was intended, in part, to offer a last opportunity for the unresponsive figure on the death bed to show some sign of revival. Generally, however, vegetative functions did not persist for long. From the observer's standpoint, the moment of death might appear as an almost imperceptible "slipping away"—a sudden stiffening, coldness, and loss of color. This transition from life to death presumably was not experienced by the decedent, whose mental functioning had ceased some time previously. Not all people died in this way; some were alert and engaged in conversation until the very end. But it had long been obvious that mental (and, therefore, by assumption) brain function might be survived by vegetative processes of the body for either a brief or, more rarely, a rather extended time.

Emergence of the "Brain Death" Concept

The long-known fact that vegetative processes may persist after the disappearance of demonstrable mental functions did not in itself lead to the concept of "brain death" nor make this idea seem particularly important. The significance now attached to brain death derives from many circumstances, of which the following may be regarded as especially salient.

The Shift from Heart to Brain. It was long believed that the heart was both the "seat of the soul" and the key to life. Today there is a romantic residue of this belief in such expressions as "She's very good-hearted" or "He has his heart in the right place." Only with the development of a more scientific approach to anatomy and physiology did it become clear that, for all its importance, the heart must give way to the brain as the center of reason, memory, and judgment. Gradually, the heart also became dislodged as the unquestioned arbiter of life and death. Although the vital connection between cardiac action and survival is not doubted, it became necessary to consider as well the role of the brain and the entire central nervous system. The contemporary view is that "In all higher organisms, behavior is a reflection of the activity of the brain. In a sense, each of us is simply a brain together with a few minor input and output appendages" (Thompson et al., 1980).

Improved Monitoring of Brain Function. The status of the brain could only be inferred from verbal and nonverbal behavior until objective techniques were developed to monitor cerebral activity. Today the electroencephalogram (EEG) is the best known and most frequently used procedure of this kind. There are a variety of other techniques, however, that enable trained personnel to determine cerebral blood flow and other aspects of brain structure and function. (Some of the most advanced, such as magnetic resonance imaging (MRI) devices, are at present rarely if ever used to determine brain death.) The concept of brain death has become of more practical value, then, with the availability of the EEG and supplementary procedures for assessing cerebral functioning.

The Availability of Life-Support Technology. Throughout human history, a person who could no longer take nourishment would die within a relatively short time. An even more rapid demise was virtually certain for the person whose respiration and cardiovascular system had failed. It is one of the major differences between " then" and "now" that, in the United States alone, thousands of people in such a perilous condition are maintained in persistent vegetative states. The introduction of life-support technology has given some people, such as automobile collision accident victims, the opportunity to survive and recover varying degrees of function. However, such procedures have also been criticized as prolonging dying rather than extending life, and as being undignified, un-

acceptable, and very costly. Many individuals express a strong aversion to having life-support techniques applied to their own lives or the lives of their loved ones. This concern has been a powerful stimulus for the development of living wills and right-to-die legislation, as well as heated controversies regarding euthanasia. Within this context, brain death has emerged as a possible criterion for deciding whether or not life-support procedures should be initiated or continued.

"Medicalization" of Private Life. There has been a general expansion of bureaucratic systems throughout the twentieth century, as well as an increasing institutionalization of human services that were previously a matter for individual arrangements. The growth of the health care bureaucracy has brought death as well as life within its orbit. It has become increasingly common for people to die under medical management and for medical management itself to be subject to regulations, pressures, and conflicts that have relatively little to do with the characteristics, needs, and preferences of the particular patient. One of the most relevant outcomes has been the need for physicians and other caregivers to have clear rules of procedure, rules that will protect them from emotional, moral, or legal challenges to their actions. The brain death criterion has become important, then, as a way of guiding or rationalizing the various courses of action a physician might take with a patient whose death is in near prospect or who may even be said to have already died. Another significant and very different approach has been the popular movement to take a holistic team approach with focus on family rather than institutional support. This is the hospice approach, in which medical considerations continue to play a significant part, but in which efforts are made to avoid "medicalizing" the entire situation.

Cost. The brain death concept is often invoked as a way of preventing the expenditure of large sums of money to maintain a body on a life support system. Families and insurance companies have a significant financial stake in this matter. Hospitals may also have reason for concern when, in some circumstances, expensive care is continued with little prospect of reimbursement.

Anatomical Gifts. In recent years there has been increasing use of donor organs and increasing public awareness of this process. At times there is a conflict between the impulse to remove an organ for the benefit of another person and the unwillingness to "steal" from another. No physician or family member wants to be caught up in this kind of dilemma. One way of contributing to a solution would be through the determination of brain death. Presumably, life-support measures might then be discontinued if it is clear that the individual has no capacity for thought and experience, even if intravenous feeding and a respirator maintain some semblance of physiological functioning.

Legal Decisions and Religious Doctrine. Both the courts and the clergy have been confronted by many new difficulties that have arisen from the newfound ability to keep people "alive" in persistent vegetative states. In general, judges, attorneys, clergy, and theologians have been cautious in their approach, attempting to do justice to all the complex and emotion-laden dimensions of the situation. Many experts in law and theology have made themselves familiar with the medical side of the question. By and large, the brain death concept has been given serious attention by court and church as providing a valuable guideline, if not necessarily the entire answer.

The "Harvard Criteria"

The concept of brain death seems to have been introduced into the medical literature by two French neurophysiologists, Mollaret and Boulon (1959), who studied unresponsive patients being maintained on respirators. Some of the patients showed no electrical activity in the brain and were therefore considered to be "beyond coma." Extensive brain damage was found on postmortem examination. Soon after publication of this study, many other medical researchers were inquiring into "respirator brain." It now appeared to at least some observers that they were dealing with patients who were, for all intents and purposes, dead.

A committee of Harvard Medical School faculty later (1968) attempted to develop clear criteria for determination of brain death. The following criteria were proposed:

1. Unreceptive and unresponsive either to external stimuli or internal need
2. No movements and no breathing
3. No reflexes
4. A flat EEG (The automatic moving stylus records a straight line, not the usual pattern of peaks and valleys that indicates electrophysiological activity.)
5. No circulation to or within the brain

The Harvard report has found widespread application. The first three criteria are by no means new; they have long been employed by physicians and other expert observers. In practice, most deaths continue to be certified without resort to the monitoring operations specified in the last two criteria: there is no question about the death. The brain circulation criterion has not often been employed outside of a research setting. In actuality, then, it is the EEG assessment that is almost always called upon when the question of brain death has been raised. Although many physicians believe that a single EEG assessment is sufficient, for the peace of mind of all persons involved, a repeat assessment is often made (usually twenty-four hours after the first). The Harvard criteria have been judged essentially adequate by the President's Commission for the Study of Ethical Problems in Medicine and Biomedical and Behavioral Research (1981), although some possible flaws were also noted. Some questions arise from the difficulties inherent in trying to make death per se the subject of objective testing (Kastenbaum, 1986). In the main, however, when the concept of brain death is discussed today, reference is most likely to be made to the Harvard criteria.

What Kind of Brain Death?

Despite widespread acceptance of the Harvard criteria, questions remain. The most controversial involves the specific brain areas that should be included in the definition. Three alternatives have been proposed: (a) whole-brain death: the irreversible destruction of all neural structures within the intracranial cavity—both hemispheres and all tissue from top to the bottom (cerebellum and brainstem); (b) cerebral death: the irreversible destruction of both cerebral hemispheres—but not including the lower centers in the cerebellum and brainstem; (c) neocortical death: the irreversible destruction of the most highly differentiated brain cells, those comprising the cerebral cortex—but not necessarily any other neural tissue.

The controversy has its roots in the fact that the higher mental functions seem to require an intact neocortex. There is a wealth of clinical and laboratory evidence to affirm this conclusion. It might be asserted, then, that the person is dead when his or her neocortex is no longer capable of supporting thought and articulate, conscious experience. Lower centers of the brain may continue to function, but to what avail? The person is dead, even if some primitive operations of the nervous system persist. A more cautious interpretation along the same lines would invoke the cerebral death criteria: not only the neocortex but both hemispheres in their entirety must be irreversibly destroyed before a person can be declared brain dead.

Nevertheless, it is the whole-brain interpretation that has prevailed up to this time. This is the most conservative approach, the one that requires the most complete loss of function before brain death is affirmed. Walton (1981–1982) proposes that some form of experience or basic awareness might still persist in the deeper centers of the brain when the higher centers are no longer operative. Furthermore, hope for recovery might remain as long as the lower centers are active. On this view, it would be unwise to consider a person as dead and cease life-support operations so long as the lower centers of the brain continue to function. There have been some dramatic examples of recovery from extended periods of unresponsiveness, and our knowledge of the central nervous system, although rapidly improving, is far from complete.

At the present time, then, the conclusion that a person is "brain dead" is "reserved for the state of total absence of function of the brain" (Walker, 1985).

A Few Suggestions

An individual who has lapsed from consciousness and seems to exist in a vegetative state can present many problems for relatives, friends, and caregivers. By anticipating these problems and becoming sensitive to their implications one can often reduce the emotional stress and distress. The problems I have most often observed are as follows.

Difficulty in Gaining Psychological Closure. The person is thought of as dead and not dead at the same time. Grief is experienced, but in an incomplete and blocked manner. Family members cannot grieve fully and then try to move on with their lives, yet they cannot help but feel sorrow and anxiety. This predicament has some commonality with family members of those missing in action.

Survivors' Acceptance of the Death. Survivors are likely to differ in their emotional readiness to "accept" the death. This means that one family member may resent and resist efforts to determine brain death and withdraw life-support measures, while another at the same time may have reached a point at which it no longer seems necessary to keep up what seems to be an illusion.

Recognizing the Humanity of the Unresponsive. Some physicians, nurses, and technicians treat unresponsive patients as though they do not exist as human beings. The patients are tended to and "processed" as objects. However, other physicians, nurses, and technicians consistently treat unresponsive patients as though they were still capable of experience and understanding. In one study, my colleagues and I found that approximately half of a population of severely impaired and persistently unresponsive geriatric patients did show some capacity for interaction when spoken to and touched (Kastenbaum & Aisenberg, 1972). Other observers have also reported cases in which patients supposedly beyond response did show some awareness and ability to communicate. There are also testimonials from individuals who were themselves once among the "living dead."

It may be suggested, then, that (1) we continue to treat the comatose or "beyond comatose" patient as though still a fellow human being at all times; (2) recognize the individuality of response among friends, family members, and staff; and (3) cultivate our sensitivity to those who must at the same time grieve and not grieve for loved ones who at the same time may appear both not quite dead and not quite alive.

See also Autopsy; Euthanasia; Grief: Missing in Action Families; Hospice: Philosophy and Practice; (The) Living Will; Uniform Anatomical Act.

—ROBERT KASTENBAUM

References

Ad Hoc Committee of the Harvard Medical School to Examine the Definition of Brain Death (1968). "A definition of irreversible coma." *Journal of the American Medical Association, 205*: 337–40.

Kastenbaum, R. (1986). *Death, society, and human experience.* 3rd ed. Columbus, OH: Charles E. Merrill.

Kastenbaum, R. & Aisenberg, R.B. (1972). *The psychology of death.* New York: Springer.

Korein, J. (1978). "The problem of brain death: Development and history." *Annals of the New York Academy of Sciences, 315*: 1–10.

Mollaret, P. & Goulon, M. (1959). "Le coma depasse." *Review of Neurology, 101*: 3–18.

President's Commission for the Study of Ethical Problems in Medicine and Biomedical and Behavioral Research. (1981). *Defining death.* Washington, DC: U.S. Government Printing Office.

Thompson, R.F., Berger, T.W., & Berry, S.D. (1980). "An introduction to the anatomy, physiology, and chemistry of the brain." In M.C. Wittrock (Ed.) *The brain and psychology.* New York: Academic Press, 3–32.

Walker, A.E. (1985). *Cerebral death.* 3rd ed. Baltimore: Urban & Schwarzenberg.

Walton, D.N. (1981–1982). "Neocortical versus whole-brain conceptions of personal death." *Omega, Journal of Death & Dying, 12*: 339–44.

BURIAL: "GOING HOME"

One of America's best known traditional songs states:

> It matters not, I've oft been told,
> Where the body lies when the heart
> goes cold,

> Yet grant, oh grant, this wish to me:
> Oh bury me not on the lone prairie.

This song focuses on an important theme in the human experience of space and place: the concern of many people confronting death with the place of their burial. For most, this concern involves a desire to be laid to rest in a place for which they hold special affinity, a place thought of as "home." Most relatives will go to great lengths to see to it that a person is interred in the place he or she wished. In *As I Lay Dying,* William Faulkner (1964) devotes an entire novel to this theme.

A Longing Expressed in Many Cultures

The belief that one should be buried at home among friends and relatives finds expression in a diversity of cultures and is by no means a new phenomenon. In preliterate tribal societies it was rare for individuals to travel far; nevertheless, there are accounts of such peoples in various places, such as Africa and South America, transporting human remains long distances in order to bury them in a traditional homeland.

Because they had not solved the problem of preserving bodies, many cultures in the past transported only the bones of the deceased. For example, the bones of all Athenian soldiers killed in the Peloponnesian War were returned for funeral and burial. The bodies of Jewish dead were shipped to the Holy Land for burial in family tombs for hundreds of years after the Diaspora. By the Middle Ages it was not unusual for nobility to travel, and thus die, far from home. In many such cases the bodies were shipped home (as happened to Edmund, Earl of Lancaster, and to Henry I). Circumstances did not always permit the prompt transportation of remains, however. The followers of Charles the Bold, for example, considered it prudent to bury his body at once and to exhume and return the bones at a later time.

Long distance transportation of human remains became important in the United States in the later part of the nineteenth century. Techniques for the shipment of cadavers were largely developed during the Civil War. Many soldiers were dying far from home. The government allowed the next of kin of officers to have their loved ones returned home for burial at their expense. Several technological advances made this possible. The telegraph allowed for notification of next of kin, a rail network provided shipment, airtight caskets had been developed, and embalming techniques had been significantly improved.

By the turn of the century, the shipment of cadavers within the civilian sector of the economy had developed into a big business. And by the middle of the twentieth century, the concept of returning a body "home" had become a part of the American psyche, as evidenced by the fact that no military cemeteries have been established overseas since World War II, as well as by the continuing concern for the return of the remains of all those missing in action in the Vietnam War.

The Current Situation

Many cadavers are shipped across America today. Most are transported by air, but there are surprisingly few restrictions on how cadavers are to be transported. Some are taken on long journeys by family members in pickup trucks, campers, and similar vehicles.

Few states keep records of cadaver shipments, but several generalizations can be made from the statistics that are available. A large percentage of the dead will be removed from states with high in-migration rates. The states with the highest percentage of removals in 1983 were Nevada (23.9%), Florida (20.9%), Alaska (18.3%), and Arizona (17.1%). Removal rates will probably continue to remain high for those states, such as Arizona and Florida, that are destinations for large numbers of retirees. As these people die and are returned to another home for burial, they are replaced by other retirees and the trend continues. Those states such as Alaska to which the young are migrating can probably expect a declining removal rate. Young people tend to raise families, live in the area for many years, and develop a bond to the land.

The statistics that have been given here tend to underestimate the actual number of bodies returned home. This is because of the growing popularity of cremations. On death certificates, a cremation is considered to be the final disposition. However, many "cremains" are shipped beyond state lines to a home in another state. The number of cremains shipped out of state cannot be ascertained because no official state records are kept.

Several practical considerations may influence the decision to ship a body. Possession of a burial plot at a place of previous residence often greatly influences that decision. Another practical rationale for removal is the relatively small expense of transporting a body home for a funeral, as compared with an entire family travelling to where the loved one died. In situations where the wishes of the deceased are unknown, the body may be returned almost by default to the next of kin, whose place of residence may or may not have held the connotation of home for the deceased.

See also Cremation; Embalming; Grief: Missing in Action Families.

—MALCOLM L. COMEAUX

References

Faulkner, W. (1964). *As I lay dying.* New York: Random House.

Rowles, G.D. & Comeaux, M.L. (1986). "Returning home: The interstate transportation of human remains." *Omega, Journal of Death and Dying, 17*: 102–13.

Rowles, G.D. & Comeaux, M.L. (1987). "A final journey: Post-death removal of human remains." *Tijdschrift voor Economische en Sociale Geografie, 78*:114–24.

C

CAUSES OF DEATH

Classification

The causes of death are distributed among three major categories: degeneration, or biological deterioration of the body, such as heart disease, cancer, stroke; communicable (or infectious) diseases such as tuberculosis, pneumonia, and malaria; and deaths attributable to the social and economic environment, such as accident fatalities and suicide. Although this standard categorization scheme provides a useful analytic framework for thinking about causes of death, the three categories are not mutually exclusive. For example, cancer deaths related to asbestos in the working environment are both degenerative and socioeconomic in origin. Pneumonia deaths related to the paralysis of some stroke victims combine elements of both degenerative and infectious causes. Keeping this qualification in mind, the relative importance of various causes of death, along with the age distribution, changes with socioeconomic development. This overall change is known as the epidemiologic transition.

Some cautions are in order before examining causes of death and their changing configuration or epidemiologic transition. Of all the "hard" data on deaths, causes of death are fraught with the most numerous methodological problems. The classification of deaths according to causes generally follows the International Classification of Diseases (ICD) as set down by the World Health Organization. This classification system has gone through several revisions. The version currently in use is the Ninth Revision. Comparability of causes of death over time has been affected by these classificatory revisions, some of which have been quite substantial. Furthermore, cross-national comparisons are problematic because (1) data on cause of death are dependent upon the diagnostic skill and type of training of the certifying medical attendant, which can vary greatly across societies, and (2) in the least developed countries, no record of cause of death is kept, making comparisons impossible. A final problem is that the ICD system assumes "one death, one cause." This principle may be untenable, particularly in the case of deaths occurring to elderly persons, and is coming under increasing attack.

Epidemiologic Transition: Three or Four Stages

The epidemiologic transition describes a three-stage shift in the major causes of death (Omran, 1977). The first stage existed throughout most of human history and ended around 1800 in developed countries. It is characterized by high mortality rates attributable largely to communicable diseases that tend to select young victims. The second stage spans the years from approximately 1800 to the early decades of the twentieth century in developed countries. In this stage, epidemics lessen as major takers of life because of improvements in sanitation and nutrition as well as medical intervention. The third stage is one in which degenerative diseases predominate as the major causes of mortality, with deaths concentrated at the older ages. Recently, a fourth stage has been proposed (Olshansky & Ault, 1986). This is marked by a continuation of degenerative diseases as the major causes of death, however, deaths are now postponed to even older ages.

At the present time, developed and developing countries are located at different places in the epidemiologic transition and, accordingly, display different distributions of causes of death. Table 1 presents distributions for five selected countries, circa 1983. Even though cause-of-death data are not available for the least developed nations, the differences represented are quite striking. In the developed world, represented in the table by the United States and the Netherlands, deaths attributable to degenerative causes (cardiovascular diseases and malignant neoplasms) predominate. These comprise nearly three-quarters of all deaths. In the other countries, parasitic and infectious diseases play a larger role. Particularly notable is the lack of concentration of deaths in any particular category(ies), unlike the situation in developed countries.

Major Causes of Death in the United States

In the United States at the present time, degenerative diseases prevail as the main killers. However, there are substantial age, sex, and race differences in mortality rates attributable to the diverse causes of death (Table 2). Overall, mortality rates are higher for old than for young, for males than for females, and for blacks than for whites. Although age differences are largely biological in origin, the sex and race differentials at given ages reflect the role of social and economic factors.

Mortality rates attributable to cardiovascular diseases display the age curve typically associated with degenerative disease: increasing rates with advancing age. Except in childhood, cardiovascular death rates are substantially higher for males than for females. In general, rates for blacks are markedly higher than for whites. The age pattern for deaths related to malignant neoplasms (cancer) is similar to that for the cardiovascular diseases, although at all ages cancer mortality rates are substantially lower. Sex differentials are marked at older ages only, after age 55. Strong racial differentials emerge earlier, by age 35. It can be observed that for the oldest age category, the race differential narrows for malignant neoplasms and reverses for cardiovascular diseases. It is a point of research debate whether this pattern reflects a "real" phenomenon or is the result of data error, particularly in the self-report of age among older blacks.

Although deaths attributable to accidents account for less than 5 percent of total deaths, these are important takers of life among young people. In fact, accidents are the leading cause of death among the population aged under 25, accounting for 30 percent of all deaths. Within this cohort, white males aged 15–24 are particularly vulnerable, as shown in Table 2. A large sex differential exists in accident mortality. The racial differential is less pronounced. For both sex and race grouping, accident mortality rates are highest at the oldest ages. However, the type of accidental death varies by age: among the under-25 population, motor vehicle accidents account for 63 percent of all accident fatalities. Among the population aged 75 and over, the comparable figure is 18 percent. For the older population, accidental deaths related to falls predominate.

TABLE 1: Percentage of deaths attributable to five major causes, selected countries, circa 1983

Country	Infectious & Parasitic	Cardiovascular Diseases	Malignant Neoplasms	Respiratory Diseases	Accidents
United States	1.0	49.2	22.0	3.5	4.8
Netherlands	0.5	43.2	26.8	5.0	3.4
El Salvador	9.9	10.6	3.6	5.0	7.5
Egypt	2.4	19.3	1.9	8.9	2.0
Thailand	7.0	11.5	5.8	2.0	7.1

Source: *Demographic Yearbook, 1985* (1987). New York: United Nations Department of International Economic and Social Affairs

TABLE 2: Age-sex-race-specific mortality rates per 100,000 population by cause of death, United States, 1983

	Age								
	-1	1–14	15–24	25–34	35–44	45–54	55–64	65–74	75+
Cardiovascular									
White:									
Male	27.7	1.6	3.9	11.4	55.1	265.8	767.1	1,824.8	5,407.1
Female	21.9	1.5	2.6	5.4	18.6	86.4	294.6	895.8	4,378.9
Black:									
Male	55.0	2.9	8.2	30.6	124.7	486.5	1,201.5	2,357.2	4,712.5
Female	46.3	2.3	6.4	18.5	66.0	241.8	662.9	1,523.7	3,873.5
Neoplasms									
White:									
Male	3.4	4.6	7.0	11.9	33.9	164.9	504.2	1,021.3	1,752.6
Female	3.4	3.7	4.9	11.8	42.8	158.3	371.0	603.2	912.1
Black:									
Male	3.4	4.1	5.5	12.9	60.0	313.0	867.3	1,495.2	1,978.0
Female	2.9	3.4	5.1	16.0	59.7	211.8	444.5	685.9	859.8
Accidents									
White:									
Male	24.0	18.4	82.7	58.4	59.4	45.5	51.2	63.3	166.5
Female	19.4	10.1	24.5	14.5	12.3	15.3	19.8	32.5	107.0
Black:									
Male	49.7	24.7	48.7	64.3	67.2	83.2	102.4	119.9	194.2
Female	34.0	15.1	14.2	16.5	15.1	22.4	29.9	48.6	99.8
Suicide									
White:									
Male	—	0.7	21.4	24.8	20.5	25.2	27.7	31.8	48.6
Female	—	0.2	4.8	6.8	7.3	9.8	9.2	7.6	5.7
Black:									
Male	—	0.3	11.3	16.7	11.8	12.0	12.3	14.0	13.6
Female	—	0.4	2.7	2.6	3.0	3.0	1.7	1.3	1.3

Source: U.S. Bureau of the Census. *Statistical Abstract of the United States: 1987.* Washington, DC: U.S. Government Printing Office.

Suicide

Suicide accounts for less than 2 percent of all deaths in the United States. However, suicide mortality rates display some noteworthy characteristics. Rates for whites are higher than for blacks: suicide is one of the few causes of death for which blacks have an advantage. White males display the highest rates and are also unique in experiencing a pattern of increasing rates with advancing age.

The relatively high suicide rate for white men must be viewed in the light of high homicide rates for black men, particularly at young ages. Among black males aged 15–34, homicide is the leading cause of death, exceeding even accidents. Homicide in this age and race grouping accounts for 34 percent of all deaths. Whether or not high white suicide rates and high black homicide rates represent different responses to similar social stressors is difficult to determine. Unfortunately, it is easy to conclude that young men in the United States are prone to die by violence. If deaths caused by suicide and homicide were averted among the male population aged 15–34, nearly 18,000 lives would be saved annually.

Future Trends

The future distribution of causes of death is difficult to predict in any exact way. It is likely that degenerative diseases will play a large role in developing societies as they modernize and experience overall mortality decline. The emergence and spread of AIDS in the 1980s raises questions about the future impact of infectious disease in developed societies, but there is a consensus that degenerative diseases will continue to predominate. However, the relative importance of different degenerative diseases may change. If present trends continue, the percentage of deaths attributable to cardiovascular diseases will decline, while the percentage of deaths attributable to cancer (particularly respiratory cancer) will increase, assuming that no cure for cancer is found and no significant change occurs in smoking habits. As larger proportions of the population survive to very old ages, the percentage of deaths attributable to Alzheimer's disease and other forms of dementia will increase.

Although there is general agreement that degenerative diseases will remain the major killers in the future, there is considerable research disagreement about "compression of morbidity." This is the concept that the onset of debilitating degenerative disease(s) will be postponed until shortly before death occurs, meaning that most people will live in good health until a brief period of decline very late in life. However, at this time there is no substantial evidence to support this optimistic postulation.

The health care challenge of the future is to devise the most humane and economically efficient ways of dealing with an increasingly older population that presents degenerative health problems.

See also Acquired Immune Deficiency Syndrome (AIDS); Mortality Rate; Murder; Suicide.

—ELLEN GEE

References

Olshansky, S.J. & Ault, A.B. (1986). "The fourth stage of the epidemiological transition: The age of delayed degenerative diseases." *The Millbank Quarterly, 64*: 355–91.

Omran, A.A. (1977). "Epidemiologic transition in the United States: The health factor in population change." *Population Bulletin, 32* (2). Washington, DC: Population Reference Bureau.

Uemara, K. & Pisa, Z. (1985). "Recent trends in cardiovascular mortality in 27 industrialized countries. *World Health Statistics Quarterly, 38*: 142–62.

CEMETERIES

The history of the cemetery tells us much about human history in general—many of our most significant themes, values, fears, and hopes have expressed themselves in the places designated for final interment of our dead. Even today, the status, condition, and uses of cemeteries continue to bear testimony to the way we live our lives and relate to our deaths.

Strawberry Fields, a garden created as a memorial to John Lennon by Yoko Ono, his widow (New York City: 72nd Street at Central Park). Visitors are welcome to use this 3.5 acre garden for relaxation and contemplation. Reprinted, by permission, from Judi Culbertson & Tom Randall, *Permanent New Yorkers,* Chelsea Green Publishing Co., p. 52. © 1987 by Judi Culbertson & Tom Randall.

Instead of traditional statuary, Strawberry Fields offers a path that leads to a mosaic design offering but one word: IMAGINE, the title of a John Lennon song and, later, of a documentary on his life. Reprinted, by permission, from Judi Culbertson & Tom Randall, *Permanent New Yorkers,* Chelsea Green Publishing Co., p. 51. © 1987 by Judi Culbertson & Tom Randall.

Historical Perspective

The name given to burial grounds reflects one of humankind's most ancient and enduring metaphors for death. Cemetery derives from the Greek *(koimeterion)* and Latin *(coemeterium)* for a sleeping chamber. There is no reason to suppose that our ancestors actually mistook death for sleep. However, the analogy with sleep helped then, as it does now, to bridge the gap between the known and the unknown, as well as to soften, if slightly, the survivors' sense of loss.

Another characteristic of cemeteries from early times forward has been the attempt to represent the burial place as a kind of dwelling (See also **Lullabies of Death**). This endeavor can be seen clearly in the excavated sections of the necropolis of Cerveteri (Pallottino, 1950). Often described as a "city of the dead," this large cemetery is located on the Italian coast, its name meaning "Old Caere," an important port city for the Etruscans.

> Round the town stretched a ring of burials whose pit and trench graves, chamber-tombs and architectural tumuli testify of a continued existence from the VIIIth century B.C. to the Roman Imperial period. The most ancient groups of tombs have been found at the foot of the city. . . . These consist of both cremation and inhumation graves, usually not of a monumental character (VIIIth to VIIth century B.C.). To the right and left . . . stretched the great cemeteries of the historical period, with tumuli, chamber-tombs and sepulchral ways: real cities of the dead. (Pallatino, p. 4).

The attempt to domesticate death is visible even in the most ancient sections of the necropolis. The burial chambers are designed to imitate the dwellings of the time (a valuable feature for historians who are interested in reconstructing the daily lives of the Etruscans). For at least 2,800 years, then, the dead in this part of the world were not simply placed underground, but were relocated into a sort of housing tract that emulated the arrangements they had known throughout their lives. As time went on, the abodes became more elaborate. Furniture and decorative details were added. Those whose social status and affluence would provide them with tombs could look forward to such amenities as a "living room," several side chambers, a larger chamber for the tomb (suggestive of a master bedroom), and several windows. Designs changed over time (as they did in the world of the living), but the principle of recreating a domestic environment for the dead was obeyed generation after generation. That the dead collectively possessed a "city" as well as their own "homes" was emphasized by the introduction of a street system within the necropolis.

Still another major characteristic of cemetery symbolism can be seen in the necropolis of Cerveteri and in other ancient sites: the individual's social standing during life (often this meant the social standing of his or her family) was likely to be preserved after death. The rich and the poor each had their own well-demarcated sections.

Cemeteries through the centuries have also served five other functions in the death systems of many societies (Kastenbaum, 1986 and In press).

Separation from the Living. The cemetery cleanly separates the dead from the living. This physical separation makes it easier for people to go about their daily lives with fewer reminders of particular people who have died and of death in general. And since the dead are often thought to have a special relationship with Death (personified and, in an extreme case, vampire-ized), we can also lull ourselves into the uncritical belief that Death's place of business is restricted to the necropolis.

Respect for the Dead. The cemetery and its amenities (well-tended grass, grave markers, floral tributes, and plantings) exhibit our respect for the dead. On the level of conscious awareness, this solicitude reveals our responsible and caring attitude. On a more primitive level of thinking, however, we may be attempting to appease the dead. As Frazer (1933) and others have observed, fear of the dead is a common and powerful motivating force in pretechnological societies. This attitude has by no means disappeared from contemporary societies. The deceased person may already have reason to bear grudges against us, and failure to provide suitable rituals and disposition could unleash an angry spirit.

Visiting the Dead. The cemetery makes it possible for the survivors to visit their dead friends and relatives when they feel a need to do so. It may be personally meaningful to bring fresh flowers to the grave on a birthday or anniversary, or comforting simply to see that the cemetery is still well tended. One person may come to the cemetery alone to have a sense of being with the deceased and re-experience the life they shared together; an entire extended family may visit as a way of affirming their identity and continuity. Societies that maintain a traditional way of life over many generations often assign a significant role to the cemetery. For example, Potomia, a Greek village near Mount Olympus, still functions much as it did many centuries ago (Tsiarias, 1982). The small cemetery is the scene of frequent visitations by mourners, usually women, who spend hours talking to their dead and to each other. Although ancient, the burial grounds never become overcrowded. After five years in the cemetery proper, the corpse is transferred to the bone house where it joins the remains of many previous generations. Psychologically, the two phases of burial seem to help the mourners to work through their grief in a lengthy period in which one can say farewell to the deceased, and subsequently be willing to let go.

The cemetery may also represent events as well as people from the past that the survivors believe should never be forgotten, as in the large military cemetery in Hawaii where many American war dead are memorialized.

Affirmation of Custom. The cemetery affirms some of the motives and regulations that govern the living and thereby contributes to an implicit symbolic victory over death. Often this involves the extension of property rights and other economic values to the fields of the dead. Toynbee (1971) gives a number of such examples from Roman times. Burial rights were specified in careful detail.

Lucius Cocceius Adiutor built (this tomb) for himself and declares that no one should burn or bury a body on the left side as one enters. If he does, he shall pay 50,000 sesterces to the city of Ostia. The informer shall receive the fourth part. . . .

But if after the death of Marcus Antonius Vitalis anyone should sell or give or in any way alienate this tomb or introduce into it or within any of its enclosure-walls the body or bones of a person with a name other than is contained in the above list, he shall pay a fine of 3000 sesterces for each body.

Specifications often included the precise size of the space that was to be set aside for a particular tomb (especially its frontage). Roman law gave abundant attention to such questions as ownership and rights to burial space and tombs. Financial considerations have remained important in cemetery access and management over the centuries. In this sense, society asserts its provenance over the dead and derives a rather sneaky sense of control; death can't be all that powerful if we can subject it to our fondness for taxation, regulation, and profit.

Preparation for Death. The cemetery can be helpful in preparing ourselves for our own deaths. Although not all cemeteries have a positive effect, a cemetery that gives the impression of such positive qualities as dignity, beauty, and enduringness may provide one useful element in the total construction of the idea of personal death. Serving as a *memento mori*, the cemetery by its very existence may suggest that each of us should give some thought to death as well as to life. This does not mean that such sights and thoughts are pleasurable, but under favorable circumstances the cemetery may make them more acceptable.

Menace and Reform

Cemeteries took on a menacing aspect as population increased and people thronged together into cities. The high density of the living resulted inexorably in a high density of the dead. A churchyard's burial grounds may have met the needs of the parish for several generations. However, population pressure soon exceeded the available space. Furthermore, it became increasingly difficult to extend the burial grounds as surrounding areas also became more populated. Compromises were made in an effort to provide for the local dead, and some of these attempts (e.g., placing one corpse atop another in a limited space) created further problems.

The pressures became overwhelming when epidemics struck. Not only was it difficult to absorb all the new bodies within a limited time, but social organization was likely to fail. Who has the right to make decisions? Who was going to pay for all the burials? And who could be made to dig the graves and handle the diseased corpses? Mass burials were sometimes the only solution that a hard-pressed city could find, as at the peak of the Black Death. There might be few able-bodied people available to haul away the bodies, dig, and cover the graves. In the worst of times, the graves might remain open for long periods of time. Apart from the emergencies that occurred periodically, the standards for managing a burial ground often did not keep up with the needs.

Cemetery conditions deteriorated further as the Industrial Revolution took hold in Europe. Rapid urban growth, the emergence of new industries, and dislocation from traditional values were generating a new and confusing social environment. Neglect of proper burial arrangements and neglect of cemetery maintenance were among the disturbing consequences. The dangers of the situation were well recognized by a London physician, George Alfred Walker. In *Gatherings from Graveyards* (1830/1977), Walker not only described many of the problems but also proposed corrective measures.

Walker leads the reader on a tour of metropolitan burial grounds. His detailed descriptions make it clear that Londoners were often exposed to distressing sights and smells. In some neighborhoods there were several improperly tended cemeteries whose stench mixed with other noxious odors (such as slaughter yards). The residents could not avoid the stench of decay from all sides. But it was not simply that the environment had become exceedingly unpleasant—it was also exceedingly unhealthy. Speaking of one such neighborhood, Walker observed, "Typhus fever in its aggravated form has attacked by far the majority of the residents, and death has made among them the most destructive ravages."

Walker's descriptions are distressing to read. They include examples of bodies improperly buried (hardly buried at all), graves robbed and desecrated, and elementary principles of social responsibility and decency neglected. As a physician Walker was able to point out serious public health consequences. The body-handlers and gravediggers were at very high risk for communicable diseases, as were those living and working in the vicinity of cemeteries.

Walker and other articulate observers eventually aroused public opinion and stimulated major reforms in burial procedures and cemetery management. The reform movement made important advances throughout the nineteenth century in many parts of the world. It is difficult to imagine how modern cities would have survived at all had not such actions been taken.

But the nineteenth century produced more than reform. There was also a new vision (or renewed, for there are historical precedents) of how a cemetery should look and how it should be used. The cemetery as an inviting, landscaped park was first introduced on the outskirts of Cambridge, Massachusetts, in 1831. Mount Auburn Cemetery was soon followed by two other American versions, Laurel Hill (Philadelphia) and Greenwood (Brooklyn). Very well accepted by the public, new cemeteries of this type offered attractive features such as woodlands and terraced lawns, sometimes ponds and streams as well. A visit to the new type of cemetery could be seen as a refreshing and inspiring family outing—a long way from the repulsive boneyards of poorly managed cemeteries in the old world.

Cemeteries Today

The "great age" of cemetery development has come and gone. Changes in property values and priorities and continued population growth have resulted in heightened competition among possible land uses. Relatively few new cemeteries have been established in recent years, and pressure mounts to yield some older cemeteries to housing and commercial interests. A number of cemeteries are also in difficulty because of massive changes in their local environments; for example, many generations of ethnic neighborhoods having been replaced by mills and factories that themselves have shut down.

However, a heritage does remain in the form of attractive and well-maintained cemeteries from the early years of the memorial park, as well as some later examples. There are also a number of vast cemeteries that one would hesitate to describe as beautiful or serene, but which do faithfully preserve gravemarkers and tombs from earlier generations. Armchair tours of some memory-laden cemeteries can be had through such books as *Permanent New Yorkers* (1987) and *Permanent Parisians* (1986), both by Culbertson and Randall.

See also (The) Black Death; Cremation; Death System; Embalming; Epitaphs; Funerals; Lullabies of Death; *Memento Mori*.

—ROBERT KASTENBAUM

References

Culbertson, J. & Randall, T. (1986). *Permanent Parisians.* Chelsea, VT: Chelsea Green.

Culbertson, J. & Randall, T. (1987). *Permanent New Yorkers.* Chelsea, VT: Chelsea Green.

Frazer, J.G. (1933/Reprint 1977). *The fear of the dead in primitive religion.* New York: Arno.

Kastenbaum, R. (1986). *Death, society, and human experience.* Columbus, OH: Charles E. Merrill.

Kastenbaum, R. (In press). *The psychology of death.* 2nd ed. New York: Springer.

Pallottino, M. (1950). *The necropolis of Cerveteri.* Rome: Ministero della Pubblica Istruzione.

Toynbee, J.M.C. (1971). *Death and burial in the Roman world.* Ithaca, NY: Cornell University Press.

Tsiarias, A. (1982). *The death rituals of rural Greece.* Princeton, NJ: Princeton University Press.

Walker, G.A. (1930/Reprint 1977). *Gatherings from graveyards.* New York: Arno Press.

CHARON

In Greek mythology the souls of the dead must cross the Styx and other rivers of the lower regions in order to reach their destination in the underworld. Charon (ká-ron) is the ferryman who provides this service—for a fee. The earliest mention of the boat fare appears to be in Aristophane's comedy, *Frogs*. The payment was sometimes conveyed by placing a coin between the teeth or under the tongue of the deceased, the coin itself being either a regular piece or one prepared specifically for this final voyage.

Charon himself may not have become a part of Greek mythology until approximately the fifth century BC, when an inscription praised him as "you who release many men from toil." He is often portrayed as a stern and formidable old man who insists that the rules be respected. This is well illustrated in Bulfinch's retelling of an incident first described by Virgil:

> Charon, old and squalid, but strong and vigorous . . . was receiving passengers of all kinds into his boat, magnanimous heroes, boys and unmarried girls, as numerous as the leaves that fall at autumn, or the flocks that fly southward at the approach of winter. They stood pressing for a passage and longing to touch the opposite shore. But the stern ferryman took in only such as he chose, driving the rest back. Aeneas, wondering at the sight, asked the Sibyl, "Why this discrimination?" She answered, "Those who are taken on board the bark are the souls of those who have received due burial rites; the host of others who have remained unburied are not permitted to pass the flood, but wander a hundred years, and flit to and fro about the shore, till at last they are taken over."

Aeneas, displaying the sacred golden bough, finally persuades Charon to make an exception and allow him, one of the living, to cross into the realm of the dead in order to bury a fallen comrade and see his father. It is from the account of this highly unusual round trip that we have some of our most detailed impressions of the "lower world" in which the souls of the dead are to be found.

Although in classical mythology he is usually imagined as a grim figure with an awesome task to perform, Charon has also been portrayed with humor and even tender passion. Writing in the second century AD, for example, Lucian offered a *Dialogue of the Dead* in which Charon quarrels with Menippus, a philosopher who demands a free ride. At one point, Charon asks, "Didn't you know that you had to bring the fee?" "I knew," replies Menippus, "but I didn't have it. What was I to do? Not die?" This displeases Charon: "So you will be the only one to boast that you were ferried across free?" Menippus shows that he is a reasonable sort of a person—for a philosopher—by offering to allow Charon to bring him back to life instead. The vexed old ferryman finally allows Menippus free passage, complaining all the way that his philosopher-passenger is babbling and singing instead of moaning as do ordinary dead souls.

The nineteenth-century poet, Walter Savage Landor, offers a very different imagining of Charon as the beautiful Dirce steps into his boat to cross the Styx:

> Stand close around, ye Stygian set,
> With Dirce in one boat conveyed,
> Or Charon, seeing, may forget
> That he is old and she a shade.

Charon and the stories that surround him emphasize the view of death as a voyage or crossing, as well as the need to separate the realm of the living from that of the dead. There may also be some subtle reassurance in the belief that rules, regulations, and fees apply here as well as in everyday life.

See also Hades; Styx.

—ROBERT KASTENBAUM

References

Bulfinch, T. (1855/Reprint 1979). *Bulfinch's mythology. Part I. The Age of Fable.* New York: Avenel Books (and many other editions).

Garland, R. (1985). *The Greek way of death.* Ithaca, NY: Cornell University Press.

Morford, M.O. & Lenardon, R.J. (1977). *Classical mythology.* New York: David McKay.

CHILDREN, DYING

What do terminally ill children know and what should they be told about their condition? There has been a dramatic change over the past quarter century in the views held by clinicians and researchers. It was previously thought that dying children know nothing about their condition and would not want to talk about it. More recent observations indicate that children can be quite aware of their condition and do want to discuss it.

Studies of Terminally Ill Children

Investigations by Karon and Vernick (1968), Waechter (1971), and Spinetta (1974) were among the first to indicate that terminally ill children could be well aware of their prognoses and interested in talking about them. These studies suggested that terminally ill children's reluctance to speak about their condition did not come from a lack of understanding, but, rather, from anxiety—and from awareness of the adult's reluctance to talk about it.

Nine months of intensive ethnographic fieldwork with forty leukemic patients between the ages of 18 months and 14 years showed how terminally ill children became aware of their prognoses even when nobody had told them, how they communicated that awareness, and why adults as well as children were reluctant to speak about the situation (Bluebond-Langner, 1978). Interviews, observations, and interactions at various points of the illness in the children's homes, hospital, and clinic revealed that all the children age three or above became aware that they were dying before death was imminent. This awareness developed whether or not they had been told of their prognoses. Furthermore, the acquisition of information about the disease was part of a prolonged process that involved particular experiences and changes in the child's view of self. This process is best characterized as a five-stage processual model.

In the first stage, the children learned that they had a serious illness. In the second stage, they became aware of the names of the drugs and their side effects. In the third stage, they concentrated on the purposes of various treatments and procedures. By the fourth stage, they were able to put all these isolated bits and pieces of information into a larger framework. Now they could see the disease as a cycle of relapses and remissions. At this point, however, they still did not incorporate death into the cycle. It was only when they reached stage 5 that the children saw death as part of the process.

Overall, the children moved from a view of themselves as "seriously ill" to "seriously ill but likely to get better," and then to "always ill but likely to get better." This was followed by a perception of self as "always ill and not likely to get better" and, finally, to a view of themselves as dying.

In order for the child to pass through these stages, certain significant events or experiences had to occur. For example, passage to stage 1 came after the child observed the dramatic shifts in the behavior of parents and other adults toward him or her once the diagnosis had been confirmed. Passage to stage 2 came after the first remission. Passage to stage 3 came after the first relapse. Passage to stage 4 came after a number of relapses and remissions, and passage to stage 5 came after the death of a peer.

Information was cumulative. If, for example, a child were at stage 2 and another child died, he or she did not immediately come to the conclusion that the disease had a terminal prognosis and that he or she, too, would die. The child had to be at stage 4 in order for that awareness to be achieved. Similarly, if a child were at stage 4 and no other child died, then the child did not move to stage 5.

The children's awareness was reflected in their behavior. For example, children at stage five—aware of their terminal prognoses—would not play with toys from deceased children. They also avoided mentioning the names of deceased children, talked about future events far in advance of when they were to happen, avoided discussing their own progress, introduced disease and death imagery into their conversation and play, and distanced themselves from others through displays of anger, withdrawal, and banal chit-chat. The children gradually assimilated a great deal of

information and came to the conclusion that they were dying.

> **Benjamin**: Dr. Richards told me to ask you what happened to Maria. (Note: Dr. Richards had said no such thing.)
> **Myra**: What do you think happened to Maria?
> **Benjamin**: Well, she didn't go to another hospital.
> **Myra**: (Nods head, no.)
> **Benjamin**: Home?
> **Myra**: No. She was sick, sicker than you are now, and she died.
> **Benjamin**: She had nosebleeds. I had nosebleeds, but mine stopped. (Note: Benjamin went through this type of conversation with everyone he saw that day.)

This type of conversation and pithier statements like, "I won't be here for your birthday," or "They don't buy me clothes to grow into," reflected not only the child's awareness but also his concern about his prognosis.

Embedded in the children's statements and behaviors are a variety of views of death. Death represented separation, mutilation, loss of identity, and the end of a biological process that is inevitable and irreversible. The children simultaneously held seemingly contradictory views. For example, a 5-year-old was concerned about separation, talked about worms eating him, and refused to play with toys from deceased children. But this was the same 5-year-old who knew that the usefulness of the drugs had run out, and who demanded that time not be wasted. So, too, the 9-year-old who drew pictures of herself on blood-red crosses and knew that it was the medication that was causing liver damage was the same 9-year-old who never mentioned the names of deceased children and couldn't bear to have her mother leave her for a moment.

Each of these children held some views one would expect from children of their age, as well as views one would not expect from those so young (See **Children and Death**). In a sense, this is not surprising, given that the dying child's experiences—separation from parents, painful procedures, death of peers—are so different from those of most children.

Mutual Pretense

Many of the behaviors the dying children exhibited at stage 5 helped to maintain the delicately balanced drama of mutual pretense (Glaser & Strauss, 1965). Although it was obvious from the children's behavior that they were aware of their prognosis, they chose not to discuss it. In other words, they behaved in the same way as many of the adults with whom they interacted.

Mutual pretense is not practiced as extensively as it once was, but it does continue to exist. Dying children engage in mutual pretense with some individuals and open awareness with others. Furthermore, there are often shifts back and forth even with those with whom they share open awareness.

If mutual pretense is to continue, then the individuals involved must focus on safe topics (the weather, food, parking), avoid discussion of dangerous topics (the future, deceased children, prognosis), and use props to sustain the illusion that the patient is getting better (continue medical procedures, even if no longer very useful). The strategies used to maintain mutual pretense allow parents to act as if they are nurturing and protecting. Physicians are allowed to act as if they are healing, and the children themselves to act as if they are still growing up, still becoming. Each is able to assume the roles and responsibilities prescribed for parents, physicians, and children in society. By fulfilling the prescribed roles and responsibilities, individuals retain membership in society and, hence, are not abandoned. Individuals are often ostracized and abandoned when they do not meet society's expectations, and when they present challenges and problems others cannot face. For these children and their parents, the prospect of abandonment was a great and ever present source of fear and concern.

Many adults felt that open awareness was extraordinarily difficult to maintain. Parents and staff who practiced open awareness reported difficulty when asking the child to go through painful procedures that would not offer any long-term benefits. Several parents reported that the feelings of guilt, frustration, anger, and sadness did not diminish with open awareness

as they thought they might. Some wondered whether one should maintain open awareness all the time, even if this were possible.

Taking Cues from the Child

It is important to recognize the various problems that follow from the practice of mutual pretense and open awareness, as well as children's abilities to learn about their illness regardless of whether or not adults choose to tell them.

Terminally ill children have different needs, concerns, and desires at different stages of the illness, and these do not necessarily match those of adults. Their strongest desire is to keep those they care about around them. This desire leads terminally ill children to follow whatever rules for interaction adults establish. It is, therefore, most important to take one's cues from the child; answer what the child wants to know in ways that the child can understand. The issue is not whether "to tell or not to tell" but, rather, what to tell, when to tell, how to tell, and who should do the telling.

See also Awareness of Dying; Children and Death; Hospice: Children; Siblings of Dying Children.

—MYRA BLUEBOND-LANGNER

References

Bluebond-Langner, M. (1978). *The private worlds of dying children.* Princeton, NJ: Princeton University Press.

Glaser, B. & Strauss, A. (1965). *Awareness of dying: A study of social interaction.* Chicago: Aldine.

Karon, M. & Vernick, J. (1968). "An approach to emotional support of fatally ill children." *Clinical Pediatrics, 7*: 274–80.

Spinetta, J.J. (1974). "The dying child's awareness of death: A review." *Psychological Bulletin, 81*: 256–60.

Spinetta, J.J. & Deasy-Spinetta, P. (1981). *Living with childhood cancer.* St. Louis: C.V. Mosby.

Vernick, J. & Karon, M. (1965). "Who's afraid of death on a leukemia ward?" *American Journal of Diseases of Children, 109*: 339–97.

Waechter, E.H. (1971). "Children's awareness of fatal illness." *American Journal of Nursing, 71*: 1168–72.

CHILDREN AND DEATH

Whether from personal apprehension, erroneous assumptions about children's capacities, or adherence to certain theoretical orientations, adults have often thought children to be incurious, unthinking, and unfeeling about the subject of death. Until fairly recently, few professionals systematically studied children or adolescents in relationship to death, although volumes of research accumulated on adults. This is true especially for dying, bereaved, and suicidal children and adolescents, and for death-related fears and anxieties among children and adolescents in general. In the past few years such researchers as Bluebond-Langner (1978), Martinson (1978), Pfeffer (1984), and Peck (1984) have sought to close some of the gaps in our knowledge. Their pioneer efforts have helped us to gain important understandings of the intrapsychic and interpersonal dynamics of children and adolescents who encounter death or contemplate terminating their own lives. These pioneers not only have helped to break through formidable barriers but also have stimulated others to follow their lead and to debunk some of the more romantic notions about children and death.

Understanding Death

Fewer barriers have existed to the study of children's understanding of the meanings of death. Our knowledge in this area is therefore more thorough and comprehensive although not entirely without inconsistencies and contradictions. The almost compulsive focus of so many studies on children's death-related thoughts, and the tiptoeing around their feelings, illustrates our discomfort with the subject of death-related fears and anxieties. In fairness to the researcher, however, it should be acknowledged that the most frequently applied theoretical model for this line of inquiry, Jean Piaget's theory, itself tends to neglect emotional development. Additionally, professional ethics dictate extreme caution to avoid arousing anxiety. Most participants for this type of research have been healthy children and adolescents, ex-cluding both those who are terminally ill and those who have been recently bereaved.

There is a tradition of research in this area that dates back more than half a century. Most of the early work was done in Europe and, with few exceptions, is also available in English. Piaget's (1929) observation of animistic thinking in the child of approximately 2 to 5 years gave impetus to a number of studies on "child animism" and the concept of "alive," as well as to controversy over definition and measurement (e.g., Klingberg, 1957). Today's researcher may still find this literature of interest. Piaget suggested animistic reasoning as one explanation for the young child's inability to grasp the concept of death. Considering the relationship between the child's notions of life and death seems logical. Safier (1964), while not examining the concepts themselves, discovered a positive relationship between the child's views of life and death and parallel stages in their development.

Other early researchers focused on the development of death-related concepts. Perhaps van Hug-Hellmuth's study, originally published in 1912, was the first of this series. He and, later, Cousinet (1939), using case history approaches, concluded that the child's understanding of death develops in an orderly sequence from less to more mature. Several other researchers studied the question systematically with large samples of children. A classic is Nagy's (1948) study of nearly 400 Hungarian children, ages 3–10 years, in the 1930s. She identified three stages in the development of the concept of death.

Nagy's stage 1 characterizes children less than 5 years of age. They do not know the meaning of death, understanding it as a departure, sleep, or other state of restricted functioning. For instance, even though the dead are in a coffin and buried in the cemetery, they still breathe, eat, think, and feel. Stage 2 is present between ages 5 and 9. The child now understands that death is final and focuses on causation, viewing death as an externally imposed and capricious event. Nagy described this stage as personification of death, reporting that the child tends to view death as a skeleton, an angel, the embodiment of a spirit, or as the dead person himself. At stage 3 (ages 9 or 10 and above), children recognize that death is not only final but inevitable.

More recent studies strongly support most of Nagy's findings of developmental stages in the understanding of death. These stages in the comprehension of death seem closely related to Piaget's theory of cognitive development in general. In a study of children between the ages of 3 and 12, Kane (1979) also identified three stages. In stage 1, death is viewed as a state of temporary immobility. In stage 2, children view death as irrevocable, universal, and internally caused. In stage 3, children are able to think of death in the abstract and speculate about issues of life and death. Kane pointed to the close correspondence of her stages with Piaget's three stages of preoperational thought, concrete operations, and formal operations. Earlier, Koocher (1973) had arrived at a similar description of stages and agreement with Piaget's theory with a sample extending in age to 15 years.

Both Kane and Koocher, however, noted a discrepancy between their findings and those of Nagy concerning the personification of death at stage 2 (ages 5–9). None of Koocher's respondents and only 4 percent of Kane's made personification responses. Those few who did give personifications were among the older children. In a recent study, Wenestam and Wass found that among Swedish and American children, personification responses were not common, and occurred chiefly among the older children. (Wenestam & Stillion, 1987; Wass & Stillion, 1987).

Aside from this discrepancy, however, the overall research literature suggests that there is a stage-based progression in the development of children's understanding of death, one that is generally consistent with Piaget's theory of cognitive growth. Thus, very young children at the preoperational level of thought have inaccurate concepts of death, thinking it to be a temporary restriction, a reversible condition. They perceive death as being caused by external forces, either violent or accidental. During middle childhood and preadolescent years, when children reach the level of concrete operational thinking, physical causality replaces animistic, magical, and other modes of earlier thought.

Children now understand the cessation of functions and the irreversibility and universality of death. They develop concrete and nonspecific ideas about life and death. In adolescence, the period of formal cognitive operations (propositional and hypothetical-deductive thinking), children develop sophisticated and abstract philosophies and theologies about the nature of death and existence after death.

The most striking consistency of findings concerns the young child's notion of the reversibility of death; the idea that the dead can be "fixed up" and otherwise restored to their previous state. This finding holds across several generations (from the 1920s to the 1980s), several Western societies (England, France, Germany, Canada, United States), and widely divergent methodologies (interviews, questionnaires, observation, and projective techniques).

One obvious disagreement in the research literature concerns the chronological ages at which children progress through levels of understanding. Most contemporary studies show children attaining mature concepts at earlier ages than Piaget estimated for the development of concepts in general. Attempts to establish rates for various aspects of development by chronological age have always been subject to error because of large individual differences in development, differences that tend to increase as children grow up. It is possible that individual differences may obscure any sequence that exists in the child's understanding of death—or there may be no universal sequence at all for older children. Instead, the concepts may be obtained in fluid or uneven patterns.

This, of course, raises the fundamental question of the impact of different environments on the development of death-related concepts. Tallmer and her colleagues (1974), for example, reported some relationships between children's concepts of death and demographic variables. In fairness to Piaget, he never claimed to study development under divergent environmental conditions. His basic view is that cognitive development is an active process that occurs in dynamic interaction between child and environment. Because Piaget's work is usually read in translation—and because even in his native language the style of writing is somewhat obscure—it is understandable that some researchers not intimately familiar with the full range of his publications have misinterpreted his work or even dismissed it as "biological determinism." In actuality, the differences between environmentalists and those who favor Piaget may be far more apparent than real. It is unlikely, for example, that Piaget would deny that children faced with a life-threatening disease would not have any understanding of their conditions.

Nevertheless, Piaget's underestimation of the cognitive capacities of young children also seems apparent in his assertion that infants cannot yet conceptualize. Although this may be correct in the strict sense of the word, recent studies (as reviewed by Gratch, 1977) suggest that infants are more advanced in their intellectual development than Piaget recognized. Kastenbaum (1986a) and Lonetto (1980) have both noted communications from older infants that suggest they had achieved some sort of intuitive knowledge or intimations of the finality of death. We do not yet know to what degree the verbal and symbolic communications of very young children adequately represent their images, perceptions, and ideas. Many of us may not be attuned to such early communications and thus may often miss the messages that are sent.

Death in Daily Life

Life expectancy is significantly higher than in previous centuries or even the early years of the twentieth century. Infant mortality has declined dramatically. Three-fourths of those who died in 1986 were 65 years of age or older. Furthermore, most people die away from home, without children present and often children do not even attend the funeral. Based on these observations, Fulton (1988) has suggested that today's young are the first "death-free" generation in recorded history. Many children grow well into adulthood before any of their family dies. Of course, many of our young still do experience the death of a loved one. The death of a pet may cause pain and grief. Still, the absence of a significant personal death experience on the part of many children and adolescents

seems to be an unusual feature of contemporary life.

In an era of personal remoteness from death, children are nevertheless surrounded by an abundance of indirect, abstract death, most of it violent, much of it obscene.

Death on the Air

Prime time television action/detective shows seem benign compared with the recent outpouring of violent feature films such as the Rambo series. These, in turn, look almost innocent in comparison to some of the multiple murder movies such as *Nightmare on Elm Street* that cater to adolescent audiences. And, indeed, older children and adolescents are fascinated by frightening mass-murder and occult films (Wass et al., 1987b). Recently, some unrated videotapes that defy any reasonable standards of decency in the way death is treated have come on the market (some video stores have now decided to stop selling them). One of the most offensive of these tapes contains lengthy footage with close-ups of killing, mutilation, and cannibalism. It has been readily accessible to teenagers and is apparently a popular rental item. How does such depiction of death affect children's perceptions of social reality? What does it teach them about the dignity and value we assign to human life and to our physical as well as our psychological being? What sort of emotions are aroused in them, and how do they handle these emotions?

Of course, children need only turn on the evening news to find such values violated daily by reports showing starving people in Third World countries, bodies strewn about after a terrorist attack, or a scene from one of the numerous wars going on in various parts of the world where killing is a major objective. Children and adolescents rate the evening news as among the most violent of the standard television fare (Wass et al., 1987b). These news portrayals may lack the pornographic aspects of the fictional or dramatic materials but may have a greater impact because it is reality they report.

Additionally, some of the popular hard rock groups bombard their adolescent fans with music whose lyrics explicitly encourage deadly violence against self or others. There is controversy between the recording industry and various child advocacy and professional organizations regarding the negative influences of such lyrics and how to protect the young from exposure to them. Again, there are no definitive studies to tell us how violent themes in contemporary rock music may affect children and adolescents. It is not even clear what proportion of our young are attracted to this type of music. In one preliminary study it was found that 17 percent of rural and 24 percent of small city high school students listed among their favorites music explicitly promoting homicide, suicide, or occult practices (Wass et al., 1987a).

Deadly Toys and Games

Children are not only passive viewers of violent death but also handle "killing" toys from the simple play gun to the high tech Laser Tag. A wide array of other toys and games with destructive intent are made for the child and adolescent market, including video games in which entire galactic systems are destroyed in milliseconds. Playing with toy weapons and games teaches children many ways in which people can attack each other. It allows them to play the role of the attacker (they far less often elect to play the attacked). Lethal violence in imaginative play and for entertainment is a common aspect of modern children's socialization, especially for boys. Is this an essential effort to instill patriotism in the young, for teaching them self-preservation, or peaceful coexistence? Or have we simply been "good consumers," responding to effective advertising by the industry?

Symbolic Violence

Turning to psychology for an answer to this question, we find fundamental disagreement between two widely respected theories: psychoanalytic and social learning. No integrating views are currently in sight.

According to psychoanalytic thinking, we are all born with destructive drives that dwell in the dark recesses of our unconscious psyches where they are an ever-present threat to ourselves and others. To control these impulses and the anxieties they arouse, we need to externalize, confront, and "work them through." This process of coping with innate destructive tendencies is considered essential to healthy personality development. The process can be aided by certain types of symbols. Bruno Bettelheim (1977), a contemporary exponent of this view, advised parents to make use of the old uncensored Central European fairy tales (as distinguished from the altered and watered down versions that have gained more currency). Almost everyone of these original fairy tales presents as its main characher a monstrous killer. According to the psychoanalytic view, as interpreted by Bettelheim and some others, such symbolic activities as reading and play-acting can help children appease their secret destructive instincts as well as to find release from their deep-seated anxieties surrounding death and mutilation. The child can experience killing in a vicarious sense without doing any actual harm or developing fear and guilt as a result.

It is tempting to adopt this theory and apply it as well to the violent death themes so common on film, television, and record. Doing so would permit parents and professionals to adopt a laissez-faire attitude toward the multitude of violent symbolic stimulations to which children and adolescents have easy access. Unfortunately, however, psychoanalytic theory has proven very difficult if not impossible to verify. We may all have opinions about the existence of unconscious drives, but there have been no convincing studies of what might be essentially an unverifiable proposition. Nevertheless, there is some support for this hard-to-test view. Children and adolescents do seem attracted to gory movie, television, and video fare and—as a group—also seem to come away unscathed. Or do they? One obvious fact is that our young have not become mass murderers.

Support for the psychoanalytic view can also be found in the "sick" jokes that are often popular among youths. Some of these, for example, the "dead baby" genre of jokes that has circulated among older children and adolescents, are extremely offensive to adults. What function can such humor serve? Psychologists have long suggested that children ward off or mitigate anxieties through humor. Recent events support this explanation. Immediately following the explosion of the *Challenger* spaceshuttle in 1986, a number of gruesome jokes began circulating among children and adolescents, stories concerning the violent manner of the astronauts' deaths (Blume et al., 1986; Children, 1986). It is easy to condemn those who create and pass along these jokes as calloused or "sick," but their popularity still needs to be explained.

Social learning theory is in sharp contrast to the psychoanalytic view. As presented by Bandura (1977) and others, this approach holds that behavior, attitudes, and feelings can be learned by observing the actions of other people. Children do not necessarily have to experience everything directly and have this experience confirmed by positive reinforcements; they can also learn by modeling themselves after others.

Many studies have supported this general view. Learning extends beyond the actual persons in the child's life (parents, teachers, siblings, peers) to include the symbolic models they see on film and videos, hear on records, or read about in print. Despite the fact that social learning theory has lent itself to scientific testing in a number of circumstances, it has not yet been possible to establish the specific effects of televised aggression on children's behavior, even after more than thirty years of research. The difficulty lies in the fact that human behavior and attitudes are formed through complex interactions of many variables. Isolating and determining the effect of a single variable (such as television violence) is almost impossible. However, the weight of the evidence is strong, given certain circumstances and specified conditions; from the perspective of social learning theory it is best to keep children and adolescents away from direct or indirect lethal violence (National Institute of Mental Health, 1982).

Obviously, this approach cannot be applied successfully in many instances, nor does the theory hold in all cases. We know that not all adolescents who listen to Ozzy Osbourne's "Suicide Solution" or to Metallica's eerily melodic "Fade into Black" are influenced to kill themselves. But, frighteningly, a few have done so, apparently after listening to these very songs.

Basic questions are: Who are those at risk among our children and adolescents? What circumstances and conditions make them vulnerable to influences by others' violent behaviors and suggestions? For whom are such exposures actually helpful and therapeutic? We have two conflicting views—psychoanalytic and social learning—and insufficient evidence to resolve the issues. In such situations we may find the observations of experienced developmental psychologists helpful.

Elkind (1981) points to the "hurriedness" of children's lives and the extreme stresses such hurriedness produces. He believes that the problem with television violence is not so much one of negative modeling but of being bombarded with observations and stimulation that are too difficult to digest at the level of their experience and emotional maturity. Kastenbaum (1986b) has made some lucid observations, asked compelling new questions, and shared profound reflections on what it may mean to be an adolescent in the process of transition and reconstruction of self, purposes, and goals—and particularly to be an adolescent in the present era of colliding and confused attitudes about life and death. These observations of Elkind and Kastenbaum provide a broad context for the issues presented here. One thing seems clear: the major burden of responsibility rests with the home. Parents are potentially the most significant persons to mediate, monitor, and assist. Children and adolescents alike need their parents' help in coping with the fundamental issues of death, the bewildering onslaught of death-related stimuli, and the deep anxieties and concerns they almost certainly experience.

See also Adolescence and Death; Causes of Death; Children, Dying; Hospice: Children.

—HANNELORE WASS

References

Bandura, A. (1977). *Social learning theory.* Englewood Cliffs, NJ: Prentice-Hall.
Bettelheim, B. (1977). *The uses of enchantment—the meaning and importance of fairy tales.* New York: Vintage Books.

Bluebond-Langner, M. (1978). *The private worlds of dying children.* Princeton, NJ: Princeton University Press.

Blume, D., Whitely, E., Stevenson, R.G., Van Buskirk, A., Morgan, M.A., & Myrick, R.D. (1986). "Challenger 10 and our school children: Reflections on the catastrophe." *Death Studies, 10*: 95–118.

"Children's reactions to the space shuttle tragedy." (1986). *Death Studies, 10*: 507–18.

Cousinet, R.L. (1939). "L' idee de la mort chez infant." *Journal du Psychologie Normale et Pathologie, 36*: 65–75.

Elkind, D. (1981). *The hurried child: Growing up too fast, too soon.* Reading, MA: Addison-Wesley.

Fulton, R.C. (1988). "The funeral in contemporary society." In H. Wass, F.M. Berado, & R.A. Neimann (Eds.) *Dying—facing the facts.* 2nd ed. Washington, DC: Hemisphere, pp. 257–72.

Furman, E. (1974). *A child's parent dies.* New Haven, CT: Yale University Press.

Gratch, G. (1977). "Review of Piagetian infancy research: Object concept development." In W.F. Overton & J.H. Gallagher (Eds.) *Knowledge and development.* Vol. 1. New York: Plenum Press, 81–104.

Kane, B. (1979). "Children's concepts of death." *Journal of Genetic Psychology, 134*: 141–53.

Kastenbaum, R. (1986a). *Death, society, and human experience.* 3rd ed. Columbus, OH: Charles E. Merrill.

Kastenbaum, R. (1986b). "Death in the world of adolescence." In C.A. Corr & J.N. McNeil (Eds.) *Adolescence and death.* New York: Springer, 4–15.

Klingberg, G. (1957). "The distinction between living and not living among 7–10 year-old children with some remarks concerning the so-called animism controversy." *Journal of Genetic Psychology, 90*: 227–38.

Koocher, G.P. (1973). "Childhood, death, and cognitive development." *Developmental Psychology, 9*: 369–75.

Lonetto, R. (1980). *Children's conceptions of death.* New York: Springer.

Martinson, I.M. et al. (1978). "Home care for children dying of cancer." *Pediatrics, 62*: 106–13.

Nagy, M. (1948). "The child's theories concerning death." *Journal of Genetic Psychology, 73*: 3–27. From *The child and death,* published in Hungary, 1936.

National Institute of Mental Health (1982). *Television and behavior: Ten years of scientific progress and implications for the eighties.* Vol. 2: *Technical reviews.* Washington, DC: U.S. Government Printing Press.

Peck, M. (1984) "Youth suicide." In H. Wass & C.A. Corr (Eds.) *Childhood and death.* Washington, DC: Hemisphere, 279–92.

Pfeffer, C.R. (1984), "Death preoccupations and suicidal behavior in children." In H. Wass & C.A. Corr (Eds.) *Childhood and death.* Washington, DC: Hemisphere, 261–78.

Piaget, J. (1929). *The child's conception of the world.* London: Routledge and Kegan Paul.

Safier, G. (1964). "A study in relationships between the life and death concepts in children." *Journal of Genetic Psychology, 105*: 283–94.

Tallmer, M., Formanek, R., & Tallmer, J. (1974). "Factors influencing children's conceptions of death." *Journal of Clinical Child Psychology, 3*: 17–19.

van Hug-Hellmuth, H. (1912/Reprint 1965). "The child's concept of death." *Psychoanalytic Quarterly, 34*: 419–516. (Originally published as "Das Kind und Seine Vorstellungen vom Tode," *Imago, 1*: 286–98.)

Wass, H., Cerullo, K., Martel, L.G., Mingione, L.A., Raup, J., & Sperring, A.M. (1987). "Murder, suicide, and occult themes in contemporary hard rock music and adolescents' rock music preferences and views on such themes." Presented at the Annual Conference of the Association for Death Education and Counseling, London, Ontario (May 8).

Wass, H. & Stillion, J.M. (1987). "Death in the lives of children and adolescents." In H. Wass, F. M. Berardo, & R. Neimeyer (Eds.) *Dying—facing the facts.* 2nd ed. Washington, DC: Hemisphere.

Wass, H., Stillion, J.M., & Fattah, A.F. (1987). "Exploding images: Gifted children's view of violence and death on television." In C.A. Corr & R.A. Pacholski (Eds.) *Death: Completion and discovery.* Lakewood, OH: Association for Death Education and Counseling, 201–28.

Wenestam, C.G. & Wass, H. (1987). "Swedish and U.S. children's thinking about death: A qualitative study and cross-cultural comparison." *Death Studies, 11*: 99–121.

CHILDREN'S HOSPICE INTERNATIONAL

Children's Hospice International (CHI) creates a world of hospice support for children by providing medical and technical assistance, research, and education for dying children, their families, and health care professionals throughout the United States and abroad. CHI was founded in 1983 as a nonprofit organization to (1) promote hospice support through pediatric care facilities; (2) encourage the inclusion of children in existing and developing hospices and home care programs; and (3) include the hospice perspectives in all areas of pediatric care, education, and the public arena.

Definition of Children's Hospice Care

Children's hospice is a concept of care for children and adolescents in the final stages of a life-threatening condition. Hospice care can take place anywhere—in the patient's home, hospital, or other appropriate location. In hospice care, the use of the term "patient" may refer to the patient himself or herself as well as the patient's immediate support system, be it family or any combination of significant others.

Pediatric hospice care is achieved by addressing and balancing the individual needs of the patient and those of the family. This includes the developmental, psychosocial, and spiritual as well as the physical aspects of care. Support of anticipatory grief begins at the time of referral. Bereavement support is provided to the family for a period of at least one year after the death of the child.

Services must include (but are not limited to) those of physician and nurse, psychosocial, spiritual, bereavement, and any other additional services necessary for appropriate care of the patient and family. Consultation with a registered nurse must be made available twenty-four hours a day as needed by the patient and family.

Children's hospice care facilitates the participation of parents in assuming the role of primary caregiver and supports the inclusion of patient and family in making the best decisions they can commensurate with their desires. The hospice team supports the patient and the family. In turn, support of the hospice team is provided through scheduled access to ongoing education and training programs.

Resources Available

The following resources and services are provided by CHI:

- Publications, audiocassettes, videotapes, and film rentals.
- Conferences, seminars, and inservice training programs.
- Speakers and conference planning assistance: providing speakers on a wide variety of hospice-related topics, working with individual organizations, assisting in the design of conferences and workshops.
- Consultation on hospice program implementation.
- Referral service: responding quickly and directly to the needs of special children, their families, and health care providers.

CHI is presently working on an innovative program of care and outreach to fill the gap not being met by hospice programs that primarily serve adults. Videotapes and textbooks will be produced using the expertise of leading authorities in the field of child care. These materials will provide vital information to hospices, hospitals, home care, and long-term facilities as well as community-based organizations.

For additional information contact:

Ann Armstrong Dailey, Founding
  Director
Children's Hospice International
1101 King Street, Suite 131
Alexandria, VA 22314
(800)-24-CHILD
(703) 684-0330 in Virginia.

See also Children, Dying; Children and Death; Hospice: Children.

—ANN ARMSTRONG DAILEY

COMPASSIONATE FRIENDS

The Compassionate Friends (TCF) is a self-help group of bereaved parents offering friendship and understanding to bereaved parents in order to promote and aid a positive resolution of grief.

TCF was founded in England in 1969 by the Reverend Simon Stephens, a hospital chaplain. TCF now has chapters in the United States (approximately 600), England (40), Australia (15), South Africa (4), and at least one chapter each in Switzerland, Hong Kong, the Netherlands, West Germany, Brazil, Israel, New Zealand, Mexico, and Bolivia. There is no international organization, but contact is maintained by correspondence and personal visits.

Local chapters form the basic unit of TCF. In the United States, a national board maintains an office that functions primarily as a support service to local chapters.

There are limited empirical data on the activities of local chapters. However, the great majority have at least one regular meeting per month, publish a newsletter, offer a network of telephone contacts, and engage in activities to educate the community on the needs of bereaved parents. There is great variation in the use that bereaved parents make of the group. Many read the newsletter but never attend meetings. Among those who attend, some come only a few times, some attend for a year or two, and some move into leadership positions in the chapter and continue attending for several years.

Two dynamics characterize the relationship of the bereaved parent to the group. First, parents receive help with experiential difficulties such as how to celebrate the holidays or how to handle strained relationships within the family. Second, parents develop deep interpsychic bonds that are an extension of the bond the parent had with the dead child.

The TCF "credo" reads:

> Whatever pain we bring to this gathering of The Compassionate Friends, it is pain we will share just as we share with each other our love for our children. We are all seeking and struggling to build a future for ourselves, but we are committed to building that future together as we reach out to each other in love and share the pain as well as the joy, share the anger as well as the peace, share the faith as well as the doubts, and help each other to grieve as well as to grow.

See also Grief; Grief: Death of a Child.

—DENNIS KLASS

References

The Compassionate Friends. (1983). *Grieving, healing, growing.* Hinsdale, IL.: West Suburban Chapter of the Compassionate Friends.

Edelstein, L. (1984). *Maternal bereavement: Coping with the unexpected death of a child.* New York: Praeger.

Klass, D. (1988). *Parent grief.* New York: Springer.

CONCERN FOR DYING

Concern for Dying, a not-for-profit educational organization, was founded in 1967 to improve the care and articulate the rights of dying patients. The organization attempts to increase professional and public understanding of, and communication about, the multifaceted aspects of the dying process and, particularly, decisions to forgo life-sustaining treatment. In addition to educating students and practitioners of medicine, nursing, law, school counseling, chaplaincy, and other health-related fields, Concern for Dying also provides forums and materials for laypersons, including the living will and information about the durable power of attorney and other legislation.

Concern for Dying recognizes the importance of the law in articulating and protecting patients' rights, and it participates as advisor and amicus in selected cases. Nevertheless, it believes that forgoing life-support is not simply a legal matter but one that involves cultural, psychological, professional, and organizational aspects as well. Thus, the need remains to educate successive generations of caregivers on all these aspects of care in addition to familiarizing them with the points of law that have been made clear by judicial decisions, statutes, and regulations.

Concern for Dying's educational program is known as The Collaboration: A Multi-Professional Network for Death, Dying and Decisionmaking. This program brings together students and practitioners in health-related fields to address the issues of terminal care and decisionmaking. The workshops also help participants to build skills in order to deal with terminally ill patients and their families and provide a supportive network for students and practitioners.

Resources provided by Concern for Dying include:

- A quarterly newsletter that offers an update on Concern for Dying's work and on current national issues related to death and dying, upcoming educational events, and reviews of current pertinent literature. The newsletter is sent to anyone who has contributed $5 or more to the organization.
- Films and videotapes for rental and purchase.
- The living will and related information.
- "A Legal Guide to the Living Will."
- The landmark report issued by the President's Commission for the Study of Ethical Problems in Medicine and Biomedical and Behavioral Research: *Deciding to Forgo Life-Sustaining Treatment.*
- Guidance of a staff attorney as well as a Legal Advisors Committee, in legal questions related to patients' rights.
- Workshops for students and practitioners in health care on such topics as medical ethics, AIDS, and terminal-care decisionmaking.
- A national network of health care professionals and laypersons to speak about the various issues involved in death, dying, and decisionmaking.

Further information can be obtained by contacting:

Concern for Dying
250 West 57th Street, Room 831
New York, NY 10107
(800) 248-2122
(212) 246-6962 in New York State

See also (The) Living Will.

—PENNY B. WEINGARTEN

CREMATION

What is to be done with the physical remains of a dead person? Several approaches have been taken. The body has been placed beneath the earth in ground burial or inhumation. The body has been exposed to the natural elements until only the bones remained and these were then either buried or kept as a remembrance. The body has been embalmed and enclosed in one or more protective structures. Both burial at sea and unceremonious casting of a dead body overboard have also been practiced.

Cremation rivals all these methods in both historical pedigree and current utilization (it is now, for example, by far the most common means of body disposal in China). Consigning the body to flames was already an ancient practice when it acquired its familiar Latin-derived name (from *cremare,* "to burn"). Although the attitude toward and popularity of cremation has been far from constant over the centuries, it does remain one of the basic links between the Stone Age and contemporary life.

Historical Perspective

It is clear from archeological evidence that cremation was practiced in eastern and northern Europe during the Stone Age and became even more widely utilized as previously isolated populations encountered each other in the Bronze Age. There is reason to believe that at least some of the cremations were part of rituals associated with early cults of the dead (James, 1957). Fire had become a vital symbol, often associated with purification rituals. Although the meaning of ancient fire rituals is unknown, the surviving artifacts indicate that cremations were often conducted in an orderly and consistent manner. Cemeteries have been found (dating from as long ago as 1500 BC) in which numerous urns had been placed, each containing ashes. Inhumation and cremation seem to have been practiced at the same time by ancient peoples, a phenomenon that still occurs today. It was not unusual for both methods to be applied to the same body, as when Babylonians would wrap the corpse in combustible material, encase it in clay, and burn it on a brick platform. The ashes would then be placed in a jar and accompanied by objects thought to be useful to the deceased in the next life (Irion, 1968).

The early Christians lived in a world in which cremation was a common but by no means a universal practice (for very different reasons, Chinese, Egyptians, and Jews preferred other methods). The Greeks had cremated their fallen warriors to prevent abuse of the corpses by the opposing armies. In the time of Pericles, cremation became a public health measure. Recognizing that some diseases can be transmitted through the food supply and other forms of contagion, Greek leaders urged that no further burials be made in inhabited areas and cultivated fields. Cremation was advocated as a prophylactic approach. (Widespread cemetery reform would still be needed throughout much of Europe more than a thousand years later.) Social class distinctions made themselves apparent in body disposal practices in classical Greece, as they have in many other times and places. It was only the wealthy citizen who could afford a proper and efficient cremation. A telling insult would be to describe somebody as "half-burned," perhaps the ancestor to later jibes about "half-baked" schemes.

Cremation was viewed as barbaric and wrong-headed by the soon-to-be-dominant Christian cult. Resurrection in the flesh was thought by some to require an intact body. However, not all Christians agreed with this belief; instead, burial was preferred because this was more in keeping with the entombment and resurrection of Jesus. As a rather troublesome element in the Roman world, the early Christians were at odds with the prevailing belief that the soul, but not the body, survives physical death. Rejection of cremation, then, was one of the major principles differentiating Christianity from the opinion of the time.

Evidence that the method of body disposal had become a bone of contention includes Roman attacks and Christian replies such as the following (both cited by Rush, 1941, p. 236). The criticism is by Minucius Felix, the defense by Octavius:

it is easy to understand why they curse our funeral pyres and condemn cremation; just as if every body, although withdrawn from the flames, were not reduced to dust as the years roll on, just as if it makes any difference whether our bodies are torn to pieces by wild beasts, swallowed up in the sea, covered with earth, or destroyed by fire. Any kind of burial must be a punishment to them, if they have any feeling after death. If they have not, cremation must be regarded as a beneficient remedy in the rapidity of its effect.

We are not, as you imagine, afraid of any injury from the manner of burial, but we practice the old and better practice of interment.

Cremation was practiced widely in many Asian cultures (with the already noted exception of the Chinese, who today are in conflict between government pressures for the economics of cremation and the resurgence of support for traditional burial rituals). Various rituals and meanings were associated with cremation. The Hindu *Rig-Veda*, among the most ancient surviving scriptures for any religion, includes a funeral hymn that beseeches the fire god to offer safe conduct for the deceased. The now illegal practice of suttee *(Sati)* called for Hindu widows to immolate themselves along with their deceased husbands on the funeral pyre.

The spread of Christianity was accompanied by a strong preference for earth burial over cremation. Most existing crematoria were not maintained, and the practice was criticized as pagan. Cremation was even regarded as a severe punishment and was invoked as such upon the corpse of John Wyclife, who had been condemned and executed as a heretic more than forty years before his remains were reduced to ashes and thrown upon the waters.

Not for many years did Christian society care to look upon cremation as an acceptable alternative. Curiosity was stimulated by Thomas Browne's (1658) open-minded description and analysis of "sepulchrall urnes lately found in Norfolk." These were Roman "cremains" (to use a term that has become familiar in our own time). Although he was not himself a firebrand who demanded the reinstatement of cremation, Browne showed an independent mind:

Men have lost their reason in nothing so much as their religion . . . and since the religion of one seems madnesse unto another, to afford an account or rationall of old Rites requires no rigid Reader. . . .That they washed their bones with wine and milk, that the mother wrapt them in Linnen, and dryed them in her bosome, the first fostering part, and place of their nourishment; that they opened their eyes towards heaven, before they kindled the fire . . . were no improper Ceremonies (Browne, 1658, pp. 56–57).

Cremation gradually regained a place in Western custom as the conditions of everyday life were transformed by science, technological change, urbanization, and other forces. A major contributing factor was growing public concern about the poor condition of burial grounds, especially in expanding and overcrowded cities. Furthermore, an increasing number of religious leaders presented the view that cremation was compatible with Christian dogma and had some advantages worth considering; in nineteenth-century Italy, for a particularly influential example, some priests showed themselves willing to participate in funeral services for the cremated dead (Erichsen, 1887).

Current Practices and Issues

One collective nightmare for the human race has created a horrifying association with cremation. Moving from a distorted version of euthanasia (not deserving that term at all) to outright genocide, Nazi Germany killed and cremated millions of men, women, and children (for two different types of accounts, see Lanzmann 1985; Lifton, 1986). Residents in nearby cities could see and smell—could literally breathe in—the ashy smoke of Nazi victims. Although this association has more to do with the destructive side of human nature than with the act of cremation as such, it is also an association that many will never be able to forget.

Today cremation is a readily available option in most parts of the world. The heated controversy of the past seems to have given way to personal, family, and ethnic preferences. England has proven especially receptive to the cremation alternative, with approximately 60 percent of all deceased disposed of by this means

(Ragon, 1983). There is considerable official encouragement, as cemetery space is in very short supply.

In the United States, the choice of cremation usually does not affect the overall pattern of funeral and memorial observances. The body of the deceased can be viewed, if that is the preference, and the survivors can arrange whatever services and observances they consider appropriate. The difference occurs at the conclusion of the services. At this point the body is transported to a crematorium. The body may first be brought to a room known as the committal chamber. Here family and friends can engage in a final leave-taking with the body of the deceased, if they so choose.

The body, enclosed by a casket, is introduced into a furnace where intense heat is provided by oil or gas flames. The physical remains are rapidly dehydrated by the heat, and the carbon-containing components of the body are reduced to ashes. Fragments of bone usually are found among the ashes. These fragments may be reduced to the size of small stones through use of a crushing device, or they may remain in pieces of various size. Next of kin who wish to have all the ashes completely reduced to powder may find it useful to make these arrangements in advance. The cremated remains (often called "cremains") generally weigh between five and seven pounds.

A survey sponsored by the National Foundation of Funeral Service (Adams, 1986) indicates that cremation is usually the direct choice of the deceased person. A perhaps more unexpected result: "While stereotypes hold that those who arrange cremation are more interested in convenience and efficiency, quite the opposite is true. The burial sample was significantly more interested in convenience/efficient arrangements. The implication . . . is that the funeral service practitioner must not assume that the family selecting cremation wants minimal services" (Adams, 1986, p. 84). Two other stereotypes failed to hold up. There were no significant differences between an interest in "keeping expenses low" and "concern for use of land" between those who selected cremation and those who selected burial. Furthermore, there is no clear pattern of differences between the two groups in the causes of death or length of illness. Age and gender also seem to have no bearing on the choice between cremation and burial. What are the differences? According to the survey, people who select cremation tend to be more educated, have higher employment (but not higher income) levels, and be less active in religious affairs. Protestants are more likely to choose cremation than are Catholics.

It should also be noted that cremation does not preclude burial. In fact, having the ashes buried was the most common choice made.

Inadequate or miscommunication between the family and the funeral director sometimes transpires with respect to cremation. For example, some family members neglect to instruct their funeral directors on what they want to be done with the ashes, and some funeral directors have presented the cremains to family members without adequate preparation. As in any interaction between a family and a service provider, mutual respect and the opportunity for thorough exchange of information and views is much to be favored.

See also Cemeteries; Funerals; Survival Beliefs and Practices: Hindu; Survival Beliefs and Practices: Roman Catholic; Suttee (Sati).

—ROBERT KASTENBAUM

References

Adams, J.A. (1986). "Project Understanding: A national study of cremation." *Research Record, 3*: 73–96.

Browne, T. (1658). *Hydrotaphia.* London: Sign of the Gun.

Erichsen, H. (1887). *The cremation of the dead.* Detroit: D.O. Haynes.

Irion, P.E. (1968). *Cremation.* Philadelphia: Fortress Press.

James, E.O. (1957). *Prehistoric religion.* London: Thames & Hudson.

Lanzmann, C. (1985). *Shoah.* New York: Pantheon Books.

Lifton, R.J. (1986). *The Nazi doctors.* New York: Basic Books.

Ragon, M. (1983). *The space of death.* Translated by Alan Sheridan. Charlottesville, VA: University Press of Virginia.

Rush, A.C. (1941). *Death and burial in Christian antiquity.* Washington, DC: Catholic University of America Press.

"CROSSING THE BAR"

Perhaps no other poem in the English language has so often been called upon to offer consolation in the face of death. "Crossing the Bar" is one of the last of the many poems written by Alfred, Lord Tennyson (1809–1892), then England's Poet Laureate.

"Crossing the Bar" was both years and but a few minutes in creation. Tennyson was seriously ill late in 1888. Considering his history of health problems and his advanced age, there was much concern for his survival. Tennyson rallied somewhat, however, and, in an invalid chair, accompanied his family on a trip that included a passage by ship. The journey started out in a pleasant vein, but Tennyson's spirits were depressed when he learned that a dog had been accidentally killed enroute. At the end of this trip, his health again deteriorated and the aged poet became preoccupied with the death that seemed to be impending. His wife, Emily, observed at that time: "The face of the clock seemed to him to expand & fill up the whole end of the room. The clock pointed to a quarter past six & he said superstitious people would say that he would die then" (quoted by Martin, 1980, pp. 567–68).

It was a year later that the recovered poet was urged by his nurse to write a poem in thanksgiving. That day the Tennysons again made the same short crossing of the Solent on their way home to Farringford. As Martin (p. 570) tells the incident:

> In a fit of instantaneous inspiration, the sixteen lines of "Crossing the Bar" sprang into his mind in almost their final form. Less than twenty minutes later, when the boat pulled into Harmouth, it was written down on a piece of used paper. That Evening Nurse Durham came into his study to light the candles and found him sitting alone in the dark. "Will this do you for, old woman?" he asked gruffly and recited the poem. Forgetting that she had asked him for a hymn of thanksgiving, she thought that he had . . . composed his own death song; in her agitation she fled without replying.

This was not Tennyson's last poem, for he outlived "Crossing the Bar" by three years. Nevertheless, it is generally considered his final statement of belief, and Tennyson himself asked that it be placed at the very end of his collected poetry.

The faith expressed in this poem did not come easily to Tennyson. He suffered doubts about immortality throughout his life, partially because he was well aware that a new scientific world view was emerging that called traditional beliefs into question. Even in his last days there were times when the old doubts returned, although it seems probable from the circumstances that he ended his life with a sense of faith and trust similar to that expressed in "Crossing the Bar."

The poem is simple in structure yet displays the subtle sense of sound and meter found in Tennyson's best works. Ricks (1972, p. 314) finds that "Its simple dignity is yet consonant with a fine patterning and subtle variety. The third line of each stanza, longer than the preceding line, swells into a release of feeling. But what saves this from self-indulgence . . . is the immediate curbing effect of the stanza's shortened concluding line, reining and subduing that feeling. . . . The poem itself 'turns home again.'" Ricks concludes that this poem, within its brief compass, perfectly illustrates Tennyson's most characteristic movement, "a progress outward which is yet a circling home."

Tennyson's reputation was once of the very highest. He and other Victorian poets were later subjected to criticism and parody. It was fashionable for some years to dismiss Tennyson in a rather condescending way. Today, however, it appears that his enduring qualities are better appreciated. T.S. Eliot is among his admirers: "Tennyson is a great poet, for reasons that are perfectly clear. He has three qualities which are seldom found together except in the greatest poets: abundance, variety, and complete competence" (Eliot, 1950/1985, p. 11). In "Crossing the Bar" Tennyson has also shown the rare quality of touching and consoling those for whom death has become a matter both urgent and personal.

Crossing the Bar
Sunset and evening star,
And one clear call for me!
And may there be no moaning of the bar,
When I put out to sea,

But such a tide as moving seems asleep,
Too full for sound and foam,
When that which drew from out the boundless deep
Turns again home.

Twilight and evening bell,
And after that the dark!
And may there be no sadness of farewell,
When I embark;

For though from out our bourne of Time and Place
The flood may bear me far,
I hope to see my Pilot face to face
When I have crost the bar.

See also "Thanatopsis."

—ROBERT KASTENBAUM

References

Eliot, T.S. (1950/Reprint 1985). "In memoriam." In H. Bloom (Ed.) *Alfred Lord Tennyson.* New York: Chelsea House Publishers, pp. 11–18.

Martin, R.B. (1980). *Tennyson: The unquiet heart.* New York: Oxford University Press.

Ricks, C. (1972). *Tennyson.* New York: Macmillan.

CRYONIC SUSPENSION

It has been known for many years that reducing the body temperature of a living organism can serve a number of useful purposes. For example, in the days before effective anesthesia techniques, surgeons would sometimes attempt to dull the pain of knife and saw by packing the injured limb in ice. Cryonic (from the Greek *kyros,* icy cold) techniques continue to have a place in medical care today, as well as in a variety of commercial and research applications.

The term cryonic suspension, however, refers to a more extreme application of the temperature reduction principle. Advocates claim that it is possible for a person to be maintained in a state of hypothermia for an extended period of time and then restored to normal life. It is pre-

Cryonic suspension storage units. Large unit (9′ tall) stores one or two whole bodies. Small unit is for neurosuspension (head only) storage and holds up to four heads. Photo reprinted by permission of Alcor Life Extension Foundation, 12327 Doherty Street, Riverside, CA 92503, (714) 736-1703.

sumed that technology will become available for "repairs" that are not now possible. Whether described as cryonic suspension or "solid-state hypothermia," this phenomenon is regarded by some people as a new and viable method for overcoming death.

The Prospect of Immortality

Cryonic suspension first came to general attention in the United States through the writings and lectures of Robert C.W. Ettinger. In the first sentence of his much discussed book, *The Prospect of Immortality* (1964, revised 1966), Ettinger suggested that "Most of us now breathing have a good chance of physical life after death—a sober, scientific probability of revival and rejuvenation of our frozen bodies." He further claimed that "At very low temperatures it is possible, right now, to preserve dead people with essentially no deterioration." Medical science will eventually make it possible to repair almost any damage that a human body might suffer. Therefore, a person who has "died" in the usual sense of the term could have his or her body preserved in a cryonic condition until a cure has been discovered for whatever disability resulted in the "death." Ettinger insisted that "No matter what kills us, whether old age or disease, and even if freezing techniques are still crude when we die, sooner or later our friends of the future should be equal to the task of reviving and curing us" (p. 15).

In the ideal case, the following events would occur:

- A person with a life-threatening illness specifies that he or she wishes to be placed in cryonic suspension when death occurs.
- Friends and family support this plan.
- The dying person's physician supports this plan.
- Hospital administration and staff support this plan.
- Experts and equipment are available to initiate the cryonic procedures.
- Financial arrangements have been made to take care of the immediate and continuing expenses.

These favorable circumstances might not be sufficient, however, unless:

- The death actually occurs in a situation that makes the cryonic procedure possible (e. g., the person does not die in a different part of the world that lacks the provisions or willingness to assure cryonic suspension), and
- All the elements that are critical to the initiation of the cryonic suspension procedure are actually in place when the death occurs.

This final point is an important one. Delay in the certification of death could result in further physical deterioration prior to the initiation of cryonic procedures. Furthermore, any number of problems may arise despite the original state of mutual agreement and preparedness, e.g., the consenting physician may not be available, the hospital staff on duty at the time may refuse to cooperate, etc. These are complications that have actually developed when some efforts toward cryonic suspension have been made (Nelson, 1968).

The next set of requirements for the ideal case of cryonic suspension would involve:

- Proper maintenance of the body until medical knowledge and expertise make it possible to treat the corpse successfully for the condition(s) that resulted in death, and
- Techniques have been perfected for raising the body temperature and reversing the cryonic condition without inflicting significant damage in the process.

There is at least one other critical factor that must hold true:

- The health care system at the time of the attempted revival—indeed, society in general—must be willing to invest the effort required both for the recovery procedure and any prolonged rehabilitation that might be required.

Ettinger recognized that there would be many technical and social problems involved, and that the hope for his "prospect of immortality" also rested upon continued progress in the medical sciences. Nevertheless, his vision of the cryonic alternative to death attracted considerable public attention at the time. Some individuals were enthusiastic enough to form organizations to foster the exchange of information and to encourage the development of the equipment and techniques thought necessary for cryonic suspension. For a period of several years subsequent to publication of *The Prospect of Immortality,* these efforts showed some energy and growth. General public interest declined, however, and gradually a number of early enthusiasts deserted the movement. Nevertheless, a core of individuals (including Ettinger himself) continue to be dedicated to the possibility of cryonic suspension. Newsletters such as *Venturist Monthly News* (1355 Peoria Ave., Phoenix, AZ 85020) provide a source of advocate information and opinion on this topic.

Critical Response to the Cryonic Suspension Movement

Objections to the cryonic thesis have been made from psychological, social, economic, moral, and scientific standpoints. From this writer's surveys of allied health care professionals and university students in the years immediately following publication of Ettinger's book it was clear that most respondents were repelled by the idea. The most common objection included elements of psychosocial, social, economic, and moral criticism. Respondents most often thought it was wrong to tamper with life and death in this manner. There were specific aversions to the idea of freezing and storing human bodies, to the expense involved, and to the ways in which this procedure might disrupt the lives of the survivors (e.g., "How could you remarry, if your first spouse is in a freezer some place, waiting for a second chance?"). Additionally, there were strong feelings expressed about "How greedy it is to expect another life . . . and maybe another life after that and so on." Others said much the same thing with a statement such as, "We all owe Nature a debt." The moral objection was most often embodied in statements such as, "Life is a gift from God," and "The Lord has His own plans for us." A more socially conscious type of moral objection was also expressed by some respondents: "Who will be thawed out? Only the power brokers, the people with money—just one more kind of discrimination, who needs that?"

It is possible that many of these objections could be explained as a familiar type of response to unfamiliar ideas, e.g., "If God had meant man to fly, he would have given him wings." Among the responses was a jest that seemed to come spontaneously to many people: "Many are cold, but few are frozen." The curiosity of the general public seemed to be piqued by the cryonic movement for a time, but there were relatively few who welcomed this prospect of immortality in a wholehearted manner.

Ettinger was well aware of the social, economic, and moral complications that could arise if cryonic suspension became a reality. In fact, his discussion of these issues remains of interest today, whether or not one is an advocate or believer. He pointed out, for example, that legal definitions of death would be challenged, life insurance provisions would need to be revised, and the marital vow "until death do us part" might take on a different meaning (Ettinger, 1966). In a scholarly preface, Gerald J. Gruman suggests that "Bringing up the question of the nature of death is a major contribution of this book. . . . We tend to accept uncritically as absolute such concepts as 'irrevocable damage,' 'biological death,' etc., and we overlook the insidious nature of this 'hardening of the categories,' an intellectual flaw as prevalent and as hampering as hardening of the arteries" (p. 12). In other words, the issues that lead some to dismiss cryonic suspension abruptly are the very issues that deserve fresh and incisive attention. Ettinger's own treatment of these issues leaves much room for further considerations.

Although many types of concern have been expressed about cryonic suspension, the most critical test involves its scientific credibility. What are the realistic prospects for actualizing the goal of eventual restoration to life and health for those who are cryonically suspended? Evaluation of this prospect is very difficult because the concept of "eventual" eludes precise definition. It is almost certain that there will continue to be advances in the fields of technology that bear upon cryonic suspension and reversal, but scientific opinion is sharply divided regarding the rapidity and extent of such future advances.

Opponents of cryonics emphasize the fact that no large organ or mammal has yet been revived from a solidly frozen state, as well as the difficulties that appear to preclude such resuscitation—mainly, freezing damage and lack of a perfected freezing technique. Although some individual cells are routinely recovered in viable form from liquid nitrogen storage, many cells do not recover. Furthermore, there is no known way of preventing substantial and lethal cell loss, disruption, and chemical imbalance throughout a larger organ or organism. One problem is that different cells, found in close proximity in the same organ, may require different specific techniques for thawing to a viable state. Then, too, even under the best of known conditions, some types of cells do not survive solid freezing (Mazur, 1984). The brain, which is the all-important organ that encodes the personality in its structure and memory traces, is likely to offer significant additional difficulties in view of its great delicacy and complexity.

Proponents of cryonics concede that existing techniques do not allow for resuscitation of whole mammals (including humans). However, they also point out that technology is continuing to advance rapidly. Substantial future advances can be expected. Advances relevant to cryonics might involve both the freezing process and "thawing" or resuscitation. For people today, perhaps the most crucial question is whether humans frozen by currently available methods can be resuscitated by tomorrow's science. This, the advocates say, is at least a reasonable possibility given the high degree of structural preservation seen in frozen brain and other tissue, and the fact that such tissue, preserved at liquid nitrogen temperature, does not deteriorate over time. They forecast a future in which atom-by-atom manipulation of matter will be possible, allowing repair devices on the cellular and subcellular levels to correct deficiences that seem insuperable today. A discussion of how this new level of technological advances might work has been presented by K. Eric Drexler (1986).

Our day-to-day existence is already dependent on continuous repair and maintenance processes that take place in our bodies. All that appears to be lacking, according to cryonic proponents, is a method for controlling these processes ourselves. With such control it would not be necessary to preserve the functional integrity of an organism through freezing. Much freezing damage, presently lethal and irreversible, could be tolerated. The only requirement would be that the frozen tissue must contain enough intact structure to allow eventual inference of what should be there from what still is there. The problem of cryonic resuscitation is seen, then, as ultimately one of information recovery, rather than primarily a "biological" or "medical" problem, as these concepts are usually understood today.

In balance, cryonic resuscitation would seem to offer great difficulties, and no guarantee that they can be solved, but likewise no proof, as yet, that they will never be solved. Some people embrace the possibilities of cryonics and consider the potential benefits to far outweigh the cost. While most at present do not share this optimism, the history of science is studded with so many remarkable achievements that it might be foolish to say at this time that resuscitation from cryonic suspension will never be a reality.

A Perspective on Cryonic Suspension

The movement to "Freeze-Wait-Re-animate!" may tell us as much about ourselves as about the still developing science of cryonics. The prevailing negative response seems in part to represent a skeptical view that is well supported by the present state of knowledge. Many people with biomedical expertise judge that it simply will not work. Others, however, argue that the problem is not primarily a "biomedical" one, and that the real experts to consult are in fields such as computer science, mathematics, and nanotechnology (the newly-developing study of controlled manipulation on the atomic scale).

Some of the psychological objections, however, may reflect upon the public's own uneasiness with the subject of death. Thinking about cryonic suspension also requires thinking about one's death and the circumstances that surround it. Those who resist thinking about their own mortality are not likely to enjoy dwelling on the details of cryonic suspension. The moral objections to cryonic suspension may also deserve closer scrutiny. Society's view of what should and what should not be done to preserve life has been challenged repeatedly through biomedical innovations. If cryonic suspension were encompassed within the larger framework of methods potentially available to preserve life (e.g., organ donation and other "heroic" techniques), then a more coherent moral position might be developed. The social, legal, and economic ramifications of cryonic suspension would certainly require attention from the general public, health personnel, and decision-makers of various types. However, society is already engaged in reconsidering many other issues relevant to health and welfare, so perhaps even the radical-sounding implications of cryonic suspension are not that unusual or even that radical any more.

The negative or apathetic response to the cryonic thesis also suggests that people do not necessarily consider longer (or renewed) life as their top priority. Offered at least the prospect of immortality, many have found reasons in themselves to decline the option (at least in its present guise). The immortalist tradition (See **Prolongation of Life**) may well take still other forms in the years ahead but, judging from the response to cryonics, there may continue to be some hesitancy and resistance.

In the meantime, the physical remains of a retired professor of psychology continue to exist inside a frozen capsule (paradoxically, in a near-desert climate in Arizona). Dr. James H. Bedford, the first human to be cryonically suspended under controlled conditions, was frozen in January 1967. His body was perfused with dimethylsulfoxide (DMSO) and packed in dry ice, then transferrred to liquid nitrogen storage. Others have undergone cryonic suspension (e.g., Darwin, 1988); more modern techniques introduce a larger amount of a better protective agent, glycerol, through perfusion. Some now have only their heads frozen, this approach being based upon the idea that the technology to resuscitate them will also be able to provide a newly-reconstructed body. Some have had their cryonic plans aborted for a variety of circumstances, a problem that cryonics organizations are working to overcome.

Should Dr. Bedford one day have the opportunity to write his own postmortem autobiography, then many will have occasion to revise their thinking. In the meantime, one might draw some interesting inferences from the cryonic thesis in theory and practice (e.g., Drexler, 1986; Harrington, 1969, Chapter 18).

See also Brain Death; Prolongation of Life.

—ROBERT KASTENBAUM
(R. Michael Perry, Consultant)

References

Darwin, M. (1988). "Long time Alcor member enters biostasis." *Cryonics, 9*: 2–13.

Drexler, K.E. (1986). *Engines of creation.* New York: Anchor/Doubleday.

Ettinger, R.C.W. (1966) *The prospect of immortality.* New York: Macfadden.

Harrington, A. (1969). *The immortalist.* New York: Random House.

Mazur, P. (1984). "Freezing of living cells: mechanisms and implications." *American Journal of Physiology, 247*: C125–C142.

Nelson, R.F. (1968). *We Froze the First Man (As told to S. Stanley).* New York: Dell.

D

DANCE OF DEATH (DANSE MACABRE)

The image of a "last dance" lingers in our own times although its most pervasive and powerful manifestations belong to the late Middle Ages. Several very popular classical music compositions have associations with this image. The most obvious example is the tone poem, *Danse Macabre* by Camille Saint-Saens (1835–1921). Death is portrayed musically as a demonic fiddler in this eerie piece. One of the most familiar compositions by Jean Sibelius (1865–1957) is the graceful but deeply melancholic *Valse Triste*—part of his incidental music for *Kuolema* (Death), a play written by his brother-in-law, Arvid Jarnefelt. Death makes an appearance here as an almost compassionate figure who calls upon a dying old woman for one last dance. This image resonates with the final scene of the Stephen Sondheim musical, *A Little Night Music.* Here, again, an old woman slips away peacefully to the sound of a waltz whose opening measures bear a striking similarity to *Valse Triste.* Maurice Ravel's brilliant tone poem, *La Valse,* has been used effectively for an historically updated dance of death ballet. And when Woody Allen and Death become dance partners in the closing scene of his film, *Love and Death,* we know once again that the ancient image has not yet exhausted all its possibilities.

The origins of the dance of death image have been traced to a thirteenth-century poem: "The Encounter of the Three Living and the Three Dead." (It may well have drawn upon even earlier traditions.) Three brave knights, in the prime of life, encounter a like number of corpses—who turn out to be themselves. This theme soon became expressed in the visual arts where the living and the dead are portrayed as engaging in a solemn dance together. Versions of the dance of death appeared in books of hours, paintings, tapestries, and frescoes on church walls. One of the earliest known examples was a danse macabre painted on the cloister walls of the Innocents, a religious order in Paris during 1424–25. This image has survived in the form of woodcut editions from the late fifteenth century and their facsimile copies.

The term itself, *danse macabre*, is thought by some scholars to represent a corruption over time of the Greek *macarius,* the blessed (the dead) plus the Latin *chorea*, dance. The resulting Latin term, *chorea machabaeorum,* is still one leading candidate for the root of *danse macabre.* In more recent times, *macabre* has been increasingly associated with bizarre and shocking elements. Some, but not all, depictions of the dance of death are dominated by macabre features. Aries (1981, p.116) offers a plausible alternative with a French slang word for corpse: *macchabe.* He finds it "not surprising that around the fourteenth century the dead body—the word cadaver was seldom used—was given the name of the holy Maccabees. The Maccabees had long been honored as patron saints of the dead because they were believed, rightly or wrongly, to be the originators of the prayers of intercession for the dead." Still another theory is that in even more ancient times, especially in Persia, there were ac-

A grant danse macabꝛee
des hōmes ⁊ des femmes
hystoꝛiee ⁊ augmentee de
beaulx ditz en latin.

Le debat du coꝛps ⁊ de lame
La complaincte de lame damnee
Exhoꝛtation de bien viure ⁊ bien mourir
La vie du mauuais antecheist
Les quinze signes
Le iugement.

The dance orchestra of Death. From *La grant danse macabre des hommes et des femmes,* Troyes, 1496. Reprinted, by permission, from Ernst & Johanna Lehner, *Picture Book of Devils, Demons and Witchcraft,* p. 103. © 1971 by Dover Publications, Inc.

tual dances of a pantomime character performed by gravediggers as part of their annual rituals—magic funeral dances (cited by Meyer-Baer, 1970). Precisely how these festivities influenced either the medieval dance of death tradition or its danse macabre appellation remains obscure. Among German-speaking people, the dance of death tradition was well represented under the title, *Totentanz.*

Among the most significant artistic representations of the dance of death are the forty-one woodcuts created by Hans Holbein the Younger (first published in 1538). The Black Death had passed and some of the other overwhelming horrors of the fourteenth century had abated by this time, but the emotional memory lingered and life remained frought with peril. One should not expect to find literal dancing in all of Holbein's scenes. The guiding concept is subtler; it is closer to his intent if we think of a dance of life that is shadowed relentlessly by death. The band does not suddenly strike up for a dance of death. Death has been waiting and watching all the time as we move in a self-absorbed manner through the days of our lives. Holbein's moral purpose is conveyed by the captions as well as the images. The Last Judgment scene, for example, is accompanied by these words:

Before the mighty Judge's chair
Comes reckoning for each man alive;
Fear, then, the judgments rendered
    there:
You know not when he will arrive.

In Holbein's and some later dance of death series, there are a variety of attitudes assumed by Death. He is abrupt and vengeful, for example, when seizing a monk "who hast never felt remorse nor care," but gentle with the exhausted old woman: "Then come along to rest with me, For Death is better now than life." By Holbein's time, if not before, Death had become a commentator for social and moral criticism as well as a figure of dread.

Death became a theatrical figure as well, often a skeletal, hooded personage who delighted in shock and destruction. There was often an element of parody as well—the Death character could somehow terrify and amuse at the same time. Generally, the dance of death was consistent with the prevailing spirit of the times, *Ars*

moriendi: a mutual reminder that humans are mortal and will have to reckon with God's judgment. Although Death became deputized as an enforcer of the moral order, farce and even obscene humor were seldom absent for long. The shock value of Death was well appreciated by artists, writers, and actors. The dance of death was also sensitive to social rank and class. The Death figure often passed judgment on peasants, merchants, clergy, and royalty, each of whom were thought to have specialized in particular forms of sloth and vice.

Actual dancing did take place, although the tradition seems to have been most fully expressed through its visual and poetic representations. As far as can be determined, it appears that when people enacted the dance of death it was usually in a measured, almost ritualistic manner. A late fifteenth-century woodcut by Guyot Marchand suggests the type of musical accompaniment that might be expected: four skeletal figures perform on the bagpipe, portative organ, harp, pipe, and tabor (a small drum). The dance element seems to have become somewhat more dominant in Germany, especially in the woodcuts known as the Heidelberger *Totentanz*. In most other depictions, we are shown more of a stately procession than what to modern eyes would look like a dance. Meyer-Baer (1970) offers a rare example of a song that might have accompanied a dance of death. The text emphasizes that only Christ and the Holy Virgin can save one from eternal death.

The image of the dance of death arose in a world sorely tested by catastrophes over which the inhabitants had little control. Although the tradition has changed over time, artistic expression of this powerful, haunting image is likely to endure.

See also *Ars Moriendi;* (The) Black Death; Death Themes Through History; *Memento Mori.*

—ROBERT KASTENBAUM

References

Aries, P. (1981). *The hour of our death.* New York: Alfred A. Knopf.
Holbein, H. (1538/Reprint 1971). *The dance of death.* New York: Dover.

Meyer-Baer, K. (1970). *Music of the spheres and the dance of death.* Princeton, NJ: Princeton University Press.

Tuchman, B.W. (1978). *A distant mirror.* New York: Alfred A. Knopf.

Warthin, A.S. (1931/Reprint 1977). *The physician of the dance of death.* New York: Arno Press.

Weber, F.P. (1910/Reprint 1971). *Aspects of death and correlated aspects of life in art, epigram, and poetry.* College Park, MD: McGrath.

White, F. (1931/Reprint 1970). *The dance of death in Spain and Catalonia.* New York: Arno Press.

DAYS OF THE DEAD

The Roman Catholic observances known as the days of All Saints (November 1) and All Souls (November 2) are celebrated in an unique way by Indian traditionalists in Mexico. Both holidays are known collectively as *Dias de Todos Muertos,* or Days of the Dead. Based upon her observations in the city of Oaxaca, Judith Strupp Green (1972, p. 242) has provided this description:

> Among those raised in the Western heritage of death-avoidance, the observation of the Days of the Dead in traditional parts of Mexico often elicits a reaction of mild shock and even repulsion. Death iconography mingled with gustatory delights (sugar skulls, coffin candies), toys for children (skeleton puppets), and politics (the calvaveras news-sheet) and the ordinary pursuit of the living grates against contemporary North American and European attitudes toward death. Certain customs carried out in graveyards on these days or nights, such as gambling or playing board games on the tombstones, or eating a picnic lunch there, have the same effect. Although these customs are actually peripheral . . . to the ritual itself, they are consonant with the ancient indigenous beliefs about the dead.

The Days of the Dead festivals are both important and expensive. No matter how poor the family, the women purchase new dishes to please the spirits, create an altar in the home, and prepare food for guests. On October 31, the night of Allhallow's Eve (Halloween), the family stays up to prepare the foods, and the boys ignite firecrackers in celebration when the tamales begin to steam. Those who have sufficient space in the house are likely to set up a special altar in memory of dead children, *angelitos,* ("little angels") which includes tiny candleholders, small fruit and vegetables, and toys.

Green's informants believe that the spirits of dead children arrive at 4 AM on November 1. A tiny candle is lit for each of these visitors. Four hours later, the *angelitos* leave, and the candles are snuffed and removed. A mass is said in church later that morning. At about 3 PM, the adult spirits are said to arrive and a full-sized candle is lit for each visitor. The food placed on the altar for the spirits is not touched by the family for fear of antagonizing the dead; similarly, it would provoke the spirits if the food and gifts are not adequate. A rosary is said by the family that evening, and the adult spirits depart as several masses are said in church. Rituals for the dead are conducted throughout the day, including blessing and sprinkling their graves with holy water. The graveside rituals are likely to continue beyond the *Dias de Todos Muertos* in order to make sure that all the deceased have been honored.

At sundown on the second day, villagers decorate the graves with flowers, candles, and incense. The most elaborate treatment is given to children's graves, which are likely to include cardboard or plastic figures representing the dead or their status in the afterlife. Around this time there are also rounds of visiting by relatives and friends who pray at the home altars and offer gifts to the dead souls. The gift is known as a *muerto* and is most likely to be food prepared specially for that day. (For example *pan de los muertos,* "bread of the dead," is shaped or decorated with such religious symbols as a winged angel or hearts and crosses).

Various ritual objects are associated with the Days of the Dead. Some of these represent death, for example, skeletal figures dressed in various ways, including comical impersonations of bishops and scholars. Especially popular are edible representations of death, such as sugar candies molded in the shape of skulls.

Scholars believe that contemporary Days of the Dead observances in Mexico (also to be seen in some areas of the southwestern United States) combine Roman Catholic beliefs and customs with ancient Aztec rituals (Green, 1969; Leon-Portilla, 1963; Sahagun, 1950). It is considered probable that the cardboard and plaster representations used today are substitutes for actual skulls and sacrificial animals employed in the past. The Spanish influence on the native populations of Central America was also marked by its own traditions of feeding and interacting with the dead. The Dance of Death was especially prominent in Spain (where it may have originated) through the fifteenth and sixteenth centuries, and, as Green (1972) notes, "Spanish devotion to the dead was so great as to amount to a death cult" throughout the seventeenth and eighteenth centuries as well.

Green offers another observation that is worth considering by all who are interested in the way that the circumstances of everyday life influence and may be influenced by ritual and belief: "The transference of death themes to toys and candies for children is entirely consonant with ancient and modern Indian beliefs regarding childhood participation in religious ritual. And there is no need to hide the facts of death from the Indian child. It is an event with which he is intimately familiar, not only because of the depressingly high mortality rate, but because death, like birth, takes place in the home and with the family."

See also Children and Death; Dance of Death (*Danse Macabre*); Survival Beliefs and Practices: Roman Catholic.

—ROBERT KASTENBAUM

References

Green, J.S. (1969). *Laughing souls: The Days of the Dead in Oaxaca, Mexico.* San Diego: San Diego Museum of Man, Popular Series, No. 1.

Green, J.S. (1972). "The Days of the Dead in Oaxaca." *Omega, Journal of Death and Dying* 3: 245–61.

Leon-Portilla, M. (1963). *Aztec thought and culture: A study of the ancient Nahuatl.* Norman, OK: University of Oklahoma Press.

Sahagun, B. (1950). *General history of the things of New Spain: Florentine codex.* Translated and annotated by A.J.O. Anderson and C.E. Dibble. Sante Fe, NM: School of American Research.

DEATH ANXIETY: MEASURES

Although religion and the humanities have addressed the matter for centuries, the behavioral sciences and mental health disciplines virtually ignored death anxiety until the second half of the present century. In a pioneering investigation, Herman Feifel (1955) administered to psychiatric patients a semistructured interview regarding death attitudes. Some researchers employed projective techniques but did not attempt to determine the reliability or validity of their instruments.

The Boyar (1964) Fear of Death Scale (FODS), reported in an unpublished dissertation, appears to have been the first psychometric instrument to assess death anxiety. Boyar obtained an initial pool of items on the basis of individual interviews. He then had judges rate the adequacy of his items. Next, the items were embedded in filler (nondeath) items. The split-half reliability was determined, and item-item and item-test correlations were computed. To determine the validity of the 18 Likert-type items, respondents were administered the scale before and after a movie intended to increase death anxiety. Since the FODS scores for the experimental group increased to a significantly greater extent than did those of the control group shown an innocuous movie, Boyar concluded that the validity of his scale was established.

The most widely used psychometric instrument in this area is now the Templer (1970) Death Anxiety Scale (DAS). Templer viewed Boyar's items as reflecting too narrow a range of life experience, primarily the act of dying, the finality of death, and corpses and their burial. Templer attempted to devise items that cover a wider array of life experiences.

The initial forty true–false items were subjected to face validity judgments and internal consistency determinations. The fifteen surviving items were found to have good internal consistency and reliability over time. Most of the fifteen DAS items are quite straightforward. Nine of the items are keyed for a true answer (e.g., "I am very much afraid to die," and "The subject of life after death troubles me greatly"). Six of the items are keyed for false (e.g., "The thought of death never bothers me" and "It doesn't make me nervous when people talk about death").

Construct validity determination included correlations with the Minnesota Multiphasic Personality Inventory and with psychiatric conditions appraised as having high death anxiety. There was also, ironically, a rather high correlation with Boyar's scale, an instrument Templer originally had reservations about.

Subsequent research demonstrated that DAS score correlates positively with other measures of psychopathology and between members of the same family. Females tend to have higher DAS scores (Templer et al., 1971). Highly religious persons tend to have lower death anxiety, as do elderly persons in some populations investigated. Two studies reported lower DAS scores in terminal cancer patients as compared with controls, who were not terminally ill (Gibbs & Auhlerberg-Lawlis, 1978; Dougherty et al., 1986). DAS scores have been found to be associated with diverse behavioral variables such as resistance to rape and being a motorcyclist. A number of factor analyses have been carried out, with cognitive and affective reactions to death, physical changes, concerns about flow of time, pain, and stress being the sort of factors most commonly reported (Lonetto & Templer, 1986). The DAS has been translated into Arabic, German, Spanish, Hindu, Chinese, Korean, Afrikaans, and Japanese. American norms have been provided (Stevens et al., 1980). A Likert format has been established (McMordie, 1982) in addition to the original true-false format. This Likert format would appear to have a greater sensitivity for detecting change over time.

The DAS has been administered before and after various intervention strategies. Some of these investigations have reported a decrease in anxiety, some an increase, and some no change. A "consolidation" effect first reported by Murray (1974) reveals no pre-post change but a subsequent lowering at follow-up testing after several weeks. Some of the intervention studies were formulated on the basis of Templer's (1976) two-factor theory of death anxiety—that degree of death anxiety is determined both by general psychological health and by experiences with death.

A table presenting the DAS correlations with nine other psychometric death anxiety instruments, and a brief review of the more frequently used of these, is included in a 1986 book by Lonetto and Templer. One of the more useful and innovative of these other instruments is the Collett-Lester Fear of Death Scale (Collett & Lester, 1969), which has separate scores for fear of death of self, fear of death of others, fear of dying of self, and fear of dying of others. This scale has thirty-six items with six response alternatives ranging from strongly agree to strongly disagree. As an example of its utility, the Collett-Lester Scale is currently being employed in a study to determine the death attitudes of homosexual men as a function of religion, whether or not they have AIDS, and whether or not a lover or friend has AIDS.

Which death anxiety instrument to use should be a function both of the purpose of the assessment and the construct validity of the instrument. In general, the various scales provide similar findings, so one can have security in the knowledge that they do tap a common understructure.

The scales all share the limitation of assessing primarily the death anxiety that one is aware of and willing to acknowledge.

See also Death Anxiety: Reduction; Death Fears and Anxiety; Death Threat Index (TI).

—DONALD I. TEMPLER

References

Boyar, J.I. (1964). "The construction and partial validation of a scale for the measurement of the fear of death." *Dissertation Abstracts, 25*: 20–21.

Collett, L. & Lester, D. (1969). "The fear of death and the fear of dying." *Journal of Psychology, 72*: 179–81.

Dougherty, K., Templer, D.I., & Brown, R. (1986). "Psychological states in terminal cancer patients as measured over time." *Journal of Counseling Psychology, 33*: 357–59.

Feifel, H. (1955). "Attitudes of mentally ill patients toward death." *Journal of Nervous and Mental Disorders, 122*: 375–80.

Gibbs, H.W. & Achterberg-Lawles, J. (1978). "Spiritual value and death anxiety: Implications for counseling with terminal cancer patients." *Journal of Counseling Psychology, 25*: 563–69.

Lonetto, R. & Templer, D.I. (1986). *Death anxiety.* Washington, DC: Hemisphere.

McMordie, W.R. (1982). "Concurrent validity of Templer and Templer/McMordie death anxiety scales." *Psychological Reports, 51*: 264–66.

Murray, P. (1974) "Death education and its effect on the death anxiety level of nurses." *Psychological Reports, 35*: 1250.

Stevens, S.J., Cooper, P.E., & Thomas, L.E. (1980). "Age norms for Templer's Death Anxiety Scale." *Psychological Reports, 46*: 205–06.

Templer, D.I. (1970). "The construction and validation of a Death Anxiety Scale." *Journal of General Psychology, 82*: 165–77.

Templer, D.I. (1976). "Two factor theory of death anxiety: A note." *Essence, 2*: 91–94.

Templer, D.I., Ruff, C.F., & Franks, C.M. (1971). "Death anxiety: Age, sex, and parental resemblance in diverse populations." *Developmental Psychology, 4*: 108.

DEATH ANXIETY: REDUCTION

Almost all published studies of attempts to reduce death anxiety have been group-centered and have involved adolescents or adults from normal populations. These studies have used death education, behavioral techniques, group processes, or some combination. The Death Anxiety Scale (DAS) of Templer (1970) was administered before and after the intervention of educational programs in most of this research. Some authors reported a significant decrease, some a significant increase, and some no change in death anxiety score. Lonetto and Templer (1986) suggested that the interventions that were most effective had a strong experiential component and provided sufficient opportunity for a cognitive and affective "working through" of the material.

Murray's (1974) study was important in that she found no change in DAS score from the pretest to the completion of a six-week program but a significant decrease four weeks later. Murray suggested that some type of "consolidation" takes place during this time period. Subsequent researchers have replicated Murray's finding of a decrease in death anxiety at the time of follow-up.

Zuehlke and Watkins (1975) found an increase in both death anxiety and purpose in life scores in terminally ill cancer patients after they experienced logotherapy, (based on the work of Victor Frankl), a finding they interpreted as lessened denial of impending death. Their discussion of therapeutic, theoretical, and ethical implications is worth further attention.

It is probably premature to propose detailed and fixed guidelines either for clinicians working with physically healthy populations or those working with dying persons. However, researchers should consider using death attitude factor scores and Likert response formats to provide greater sensitivity to changes over time (McMordie, 1979).

See also Death Anxiety: Measures; Death Fears and Anxiety.

—DONALD I. TEMPLER

References

Lonetto, R. & Templer, D.I. (1986). *Death anxiety.* Washington, DC: Hemisphere.

McMordie, W.R. (1979). "Improving measurement of death anxiety." *Psychological Reports, 44*: 975–80.

Murray, P. (1974). Death education and its effect on the death anxiety level of nurses. *Psychological Reports, 35*: 1250.

Templer, D.I. (1970). "The construction and validation of a Death Anxiety Scale." *Journal of General Psychology, 82*: 165–77.

Zuehlke, T.E. & Watkins, J.T. (1975). "The study of psychotherapy with dying patients: An exploratory study." *Journal of Clinical Psychology, 31*: 729–32.

DEATH CERTIFICATE

Both the certificate of birth and the certificate of death have become core documents in modern society (Kastenbaum, 1988). This is easily demonstrated whenever a person is required to furnish proof of his or her identity or a survivor attempts to collect on a life insurance policy. Apart from their individual applications, however, certificates of birth and death are relied upon for the development of statistical information on entire populations (Preston, 1972). Governmental agencies, commercial interests, and researchers all make substantial use of the information provided through these forms.

Church registry books were perhaps the most significant forerunners of the modern death certificate. Births and deaths were recorded at the local church throughout much of Europe. It was part of the clergyman's function to monitor the comings and goings of his people and see that all had the benefit of ritual, instruction, and care. These records were also called upon when questions of kinship, property rights, and inheritance arose. Some church registries have survived intact over the centuries and have proven invaluable to cultural and medical historians.

A major step was taken toward the establishment of the modern death certificate as a result of some disturbing and bizarre practices that prevailed in England throughout the eighteenth and into the nineteenth centuries (Williams, 1987). Professional "body-snatchers" had been furnishing cadavers to physicians for their instruction and research. There were many abuses, culminating in scandals that revealed some unfortunate people had been murdered for their bodies. As part of an effective reform movement in 1832, Parliament required authenticated certificates for every death. It was not until 1911, however, that Sweden took the lead in collecting data on cause of death for an entire nation. Today, death certificates are collected throughout the world (although experts have doubts about cause of death data from some countries).

In the United States the typical death certificate requires several types of data: (1) decedent information, such as name, sex, date and place of birth, race, marital status, citizenship, place of residence, occupation, next of kin, and Social Security number; (2) names of parents; (3) disposition of body (burial or cremation); (4) circumstances of death: time (hour as well as date), place, and immediate and contributing causes. The certificate must be signed by a physician. Notation is made if a medical examiner has been called upon to investigate the cause of death (when homicide is a possibility or a contagious disease that could threaten the population at large). It is also common practice now for states to require a special certificate in the case of fetal death. In addition to the information obtained through the standard death certificate, the fetal form also includes information on the course of pregnancy and birth.

Those interested in drawing conclusions from death certificate information should familiarize themselves with changes over time in the classification system as well as other factors that require some caution in interpretation.

See also Autopsy; Causes of Death; Death System; International Classification of Diseases (ICD).

—ROBERT KASTENBAUM

References

Kastenbaum, R. (1986). *Death, society, and human experience.* 3rd ed. Columbus, OH: Charles E. Merrill.

Preston, S.H., Keyfitz, N., & Schoen, R. (1972). *Causes of death.* New York: Seminar Press.

Williams, G. (1987). *The age of miracles.* Chicago: Academy Chicago Publishers.

DEATH EDUCATION

Death education is a term applied to a wide variety of planned educational experiences that improve knowledge and understanding of the meaning of death, the process of dying, and grief and bereavement. Topics are numerous and diverse, ranging from health care of the terminally ill, bioethical issues of machine-dependent survival, epidemiology of suicide, training for hospice volunteers, and bereavement counseling to cremation practices in Nepal.

The goals of the death educator reflect the needs of the individuals who seek death education. These needs appear to fall into four major categories: (1) personal concern because of some previous experience that has not been resolved; (2) personal concern because of some ongoing experience, such as the critical illness or very recent death of a close family member; (3) involvement with a relevant form of work, such as nursing, medicine, social work, the ministry, or volunteer service through a hospice organization; or (4) a wish to understand better what death means or how to cope more effectively with one's own death or the death or grief of others.

The form of death education is variable. A great deal of death education can be categorized as either cognitive/informational or personal/affective. The former, perhaps with this article as an example, is an attempt to communicate information; the latter attempts to help people understand their own values and to behave as effectively as possible when confronting death-related issues. These two broad categories may be less differentiated in practice than in theory. Information may help people understand and, therefore, handle their feelings in ways, that provide greater personal satisfaction, while the process of becoming able to handle one's feelings and accept one's values can be cognitively instructive at the same time.

As commonly used, the term *death education* is limited to those instances in which education or training form the basis or intent of the educational experience. Therefore, a parent who takes a child to a funeral to help the child learn about death is providing a form of death education; a parent who takes a child to a funeral without any educational intent is not providing death education, although the child will undoubtedly learn something about death. This differentiation, however, will not find universal agreement among either experts or the general public.

Among the settings in which death education is most frequently provided in contemporary Western societies, and in the United States and Canada in particular, are university, college, and high school classrooms and other programs; religious services and other church-related settings (adult education); and special in-service training for people whose work brings them into regular or sporadic contact with death, dying, and grief (health care professionals, clergy, counselors, psychotherapists, teachers, and social workers).

Given the wide range of settings in which death education occurs, innumerable individuals provide death education at one time or another. However, just as many people give financial advice without being financial counselors, many people provide death education without being death educators.

The Role of the Death Educator

Much of the early writing and teaching in death education was critical of health professions and systems, with particular antipathy to the care given by physicians and hospitals. This coincided with the beginning of the hospice movement. Claims were commonly made that physicians as individuals and hospitals as systems were not sufficiently sensitive to the needs of dying and grieving persons and that the dying person too seldom received compassionate health care, adequate pain management, and sufficient contact with family members and close friends. Further, the emphasis on maintaining life or existence without apparent regard to its quality became a significant health concern.

Needless to say, many physicians were distressed by these criticisms, and the criticisms themselves did injustice to those members of the medical profession who were, in fact, sensitive and caring. The development of the hospice movement was a response to the perceived inadequacies of the treatment of dying persons, thus making hospice itself a kind of criticism of prevailing medical and hospital practices.

Although these criticisms are still heard, two factors seem to have reduced their intensity. First, the medical profession plays a major role in hospices, and many hospices are tied to hospitals, thus diminishing the tensions in that arena. Second, some combination of death education and the spirit of the times has led to improved sensitivity to the dying on the part of hospitals and physicians.

The contributions of the nursing profession to the improved climate are considerable. Since nurses are more likely than other professionals both to provide on-going caring relationships to dying persons and to meet with visiting family members, they were greatly affected by the lack of adequate psychosocial care for the dying. Further, the advent of the death-awareness movement coincided with increasing concern among nurses for their own professional status. These two factors led to a significant demand in nursing for death education for themselves as well as for others.

One analysis of the increase in public and professional criticism of the medical profession uses a religious metaphor. In this analysis, religion is defined as one's "ultimate concern" (after Paul Tillich) and the clergy are viewed as individuals who enable others to attain what they seek in this regard. If long and healthy life, rather than traditional spiritual or religious goals, are what one seeks, then physicians emerge as the contemporary priesthood. Since the traditional priesthood made promises that were to be kept only after death, their ability to keep these promises could never be ascertained. The medical priesthood, however, may be seen to promise long and healthy life, and since everyone does eventually die, this new priesthood may be perceived as making promises it cannot keep. Also, the new priesthood is much better paid than the old priesthood, which offers an obvious basis for anger.

Death educators, according to this analysis, are the deacons, much less likely to elicit anger but nonetheless intruding into sacred territory. Therefore, they need to anticipate not only the thanks of those they help but criticism of any action that appears to arise from vanity, greed, or self-aggrandizement (Kalish, 1980–81).

As long as these "deacons" provide support for the "priests" and do not challenge their authority, they are welcome. However, overstepping their boundaries or seeming to be critical of those in power can lead to a curtailment of their own influence. This is an even greater issue for death counselors.

The History of Death Education, 1955–1975

In common with other forms of education, death education first occurred informally through family members, neighbors, and participation in sacred rituals. With the advent of the death-awareness movement, which we would arbitrarily set as the second half of the 1950s with the publication of the books and articles of Herman Feifel (e.g., 1959) and others, it became obvious to the pioneers in this field that death had become a taboo topic and that neither cognitive nor affective understanding of the issues were being fostered through available educational challenges. One early author compared the status of death to that of sex, referring to death as the "new pornography" (Gorer, 1959).

University courses on death began to be taught some ten years later. Books were also appearing, and professional journals started to publish increasing numbers of academic articles, including empirical research, theory, and programmatic presentations. There had always been some academic and professional writings on death. Treatises on how to die and how to be consoled date back many centuries (See **Ars Moriendi**).

In this era, outstanding authors such as sociologist Thomas Eliot, psychiatrists Walter Bromberg and Paul Schilder, psychologist G. Stanley Hall, physician Alfred Worcester, and, of course, Sigmund Freud, had been publishing on death-related topics from shortly after the turn of the century through the 1930s. It appears, however, that educational opportunities in addition to reading were limited to a few minutes in medical school or a church sermon.

By 1965 a small number of credit courses were being taught in universities, while relevant training programs were initiated in some hospitals and long-term care facilities (the hospice movement was still in the future). A book with death education in its title appeared in 1971 (Green & Irish), and a newsletter, later to become the journal *Omega*, was distributed on a regular basis, starting in 1966 and coedited by Robert Kastenbaum and Richard Kalish.

Among those offering either university courses or formal training programs in these early days were philosophers (e.g., Jacques Choron), sociologists (e.g., Robert Fulton, Barney Glaser, Anselm Strauss), psychologists (e.g., Herman Feifel, Richard Kalish, Robert Kastenbaum, Leonard Pearson, Lawrence LeShan), nurses (e.g., Jeanne Quint Benoliel), the clergy (e.g., Earl Grollman, Edgar Jackson), psychiatrists (e.g., Avery Weisman), and oncologists (e.g., Melvin Krant).

The first university courses drew very small numbers of students. By the end of the 1960s, however, students had become aware of the courses and were flocking to them. It was not unknown for between 50 and 200 students to attend an upper-level undergraduate course on death, and slowly the courses were incorporated into the regular curriculum. The particular academic departments in which these courses appeared reflected the interests of those individual faculty members who were highly motivated to request to teach on a topic that at the time received little approval from their colleagues.

At first, the courses were primarily in psychology and sociology departments and schools of nursing. There were also occasional listings in theological schools, schools of public health and social work, and departments of philosophy. Later courses appeared in anthropology, education, literature, religious studies, allied health sciences, and elsewhere. Even schools of mortuary science, which previously had provided little education on psychological aspects of death, had eagerly added such programming by the late 1960s.

Events Outside Educational Institutions

The hospice movement initiated through the efforts of Cicely Saunders in England was gaining attention in North America by the late 1960s. A few years later attention of both the general public and relevant professions was drawn to the work of Elisabeth Kubler-Ross. Less well known but influential in its own way was a 1968 international conference in Aberdeen, Scotland, on social science and medicine, in which death and dying was selected as one of the major foci. Participants included John Hinton and C. Murray Parkes (England), Loma Feigenberg (Sweden), Kalle Achte (Finland), Jan Matse and M.A. Munnichs (Netherlands), and Robert Kastenbaum and Richard Kalish (United States), all of whom were actively involved in university education, hospital training, or both. This was the beginning of significant international linkages in death education.

Another contributing event was the establishment in 1973 of Ars Moriendi, an organization devoted to death education. Centered in Philadelphia and led by psychiatrist John Fryer, this organization further stimulated cooperation among those active in death education, clinical services, and research. Two years later, the Forum of Death Education and Counseling (now **Association for Death Education and Counseling**) was established under the leadership of health educator Dan Levitan. It has held annual meetings and occasional training workshops since that time.

The History of Death Education: 1975 to the Present

By the middle of the 1970s, probably every major college and university and most community colleges had at least one course on death. It was not unusual for a course on death to be cross-listed in two or more departments or team-taught on an interdisciplinary basis. Often a college or university would offer a course on death in one department in the fall and in another department in the spring, with overlapping but far from identical content.

The field of nursing responded in a particularly timely and vigorous manner to the emergence of death education. Many courses appeared in schools of nursing, and death education also became an important topic for in-service training. Journals in the field of nursing supported this surge of interest by publishing an increasing number of articles, many describing the experiences of nurses in working with terminally ill patients. Although medical schools were much less likely to include death-related issues as a formal part of their curriculum, they did provide individual speakers and workshops on the topic.

High schools and even elementary schools have also offered death education. In a few instances, such programming became politically controversial in somewhat the same way that sex education has been the subject of controversy, although usually with much less intensity. In effect, it was considered by some parents, teachers, and administrators that the topic of death was too emotionally upsetting to be presented in schools, and that even adolescents were too immature to discuss it or even to give it serious thought. Nonetheless, many school systems and countless individual teachers recognized the need for children and adolescents to learn something about death and grief and to have an opportunity to explore values and personal feelings. Interestingly, in 1973 one seventh-grade English teacher realized that *Romeo and Juliet* stirred up as much strong feeling about the meaning of death as it did about the meaning of love. A local expert on the topic was invited to meet with the students, and he reported that these young people asked the same questions and expressed the same views as university students and adults.

Evaluating Death Education

There have been numerous attempts to evaluate death education systematically. These vary greatly in terms of the nature of the death education program being evaluated, the audience, and the research methodologies. Both the cognitive/informational and the affective/personal modes of death education have been evaluated. It is inevitably easier to determine whether someone has learned new information than to determine whether someone has changed in terms of feelings, attitudes, values, or behavior.

After examining the research literature on seven criteria for evaluating the effectiveness of death education, Kalish (1985) proposed the following: (1) participants do learn factual information; (2) they probably become more aware of their own feelings; (3) they may claim to be better able to relate to dying and grieving persons, but there is no evidence one way or the other; (4) they claim that death-related fears and anxieties diminish, and this claim may well be valid; (5) they may learn to be more sensitive to death themes in art, literature, and so forth, but there is no research evidence; (6) they probably become more appreciative of philosophies of death, although again there is no systematic evidence; and (7) they probably become more capable of developing or working in death education or death counseling programs.

The Present Status of Death Education

It would appear that death education is well established in numerous settings. Although some of the excitement and fervor of the 1960s and early 1970s has disappeared, death education and training are likely to persist. Credit and noncredit courses in all levels of higher education are now expected. Training programs for professionals, paraprofessionals, and volunteers are commonplace, as, for example, in hospice programs. Death education is a formal or informal part of many primary and secondary schools. Both churches and public agencies offer frequent workshops and presentations on relevant topics. Additionally, numerous individual speakers, some coming from the earlier human potential movement, and others more focused on what is often referred to as New Age or transpersonal issues, offer innumerable workshops and seminars on death, almost all centering on the affective/personal elements. In fact, although attention in this article has focused on higher education, by far the greater part of death education, in prevalence, though not necessarily in depth, occurs outside the university classroom.

New issues continue to arise. Most recently, for example, the impact of the death of a sibling—either the immediate death or a much earlier death—has received attention. There has also been a reexamination of how best to help parents of stillborn infants cope with their grief. And, perhaps most significantly, the advent of AIDS and its potential to reach epidemic proportions have required a careful look at some new health and personal care issues. The San Francisco-based organization, Shanti, which initially offered counsel and support to anyone for whom death was an immediate concern, now provides extensive services to AIDS patients.

Although systematic data are lacking, it does appear that interest in university courses on death may have leveled off, and has perhaps even diminished slightly. However, the courses are very much part of the regular curriculum, taught by professors who are often deeply committed to the topic.

Some university-based death educators base their commitment on the enjoyment of relevant scholarly activity, with substantial numbers having completed dissertations and other significant academic writings on these matters. For others, the commitment arises from their belief in the importance of helping students handle their own personal death-related issues. And, of course, some professors combine both interests and have also had significant clinical experience. It would appear that, as long as student enrollment is maintained, these courses will remain on the books.

Two universities (Brooklyn College: Department of Health Science, and University of Florida: School of Education) now offer master's degree programs with an emphasis in death, dying, and grief. No accredited university has established a Department of Death and Grief (or of Thanatology), although there have been centers devoted to death-related topics, such as the pioneering one established by Robert Fulton through the Department of Sociology at the University of Minnesota. The belief is often expressed that knowledge regarding death needs to be embedded in one or more academic disciplines or professional fields, rather than established as a free-standing program.

An emerging concern for death educators, more political and economic in nature than academic, is that of certification. The Association for Death Education and Counseling offers certification. A certified death educator should have established both significant work experience and extensive knowledge of theory, research, and skills in the field of education in general as well as in regard to death-related matters. The question whether such certification is relevant is difficult to answer. Death educators function in numerous contexts, each of which calls for somewhat different knowledge and skills. A hospital chaplain who provides in-service training for hospital staff may be expected to offer a very different educational package than the professor who teaches in a sociology department.

In summary, it appears that within the past twenty-five years or so, death education has developed from fad to fashion to a moderately well-entrenched part of the educational system. Although rapid growth no longer seems to be occurring, the interest and activity continue. Two academic journals are published regularly (*Death Studies* and *Omega, Journal of Death and Dying*), and the Association for Death Education and Counseling holds regular programs, as does the National Hospice Organization. And, perhaps most significant, death education programs continue within and outside of traditional education institutions on a regular basis.

See also Association for Death Education and Counseling; *Death Studies* (Journal); Hospice: Volunteers; National Hospice Organization; *Omega, Journal of Death and Dying*; Siblings of Dying Children; Sudden Infant Death Syndrome (SIDS).

—RICHARD A. KALISH

References

Feifel, H. (Ed.) (1959). *The meaning of death.* New York: McGraw-Hill.

Gorer, G. (1959). "The pornography of death." In W. Phillips and P. Rahv (Eds.) *Modern writing.* New York: McGraw-Hill, pp. 157–88.

Green, B.R. & Irish, D.P. (1971). *Death education: Preparation for living.* Cambridge, MA: Schenkman.

Kalish, R.A. (1980–1981). "Death educator as deacon." *Omega, Journal of Death and Dying, 11*: 75–85.

Kalish, R.A. (1985). *Death, grief, and caring relationships.* 2nd ed. Monterey, CA: Brooks/Cole.

Kastenbaum, R. (1977). "We covered death today." *Death Education, 1*: 862–92.

Knott, J.E. (1979). "Death education for all." In H. Wass (Ed.) *Dying: Facing the facts.* New York: McGraw-Hill, 385–403.

Levitan, D. (1977). "The scope of death education." *Death Education, 1*: 41–56.

DEATH FEARS AND ANXIETY

Fear death?—to feel the fog in my throat,
The mist in my face. . . .

Robert Browning is but one of a great many writers who has taken the fear of death and dying as subject-matter. Emily Dickinson also takes us right to the moment of death:

I heard a Fly buzz—when I died—
The Stillness in the Room
Was like the Stillness in the Air
Between the Heaves of Storm. . . .

In both of these very well-known poems, the author begins with a vivid imagining of the final moments of life and concludes with a kind of victory over fear (or is it anxiety?). Storm imagery is invoked by Browning as well as Dickinson when he envisions:

The power of the night, the press of the
storm,
The post of the foe;
Where he stands, the Arch Fear in a visible
form,
Yet the strong man must go

In speaking of this as the "Arch Fear," Browning is expressing a view that has since been endorsed by a number of existential thinkers: death anxiety as the deepest source of all other fears and as a prime motivating force of human behavior. In *Prospice,* Browning also offers his own orientation toward this ultimate fear:

I was ever a fighter, so—one fight more,
The best and the last!
I would hate that death bandaged my eyes,
and forbore,
And made me creep past.

Browning observes that "the black minute" will have its end. He is willing to suffer and in this minute pay "life's arrears of pain, darkness and cold." When this moment passes, there will be "first a peace out of pain, then a light," and he will be with God. Dickinson reveals another way to transcend fear of death at the same time that one acknowledges it—the poem places her at a retrospective distance from death: the living woman writes as though she had already passed through her final moments. It is not really surprising that Browning's "peace out of pain, then a light" anticipates contemporary research on near-death experiences, or that Dickinson's anticipates some death education efforts to help people integrate the prospect of death into their lives. The insights of creative artists have often preceded science and technology.

However, in art as well as in life, one does not always overcome fear and anxiety. Shakespeare's Hamlet, for example, is obsessed with death in an almost pornographic sense. He tells the king that the slain Polonius is "At supper!" "Where?" "Not where he eats, but where he is eaten: a certain convocation of politic worms are e'en at him. Your worm is your only emperor for diet: we fat all creatures else to fat us, and we fat ourselves for maggots." As the king shudders, Hamlet cheerfully continues that "A man may fish with the worm that hath eat of a king, and eat of the fish that hath fed of that worm." When the king wonders what all this morbid discourse means, Hamlet replies, "Nothing but to show you how a king may go a progress through the guts of a beggar." Here Shakespeare shows us how death can be presented in a degrading manner to intensify the distress of others—death anxiety as a weapon.

And, in perhaps the theater's most celebrated monologue, Hamlet proceeds from "To be, or not to be" to "the dread of something after death, the undiscover'd country from whose bourn no traveller returns." In this case it is not a fear of extinction but "the dread of something after death" that gives one pause. Were death only death, why, then, one might escape from "the slings and arrows of outrageous fortune" by taking a "bare bodkin" in hand and ending the torments of life. Fear of death may take more than one aspect; the "dread of something" can be quite competitive with the dread of nothing.

It is simplistic to think that a person must either fear or welcome death. Hamlet's ambivalence has been expressed by many others as, for example, Anne Sexton, a brilliant poet who made repeated suicide attempts, often explored the relationship between death fears and longings. In

"Hurry Up Please It's Time" (1974), she asks, as though hypothetically:

> Say the woman is forty-four.
> Say she is five seven-and-a-half.
> Say her hair is stick color.
> Say her eyes are chameleon.
> Would you put her in a sack and bury her,
>   suck her down into the dumb dirt?

Sexton's own answer:

> Some would.
> If not, time will.

World literature and history provide us with many examples of people attempting to face not only death but the fears or anxiety associated with death. The outcomes are variable. Socrates calmly tells his friends why there is nothing in death to fear before he quaffs the fatal hemlock, but Tolstoy's *Ivan Ilych* screams for three days in anguish until he finds peaceful resolution, and the philosopher Jean-Jacques Rousseau states flatly that "He who pretends to look on death without fear lies."

Theories of Death Fear and Anxiety

How do modern psychologists, psychiatrists, and philosophers conceive of death fear and anxiety? The reader can be assured that there is disagreement on some fundamental issues. However, there is considerably more interest in this topic than was the case prior to World War II. Not long ago, psychiatrists tended to regard *thanatophobia* as just one symptom of neurosis (or psychosis) among many others. "Normal" people did not trouble themselves with death-related fears. Today it is more widely recognized that everybody—children as well as adults, those with a firm hold on their lives as well as those in difficulty, those in good health as well as those with life-threatening illnesses, has death-related thoughts and feelings.

It is also important to emphasize that not all our thoughts and feelings about death are of a fearful nature. There may be curiosity, for example, common among children but often suppressed when they learn this topic makes adults uncomfortable. Sorrow about death is also to be distinguished from fear; people may feel a keen loss in the death of others and be reluctant to "leave the show" themselves, but this is not necessarily accompanied by overt fear regarding death itself. And, as already illustrated, a person may long for death, hoping to be reunited with a deceased loved one, or weary and discouraged with life. It would be misleading to offer a definitive list—the human mind is almost infinite in its variety when confronting the thought of death at a distinct moment.

The principal terms of our discourse require attention before we turn to the major theories. "Fear" and "anxiety" are sometimes used interchangeably. Both imply a state of discomfort and a disposition toward aversion. We feel upset; we want to get away from whatever we think is causing this upset. We dislike feeling this way and want to put an end to this condition. There are only three basic maneuvers by which relief can be obtained. We can eliminate the source of the distress, avoid contact with the threat, or change the way we think about it. Fear of contracting AIDS through transfusions has been sharply reduced by improved screening techniques. This is an example of eliminating a source of threat. A person with a strong fear of being killed in an airplane crash might decide never to fly, thereby avoiding activation of this fear. "Cognitive restructuring" (Deffenbacher & Suinn, 1987), whether through psychological therapy or by other means, can help a person either to recognize that what seems to be a menace is actually innocuous, or that one has the ability to cope with it. For example, a patient may expect to die because a friend with similar symptoms died. This fear might well be relieved in just a few minutes when a doctor or nurse carefully explains the actual nature of the condition and how it will be treated.

A fear may be realistic or exaggerated but it can be specified or articulated. By contrast, anxiety is a generalized state of being. We feel unsettled, apprehensive, unsure of ourselves. The body refuses to behave normally; we may sweat, twitch, hyperventilate, tense up, and have difficulties in sleeping, among other symptoms. The mind also tends to become less dependable; we pay too much attention to some things and too little to others; concentration and memory are apt to fall off; restlessness contends with immobility. The usual flexibility and openmindedness we pride ourselves on has given way to a more driven, less coherent mental state. Anxiety is fatiguing because one cannot readily locate the threat. One may well have a variety of fears as well, but the overall feeling is one of helplessness in the face of some obscure but formidable threat that could destroy us in some unspecified way in some unspecified place at some unspecified time.

Early research usually focused on specific death-related fears. A pioneering self-report study by Means (1936), for example, asked a thousand female college students to respond to a list of 349 stimuli that one might or might not find fearful (e.g., high places, dentists, wild parties). The most common fear expressed by these young women was of snakes (would this hold true today?). However, a variety of death-related words were among those most often selected as fearful (e.g., sudden death, slow death, death by suffocation). Words that suggest a prelude to death were also frequently selected as fearful (e.g., cyclones, pistols, reckless driving).

Some more sophisticated studies later suggested that differences could be observed between fear and anxiety. Alexander and Adlerstein (1959), for example, found that some of their male college student respondents admitted and some denied being fearful of death. But nearly all the respondents showed a heightened psychogalvanic skin response (PSR) when exposed to death words. (The PSR is one of the measures included in polygraph or so-called lie detector tests.) This pattern of findings indicates that a person may show psychophysiological signs of anxious arousal although at the same time claiming to be free of death fear. Similar findings were obtained by Feifel and Branscomb (1973), who also assessed orientations toward death on several different levels of awareness within the same individuals. As in the previous study, responses to direct questions about death differed. However, all the respondents evidenced anxiety on projective and indirect measures when exposed to death-related stimuli. Studies of this kind suggest that what we choose to report about our death attitudes (or even to allow into conscious awareness) does not tell the whole story. Furthermore, the general pattern seems to be an underlying

agitated arousal to death-related stimuli whether or not this is accompanied by the self-report that we fear death.

Two strongly contrasted theories have received most of the attention. Sigmund Freud recognized that anxious people sometimes spoke of death. However, these expressions of death fear are somewhat superficial; they only hint at what really troubles the person. According to Freud, we are unable to imagine our own death because whenever we try to do so "we really survive as spectators." In other words, "I" am still here, full of life, thinking of "me" dead. Furthermore, our deepest psychic level, the unconscious, "knows nothing whatever of negatives or of denials . . . and so it knows nothing whatever of our own death, for to that we can give only a negative purport. It follows that no instinct we possess is ready for a belief in death" (Freud, 1915/1953).

Freud traced death fears to unresolved psychological conflicts whose roots are often to be found in infancy and childhood. For example, castration anxiety may be reactivated in adulthood and take the form of thanatophobia. "I'm afraid to die!" could be a coded way of expressing the little boy's anxiety that "Father's going to punish me for wanting Mother!" This is not the only possible derivation for death concern in adults, but it typifies the Freudian approach: if a person seems to be afraid of death, we should try to help him or her discover the "real" source of concern. (Freud did take death more seriously as a primary problem as he grew older and continued to see how violent and ruthless human aggression could become. His not well accepted death instinct theory attempted to explain both outer and inner directed explosions of destructive behavior.)

An opposing view is held by a number of existential thinkers such as Ernest Becker (1973). He argues that death anxiety is the most basic driving force for the individual and society. Aware of our mortality, we must find a way to keep this awareness from becoming too painful, too terrible. For this reason, the denial of death has become a popular and widespread characteristic of modern society. What happens when this denial breaks down and the individual comes face-to-face with the reality of personal death? The answer can be found in psychiatric wards, according to Becker—psychotic depression and schizophrenia are among the pathological states that may follow when death-denial fails.

While Freud would seek the "real reasons" for manifest death anxiety, Becker would look for the ways in which death anxiety and its denial underlies many individual and sociocultural phenomena. His work, like that of Weisman (1972) and some others, calls valuable attention to the many ways in which we try to avoid acknowledging our own mortality.

There are, however, two important similarities between these contrasting views: (1) Both do suggest that we cannot become complete and mature adults unless we live with the full realization of our mortality, and (2) neither have been firmly supported by empirical research (Kastenbaum, In press). The theories offered by Freud and Becker are formulated on a level of generalization that has proven difficult to test in controlled research. It should be added that very few have *tried* to test these theories. One may find much of interest in both sets of ideas, but neither have been subjected to enough appropriate research to draw reliable conclusions.

A third approach has been proposed that is intended to be more amenable to research and evaluation: Perhaps we *learn* to fear death. Death-related concerns may develop as part of the general interaction between the individual's level of maturation and his or her distinctive life experiences. How a person copes with death-related concerns is best understood within the context of his or her overall strategy for dealing with threats of all kinds. Significant problems in coping with death-related concerns are likely to derive from difficulties in developmental learning as well as with the topic of death itself. Within this approach it is considered important to take the individual's total personality and situation into account, not simply thoughts and feelings about death. And, if death-related fears are mostly learned, then it is also through learning that problems can be remedied.

Some Major Findings

Although the research literature does not clearly support any one theory of death fear or anxiety, there have been a number of findings that have occurred frequently (Kastenbaum, 1987–88; Lonetto & Templer, 1986). These include:

1. Higher expressed death fear or anxiety for women as compared with men. (This does not necessarily mean that women are "too" anxious; a viable alternative is that women are more open to emotional experience, as shown also by the predominance of women in providing direct care to people with life-threatening illnesses.)
2. Death fear or anxiety tends to be somewhat higher among adolescents and young adults than at other points in the life course. As a rule, elderly adults tend to express less death anxiety than do younger adults.
3. Dying people do not necessarily express intense death-related fears. However, a dying person may have significant concerns about other matters, such as pain, finances, and the well-being of his or her loved ones.
4. In some instances, expressed fears of death may result from other causes (as Freud has noted), while in other instances, it is death anxiety that underlies other types of disturbance (as Becker has noted).
5. People differ in precisely what it is about death that most concerns them (the dying process, fear of extinction, fear of punishment after death, etc.). It is wise to learn what it is that troubles a particular person rather than assume that everybody has the same concern.

There is nothing weak or pathological in a person's thinking of death, including possible sources of anxiety. How could a reflective person *not* think every now and again about this central fact of our existence? Fortunately, the denial tendencies described by Becker, Weisman, Feifel, and others have now loosened their hold somewhat and there is more opportunity to share death-related thoughts and feelings with others.

See also Acquired Immune Deficiency Syndrome (AIDS); Death Anxiety: Measures; Death Anxiety: Reduction; Death Instinct; Death Threat Index (TI); Deathbed Scenes; Humor and the Fear of Death; Near-Death Experiences; Old Age and Death; Socrates' Death.

—ROBERT KASTENBAUM

References

Alexander, I.E. & Adlerstein, A.M. (1959). "Death and religion." In H. Feifel (Ed.) *The meaning of death;* New York: McGraw-Hill, 271–83.

Becker, E. (1973). *The denial of death.* New York: Free Press.

Browning, R. (1956). *Poems of Robert Browning.* Boston: Houghton Mifflin.

Deffenbacher, J.L. & Suinn, R.M. (1987). "Generalized anxiety syndrome." In L. Michelson & L.M. Ascher (Eds.) *Anxiety and stress disorders.* New York: Guilford Press, 332–60.

Dickinson, E. (1961). *Final harvest. Emily Dickinson's poems.* Boston: Little, Brown.

Feifel, H. & Branscomb, A.B. (1973). "Who's afraid of death?" *Journal of Abnormal Psychology, 81*: 282–88.

Freud, S. (1915/Reprint 1953). "Thoughts for the times on war and death." In *Collected papers, Vol. 4.* London: Hogarth Press, 288–317.

Kastenbaum, R. (1987). "Death-related anxiety." In L. Michelson & L. M. Ascher (Eds.) *Anxiety and stress disorders.* New York: Guilford Press, 425–44.

Kastenbaum, R. (1987–1988). "Theory, research, and application: Some critical issues for thanatology." *Omega, Journal of Death and Dying, 18*: 397–410.

Lonetto, R. & Templer, D.I. (1986). *Death anxiety.* New York: Hemisphere.

Means, M.H. (1936). "Fears of one thousand college women." *Journal of Abnormal and Social Psychology, 31*: 291–311.

Sexton, A. (1974). *The death notebooks.* Boston: Houghton Mifflin.

Shakespeare, W. (1984). "Hamlet." In *The annotated Shakespeare.* New York: Crown.

Weisman, A.D. (1972). *On dying and denying.* New York: Behavioral Publications.

DEATH INSTINCT

Within all living creatures there is an instinct, drive, or impulse to return to the inorganic stratum from which they arose. This is the core of the controversial death instinct theory proposed by Sigmund Freud in *Beyond the Pleasure Principle* (1920). Although neither the first nor the last death instinct theory, it is Freud's version that has attracted the most attention over the years. One has the option of disregarding Freud's own intentions and treating the death instinct theory as a concept to be accepted or rejected on its own terms. A serious examination of this theory, however, would consider its origins, context, and functions within Freud's overall psychoanalytic system.

Eros and Thanatos: A Dual Instinct Theory

At the end of World War I, Freud had much to think about. His faith in the ability of civilization to tame and sublimate humankind's destructive impulses had been badly shaken. From this point forward he would be deeply concerned for the very survival of our species. He also had an abundance of new clinical data to consider, especially on the victims of traumatic war neuroses who seemed determined to relive over and again their most disturbing experiences. It is possible that several suicides among friends and colleagues also contributed to his reconsideration of self-destructive forces. Additionally, Freud was no longer entirely satisfied with his own general account of psychosexual development. *Beyond the Pleasure Principle* addressed these and related issues.

Freud's new approach was built upon a reorganization of the instinct components of psychoanalytic theory. It was more useful, proposed Freud, to group fundamental human strivings under two broad rubrics. One set of instinctual tendencies leads to the generation and expression of higher levels of tension. The term *Eros* (one of the Greek forms for love) was applied by Freud to all such tendencies that embody love of self or others or which attempt to develop and preserve everything we hold valuable. Freud gave the name *Thanatos* to the set of strivings that tend toward the reduction of tension or the expression of destructive impulses. When Thanatos is dominant, the individual is no longer driven primarily to seek the pleasurable build-up and reduction of tensions, but, rather, to reach a state of absolute quiescence.

The active ingredient in our strivings for gratification, a kind of sexual energy, was given the name *libido*. Freud could not find a parallel stuff, even conceptually, to underpin Thanatos. He wrote instead (in various contexts) of a Nirvana Principle, and a *Todtriebe* (drive toward death).

Freud regarded the death instinct (or drive) and Eros as partners in human development. Our most significant thoughts, feelings, and actions usually involve a blending of the two components. Both tenderness and aggressivity, for example, are commonly found in sexual love. In normal development, destructive impulses are expressed outwardly in the form of aggressive copings with the world. The child has a natural need to aggress and destroy—society's failure to channel this need into constructive adult purposes was seen by Freud as a precondition for war and acts of individual violence. Depression and suicidality may be expected to result when these impulses are turned inward. The repetition compulsion observed in war neuroses and in some other conditions is another unfortunate expression of the death instinct intruding upon constructive adaptation. Eventually, in old age, the death instinct tends to gain a natural dominance.

Critical Response to Freud's Death Instinct Theory

The theory offered by Freud was grand in scale and complex in its levels and spheres. A thorough evaluation would take into account biological, philosophical, sociocultural, psychopathological, and psychological components. Critiques by Levin (1951) and Symons (1927) add theoretical physics and mathematical logic to that already imposing list. Although there are articulate supporters of Freud's death instinct theory (e.g., Eissler, 1971), the overall response has been critical, even among

psychoanalysts. It has often been rejected as an overly philosophical concept that cannot be firmly tested by empirical studies or applied usefully in clinical situations.

However one chooses to judge the truth-value of Freud's death instinct theory, it stands as one of the boldest efforts to integrate both the human propensity for destruction and the fact of mortality into an encompassing view of human development. A conclusion drawn from a more intensive analysis of death instinct theory (Kastenbaum, In press) suggests that, right or wrong, this approach continues to invite close observation and intellectual ferment in a variety of death-related areas.

See also Adolescence and Death; Suicide.

—ROBERT KASTENBAUM

References

Eissler, K.R. (1971). "Death drive, ambivalence, and narcissism." *International Journal of Psychoanalysis, 26*: 25–78.
Freud, S. (1920). *Beyond the Pleasure Principle*. New York: W.W. Norton.
Kastenbaum, R. (In press). *The psychology of death*. 2nd ed. New York: Springer.
Levin, A.J. (1951). "The fiction of the death instinct." *Psychiatric Quarterly, 25*: 257–81.
Symons, N.J. (1927). "Does masochism necessarily imply the existence of a Death Instinct?" *International Journal of Psychoanalysis, 8*: 38–46.

DEATH PENALTY

The death penalty—or capital punishment—is among the most ancient rights claimed and exercised by the state. When the rulers of Babylonia had their laws carved into a stone column more than four thousand years ago, they made sure that the death penalty was included. Most societies throughout history have employed the death penalty, although not necessarily for the same crimes. Although usually reserved for the most serious offenses, such as murder and treason, the death penalty has also been exacted for stealing a loaf of bread or making fun of a dignitary.

There have also been significant differences in the way that capital punishment has been inflicted. The emphasis today is upon swift and painless execution, even if this goal is not always achieved. Despite strong controversy between advocates and opponents of capital punishment, there is little if any support for a painful and degrading mode of execution. It is considered sufficient punishment to take a person's life. In the past, however, executions were often conducted in a singularly cruel manner. For example, a thief might be imprisoned in a wall where he would slowly perish of thirst and hunger, or a stake might be driven through his body and into the ground, leaving the victim in unspeakable agony until released by death.

The most painful deaths have often been reserved not for common criminals but for those considered to be enemies of the regime because of their political activities or religious beliefs. In thirteenth century England, for example, a man accused of being a traitor was likely to be hanged, drawn and quartered, beheaded, disemboweled, and burned (Jankowsky, 1979). Any one of these actions would have resulted in his death, but the state wanted to make its displeasure very clear and discourage others from treasonous activities. Four centuries later, British rulers continued to exact pain as well as life from those considered enemies of the realm. The victims most put to suffering were priests who refused to recant and convert to the Church of England (Knowles, 1980). The priest might be dragged through the cobblestone streets, then placed on the gallows. The executioner was expected to half-hang the condemned man to produce shock and agony just short of death. The next step would be to plunge a knife into his body, tear out the entrails and show them to the still living victim. The offender might then be drawn and quartered while, possibly, still alive. In practice, a compassionate executioner and a crowd urging mercy might dispatch the victim early in the process to spare the entire sequence of suffering that had been ordered by the crown.

The view that executions should be public and horrifying prevailed in many places until the success of reform movements, generally in the nineteenth century. Execution remained a public drama in Australia, for example, as the "showcase" of a law enforcement system that was based fundamentally on terror (Sturma, 1986–87). Eyewitness accounts suggested here, as in other societies, that public executions were more likely to produce a hardened attitude or an attitude of sympathy for the offenders, rather than a dread that might lead others to avoid criminal activities.

The Death Penalty Today

There has been a reduction in the use of capital punishment throughout the world. The death penalty has been abolished in Canada, Denmark, England, Finland, France, Portugal, Sweden, and Venezuela. In some other nations, such as Belgium and Ireland, capital punishment is still on the books but very rarely invoked. Furthermore, the type of offenses for which the death penalty may be exacted has been restricted in some nations, such as Israel and Morocco (Szumski et al., 1986). However, despite this trend there are still significant international differences in the type of offenses for which the death penalty is applied and the number of executions actually carried out.

In the United States, the Supreme Court made a landmark decision in 1972 by the closest possible margin, 5–4, that abolished capital punishment throughout the nation. This ruling was based upon the judgment that the death penalty had too often been applied in an arbitrary manner. Four years later, the Court revised this ruling, upholding statutes in Florida, Georgia, and Texas. This action provided guidelines by which each state could make its own decision regarding the reinstatement of capital punishment. The effect of the new guidelines was to reduce the likelihood that arbitrary decisions would be made as to when a person convicted of a capital offense would or would not be executed. In consequence, the United States has become and remains the only nation in which the law provides for capital punishment within some jurisdictions and not within others (Siegel et al., 1988). States that currently do not permit capital punishment are Alaska, Hawaii, Iowa, Kansas,

Maine, Massachusetts, Michigan, Minnesota, New York, North Dakota, Rhode Island, West Virginia, and Wisconsin. The death penalty has also been abolished in Puerto Rico, the Virgin Islands, and the District of Columbia. (Wisconsin and Michigan were the first states to abolish the death penalty, in 1853 and 1854, respectively.)

Lethal injection and electrocution are the most commonly employed methods of legal execution in the United States today, followed by the gas chamber, hanging, and the firing squad (Idaho and Utah only, with lethal injection as an option).

There have been few executions carried out in the United States in recent years. According to the Bureau of Justice Statistics (1987), a total of ninety-three prisoners were executed between 1977 and 1986. Interestingly, all but six of these executions took place in southern states. This follows a long pattern in which the South has dominated in number and percentage of executions. Almost all of the executions were for murder, with the remainder being for rape. The only states in which capital punishment has actually been enforced since 1977 are Alabama, Florida, Georgia, Louisiana, Mississippi, North Carolina, Ohio, Pennsylvania, Texas, Virginia, West Virginia, Nevada, and Utah. There continues to be a race differential in the proportion of executions. From 1985 through 1987, for example, twenty-six blacks and twenty-nine whites were subjected to capital punishment. This is an obvious overrepresentation of blacks in light of the black/white distribution in the general population. This kind of discrepancy, long observed, has led some analysts to argue that the laws are being unequally and unfairly enforced.

The number of executions in the United States had been declining even before the 1972 Supreme Court ruling and, with the continued reduction, there has been a gradual build-up of "death-row" prisoners (almost 2,000 throughout the nation). Almost all are men; only twenty are women (about 1 percent). Siegal et al. (1988, p. 57) found:

> The average condemned prisoner had been on death row 40 months, up from 33 months two years before. The average prisoner executed between 1977 and 1986 had spent over six years in prison between the time of sentencing and the time the sentence was actually carried out. . . . The average killer had a 1 in 6,375 chance of having to die for his or her crime.

The Controversy

Many public-spirited individuals and organizations disagree on the effectiveness and morality of capital punishment. (This disagreement became a factor in the 1988 presidential election campaign.) The pro and con arguments are often intensified by reference to particular cases. Advocates of capital punishment, for example, may emphasize the shocking and brutal way in which a helpless victim was murdered. Opponents may emphasize a case in which a person was executed—or barely escaped execution—for a crime that facts subsequently showed he or she did not commit. There is little doubt that such cases will continue to come to public attention and arouse strong feeling on both sides of the issue.

Statistics have also become important in the attempt to influence public opinion. Obviously, the deterrence argument would have more impact if it could be shown that murder and other capital offenses have become less frequent where capital punishment is in effect. Overall, however, the death penalty has not been demonstrated to be a clear deterrent to murder and other violent crime. In a careful and critical review of the research literature, Bailey (1979–80) found that the deterrence hypothesis was not supported by homicide statistics; murder rates did not seem to be affected by the existence or absence of a capital punishment provision. Bailey's conclusion is that "policies aimed at improving socioeconomic conditions will have a much more important effect on the level of homicides than would making greater use of the death penalty" (p. 256).

Most advocates of the death penalty acknowledge that the statistical data do not support this view. However, they often raise questions about the adequacy of the data. Carrington (1986, p. 121), for example, observes:

> there is absolutely no way that we can ever know with any certainty how many

would-be murderers were in fact deterred from killing. By definition, they *were* deterred, they did *not* kill, and therefore we can never know what numbers to enter on that side of the statistical equation.

Furthermore, Carrington and others report that some criminals said that the threat of capital punishment did deter them from killing.

Advocates and opponents of the death penalty also differ in their moral assessment of the tradition of taking "a life for a life." Political scientist Walter Berns (1988, p. 72), for example, argues that the law should respect the rightful anger we feel when a criminal act is perpetrated against a fellow citizen. By supporting this moral outrage with the ultimate punishment, society affirms the position that "the taking of a human life is a terrible, terrible crime. The law, I argue, must somehow inculcate that in our hearts and minds."

Some Christian scholars and theologians support the death penalty on religious grounds (Gow, 1986). The biblical commandment "Thou shalt not kill" must apply to the murderer as well as to society. The lives of victims are no less sacred than the lives of the killers. The sadistic murderer is often identified as a person who has violated the laws of God and society and must be eliminated to safeguard the common good. Individuals who are threats to the lives of others thereby lose their own right to live.

The opposition often agrees that human life is sacred but argues that capital punishment adds one violent death to another. Wertham (1966) believes that the death penalty often is exacted not so much as punishment but as a kind of exorcism, "a way of cleansing the scene after a homicide, as if the murder were an infection affecting the whole community." We should be able to find better ways of restoring security and order after a death, and better ways to prevent all forms of violence. Wertham, a psychiatrist, is among those who argue that our rising homicide rates are a symptom of serious problems in our society that must be addressed in a fundamental way, not simply isolated cases of individual violence.

Civil rights leaders continue to oppose capital punishment on the grounds that racial discrimination and other inequities continue to operate in the United States and would result in miscarriages of justice and, therefore, improper decisions to execute an accused offender. Among the opponents is Coretta Scott King, widow of Martin Luther King, Jr., who has said on this subject:

> The truth is, we all pay for the death penalty because every time the state kills somebody, our society loses its humanity and compassion and we sow the seeds of violence. We legitimize retaliation as the way to deal with conflict. . . . And in this sense the death penalty means cruel and unusual punishment for not only the condemned prisoner but for the innocent as well, for all of us (quoted by Vodicka, 1986, p. 78).

Fortunately, on this difficult and divisive issue it is possible for thoughtful people to express their views and seek more effective ways to reduce murder and other major offenses against the individual and society.

See also Death System; Murder.

—ROBERT KASTENBAUM

References

Bailey, W.C. (1979–1980). "Deterrent effect of the death penalty: An extended time series analysis." *Omega, Journal of Death and Dying, 10*: 235–60.

Berns, W. (1988). *Testimony before the Committee on the Judiciary,* United States Senate (1981). Quoted in M.A. Siegel, C.D. Foster, & N.R. Jacobs (Eds.) *Capital punishment.* Wylie, TX: Information Aids, Inc., 72–73.

Carrington, F. (1986). "Inconclusive evidence does not invalidate deterrence." In B. Szumski, L. Hall, & S. Bursell (Eds.) *The death penalty.* St. Paul, MN: Greenhaven Press, 120–26.

Gow, H.B. (1986). "Religious views support the death penalty." In B. Szumski, L. Hall, & S. Bursell (Eds.) *The death penalty.* St. Paul, MN: Greenhaven Press, 79–85.

Jankofsky, K.P. (1979). "Public executions in England in the late middle ages." *Omega, Journal of Death and Dying, 10*: 433–58.

Knowles, L. (1980). *The prey of the priest catchers.* St. Paul, MN: Carillon Books.

Siegel, M.A., Foster, C.D., & Jacobs, N.R. (Eds.) (1988). *Capital punishment.* Wylie, TX: Information Aids, Inc.

Sturma, M. (1986–1987). "Death and ritual on the gallows: Public executions in the Australian penal colonies." *Omega, Journal of Death and Dying, 17*: 89–100.

Szumski, B., Hall, L., & Bursell, S. (Eds.) (1986). *The death penalty.* St. Paul, MN.: Greenhaven Press.

Vodicka, J.C. (1986). "The death penalty degrades society." In B. Szumski, L. Hall, & S. Bursell (Eds.) *The death penalty.* St. Paul, MN: Greenhaven Press, 73–78.

Wertham, F. (1966). *A sign for Cain.* New York: Macmillan.

DEATH STUDIES (JOURNAL)

The scholarly and professional bimonthly journal *Death Studies* has been published since 1977. It first appeared as an international quarterly under the title *Death Education.* In 1985 the title was changed when publication became bimonthly. *Death Studies* publishes original manuscripts in the areas of death education, death-related counseling, terminal care, and ethical, legal, and professional issues, and controversies related to death. Research reports, critical reviews, and theoretical papers on psychosocial and cultural aspects of dying, death, and bereavement are published. In addition to standard manuscripts, consideration is also given to Personal Communications from authors relating personal and professional experiences, making informal suggestions, or responding to significant events. Approximately once a year an entire issue of the journal is devoted to a single theme of current widespread interest such as "Death in Contemporary Society" (Herman Feifel); "Personal Meanings of Death" (Franz Epting & Robert Neimeyer); and "Survivorship: The Other Side of Death and Dying" (Felix Berado). Occasionally a supplement on a special topic is produced. The guest editors for these special issues are internationally known scholars.

Death Studies has an extensive Media Review section that presents reviews and annotations of new books and various types of audiovisuals dealing with death. The Department of Law and Ethics brings commentaries on legal and ethical issues to the reader. There is also a News and Notes section.

Contributors, the readership, and the journal's editors and editorial board reflect a broad interdisciplinary scope. They include in their number educators, psychologists, philosophers, sociologists, nurses, social workers, physicians, psychiatrists, clergy, and others. The editorial board is composed of thirty-three leaders in the field drawn from ten different nations. A sampling of recent titles illustrates the diversity of topics published in *Death Studies:* "Loss and Adaptation: Circumstances, Contingencies, and Consequences" (Jeanne Quint-Benoliel); "Cognitive Structure and Death Anxiety" (Robert A. Neimeyer et al.); "Clergy's Attitudes Toward Suicide and Recognition of Suicide Lethality" (George Domino); "Stress Coping, and Mental Health Outcomes Following a Natural Disaster" (Shirley A. Murphy); "The Shuttle Tragedy, Community Grief, and the Schools" (Robert G. Stevenson); "Professions, Families, and Control in the Management of Cadaver Organ Donors" (Jeffrey C. Salloway & Paul J. Volek); "Special Issues in the Grief of Parents of Murdered Children" (Mary R. Peach & Dennis Klass); "The Age of Maturity for Death Education: Socio-Historical Portrait of the Era 1976–1985" (Vanderlyn R. Pine); and "Life After Death: Vietnam Veterans' Struggle for Meaning and Recovery" (Erwin R. Parson).

Information for Authors

Manuscripts should be submitted in triplicate to:

Hannelore Wass
Editor, *Death Studies*
Educational Psychology
1418 Norman Hall
University of Florida
Gainesville, FL 32611

Abstracts of not more than 250 words, typed on a separate page, are required. Submission of a manuscript is understood to imply that it or substantial parts of it have not been published, accepted, or submitted for publication elsewhere. Specific guidelines for preparing manuscript appear near the front of each issue and can also be obtained by writing to the editor. Manuscripts are acknowledged immediately on receipt. The review process typically requires about two months. An accepted manuscript is published approximately one year after receipt of the copyright release from the author.

For subscription information write to:

Hemisphere Publishing Corporation
Journal Division
79 Madison Avenue
New York, NY 10016

For other business information write to:

Hemisphere Publishing Corporation
1010 Vermont Avenue, N.W.
Suite 612
Washington, DC 20005

—HANNELORE WASS

DEATH SYSTEM

Every life and death is deeply personal and unique. Realization of this fundamental fact is expressed by anyone who complains about being treated "like a statistic." It is central to the philosophy of care endorsed by the hospice movement and by others who are sensitive to the dignity of the individual personality. However, there is also a social, public, and, yes, a statistical side to every life and death as well. Some external aspects are obvious and familiar: for example, the death certificate required by law, the changing profile of a society's "causes of death," the regulations governing funeral practices. Other aspects and dynamics, although subtler, may be even more significant. Infant and child mortality rates, for example, are affected by many sociocultural and economic factors. Within the same American city one can find low and high infant mortality rates. Within the same city, the nature and extent of life-saving emergency care may differ appreciably from one medical facility to another. Still another example can be seen in the connection between decades of massive cigarette advertising and the continued high death rate from chronic obstructive pulmonary disease and lung cancer. In many ways and on many levels, there are critical connections between soci-

ocultural beliefs and practices and the lives or deaths of its individual citizens.

The Concept

The "death system" concept was introduced (Kastenbaum, 1972) as an approach to understanding the dynamic relationship between society and the individual. Death system is defined as "a socio-physical network by which the relationship to mortality is mediated and expressed" (op. cit., p. 310). Whether our primary aim is to understand a particular individual or the larger forces at work in a society, it is useful to encompass both the individual and the sociophysical factors and their relationships.

Every society has its own death system, and these systems change over time in response to such factors as population growth or decline, prosperity or depression, war or peace, technological innovation, and unique events. All death systems can be analyzed in terms of their components and functions (Kastenbaum, 1986).

The components of a death system include people, places, times, objects, and symbols. Although everybody is a potential component in the death system, at any single moment some people have a more central role, while still others serve as continuing participants (e.g., the funeral director, "life insurance" salesman, and an attorney who draws up wills). People in a variety of occupations earn their livelihoods, in whole or part, from services they perform in connection with death. The people who operate slaughterhouses, for example, are part of the death system, and so, in their own way, are the managers and clerks who stock and sell meat products to the public. All people involved with the design, procurement, sales, or utilization of lethal weapons are part of the death system. Their ranks include both the legislator who argues for a larger military appropriation and the one who argues for arms reduction. Once we begin to think about the way in which our lives and occupations bear relationships with death it becomes obvious that the people in a society's death system are not limited to specialists such as acute care physicians and nurses.

Places identified with death in American society include cemeteries and funeral homes, but also that house across the street that children may avoid because they heard somebody died there last week. There are places that have become famous or infamous because of specific deaths that occurred there in the past, such as The Ford Theater in Washington, DC, and places where many lives were lost in battle, such as Gettysburg. Construction of the wall of memory for Vietnam veterans is a recent example of how a place may come to be associated with death. Society may decide, however, to destroy places that had become associated with unacceptable forms of death, as in the demolition of a McDonald's restaurant in San Ysidro, California, after twenty-one people were killed by a crazed gunman. Just as death has its people, death has its places in a society.

The "times of death" can be regular public observances, such as Memorial Day, or Mexico's **Days of the Dead.** They also can be solemn anniversary occasions that are very meaningful to some people even if not widely recognized by the whole society (e.g., the massacre of Sioux by the Seventh Cavalry at Wounded Knee, South Dakota). Although the occasions differ, many societies recognize certain times as having a special relationship to death or the dead and therefore respond to these times in a special way.

Death objects include the hearse, the gallows, the electric chair, the insect spray that promises to "kill bugs dead," and many other items. Almost any object can become associated in our minds with death, and we thereafter have different attitudes and feelings toward it (e.g., "What shall we do with the bed he died in? I don't want to sleep in it!").

The death system also makes use of language and other symbols. A black arm band and a black border around a notice both signify death in our society. Slow, thickly harmonized music performed on an organ has often been called upon to accompany funeral services. We become aware of how dependent such practices are upon our attitudinal and belief systems when a different choice is encountered—the brass band pumping out "When the Saints Go Marching In" through the streets

of an earlier New Orleans, or a contemporary memorial service with a folk singer or a jazz guitar. The symbols that are chosen (and those that are excluded) on death-related occasions can tell us much about the way a society is attempting to mediate its relationship with mortality. The choice of words can also be revealing. Until recently, few people in America, for example, "died." Instead, they "passed on," "expired," or "went to their reward." The increased willingness to use such direct words as "dead," "death," "dying," and "died" is one indication of American society's movement away from avoidance and covering up to a more realistic view of death.

All death systems have a number of important functions to serve although, again, how this is accomplished can vary appreciably from one society to another and from one time to another in the same society. These functions (Kastenbaum, 1986) include the following:

Warnings and Predictions. These may come from official sources, such as weather advisory or public health agencies, or from a variety of special interest groups and individuals. One of the striking features of the American death system at present is the large number of warnings that continue to be issued on possible life-threatening events. These include the prospect of nuclear holocaust, the heating of the planet due to continued erosion of the ozone layer, air and water pollution, destruction of the natural environment in many parts of the world, and so on. As a society and as individuals we are under unusual pressure to evaluate these warnings and predictions and decide which most require our attention. It has been recognized for some time that we do not necessarily respond in a rational and effective way even when faced with warnings of a clear and immediate danger (e.g., Grosser et al., 1964), and our responses are even more in doubt when the dangers are complex and not completely understood (e.g., Rockette, 1980).

Preventing Death. American society has taken a crisis orientation toward the prevention of death. Professional, scientific, and community resources often are mobilized in the face of situations that are perceived as emergencies. Many examples can be found within the medical care system in which research support, innovation, and prestige are usually associated with approaches that cope with acutely life-threatening diseases or conditions. By comparison, much less attention is given to the prevention of death among those who are chronically ill and in circumstances that lack the drama of crisis. A socially isolated and impoverished old person, for example, may receive superb emergency treatment and then be returned to a life situation devoid of care, interaction, and hope. Society's general priorities also show up in the type and extent of effort made to prevent death. An absorbing, if controversial, example of the link between a society's general value system and its response to the threat of death is given in detail by Shilts (1987) in his analysis of American politics and the AIDS epidemic

Caring for the Dying. Until recently, the American death system was almost entirely devoted to prevention. This emphasis stimulated the development of some valuable knowledge and techniques that have, in fact, given some people a reprieve from what might have been a fatal illness or injury. However, this emphasis has also led to a neglect of systematic, sensitive, and appropriate care for those who do face death. One of the major challenges for physicians today is to learn how to shift from an approach focusing on the prevention of death to one that provides appropriate care for the dying person and his or her family. The rigid "never say die!" approach, for all its dash of heroism, is gradually becoming recognized as not appropriate to all circumstances.

Disposing of the Dead. Although both this phrase and the reality it references may be distasteful, the fact is that all societies must take some action with respect to the physical remains of deceased members. In a society as large and complex as the United States, there are a number of different attitudes and belief systems. The Amish people (Bryer, 1979), for example, do not resort to the modern practice of turning most of the process over to a professional funeral director. Instead, their religious, family-centered, agrarian life-style includes all the services involved in escorting a person from this life. In the main-stream society bitter conflicts often arise in families concerning the details of disposal of deceased loved ones: burial versus cremation, religious versus secular funeral, cost of funeral, and so on. Differences among Americans about how life should be lived continue to express themselves when decisions must be made about how the end of a life should be treated.

Social Consolidation after Death. The integrity and viability of human society is challenged by every death, some more than others. The need to affirm or restore the strength of the community against the force of death becomes especially obvious when a powerful leader has died suddenly. The assassinations of Abraham Lincoln, John F. Kennedy, and Martin Luther King, Jr., and the public response in all these cases are among the most familiar American examples. However, social consolidation also must take place after deaths that are less famous or widely noted. One way of evaluating a society's death system is to determine the effectiveness with which the survivors "close ranks" and act in the interests of the continued viability of the community.

Making Sense of Death. What does death "mean"? Why, specifically, did this person have to die at this time? All societies are concerned not only with attempting to prevent death, comforting the dying, and disposing of the physical remains but also with trying to explain death in terms that make sense to them. Many explanations of death have been offered throughout history. Especially common among preliterate societies has been the belief that deaths are caused by the malicious actions or influences of an enemy. Vengeance and retaliation, resulting in still further deaths, were often the consequence of this type of explanation. Americans today content themselves with simple fatalistic explanations ("When your number's up, it's up"), draw upon a variety of religious dogmas, attempt to derive conclusions from science, or search for answers that meet their own needs and requirements. Throughout the centuries, those who sought power over others have often attempted to "sell" their explanations of death. For example, the high priest who could persuade his populace that he alone had the answers was also in position to demand obedience and support from them. Today, despite markedly different technology and life conditions, the "why?" questions associated with death continue to challenge human reason and faith.

Killing. A society's relationship to death is not limited to its efforts to preserve life and respect the dead. People also kill, both as individuals and as part of their larger society. Hunting and the raising and marketing of animals for their flesh or fur are among the more obvious killing activities that are carried out as part of the overall death system. Capital punishment is another example, and warfare perhaps the most significant of all. We cannot develop an encompassing understanding of a society's relationship to death until we have examined how it comes to terms with all the ways people think, feel, and act with respect to taking the lives of living creatures. In the United States, one current arena in which illuminating controversy has surfaced is in the use of animals for research and educational purposes. Killing is the most neglected function of the death system as far as the death education establishment is concerned; perhaps we resist facing the possibility that people may find some psychological satisfaction in killing, and that we ever, for any reason, place ourselves in Death's employ.

See also Causes of Death; Days of the Dead; Death Certificate; Funerals; Hospice: Philosophy and Practice.

—ROBERT KASTENBAUM

References

Bryer, K.B. (1974) "The Amish way of death." *American Psychologist, 34*: 255–61.

Grosser, G., Wechsler, H., & Greenblatt, M. (Eds.) (1964). *The threat of impending disaster.* Cambridge, MA: The MIT Press.

Kastenbaum, R. (1972). "On the future of death: Some images and options." *Omega, Journal of Death and Dying, 3*: 306–18.

Kastenbaum, R. (1986). *Death, society, and human experience.* 3rd ed. Columbus, OH: Charles E. Merrill.

Rockette, H.E. (1980). "Mortality patterns of coal miners." In W.N. Rom & V.E. Archer (Eds.), *Health implications of new energy technologies.* Woburn, MA: Ann Arbor Science Publishers, 314–40.

Shilts, R. (1987). *And the band played on.* New York: St. Martin's Press.

DEATH THEMES THROUGH HISTORY

In the twentieth century great emphasis is placed on economics, the allocation and use of scarce resources. The assumption is that unless we are conscious of the scarcity of our economic resources we will not use them wisely. Until recently, time was also considered a scarce resource, precisely because people were aware of the ultimate limit of personal time, namely, death.

Although mortality rates have changed markedly over the last century, the most basic datum has not. Death is still one for every customer. Because this fact has remained constant from culture to culture and from century to century, it is not surprising that a number of basic themes have emerged. These themes include:

- Immortality in its various dimensions and manifestations (life after death as evidenced, for example, by near-death experiences, resurrection, and reincarnation)
- Religion and its recognition of and contact with the spirit world
- Funerals and other rituals
- Sacrifice of animals and, sometimes, of people, and other forms of violence
- Death with dignity and related ethical questions
- The relationship between love, sex, and death
- The relationship between death and music, art, and literature

Immortality Theme

The most basic question is that of life after death. All else follows from this doctrine, which has been called "the most essential concept of all religions" (Achté, 1979, p. 3). Most cultures have attempted to answer this question. By immortality is meant that some aspect of the human person (often described as a soul) transcends death. This transcendence is usually regarded as a natural phenomenon; that is, it does not occur as a result of special divine intervention.

Philosophers such as Plato as well as contemporary thinkers such as Moody (1975) and Currie (1978) have espoused this life-after-life view. The natural transcendence of death is said to be evidenced by near-death experiences. A modification of this view is found in the doctrine of reincarnation. Not only does the soul or person transcend death, but physical life will be resumed at some point in the future (Sundararajan, 1974). The manner in which one lives in each of these bodies is the criterion both for the need for a return to life (Counts, 1979)—a morally perfect life would warrant an immediate entrance to eternal bliss—and the manner of existence in some future state. Finally, there is the position of resurrection (Davis, 1988), holding that a special divine intervention will occur.

The Funeral

The funeral has at least three purposes: the sanitary disposal of the body; the confrontation by the bereaved of the body, thus the beginning of the grief process; and the reintegration of the community without the deceased. Perhaps the most fundamental purpose historically and cross-culturally has been the latter. The function of the funeral has generally been to reaffirm the culture, to reestablish the meaning that was disrupted by the death.

In some cultures the emphasis has been on ensuring that the dead depart in peace, not to return (Bendann, 1930). The funeral ritual provided opportunities for final reconciliation with the deceased, the family, and the society. In other cultures, the emphasis was for the spirits to remain at the disposal of the living (Becker, 1975). Given the almost universal conviction of some sort of postdeath experience, religion, which has always been the root of meaning in lives, has as its primary focus the contact with spirits and intervention with them. The philosopher Miguel de Unamuno (1954) holds that all religion begins in the cult of the dead.

The function of all ritual is to provide established ways of dealing with life events so that in crises one knows what is expected and retains control in spite of emotional turmoil. Religion and funerary ritual have the same basic function of providing control at a time of emotional disturbance.

Sacrifice

In order to maintain this control, the rituals have often required the sacrifice of some animal or, in some cultures, the sacrifice of persons so that the spirit world could be appeased. Death is most often seen as a disruption of the natural balance of the community (Huber, 1979); therefore that balance must be reaffirmed by a sacrifice. There is a possible connection here with the stages of mental development in children. A child goes through several stages in the process of acquiring a mature awareness of death as universal, natural, and irrevocable (Speece, 1986). In one of these stages of development, the child is not yet aware of the naturalness and permanency of death. If death is not part of the natural order of things, then each death must be caused; that is, there must be some sinister element involved. The consequence of this belief is the desire to take revenge on the person who caused the death of a loved one. There is some evidence that many crimes of twentieth-century cities are rooted in childhood bereavement (Feifel, 1977).

Death with Dignity

In the eleventh century, death was viewed and orchestrated as the last act of the drama of life and much effort was made to see that the dying person maintained control (Aries, 1981). This control could be exercised by drawing up wills and commanding elaborate funerals and tombs, as well as by staging final goodbyes. Today dying and the postmortem rituals for the most part have been turned over to professionals. This shift has brought with it a loss of personal and family control. In consequence, the question of personal dignity at the time of death has arisen.

Modern death-related institutions offer little dignity if by this term one means that persons are to be treated as unique loci of control. The complexity of modern medicine and its philosophy of cure have made personal control of one's dying virtually impossible. Funeral, legal, public health, and religious professionals, by controlling the disposition of the body, have further reduced the options open to the dying and bereaved. The problem of the dignity of the dying person is further complicated by the possibility of the harvesting and transplanting of organs. Not all those attending the death of the person are there at that person's wishes or have a disinterested perspective; some parties to the death process may in fact be interested in a rapid death so that the organs can be harvested more promptly. Death with dignity would have been considered the norm until the middle of the present century, but it will be a constant and troubling theme until humankind's ethical standards correspond to the technology of death.

Love and Sexuality

The uniqueness of the person has perhaps never been more commonly held than it is today. In previous times one might consider oneself a citizen first, and an individual person second—or perhaps a child of God or a member of a community. Today's emphasis on uniqueness, however, does not negate the fact that each person is incomplete. The death of the beloved is the greatest tragedy known because not only does one lose a precious companion but one is also thrown back on one's fundamental incompleteness.

The theme of the relationship between death and love has been a part of literature since the Old Testament but was greatly emphasized in the eighteenth and nineteenth centuries (Aries, 1981). Death was understood as a great tragedy, a painful separation from the beloved. A related theme is the connection between death and sexuality. There are two major factors here. The first is that sexuality reminds us of our mortality. If we were each immortal there would be no reason for the continuation of the species that is brought about by sexual activity (Becker, 1973). Second, as death is a letting go of the roles that one plays in life, so too is sex. Orgasm has often been described as a little death, and this may be a reason for the sexual abstinence required by some cultures after the death of a member of the community.

Death as a Theme in the Arts

Death sets the limits of life, and its meaning therefore is the single most relevant idea of the culture. This all-pervasiveness of death is exemplified in music, art, drama, and literature. Perhaps the most obvious examples come from music and art associated with funerals, but death themes are also found in love songs, nursery rhymes, and a wide variety of works in the visual arts. Few operas or great dramas fail to include the ultimate challenge of meaning in the face of death, which is, in the words of William James, "the worm at the core of our pretensions to happiness."

It is in contemplating death that persons are confronted with the impulse for heroism, and for assertion of the special gifts that each of us has to give the world. The theme that life takes on more meaning when its limits are truly appreciated is found in great literature from the Psalms to writings that have come out of the Vietnam conflict.

See also "Crossing the Bar"; Dance of Death (*Danse Macabre*); Life After Death?; Lullabies of Death; *Memento Mori*; Psalms of Lament; Tame Death; "Thanatopsis"; Tombs.

—JOHN D. MORGAN

References

Achté, K. (1979). "Death and ancient Finnish culture." In R.A. Kalish (Ed.) *Death and dying: Views from many cultures.* Farmingdale, NY: Baywood.

Aries, P. (1981). *The hour of our death.* New York: Alfred A. Knopf.

Becker, E. (1973). *The denial of death.* New York: Free Press.

Becker, E. (1975). *Escape from evil.* New York: Collier Macmillan.

Bendann, B. (1930). *Death customs: An analytical study of burial rites.* New York: Alfred A. Knopf.

Counts, D.R. (1979). "The good death in Kaliai: Preparation for death in western New Britain." In R.A. Kalish (Ed.) *Death and dying: Views from many cultures.* Farmingdale, NY: Baywood, 39–44.

Currie, I. (1978). *You cannot die.* New York: Methuen.

Davis, S.T. (1988). "Christian belief and the resurrection of the body." *The New Scholasticism,* 62: 72–97.

Feifel, H. (1977). "Death and dying in modern America." *Death Education, 1*: 5–14.

Huber, P.S. (1979). "Death and society among the Angor." In R.A. Kalish (Ed.) *Death and dying: Views from many cultures.* Farmingdale, NY: Baywood, 14–24.

Moody, R.A. (1975). *Life after life.* New York: Bantam.

Plato (1973). "The republic." *The Republic and other works.* Translated by B. Jowett. Garden City, NY: Anchor Press/Doubleday.

Speece, M. (1986). "Children's understanding of death: A review of three components." In G. Paterson (Ed.) *Children and death: Proceedings of the 1985 King's College Conference.* London: King's College, 71–80.

Sundararajan, K.R. (1974). "The orthodox philosophical systems." In F.H. Holck (Ed.) *Death and eastern thought.* Nashville: Abingdon Press, 97–113.

Unamuno y Yugo, M. de (1954). *The tragic sense of life in men and peoples.* Translated by J.E.C. Flitch. New York: Dover.

DEATH THREAT INDEX (TI)

The Death Threat Index (TI) grew out of the discussions of a research group at the University of Florida interested in the application of George Kelly's Theory of Personal Constructs to the area of death concerns. Based on Seth R. Krieger's master's thesis and incorporating data from Larry M. Leitner's senior honors paper, Krieger, Epting, and Leitner (1974) published the initial instrument and research findings. They noted that Kelly had nominated death as a good candidate for a threatening event, one that appears to be unavoidable and has the potential for changing the person in some very fundamental ways.

Following this theoretical formulation, it was proposed to present respondents with a set of bipolar personal meaning dimensions (personal constructs) along which the person could rate both "self" and one's own death. This would make it possible to assess the level of disparity between the concepts of self and death and to index the threat implied by this discrepancy. If a large disparity existed, then threat would be present because much change would be needed to resolve the discrepancy when self and death become as one. A paper and pencil instrument was developed to assess this concept. Since that time, extensive reliability and validity investigations as well as modifications of the original instrument have been completed and reviewed (Rigdon et al., 1979; Epting & Neimeyer, 1984; Neimeyer, 1987).

Having low death threat has been demonstrated to be related to a number of events and variables. Examples include holding death acceptance attitudes, parenting several sick children, being a terminally ill patient in a hospice, making specific body disposal arrangements, being a physician who shows little denial in dealing with death vignettes, electing to enroll in death education classes, and having a strong religious orientation. When compared with other measures of death orientation, the TI appears to be more closely related to a conceptual or cognitive understanding of death and relatively independent of the affective self-report measures of death anxiety scales. In addition, the TI has also been used as a structured interview to help people explore the issues involved in obtaining a high death threat index. The clinical usefulness of the TI is now being explored.

See also Death Anxiety: Measures; Death Fears and Anxiety.

—FRANZ R. EPTING

References

Epting, F.R. & Neimeyer, R.A. (Eds.) (1984). *Personal meanings of death: Applications of personal construct theory to clinical practice.* New York: Hemisphere.

Krieger, S.R., Epting, F.R., & Leitner, L.M. (1974). "Personal constructs, threat, and attitudes toward death." *Omega, Journal of Death and Dying, 5*: 299–310.

Neimeyer, R.A. (1987). "Death anxiety." In H. Wass, F. Berardo, & R. Neimeyer (Eds.) *Dying: Facing the facts.* 2nd ed. New York: Hemisphere/Harper & Row, 97–136.

Rigdon, M.A., Epting, R.F., Neimeyer, R.A., & Krieger, S.R. (1979). "The Threat Index: A research report." *Death Education, 3*: 245–70.

DEATHBED SCENES

The old man lies gasping in his luxurious, canopied bed. Gathered about him are his family and dearest friends. They are all affection, all concern, all eyes and ears to his every sound and motion. He tries to speak. The effort seems too much for him, but he persists. Mumbling prayers, their faces buried in their hands, the bedside visitors nevertheless are keenly attuned to the dying man's words. This is also true of the notary who is hoping to earn his fee by transcribing the last will and testament.

This tableau has many features of the classic deathbed scene. It also has a few additional features: an orchestra sawing and piping away, and a delighted audience. In Puccini's one-act comic opera *Gianni Schicchi*, the title character is an opportunistic scoundrel who is pretending to be the old fellow who died without providing a will that would be acceptable to his loving family. Schicchi (who just happens to be a sonorous baritone) works a double scam from the deathbed. The greedy entourage has joined him in this pretense with the intent of hoodwinking the notary and benefiting from the fraudulent will. Schicchi, however, bequeaths all the valuables to Schicchi! Outraged, the deceiving and deceived relatives cannot express their fury or expose the sham. The sneaky business concluded and the notary departed, Schicchi and the relatives skirmish about the room while his newly dowried daughter (who just happens to be a lyric soprano) enjoys her first kiss from her fiance (who, to stretch the coincidence, just happens to be an ardent tenor).

This is but one of a great many deathbed scenes that have appeared in opera, drama, poetry, fiction, legend, and real life. The parodistic deathbed scene has shadowed the tragic perhaps from the very beginning. An extensive review of deathbed scenes would provide a bewildering variety of circumstances, interactions, and embodied principles. This is not surprising because the deathbed provides a unique arena for the expression of meanings and motives, hopes and fears.

It is a little surprising, however, that the increased interest in death-related topics in recent years has not been accompanied by systematic research into deathbed scenes (DBS). Academic researchers have studied specific aspects of individual death attitudes, thereby amassing a sizable literature of self-reported fears. Clinical researchers have had their own set of highly selected variables to study, such as pain control and treatment costs. Almost all the death-related research has been devoted to accumulating basic data and addressing pragmatic problems. These are reasonable and, at times, valuable pursuits, but they contribute little to the understanding of complex situations such as the deathbed gathering. In its emphasis on a host of specific variables, death-related research has emulated the dominant tradition in medical and sociobehavioral science research in general. We have learned much about specifics but much less about the way that feelings, expectations, ideas, and actions come together in a particular situation at a particular time.

The Deathbed Scene as Religious Drama

Christian belief has at times made of the deathbed scene a critical test of faith and salvation. This attitude was especially prevalent from approximately the thirteenth through the fifteenth centuries. The last moments of life became a religious drama. It was not simply that a life was coming to its end, but that the fate of the departing soul was very much at stake. This represents a significant change from the way that most people had thought of and reacted to the deathbed throughout history, including earlier Christian history. Philippe Aries (1981), a leading scholar on the history of death-related attitudes and behaviors, holds that men and women usually had met their deaths in a straightforward and natural manner (See **Tame Death**).

The newly intensified approach to the deathbed grew out of a heightened fear of the Day of Judgment and the prospect of damnation. These were familiar ideas long before the thirteenth century but became more salient as people felt themselves more exposed as individuals. In the earlier

Christian tradition a collective destiny had been affirmed, with the destiny of individual people receiving relatively little attention. Gradually, however, the devil was seen as a real and present threat who, with his minions, would contend for the vulnerable soul of the dying person. The original Christian message of victory over death had somehow become darkened by the fear of damnation.

> The more firmly people believed in the possibility of their own damnation, the more they thought about divine mercy, hoping to sway it even after death. It was the idea—if not altogether new, then at least hitherto neglected—of the intercession of the living for the dead. But in order to imagine that one might succeed in modifying the condition of the dead by prayer, it was necessary to find an alternative to the idea of uncertain salvation and probable damnation. This was no small matter, and probably required profound changes in attitudes (Aries, 1981, pp. 152–53.)

An answer was found in the formulation and acceptance of an official doctrine on Purgatory, foreshadowed in the late twelfth century, and subsequently adopted by the Roman Catholic Church. This doctrine offered the hope that a sinner might be spared eternal damnation after serving long penance and becoming purged of vice and impurities. The living might have the power to intercede for the dead—and, at the same time, make what provisions they could to have others intercede for them when the time came. The emergent emphasis on avoiding damnation and interceding for the dead had a significant effect on the deathbed scene. Jacques Le Goff (1984, p. 292) reports that "the period prior to death took on a new importance. To be sure, sinners had always been warned of the danger of sudden death and urged to prepare themselves in time to escape the torments of Hell. But in order to avoid so heavy a damnation strong measures had to be taken." It was best to avoid scandal and sin in the first place, of course, and it was also advisable to take long pilgrimages and find other ways to do penance while still alive. Nevertheless, one might still be at risk for damnation. With only a few days, hours, or minutes between oneself and damnation, it became an urgent matter to demonstrate enough penance to be spared

the worst. "Life's final moments accordingly took on a new intensity: even though it was . . . too late for most sinners to hope for direct admission to Heaven, there was still time to be saved by way of Purgatory" (Le Goff, pp. 292–93).

The deathbed took a new hold on the imagination. Artists portrayed angels and devils contesting for the dying soul. What demonstrations of faith, what good deeds, what redeeming features could be found to counterbalance the abundant sins and spiritual failings? Belief in God and a life hereafter did not necessarily assure that one could pass on in a serene state of mind. It was also important to have faith in God's infinite mercy and in one's own potential for redemption. And so in the religious drama of the DBS one might draw the last breath in faith, in good conscience, in expectation of an eventual reconciliation with God—or one might feel damned, abandoned, and consigned to punishing torments.

This momentous, supercharged envisioning of the deathbed introduced a sensitivity that has survived to the present day. The dying person is important because he or she *is* a dying person. The final scene of life is important because it *is* the final scene. Whether the dying person was powerful or obscure in life, his or her last moments are crucial. A soul is a soul. Even the mighty face the peril of damnation; even the weak have the prospect of salvation.

Reports from the deathbed became of great interest. How did she die, in despair or serenity? What were his last words? Was there a sign or omen favoring forgiveness and redemption, or just the opposite? The descriptions (accurate or imagined) led others to think upon their own future demise. People attempted to learn from the death of others and to seek either inspiration or horrible examples that could help guide their own paths to salvation.

Although this heightened emphasis on the deathbed scene as religious drama eventually subsided, it left a continuing impact on succeeding generations. Jeremy Taylor's (1651) *Rules and Exercises of Holy Dying,* for example, kept the image of the deathbed very much in mind. But Taylor also exhorted people to "practice" at the end of each day, thereby cleansing themselves regularly of sins and spiritual failings while readying themselves for the final sunset. Even today, society's renewed concern for the dying person expresses the conviction that there is—or should be—value and significance in the last moments of life.

Needless Suffering at the Deathbed

Between the diminishment of the deathbed scene as religious drama and the development of the contemporary death-awareness movement with its hospice philosophy, there was a long period of time in which the dying person was often a victim of neglect, harrassment, or both. Medical practice that was as ignorant as it was aggressive turned many a recoverable illness into a deathbed scene, notably for those eminent people who could afford physicians' services. One of many examples was that of England's King Charles II, a hearty and resilient man,

> who might have recovered if the medical profession could have left him to rest quietly and regain his strength. . . . But it was not to be; throughout Monday and the following night they bled him and purged him, administered tinctures of white vitriol in peony water, juleps of prepared pearls, sneezing powders of white hellebore root, emetics of orange, infusions of metals in white wine, blistering agents, spirits of sal ammoniac in antidotal milk water to mention but a very few of their remedies. . . . His head was shaved and red-hot irons and plasters applied to his scalp and to the soles of his feet" (Bland, 1986, p. 69).

These extremely painful measures both hastened his death and made the last days of the King's life a torment.

Although medical knowledge and ethics were to improve markedly over the years, there were still many abuses, both of commission and omission. A dying person might suffer as much from misguided treatment as from the ailment itself. But physicians might also abandon the patient when it became clear that they could not effect a cure, and do so without providing either physical or emotional comfort to them. The hospital was often seen as the last resort, essentially a place people went to die. This perception did not change radically until hospital care was transformed by modern biomedical developments in the twentieth century. Many elderly people today can recall from their youth the dread that was associated with a family member going to the hospital, and many died at home or in the hospital with little provided to alleviate their distress.

The remarkable progress since made in many areas of medical care did not have much favorable impact on the deathbed scene. If anything, the increasingly technical, objective, and bureaucratic aspects of medical practice contributed to the emotional and social isolation of the dying person—and set into motion the countertrend that eventually led to hospice philosophy and care.

Current Research

Converging studies in progress are focusing on DBS within several contexts: how films and other media depict the deathbed; how people in good health envision their eventual demise as part of their total life view; and how death actually transpires under hospice care (Kastenbaum, In press).

The motion picture industry has more or less kept pace with changes in public sophistication by offering a larger variety of deathbed scenes, some of which bear a closer resemblance to "the real thing" than was true of most earlier Hollywood depictions. An example of the old Hollywood approach can be seen in 'Til the Clouds Roll By, a stupefyingly banal musical loosely based on the life of composer Jerome Kern. The relevant scene presents one of Kern's old friends on his deathbed at home. There is no medical paraphernalia in sight (this was a few years before life-support systems came into common use), and it is the storyline rather than the old friend's appearance that indicates he is near death. "Kern" is awkward and stiff. Although his friend is well aware that he is dying, Kern persists in denial—why, he'll be up again and full of life in a few days. The doctor then enters, and Kern leaves without having said anything direct and personal to his old friend. Somberly, the doctor places one hand on the patient's wrist and with the other extracts a watch from his vest pocket, then dons his stethoscope. The death is therefore official and proper.

An audience viewing this scene today would be unlikely to agree that "Kern" did the right thing. Why couldn't he accept the facts? Why couldn't he be "real" to his old friend at this critical moment? Why should he have to leave when the doctor comes in? This scene and many others from Hollywood both followed and influenced public taste. The strong and kind person denied death, and the producer who courted success at the box office would not allow too much realistic detail to intrude. By contrast, a more recent musical, *All That Jazz,* spins around the central character's death-related thoughts and experiences, depicts open-heart surgery, and challenges the viewer to follow the story's complex progression on several levels of reality and fantasy. In a sense, *All That Jazz* attempts a hyperrealistic, or surrealistic, portrayal of a lively person facing death. It cannot be taken as a typical film, but it does illustrate some of the ways in which changing public attitudes toward dying and death are being reflected in the media.

How do everyday people think of the deathbed scenes they may have witnessed, as well as their own prospective deathbed scenes? Preliminary research findings indicate that people often do think back upon deathbed scenes that have been part of their lives. One dominant motive is the need to test mentally "whether we did what we should have." This tendency can be found in professional caregivers as well as family members. For example, a nurse recalling the death of "Mr. J." reports that at the end he became toxic, would vomit from time to time, and started to lose consciousness. He gradually lapsed into a coma and did not respond to verbal stimuli. During his last hours there were no indications of anxiety or agitation. "He died peacefully . . . not even any 'worry wrinkles' on his face." The nurse knows, however, that the end could have been different. What if aggressive treatments had been continued, including, in this case, further kidney dialysis? Thinking this possibility over, the nurse concludes that "He would have initially felt better and would not have been nauseated (and) would have lived 10 days to two weeks longer (but) possibly pneumonia would

have set in (and) he would not have died peacefully and his wife would have been very tired and under more stress as a result of this prolonged death." By studying memories of DBS we are likely to learn more not only about their impact, but also about ways to protect and enhance the quality of life at those moments. Furthermore, some survivors may benefit from the opportunity to review and share their experiences with mature and attentive listeners.

One of the findings emerging from the ongoing study of hospice deathbed scenes is that household circumstances can have a major effect on how the final scene develops. In general, people who choose the option of hospice care are more likely to die at home than those who choose traditional medical care. The home is usually a more comforting location for an impending death and usually preferred by patient and family. Nevertheless, there are often family situations that complicate and even endanger the patient's final days. In several instances, for example, the primary family caregivers lost their jobs because employers would not give them the time off to look after a dying mother, father, or sibling. Not only did this impose a severe financial burden, but it also distracted the caregivers, who could not help but worry about their future employment. The dying person himself or herself was sometimes very well aware of this problem and felt distressed to have become so burdensome. The actual deathbed scenes varied in each of the situations, but all bore the mark of the additional stress that had intruded on the situation.

Another finding that has started to emerge is the determination of some people to arrange their deathbed scenes in a distinctive and carefully planned manner. One hardy old man insisted that his friends be available to have a last drink with him when the time came, and this wish was, in fact, honored. By contrast, a dying nurse kept her thoughts to herself, but fastidiously arranged circumstances so that her family members would be out of the house long enough for her to commit suicide in a rather sophisticated manner. In retrospect, it could be seen that she had already said her farewells, did not want to undergo further physical deterioration and loss of function, and seemed to prefer the solitary scene she managed to bring about. Nevertheless, the manner of her death did burden her friends and family with the feeling of having been "left out" and not given the opportunity to be with her at the end. How often and under what circumstances the dying person and his or her loved ones agree upon the kind of ending they prefer is one of many questions that remain to be answered.

Research into the deathbed scene is not intended to be intrusive or judgmental, but, rather, to improve our understanding of the ways in which we expend our last moments of life and the enduring meanings that may be inherent in these moments.

See also Dying; Hospice: Philosophy and Practice; Hospice Development in the United Kingdom; National Hospice Study; Survival Beliefs and Practices: Roman Catholic; Tame Death.

—ROBERT KASTENBAUM

References

Aries, P. (1981). *The hour of our death.* New York: Alfred A. Knopf.

Bland, O. (1986). *The royal way of death.* London: Constable.

Kastenbaum, R. (In press). *The psychology of death.* 2nd ed. New York: Springer.

Le Goff, J. (1984). *The birth of purgatory.* Chicago: University of Chicago Press.

Taylor, J. (1651/Reprint 1977). *The rules and exercises of holy dying.* New York: Arno.

DYING

A Simple Term and Some of Its Complexities

A familiar word whose basic meaning is well understood, *dying* nevertheless has proven to be an elusive and complex concept. The word itself, along with *die*, entered common usage from a somewhat unusual source. It became established in the Friesland province of northern Holland during the fourteenth century, a time during which much of the world was ravaged by the **Black Death** and other catastrophes.

An Indo-European language, Old Frisian is a Low German dialect that is still spoken today. When, soon afterward, the word made its appearance in the English language (possibly having been reintroduced), it was often spelled "dighe" or "dye." There are cognate words in several other languages, such as the Danish *doe*, and the Icelandic *deyja*.

In its origins, the word *dying* meant essentially what it does today: the act or process of ceasing to live. However, there is a tendency to forget, even today, that *dying* and *death* refer to different conditions, the latter being the outcome of the former. Significant facts can be obscured when these two terms are used interchangeably (Kastenbaum, 1975). For example, what is sometimes called fear of death (thanatophobia) proves upon closer inspection to be fear of dying. Many people, knowing they have but a short time to live, come to terms with death. Secure in their religious faith or feeling they have enjoyed a full and eventful life, they face the prospect of death without panic or despair. Others in the same circumstances are afraid. Will they become "too dependent" on others? Will it be painful? Will it go on too long? Would it be too expensive, thereby jeopardizing the financial security of their families? Attitudes toward dying and death may differ appreciably, and the same is true of behavioral and legal aspects. A dying person is still a living person with all the associated personal, moral, and legal rights. Treating a dying person as though his or her death had already occurred is a violation at all levels of the bond that links one human to all others.

There are other ambiguities to the concept of dying. This word has long been employed in a figurative as well as in a literal sense. Renaissance singers enjoyed performing "die-away ditties," songs that faded out in a subtle and provocative manner. Poetry, especially of the Elizabethan period, often played with dying as a sexual metaphor and as an intensification of any separation from the beloved. John Donne, equally celebrated for his religious meditations and his free-spirited poetry, offers many examples.

In *The Legacie*:

When I dyed last, and, Deare, I dye
As often as from thee I goe,
Though it be but an houre agoe. . . .

In *The Paradox*:

I cannot say I lov'd, for who can say
Hee was kill'd yesterday?

A phallic sex-death conflation permeates Richard Crawshaw's *Hymn to Saint Teresa*:

Thou art Love's victim; and must die
A death more mystical and high.
Into love's arms thou shalt let fall
A still-surviving funeral.
His is the Dart must make the Death
Whose stroke shall taste thy hallow'd
      breath;
A Dart thrice dipp'd in that rich
      flame. . . .
So spiritual, pure, and fair
Must be th' immortal instrument
Upon whose choice point shall be sent
A life so lov'd. . . .

Die and dying remain popular ways of expressing both personal states of mind and external situations. "I could just die!," for example, may express surprise, embarrassment, and the wish to escape from a predicament. A range-riding cowboy who has not yet purchased a portable personal CD player may be perceived as "the last of a dying breed." In both these instances and in many other possible examples, nobody is actually in imminent danger of death, but *dying* refers to a more general sense of perishing, languishing, fading away. It is a useful term to spice up ordinary conversation and remains tempting to authors who are seeking a picturesque phrase. Nevertheless, at times the listener or reader may place a mistakenly concrete interpretation on what was intended as a figurative usage. Young children are particularly apt to be confused by the figurative use of terms such as *die, dying*, and *death*. Brent (1977–78), for example, describes how his young son developed nocturnal episodes of death anxiety in part as a result of learning that the family car had "died" because it had a "dead" battery.

As word and concept, dying has encountered a number of difficulties during the twentieth century. Feifel (1962) in the United States and Gorer (1965) in England observed how clear and direct terms such as *die, dying, died, death*, and *dead* had become socially unacceptable. Even health care professionals avoided using these terms. Hospital staff engaged in systematic evasive maneuvers to avoid confrontations with death. For example, sociologist David Sudnow (1967, p. 55) describes how John, a morgue attendant, worked at avoiding conversation and interaction:

> While picking up a body from the ward, he worked quickly, taking no time out for conversation along the way. . . . Whenever he had a stretcher with him, empty or not, he avoided interaction with others, and they with him. One adaptation of his was to carry along . . . a patient's file, or a log book . . . when he was en route to get a body. Proceeding to the elevator with the body he characteristically engrossed himself in looking through whatever he had brought with him while he awaited the arrival of the elevator. This made him . . . less available for visual encounters with others. . . . As he pushed his occupied stretcher, he always looked downward, and on numerous occasions persons with whom he was acquainted and to whom he would have otherwise made an overture of greeting . . . were silently passed by along his route.

This was a quite typical example of "normal evasion." During this same period of time, I saw hospital staff regularly deployed to "spy" out of doorways to see if "the coast is clear" to wheel out a corpse, and also learned to recognize false-bottomed stretchers that appeared to be empty but actually concealed a corpse inside. Glaser and Strauss ironically chose *Awareness of Dying* as the title of their valuable book when, in fact, most of the observations they reported dealt with the ways in which physicians and nurses attempted to avoid acknowledging the awareness of dying.

Dying was too strong and direct a word for both the public and health care professionals. People would generally try to avoid the subject entirely or tiptoe around it with generalities. "He expired," or "She passed on" were the troubled euphemistic synonyms that a person might utter when something had to be said. Almost never was someone described as dying. She "hasn't gotten her strength back yet"; he "may be laid up a while." Accurate communication had fallen victim to the need to reduce emotional stress and avoid confronting mortal realities.

And, since people were almost never "dying," and seldom "died," there was little opportunity for a comforting deathbed scene. Essentially, "nobody wanted to be there when nothing happened." The dying person was avoided, as well as the words that described his or her condition.

The situation has changed appreciably in recent years. The hospice movement, death education, and a number of other developments have helped to alleviate the isolation of the dying person and made it possible to use direct language in discussing death-related topics. Perhaps surprisingly, however, *dying* has again come up against strong competition. It is true that the word now is often used instead of a euphemism or circumlocution. Other once-taboo words such as *cancer* are also employed more often. But it is also true that the legitimatization of dying and death has engendered a counterreaction. This seems to be a price that is demanded by bureaucracy in general and by the health care system in particular.

Dying and death, no longer avoidable, must be processed in ways that are acceptable to the establishment. For this reason, *dying* has been transformed into *terminal illness.* The official rhetoric of the health care system today typically inserts "terminal illness" where one might think "dying" would be just as appropriate. The difference is not as slight as it might appear. A *person* dies. A *patient* has a terminal illness. In a roundabout but nevertheless effective way, our culture's death system has once again found a substitute for the simplest and most direct word. And once again, bureaucrats and physicians can choose to "manage terminal illness" rather than face the full complexity of a unique person whose life is coming to an end. Although both terms are in fairly common usage, the present trend seems to favor the more distant and objective-sounding medical jargon, "terminal illness."

When Does "Dying" Begin?

This question is important for its practical as well as its conceptual implications. Many studies have demonstrated that we tend to treat people differently when they are dying or when we think they are. This phenomenon was clearly illustrated in a classic naturalistic study by Larry LeShan (in Bowers et al., 1964). He found that nurses took significantly longer to respond to bed calls from dying patients than from patients with a more favorable prognosis (the nurses themselves were unaware of this difference and were dismayed to learn of it).

Several answers have been proposed to the "when" question (Kastenbaum, 1986). These include the following alternatives:

1. Dying begins the moment we are born.
2. Dying begins when a fatal condition begins.
3. Dying begins when a fatal condition is recognized by a physician.
4. Dying begins when the patient is told of his or her fatal condition.
5. Dying begins when the patient realizes and accepts the facts.
6. Dying begins when nothing more can be done to reverse the condition and preserve life.

Some readers may be uncomfortable not only with the number of alternative approaches, but also with the complexities by which they are accompanied. We human beings generally seek straightforward, solid, and simple answers to questions that bear on our deepest concerns. It would not be responsible, however, to convey the impression that determining the onset of dying is a simple matter.

The first view is generally limited to philosophic statements that intend to remind us that each life ends in a death. It has proven of little value when applied to situations in which a person's death is actually in close prospect. Although the idea that we die from the moment we are born (or conceived) offers an interesting perspective, it does not stand up well to analysis on biodevelopmental grounds. There is some local necrosis (cell death) in the early phases of development, but the whole organism is overwhelmingly launched on a growth and viability trajectory. To tell a person who is concerned about the possibility of imminent death that "we are dying all the time" is almost invariably an off-putting remark.

It is a plausible but not very useful approach to say that dying begins with the inception of a fatal condition. The onset of the dying process might remain unverified for days, weeks, months, perhaps years. When did it actually begin? It might never be possible to pinpoint the date of inception for either of two reasons: (a) no definitive observations were made until some time after the probable inception, or (b) there was actually no one clear moment in time at which a hazardous condition became one that would surely lead to death. Even with careful monitoring in a high-technology medical environment, it is not always possible to know in advance whether a person will be able to survive a life-threatening condition, and some deaths occur in situations less favorable for observation. It is often of theoretical interest only to assume that the dying process had its inception at a clearly delineated time unless there are specific data to support this conclusion.

The other alternative approaches are more pragmatic. It makes some sense to say that dying begins when a physician concludes that the patient cannot survive much longer. This is a consequential judgment because it is likely to affect the physician's subsequent management of the case and his or her interaction not only with the patient but with family members and other health care professionals. It also represents a fixed and potentially verifiable point in time: after another physical examination and a review of the laboratory findings on such-and-such a date, the doctor concludes that the patient's illness is "terminal."

There are several problems with this approach, however. A physician's judgment may not be 100 percent conclusive. Aware of individual differences and the limits of medical science, the doctor may prefer to think in terms of probabilities rather than a definitive outcome. ("With this condition at this stage of severity, most people survive for two, three, four months. But I have known a few who kept going for several years, and every now and then somebody actually manages to recover.") For this and other reasons the physician may be reluctant to make a definitive judgment until death is in very near prospect.

Another problem centers on the time framework. On the basis of all available information, the physician may judge that a particular patient will not recover from his or her illness which will eventually become either the direct or indirect cause of death. However, this may also be an illness that the patient might live with for many years; it is, therefore, a "terminal" condition, but the person is not "dying" in any meaningful sense of the term. How close should death seem, then, before thinking of the patient as "dying"? This question is usually resolved by common sense and by adhering to the standards of the day. In the United States, federal regulations for hospice care and reimbursement now provide a time framework that is often employed. A person is terminally ill/dying if death is expected to occur within six months. At this point, a person may choose the option of hospice care (or continue with general medical coverage). This is merely an arbitrary formula, though. One might substitute three months, a year, or some other time framework. When a physician certifies that a patient has six months or less to live, this is a meaningful decision from several standpoints, including the bureaucratic and financial, but it does not otherwise provide a firm basis for establishing that this is when the dying process actually begins (and physicians, of course, are well aware of this problem).

A further difficulty with taking the physician's judgment as basis for the inception of the dying process leads to the next approach: the patient's awareness of the prognosis. It could be argued that the patient's frame of reference is more important than the physician's. "Am I dying?" How a person answers this question can have profound implications on all aspects of his or her life. The key, then, might be not the moment that the physician reaches the conclusion, but the moment that it is communicated to the patient. But here again difficulties exist. A person may have decided that he or she is dying long before being told by the physician. Conversely, a person may "not hear" the physician's communication and reject or ignore the message. Furthermore, the patient may be of two minds, alternating between recognition of the facts ("Of course, I'm dying . . . that's what my body's been telling me for weeks") and evasion ("I just need a good night's sleep and maybe a change in diet"). It is not at all unusual for a dying person to alternate between acceptance and denial (as we are apt to do in other crisis situations as well), and even to give out mixed signals at the same time. Important as it can be to know whether a person considers himself or herself to be dying, the answer may be complex and shift from day to day and situation to situation. Moreover, some people die without ever clearly acknowledging the facts, while others believe they are dying although they actually have no life-threatening ailment.

The last alternative described here is quite pragmatic: dying begins when nothing more can be done to preserve life. This has become an increasingly frequent criterion as the health care system continues to offer alternative forms of treatment. Physicians seldom put this definition forward in so many words. By their actions, however, often it can be seen that the physician believes he or she has "one more thing to try." The patient does not have to be viewed as dying as long as there is some additional measure that might be attempted to prolong life. It is useful to recognize this tendency in contemporary medical practice. This line of thinking helps to keep the physician in the favored role of providing active treatment and delaying the definitive conclusion that the patient is likely to die soon. Others in the situation may have legitimate concerns that the refusal to acknowledge impending death can interfere with opportunities for leave-taking with loved ones as well as the continuation of procedures certain to be intrusive and unlikely to be effective.

It is no simple matter, then, to decide when a person has become a dying person. In some instances the individual, family and friends, and health care professionals all share the same view. However, it is not unusual for a variety of views to be held, ranging from "He will die soon," to "He'll get over this soon." From a practical standpoint it is important to listen and observe carefully, make as few assumptions as possible, and respect each individual's frame of reference.

Trajectories of Dying

Whenever dying begins, it is a process that occurs over time. Research in hospital settings by Glaser and Strauss (1968) has shown that this process actually takes a variety of different forms or "trajectories."

Glaser and Strauss noted three major trajectories of dying. The *lingering trajectory* is one in which a person is gradually declining over a long period. The pattern of care tends to be largely custodial services rather than aggressive treatment. There is also a tendency for almost all of the care to be provided by lower echelon staff members. Glaser and Strauss observed that many physicians and nurses did not find the care of chronically ill patients to be interesting or rewarding to themselves. This situation may have improved slightly in the two decades since study, especially as geriatric care has become a higher priority, but the general pattern still endures. Staff generally were ready to "let go" of a patient who had been on a lingering trajectory instead of rushing in with "heroic" measures. Unfortunately, in some situations the lingering patient had become only a "bed" to be "managed," rather than a unique personality. There are also tendencies among staff members to assume that a person on a lingering trajectory (especially if an aged adult) is "ready for death," which may reflect the observer's perception but not the state of mind of the observed (Kastenbaum et al., 1981).

A markedly different pattern of care was observed for patients who were on an *expected quick trajectory*. This pattern includes those whose lives possibly could be saved by prompt and effective action. Modern hospitals are often very well organized to cope with emergency situations. The researchers observed highly trained teams of health care personnel rushing to the patient's side. State-of-the-art technology and precise intervention techniques may be employed in certain varieties of the expected quick trajectory. But there are other types of quick trajectories in which the staff can only keep the patient as comfortable as possible and wait for the end to come. Both the "pointed trajectory" (a risky procedure whose outcome can be either life or death) and the "will-probably-die trajectory" may occur in the same hospital unit, such as the emergency room or operating room.

The *unexpected quick trajectory* is particularly disturbing to hospital staff when it occurs on a unit that is not organized primarily for emergency responses. A patient whose condition had appeared stable, e.g., making a normal recovery after a medical procedure, may suddenly deteriorate and die. Even though there may have been no way of predicting the occurrence, staff may be upset that they did not see it coming, and also alarmed by this reminder that a life-or-death crisis does not necessarily restrict itself to designated areas of the hospital.

In fact, one of the major findings of this study (and one confirmed by other investigators) is how strenuously the hospital staff attempts to shield itself against surprise. There is a strong need to maintain at least the illusion of control over events that, in the last analysis, are beyond human control. It is clear that everybody in the situation—patient certainly included—seeks to retain some measure of control in a situation that threatens to go completely out of control (Kastenbaum, 1978). The dying process, then, can be seen as not only a highly personal series of events but also as a pattern of interaction with others and a pattern that can take a variety of forms through time.

A Few Guidelines

The dying person remains a living person—and a unique person. Nobody else has had this person's distinctive history and life experiences; nobody else has participated in this person's distinctive pattern of human relationships or has seen the world in quite the same way. That this unique person may not have long to live is certainly a compelling fact. If we choose to ignore or evade this fact, then we are retreating from an essential facet of reality. But it is no less unrealistic to conceive of this individual as a sort of generic dying person. The mature and sensitive friend, family member, and caregiver will keep the whole reality in mind: this unique person, living and dying in a unique situation.

Strides have been made in reducing the pain and discomfort that can accompany the dying process. For patients and their families to benefit from modern techniques of alleviating symptoms it is useful to establish and maintain clear lines of communication with the physicians and nurses. Can we talk about pain control together? Is the doctor really listening? Has he or she kept up with the field? Does the doctor have any personal quirks that interfere with providing adequate pain relief? Has the patient accepted the belief that a dying person is supposed to suffer? Open, honest, and frequent communication is often a precondition for effective relief of pain and other symptoms.

Michael H. Levy, director of a palliative care service at a cancer center, points out that pain is not only the most common symptom of terminally ill patients but also can have serious adverse effects on their families. Writing with terminally ill cancer patients in mind, Levy concludes that "Uncontrolled pain can be a significant causative factor in anorexia, weight loss, weakness, nausea, pressure sores, and insomnia. Alternatively, anorexia, constipation, nausea, and drowsiness may be toxic effects of the narcotics used to control pain" (Levy, 1987–88, p. 266). Adequate pain control can not only reduce this specific source of distress, then, but protect the patient's quality of life in general, as well as reduce anxiety and stress on the part of family members. Along with other specialists in pain control, Levy finds that too many physicians fail to take advantage of the more effective techniques that have been developed in recent years. More research is needed for the continued improvement of pain relief measures, but also needed is greater awareness and willingness to utilize the existing techniques.

There is evidence for the proposition that "how we respond emotionally to a terminal illness may affect the duration of survival. Persons who express anger, anxiety, or a dysphoric mood may live longer than individuals who are more despairing and accepting of their status" (Schulz & Schlarb, 1987–88, p. 306). It has also been found that people who have developed abiding friendships and a pattern of mutually supportive relationships are likely to have a higher quality of life during the dying process as compared with those characterized by isolated or conflicted social patterns (Weisman & Worden, 1975). Clearly, how a person copes with problems and relates to other people continues to be a significant factor as life approaches its end. We can be helpful by enabling the dying person to continue to express his or her own individuality rather than expecting conformity to some (highly questionable) idealized pattern.

See also (The) Black Death; Death Education; Death Fears and Anxiety; Death System; Deathbed Scenes; Hospice: Philosophy and Practice; Trajectories of Dying.

—ROBERT KASTENBAUM

References

Bowers, M., Jackson, E., Knight, J., & LeShan, L. (1964). *Counseling the dying.* New York: Thomas Nelson & Sons.

Brent, S. (1977–1978). "Puns, metaphors, and misunderstandings in a two-year-old's conception of death." *Omega, Journal of Death and Dying, 8*: 285–94.

Feifel, H. (1962). "Scientific research in taboo areas—death." *American Behavioral Scientist, 5*: 28–30.

Glaser, B.G. & Strauss, A.L. (1966). *Awareness of dying.* Chicago: Aldine.

Glaser, B.G. & Strauss, A.L. (1968). *Time for dying.* Chicago: Aldine.

Gorer, G. (1965). *Death, grief, and mourning.* Garden City, NY: Doubleday.

Kastenbaum, R. (1975). "Is death a life crisis? On the confrontation with death in theory and practice." In N. Datan & L.H. Ginsberg (Eds.) *Life-span developmental psychology.* New York: Academic Press, pp. 19–50.

Kastenbaum, R. (1978). "In control." In C. Garfield (Ed.) *Psychosocial care of the dying patient.* New York: McGraw-Hill, pp. 227–44.

Kastenbaum, R. (1986). *Death, society, and human experience.* 3rd ed. Columbus, OH: Charles E. Merrill.

Kastenbaum, R., Barber, T.X., Wilson, S.G., Ryder, B.L., & Hathaway, L.B. (1981). *Old, sick and helpless: Where therapy begins.* Cambridge, MA: Ballinger.

Levy, M.H. (1987–1988). "Pain control research in the terminally ill." *Omega, Journal of Death and Dying, 18*: 265–79.

Schulz, R. & Schlarb, J. (1987–1988). "Two decades of research on dying: What do we know about the patient?" *Omega, Journal of Death and Dying, 18*: 299–317.

Sudnow, D. (1967). *Passing on.* Englewood Cliffs, NJ: Prentice-Hall.

Weisman, A.D. & Worden, J.W. (1975). "Psychosocial analysis of cancer deaths." *Omega, Journal of Death and Dying, 6*: 61–65.

E

EMBALMING

"Ashes to ashes, dust to dust" is a view of life and death that would suggest a simple and direct approach to the disposition of the corpse, namely, allowing natural processes to operate without interference. If "all flesh is grass," then decomposition is the inevitable process by which the former becomes the latter. Nevertheless, as individuals and as societies, the human race has often resisted this injunction. Can a body not be spared decay, can features not be preserved from the ravages of time? For those who would counter the forces of biodegradation with human determination and ingenuity, embalming has long been a favored alternative.

Embalming in the Ancient World

The art, science, and theology of embalming seems to have been first practiced in the early dynastic period of Egypt (Johnson & Johnson, 1980; Leca, 1980). Evidence suggests that until this time, the Egyptian dead were wrapped and buried without coffins in shallow graves. The effects were not what might be supposed. Although the corpse was provided with neither protection nor enhancement, the hot sands soon dried out the tissues and preserved the remains. Paradoxically, the dead suffered a temporary reversal of fortune as Egypt rose to higher levels of prosperity and cultural development. It had become both desirable and feasible to provide the dead with a wooden or stone container. This mark of respect for the deceased was a necessity for an increasingly popular belief—resurrection of the body. When remains were disinterred (by animals or grave robbers), those who had continued to be buried in the simple, "primitive" manner usually were found to be well preserved, while those handled in the "modern" manner were decomposed. Faced with this disturbing information, the Egyptians responded by developing effective embalming techniques somewhat resembling those still in use today.

There was an obvious foundation for this innovation. Egyptians and others had long known how to preserve food, including the flesh of fish, birds, and animals. This technology was elaborated upon and incorporated into a ritualistic procedure that bestowed culturally acceptable meaning upon the mechanics of embalming.

Two documents known jointly as *The Rites of Embalming* date from the first century of our era but are copies of a New Kingdom source extant about 1500 BC. The surviving remnants of these documents describe both theological ritual and physical preparation of the body. Embalming commenced with rituals that included anointing the head and applying perfumed resins to the surfaces of the body. (From other sources it has been learned that salt solutions were also used at various times.) The viscera were then removed and placed in one or more canopic urns. The priests and their assistants would then rub the back, and start wrapping the body. The final touches included placing gold ornaments on the hands and feet, and more anointings and wrappings. The mummified remains would then receive the honor and protection of being encased in both inner and outer containers, some of striking artistic beauty, and entombed. Such other essential steps as removing the brain are not mentioned in this earliest fragmentary document, but it is known that all internal organs were removed as part of the process. At various times in Egyptian history, the removed organs were either kept in separate vessels or replaced in the body.

Embalming was not for everybody. It was an elaborate and expensive procedure that was largely reserved for important and affluent people. And, interestingly, embalming was not intended simply as a means of preserving the physical remains as such. There is reason to believe that the carefully prepared mummy was meant to function as a kind of bait for the deceased's psychic double. As Ragon (1983, p. 7) observes, "The mummy was simply a symbolic object summoning the psychic reality it represented. That is why, in order to attract the posthumous radiation of the dead man, the object-medium had to be impregnated with all his memories."

From Near Neglect to New Knowledge

Embalming became a casualty of Egypt's encounters both with barbarian invasions and the scorn of the increasingly powerful Christian movement. After about 500 AD, embalming was no longer regularly practiced in its homeland.

Through the next millenia there were occasional applications of Egyptian-based embalming techniques to the great dead of Europe. After internal organs were removed, the body would be washed internally and externally with wine and vinegar, the blood absorbed into powders, the incisions sewn up, and the entire frame swathed in bandages. Charlemagne (814) and William the Conqueror (1087) were among the notable personages whose bodies were embalmed in this manner.

The general medieval disinterest in science along with the religious establishment's disapproval of cadavar dissection combined to reduce the development of new knowledge and techniques, as well as to limit the number of embalming operations performed. In the more enlightened ambiance of the seventeenth century, however, Dutch physicians Jan Swammerdam, Frederich Ruysch, and Stephan Blanchard

successfully injected a wine-based preservative liquid into bodies whose internal organs had been removed in the traditional manner. The organs were then replaced, and the body left to dry. Another advance occurred a century later when the pioneering Scottish physician, William Hunter, successfully injected a turpentine solution without requiring evisceration of the corpse. This proved to be especially helpful in teaching anatomy and dissection to medical students.

By the middle of the nineteenth century, embalming had taken its place as a valuable tool for teaching and research, in the United States as well as Europe. However, it was still relatively uncommon as part of funeral practice.

The War Between the States

The interconnectedness of social processes bearing on death-related matters (See **Death System**) has already made itself apparent in the birth of embalming techniques from the existing technology of preserving meats. It was another and very different type of connection that led to the widespread application of embalming in the United States. The Civil War produced an unprecedented toll of casualties, including the deaths of young men far from home. As a humane action, efforts were made to return the dead to their families for proper burial. However, there were several major obstacles. In addition to the expense and the limited availability of transportation, officials were confronted by two daunting challenges. It might be cruel indeed to ship home a severely decomposed body, and yet decomposition was expected under the circumstances. The other problem was a tribute to the heightened savagery of modern warfare. Both the wounded and the dead were more likely than in past conflicts to have suffered shattering and disfiguring injuries. Again, it seemed perhaps as cruel to cause additional anguish to the family by returning a grossly disfigured body as to fail to return the body at all.

Civilian physicians and the "undertakers" of the period responded to the challenge. The doctors found improved ways to preserve the bodies for the trip home. A variety of substances were injected, including alcohol, arsenic, copper sulfate, and zinc chloride. It was also under the pressure of wartime disruption and widespread family bereavement that the forerunners of today's funeral directors started to provide restorative services to provide a semblance of the deceased's former and characteristic appearance. Recognizing the value of embalming under these circumstances, the armed services set up the first licensing system for its practitioners.

Advances in embalming and restoration techniques were made after the war and a series of further advances were made in both of these related fields (Habenstein and Lamers, 1955). Among other factors contributing to the growing popularity of embalming was its proven effectiveness in the shipment of bodies across long distances (this was also, of course, the great age of the railroads in the United States). Standards, regulations, state licensing requirements, and education and training curricula all rapidly followed as embalming became an established practice just before the turn of the twentieth century.

Embalming Today

Embalming techniques have continued to improve through the years. It is no longer necessary to remove internal organs. Preservation is accomplished by injecting two types of fluid, one into body cavities, the other into the arteries (from which most of the blood has been removed). A pumping device is used to disseminate the arterial embalming fluid throughout the body. Many funeral directors now make use of embalming fluid that is based upon a synthetic (non-organic) type of formaldyhyde that does not pose the carcinogenic hazards that have been attributed to conventional formaldyhyde. Bodies are usually kept available for viewing for only a short period of time, but occasionally there is a need to delay burial or cremation until all the family can be present. Ordinarily, there are no difficulties to maintaining preservation of an embalmed body for several weeks or months. A body that has deteriorated significantly before being embalmed is not likely to be as well preserved. Preservation is generally most effective when death occurs quickly (as in a fatal stroke or heart attack) and embalming follows soon afterward. Dehydration will occur over a period of time, the rate depending upon particular circumstances. There are marked differences in how long an embalmed corpse remains well preserved after burial, again depending upon a variety of circumstances, including climate.

Although embalming has become a familiar, even a standard part of the funerary process in the United States, it is in most cases an option that one can either choose or forego. Attitudes toward body disposition and funerals have been in flux for several decades, and a number of individuals and organizations have expressed doubts and reservations about traditional practices. A responsible funeral director will discuss these matters openly with family members, and information can also be obtained from state and county agencies that regulate funeral services.

Embalming is common in some nations today, but rare in others. Useful information is provided by Habenstein and Lamers (1981) in their classic, though now aging, survey of the subject.

See also Death System; Funerals; National Funeral Directors Association; Tombs.

—ROBERT KASTENBAUM
(Thomas Cattrick, Consultant)

References

Habenstein, R.W. & Lamers, W.M. (1974). *Funeral customs the world over.* 2nd rev. ed.. Milwaukee: Bulfin.

Habenstein, R.W. & Lamers, W.M. (1981). *The history of American funeral directing.* Revised edition. Milwaukee: Bulfin.

Johnson, E.C. & Johnson, G.R. (1980). "The development of American embalming procedures." *The Knight Letter,* March: 7–9.

Leca, A-P. (1981). *The Egyptian way of death.* Translated by L. Asmal. Garden City, NY: Doubleday and Company.

Ragon, M. (1983). *The space of death.* Translated by Alan Sheridan. Charlottesville, VA: University Press of Virginia.

EPITAPHS

Placing something on (*epi*) the tomb (*taphos*) in remembrance of the deceased person is a custom that has been practiced by many cultures over the centuries. Although the term *epitaph* refers specifically to inscriptions placed on tombs, it has come to encompass messages on gravemarkers as well. The most commonly found epitaphs are those on cemetery gravestones, but less durable wooden markers have also been used, as when pioneers were forced to bury their dead in desert wilderness.

Epitaphs appear to have four basic motivations, not all involved in every instance:

1. To keep the memory of a person alive
2. To recommend the deceased person to God
3. To show that the survivors are behaving in a responsible and caring manner toward the deceased
4. To convey a message to the living

Many ancient as well as more recent epitaphs have been collected both by trained historians and by individuals with special interest in the subject. Review of thousands of epitaphs reveals several themes that occur repeatedly in various cultures and at various times of history. It would be incorrect to refer to these themes as universal because, in fact, not all epitaphs express these themes nor have epitaphs been found in all cultures. Nevertheless, these core themes seem to have expressed the thoughts and feelings of many people in many different settings. Other epitaphs appear to speak more vividly of an individual's life or the times through which he or she lived. Epitaph studies, then, can tell us something about both common and special thoughts, feelings, yearnings, and needs that are aroused by a death. A comparison of epitaphs in the ancient world and in the United States can illustrate both the common and the special themes.

Epitaphs in Antiquity

The sorrow of a life taken before its time was often expressed in epitaphs as well as poetry. A third-century Greek epitaph (Alexiou, 1974) tells one such tragic story:

> I, Leonto, died a maiden, like a young flower
> when it bursts its bud and first shows its petals,
> —fifteen years old, just ready to be joined in wedlock,
> I have come to lie among the dead in a long sleep.

The imagery of a life being harvested before it is ripe is found in many other epitaphs as well. Charos, a Greek version of the later "grim reaper," is reprimanded by a child's parents:

> See what a time you have chosen, my Charos, to take him

The death of another youth is commented upon in the first person:

> My corn that has been husked and reaped before its time,
> reaped too soon by the reapers of Charos!

Another theme found in ancient as well as more recent epitaphs is the survivor's distress at having been abandoned to a lonely and dismal life by the deceased. A woman so accuses her dead lover:

> You have forgotten me like stubble on the plain,
> which men sow and it grows, and then they reap,
> and they take the crop and leave behind the stubble,
> they set fire to the stubble and only ashes are left.

That the surviving parents, children, or other intimates of the deceased are doomed to unending grief is one of the traditional messages of ancient Greek and Roman epitaphs, as in these lines on the death of a soldier:

> Just as a cultivated, thriving tree falls to the ground, uprooted by the wind, so too Kronios fell doomed, according to his destiny, leaving unending grief to his parents.

The image of the deceased as a fallen tree is found repeatedly in ancient epitaphs and laments, as well as in some more recent inscriptions.

Yet there are also aggressive and menacing epitaphs to be found. Lattimore (1962) offers examples such as these:

> I, Idameneus, built this tomb to my own glory. May Zeus utterly destroy anyone who disturbs it.

and:

> You who pass by, do not insult my sacred grave, lest you incur the sharp anger of Agelis and Persephone. . . .

These epitaphs were found in Asia Minor where, according to Lattimore, a particularly strong need was felt for "defensive curses" that would repel those who were not entitled to approach and touch a gravesite. The curse, or malediction, is unusual in ancient epitaphs, but there are some vivid examples, as when a murder victim threatens vengeance against his killer. The stranger who happens to come across a grave is not usually the target of a malediction unless he intends to do some harm. Interestingly, some ancient epitaphs warn politicians not to deface the stones with campaign announcements. The voice from the grave in such cases may promise to support their candidacy if they will only put their announcements someplace else!

More typical were epitaphs that counseled serenity on the part of the survivors because the death had but repaid the loan of life:

> Father, if you long for me, I pray you put away your grief;
> for this was an acknowledged loan, the daylight that I looked on.

And, even more simply:

> I have paid back my tax.

Another ancient theme seems to take up the task of helping survivors to realize what death means, to bring home the physical and psychological reality of the transition:

> I, who was such, am now a slab, a tomb,
> a stone, an image.

That strength, youth, accomplishment, and beauty all perish is a theme well known to the ancients:

Wayfarer, you behold me a corpse who once was bold in the stadium, Melanippus of Tarsus, retiarius of the second rank. No longer do I listen to the voice of the brass trumpet and the unequal flutes, and rouse the public to an uproar.

Some ancient epitaphs asserted while others denied the existence of an afterlife. Thus, one Greek inscription informs "Blessed and beloved Sabinus, it is sleep that holds you; you live as a hero and have not turned into a corpse. You sleep in your tomb under the trees as if you were still alive; for the souls of those who are very pious live on." Yet a lengthy Roman epitaph reports, in part, that "There is no boat in Hades, no ferryman Charon, no Aeacus keeper of the keyes, nor any dog called Cerberus. All of us who have died and gone below are bones and ashes; there is nothing else." And still other epitaphs express the wish for an afterlife and a reunion, rather than the certainty of such an outcome.

Of all the ancient epitaph themes, perhaps the one that has been perpetuated most frequently over the succeeding centuries is the simple reminder that the dead were once living, and the living will take their own place in the earth. One Greek inscription also includes a representation of an old man deep in thought:

> This thing is a man. Look at what you are, and what awaits you. Gaze on this image and learn what your own end will be.

With many variations, this theme in which the dead provide a reminder of mortality to the living has continued to be expressed throughout the centuries. Perhaps it is this sense of an inescapable link among people of all times and places that accounts for some of the continuing interest in ancient epitaphs.

Epitaphs in the United States

There have been several notable collections of American epitaphs. Particularly extensive is the two-volume collection compiled by the Reverend Timothy Alden in 1814 (reprinted in 1977). His work is also valuable in that many of the gravesites he visited have since been destroyed or defaced, as Alden himself had foreseen. (Alden's work is also distinctive through the supplementary notes he has added to a number of the epitaphs.) One notices in reviewing the Alden collection that many of the inscriptions are rather lengthy, detailed, and forthright. By contrast, more recently published collections tend to emphasize short, humorous, or somewhat bizarre epitaphs, probably because of their entertainment value. Without denying the interest that is held by some of the more striking and unusual American epitaphs, it is worth keeping in mind that through much of this nation's history the inscriptions were generally serious-minded and "responsible."

The following Alden (vol. 1, pp. 107–08) example from Kennebunk, Maryland, illustrates the type of pious but descriptive and straightforward epitaph that was favored through much of American history:

> Sacred to the memory of madam Sarah Little, relict of the late rev. Daniel Little, who departed this life, 19 December, 1804, aged 78. Possessed of a feeling mind enclosed in a delicate frame, with a heart transfused with the mild spirit of christianity; with the world under her feet, and the eye of faith steadfastly fixed on heavenly joys; for a series of years, she endured excruciating pain and much bodily indisposition; and, at last, calmly resigned her body into the tomb in the well assured hope of a resurrection to a blessed immortality.

This epitaph at once conveys some of the significant particularities of Sarah Little's life and underscores the value of strong religious faith under trying circumstances. In this sense, such inscriptions affirmed a value shared by many in the community and attempted to bring some consolation and meaning to a suffering life that is ended by death. Within the Alden collection one finds a great many other epitaphs that speak in praise of the deceased's character and accomplishments.

Among the most poignant epitaphs are those that record the deaths of infants and children. The high mortality rate among the very young is documented by numerous gravestone inscriptions. All too common are epitaphs such as the following from Rockingham, Vermont (Tashjian & Tashjian, 1974):

> In Memory of
> Two Infants a Son,
> and a Daughter, of
> Elijah & Lovifa
> Bellows, they Died.
> March 2th 1799.
> sleep on sweet babes
> & take your rest
> god cald you home
> he thought it best

Women were also at high risk during pregnancy, labor, and the immediate postnatal phase. Family tragedy associated with childbirth is recorded in many American cemeteries, as in this example from Eastford, Connecticut (Tashjian & Tashjian):

> Hear lies the remains of
> Mrs. Sarah Hart Wife
> To Mr Constant Hart
> Who died March the
> 12th 1752 in the 26th
> Year of Hur Age &
> Benjamin Hart Thair
> Son Whos Bearth &
> Death was on the 4th
> Of March 1752.

Although many cemeteries have been destroyed, neglected, or their gravestone inscriptions worn beyond legibility, one can still find numerous examples of survivors mourning the loss of infants, young children, and their mothers.

Wallis (1954, reprinted 1973) has observed a trend toward standardization and simplification of American epitaphs. This trend has continued to increase over more recent decades and seems to be part of a larger pattern in which memorialization of the dead has become a relatively lower priority. However, one can still discover a variety of expressive epitaphs in American burial places as well as in such books. Inscriptions such as the following (from Wallis) tell us something about American life as well as death:

> None of us ever voted for
> Roosevelt or Truman
> (Hallenbeck family monument, Elgin, Minnesota)

> Lieut. Munroe
> I'll give them the contents
> of my gun.

Lexington, April 19, 1775
died May 25, 1825, age 73
(Said to have fired the first shot of the Revolution)

John Heath
Taken from
County Jail &
Lynched
By Bisbee Mob
in Tombstone
Feb. 22nd 1884.

Killed by unskilled Dr.
(St. Mary's Cemetery, Winona, Minnesota, 1902)

In memory of Ellen Shannon
Aged 26 years
Who was fatally burned
March 21st 1870
by the explosion of a lamp
filled with "R.E. Danforth's"
Non Explosive
Burning Fluid"
(Girard, Pennsylvania)

School is out
Teacher has gone home
(Elkhart, Indiana, S.B. McCracken, 1933)

Daniel E. Cole
Born Feb. 2, 1844
Went Away
Mar. 22, 1921
I Wonder
Where He
Went.

See also Cemeteries; Funerals; Psalms of Lament; Tombs.

—ROBERT KASTENBAUM

References

Alden, T. (1814/Reprint 1977). *A collection of American epitaphs.* 2 vols. New York: Arno Press.

Alexiou, M. (1974). *The ritual lament in Greek tradition.* London: Cambridge University Press.

Lattimore, R. (1962). *Themes in Greek and Latin epitaphs.* Urbana, IL: University of Chicago Press.

Tashjian, D. & Tashjian, A. (1974). *Memorials for children of change.* Middletown, CT: Wesleyan University Press.

Wallis, C.L. (1973). *American epitaphs. Grave and humorous.* New York: Dover Press.

EUTHANASIA

This is the dawning of the age of longevity, leading to what has been called "the biomedical revolution" (Veatch, 1976). Advances in public health measures, pharmacology, surgery, and technology are prolonging lives far beyond our earlier expectations and helping people remain alive who otherwise would not have survived. However, the increase in life expectancy and improvements in medical care have created problems of their own. Many are concerned that the quantity of life is sometimes purchased at the cost of its quality. Numerous new medical and ethical decisions must be made, such as those regarding comatose people. Within this context, euthanasia has become a very controversial topic.

The dictionaries define euthanasia both as a painless, peaceful, or good death and as the means taken to bring this about. It is especially about the latter definition—the "means"—that conflict races. Attempts have been made to do away with the controversy through semantics, by banishing the word *euthanasia*. "The fact that the term can mean both 'any good death' and 'a morally outrageous death' justifies a moratorium on its use" (Veatch, 1976). However, the problems will not go away no matter what words we use.

The Case for Euthanasia

Since many lives can be prolonged today beyond the point of anything but a vegetative existence, should treatment be continued indefinitely? If not, when should it be discontinued? Should severely disabled people be forced to remain on life-support machines they have learned to detest? To such questions there are probably no answers that will satisfy everyone. However, together with the burgeoning of life-probabilities there has been a growing support of the euthanasia movement with its emphasis on permitting people to die if and when they so wish. This growth has been signaled by the increase and acceptance of such organizations as The Hemlock Society, Concern for Dying, the Society for the Right to Die, and Americans Against Human Suffering.

The euthanasia movement has provided some ground rules, of which the following are a sample. These refer primarily to cases in which the person has a choice or has someone else acting as representative or alter ego (Richman, 1987).

- Euthanasia is based upon a supreme respect for the individual, including the ability to take charge of his or her own life. The mentally competent person is the best guide for choosing when and how the end of his or her life will take place.
- Euthanasia should be considered when there is no hope, no alternative save further misery, and when medicine helps only to prolong dying, not living.

The literature provides some good examples of what not to do. For example, the *British Journal of Medicine* for 1968 (reported in Beauchamp & Chambliss, 1983), described "A Man Who Was Not Permitted to Die." This man was a 68-year-old physician with severe heart disease and a large, spreading carcinoma of the stomach. He had already been revived from one cardiac arrest episode, and had requested in writing that he be permitted to die the next time a heart attack occurred. Shortly after, he suffered five cardiac arrests in one day—and the medical team's emergency procedures revived him each time. The physician-patient spent the next three weeks in frequent episodes of projectile vomiting that alternated with generalized seizures. During this time he was kept alive by intravenous feeding, blood transfusions, and a careful twenty-four-hour monitoring of his vital signs. Finally, he could no longer breathe on his own, so arrangements were being made to place him on a respirator. It was at this moment that his heart stopped for good. When confronted with such cases, by no means uncommon, one might well judge that it would have been better medicine to let nature take its course in the first place.

- Euthanasia is advocated when there will be a severe emotional burden or financial drain upon the family, without any genuine hope for cure, amelioration, or improvement.

- No extraordinary means should be used in the absence of a clear medical goal.

Few people would argue in favor of the extraordinary means used to keep the unfortunate patient mentioned above alive for another three weeks, especially when he had requested not to be resuscitated. "Extraordinary means," however, is a vague term that has become as much a legal as a medical matter.

A landmark case of this type was that of Karen Ann Quinlan, a young woman who lapsed into an irreversible coma after ingesting an overdose of pills combined with alcohol. At the time, this case received national attention, particularly the emotional distress experienced by her adoptive parents. After some time, her adoptive parents petitioned to have her taken off the respirator that presumably had kept her alive. The courts granted their request. That Ms. Quinlan continued to breathe on her own after the respirator was turned off was an interesting development, but not the main point. The publicity accorded the case brought the public a long way towards acceptance of the idea that life support machinery could be discontinued when the person's condition is untreatable and irreversible. It should be noted that Ms. Quinlan was unresponsive throughout this long period of time and someone else had to speak in her stead.

- Euthanasia upholds the freedom and rights of a fully conscious and competent individual to rid him or herself voluntarily of unnecessary suffering and loss of personal dignity when the poor quality of life makes continued living unbearable.

Another landmark case followed from the request of Elizabeth Bouvia in California to be permitted to refuse life-prolonging measures, including food and drink. It should be noted that she was not asking that the procedures be withheld, but only that she be given the right to decide.

- Euthanasia upholds the freedom of an individual to request the ending of his or her life by others when severe disability or other conditions have made life unbearable.

An example was Jamie Martin, a woman whose neck and back were broken in an automobile accident, leaving her severely disabled. Gary Weidner loved and took care of her. Finally, at her request, he killed her. Weidner was charged and convicted of manslaughter and given the maximum penalty.

The foregoing examples have been presented roughly in order of their general social acceptability, starting with a person whose death would have occurred quickly without resuscitation and other "extraordinary measures" and moving to those in which the individuals were afflicted with severe disabilities, but not terminally ill. The death wishes of Elizabeth Bouvia, Jamie Martin, and many others shade off into "rational suicide" and assisted suicide. They all, however, are based upon the belief that wishes regarding one's own death are to be respected and followed, especially when the person has publicly declared that no extraordinary measures should be taken to prolong life. The obligation to follow the person's wishes may be further strengthened when a living will has been prepared and filed, and when someone has been appointed to use the durable power of attorney in case the individual becomes no longer capable of representing him or herself. These wishes are to be followed when the person is rational, mentally sound, and has not been unduly influenced by those who might stand to gain by the death. Thus, there are safeguards, say the advocates of euthanasia. Not so, say their critics.

The Case for Survival

This is an age of impersonality and dehumanization in medicine, where machines and laboratory tests have replaced the doctor who made home visits and had a special relationship with his or her patients. Life and death issues were a natural part of that relationship. Today, such matters have become mechanized, and the image of a stranger pulling the plug that maintains life has become the symbol of the New Euthanasia. To pull the plug more frequently is not the answer, declare the opponents of euthanasia. Indeed, concomitant with the growth of euthanasia advocacy has been the intensification of its opposition from both religious and secular quarters. Some of the arguments are as follows:

- Free choice does not mean a rejection of spiritual beliefs and principles. All human life contains a spark of the divine and is sacred, even at the end. To shorten a life even for a moment is not permitted—not even to relieve suffering, and not for those deformed, disabled, or otherwise unable to care for themselves.

- Suffering can ennoble as well as destroy. However, the impersonality of medicine and sometimes nursing encourages the last resort of ending the patient's suffering. Death to relieve suffering, however, is not even a necessary choice. In this respect, advances in pain management are a boon to the severely and the terminally ill and should be made available to all who have such needs.

- The limitations of human decision making and wisdom have led to the misuse of euthanasia both by individuals and by society. Critics point to the notorious practices of the Nazis, who put to death hundreds of thousands of "undesirables," including the retarded, the disabled, and the medically ill, as well as criminals. The purpose of maintaining German superiority and the purity of German "blood" does not stand up to either moral or scientific scrutiny, yet it was this Nazi version of euthanasia, carried out by physicians, that prepared the German people for the practice of genocide.

As George Stein (1988) has pointed out, there were ample precedents for such views in Germany and other European nations well before Hitler. Proponents of euthanasia assert that such perversions could not occur in a democracy where the emphasis is upon rational and personal choice. In response, Longmore (1987) described a form of social Darwinism and advocacy of euthanasia in the American writings of early twentieth-century biologists and anthropologists. These writings were basically similar to the German and other European forerunners of the Nazis.

- The history of euthanasia is replete with covert prejudice against the poor, the ill, the severely handicapped, elderly people, and more recently, those with AIDS.

Longmore (1987), for example, convincingly traced the inadequate treatment accorded Elizabeth Bouvia to the subtle social bias against the physically disabled. Despite the evidence of an accumulation of stresses and life crises which strained her ability to cope and broke down her self-esteem, the courts ruled that Ms. Bouvia's wish to die was due solely to her physical disability—and that this was therefore a sufficient and acceptable reason to approve her ending her life. To paraphrase the wise advice to the physician, "Euthanasia, heal thyself."

■ There has been a gradual broadening of the criteria for "no extraordinary means."

Karen Ann Quinlan had her respiratory supports removed but remained alive and breathing on her own for years, during which time she was fed by feeding tube. In a more recent similar case, Nancy Ellen Jobes was also in a coma, breathing without artificial supports. The courts granted her family's request that the feeding tube be removed, and she died. Murray Putzer also requested that his feeding tube be removed, and he, too, died of starvation and dehydration while conscious. Now, Americans Against Human Suffering are working for approval of a measure that would allow a terminally ill person to be legally put to death at his or her request through a lethal injection by a doctor. This is the slippery slope in action.

Most of the foregoing objections are in the public domain, having become prominent in the literature. I came to the study of euthanasia, however, after almost a quarter of a century devoted to the study, treatment, and prevention of suicide. What follows are observations and comparisons based primarily upon my clinical experiences.

■ Among those who choose euthanasia, there is a prevalence of "tunnel vision," defined as the absence of perceived alternatives to death, a conviction that there is no other solution. However, if there is no alternative, then euthanasia is not based upon free choice but, rather, an absence of choice.

■ There is often a failure to recognize the crisis nature of the decision to die, the implication being that crisis intervention approaches should be used.

■ There is often a failure to recognize that the crisis can include the family and important others as well as the patient, and that all these people may affect the decision. Any "one cause" reason, therefore, is highly suspect. "Being a burden," for example, is not a valid reason for choosing death. Rather, such a statement communicates the existence of tensions that should be reduced and of family problems that need to be resolved.

Discussion

Euthanasia has a place in modern medicine. The criticisms it has engendered of the prolongation of dying and its advocacy of permitting people to let go of life when death would be a merciful release are commendable. However, there are also valid criticisms of euthanasia. These include the fact that euthanasia bears many similarities to suicidal behaviors of all kinds; its supporters may not clearly understand the complex nature of personal autonomy, nor the powerful and subtle role of others in arriving at life or death decisions.

Fortunately, there are some hopeful signs that the differences between the sensible supporters and the flexible opponents of euthanasia are not entirely irreconcilable. Agreement is already present in some areas, such as the avoidance of extraordinary medical measures to prolong dying. The hospice movement also offers a major potential for mutual agreement.

Hospitals and other institutions that are involved with the seriously ill and disabled could extend their attention to the psychological, social, and family pressures faced by those patients. Fost (1987) noted that many apparently ethical dilemmas faced by medicine are often based upon a lack of knowledge. His very sensible solution, therefore, is to bring all the professions together to share the information. One can build on this proposal by suggesting that the patient, the family, and other significant persons also be included. In addition to information exchange, everyone involved in the situation should be given the opportunity to air emotional and interpersonal factors.

However, not everyone is qualified to deal with such a complex situation. The major aspect of my proposal, therefore, is the development of a team of medical and behavioral scientists who are knowledgeable about the medical and psychosocial nature of illness, disability, and dying, as well as training in family crisis intervention. This team could be made available to the medical and surgical departments of the hospital. Their goals would be to reduce the tensions and burdens in the patient and family, and help release the caring and cohesive forces, and ultimately facilitate a genuinely free choice.

See also Brain Death; Concern for Dying; *Euthanasia Review* (Journal); Hemlock Society; Hospice: Philosophy and Practice; (The) Living Will; Suicide; Suicide: Assisted.

—JOSEPH RICHMAN

References

Beauchamp, T.L. & Chambliss, J.F. (1983). *Principles of biomedical ethics.* 2nd ed. New York: Oxford University Press.

Fost, N.C. (1987). "What is an 'ideal ethical observer?'" In R. Cross (Ed.) *The value of many voices: Summary of the conference.* Denver: University of Colorado at Denver, Graduate School of Public Affairs, 58–63.

Longmore, P.D. (1987). "Elizabeth Bouvia, assisted suicide and social prejudice." *Issues in Law and Medicine, 3*: 141–68.

Maguire, D.C. (1975). *Death by choice.* New York: Schocken.

Richman, J. (1981). "Marital psychotherapy and terminal illness." In A.S. Gurman (Ed.), *Questions and answers in the practice of family therapy.* New York: Brunner/Mazel, 139–54.

Richman, J. (1986). *Family therapy for suicidal people.* New York: Springer.

Richman, J. (1987). "Sanctioned assisting suicide: Impact on family relations." *Issues in Law and Medicine, 3*: 53–63.

Stein, G.J. (1988). "Biological science and the roots of Nazism." *American Scientist, 75*: 50–58.

Veatch, R.M. (1976). *Death, dying, and the biological revolution.* New Haven, CT: Yale University Press.

Verwoerdt, A. (1966). *Communication with the fatally ill.* Springfield, IL: Charles C. Thomas.

EUTHANASIA REVIEW (JOURNAL)

The *Euthanasia Review* is a quarterly journal sponsored by The Hemlock Society and published by Human Sciences Press. Established in 1986, this publication is "dedicated to the Hemlock Society's mission to disseminate information regarding active and passive euthanasia. It will publish serious articles on the right to die, mercy killings, living wills, medical ethics, rational suicide, legal reform, religious attitudes, health costs and sociological trends in euthanasia."

The contents of a typical issue (Volume 2, Number 3) included articles titled, "Euthanasia in the Courts," "Helping a Daughter to Die," "Compassionate Crimes," "The Law of Assisted Suicide," "Theological Reflections on Euthanasia," and a book review.

Manuscripts should be sent (double-spaced, in triplicate) to:

The Editors
Derek Humphry and Ann Wickett
The Euthanasia Review
C/O The Hemlock Society
PO Box 66218
Los Angeles, CA 90066

The style given in the *American Psychological Association Publication Manual,* 3d Edition, should be employed in preparing the manuscript for editorial consideration.

Subscription and advertising information can be obtained from

Human Sciences Press
72 Fifth Avenue
New York, NY 10011

The *Euthanasia Review* is indexed or abstracted in *APA Psychological Abstracts, Philosopher's Index, A Matter of Fact, Family Research Database,* and *Family Study Abstracts.*

See also Euthanasia; Hemlock Society; (The) Living Will.

—ROBERT KASTENBAUM

EXTREME UNCTION

The Epistle of St. James (5:14–15) includes the passage: "Is any sick among you? Let him call for the elders of the church; and let him pray over him, anointing him with oil in the name of the Lord. And the prayer of the faithful shall save the sick, and the Lord shall raise him up; and if he have committed sins, they shall be forgiven him."

This is thought (Ward, 1986) to be the scriptural origin of the sacrament known as extreme unction (from the Latin *unctio extreme*, "last anointing"). The purpose of this sacrament is to ask for the forgiveness of sins and for recovery. It is understood that the prayer can only request these blessings; the disposition depends upon God's will.

Both the Eastern Orthodox Church and the Roman Catholic Church administer forms of the extreme unction. In the Roman Catholic version, a priest dips his thumb in sanctifed oil and then makes the sign of the cross on the eyes, ears, nose, lips, hands, and feet of the recipient. Speaking in Latin, the priest prays, saying, "Through this holy anointing and by His most tender mercy may the Lord pardon whatever sins you have committed . . . by your sight, by your hearing, by your hands," etc.

There had been a custom of administering extreme unction only on the verge of death. A 1963 Vatican Council decree ruled that this sacrament could "more fittingly be called 'anointing of the sick'." This has led to a broader use of the sacrament, including now for people who are seriously ill but who are not necessarily in immediate peril of death. Many Catholics have received the comfort of what was formerly known as extreme unction who have subsequently survived their illnesses. The expanded use of this sacrament may also be changing the traditional perception in hospital situations that the arrival of a priest signified a deathbed mission.

See also Survival Beliefs and Practices: Roman Catholic.

—ROBERT KASTENBAUM

References

Book of James, New Testament.
Ward, C. (1986). *The Christian sourcebook.* New York: Ballentine Books.

F

FOUNDATION OF THANATOLOGY

This organization was established in 1967 to promote improved psychosocial and medical care for patients critically ill or dying from cancer, heart disease, stroke, and diabetes, among other diseases, and for their families. Based mainly at Columbia-Presbyterian Medical Center (New York City), the Foundation operates nationally and draws upon the support of professionals from the allied health sciences. Participants in Foundation activities have included members of fourteen medical specialties, as well as representatives of psychology, dentistry, nursing, social work, law, religion and theology, funeral services, and other fields.

The major emphasis of the Foundation is to disseminate information regarding the problems inherent in contemplating life-threatening illness, and coping with loss, separation, grief, and bereavement. At the time of this writing, the Foundation has held sixty-eight educational symposiums on a variety of death-related issues. From these the Foundation has generated a large number of books, monographs, and research reports. Many additional symposiums and publications are planned.

Four periodicals are published under the auspices of the Foundation. *Advances in Thanatology* is an academic quarterly that focuses on a single theme in each issue. *Archives of the Foundation of Thanatology* is a quarterly publication that includes abstracted and selected manuscripts from Foundation symposiums. A recent addition to the Foundation's publication program is *Loss, Grief, and Care,* a quarterly thematic journal of professional practice. The other periodical is *Thanatology Abstracts.*

Those wishing further information regarding the Foundation of Thanatology are invited to telephone (212) 928-2066 or write to:

Dr. Austin H. Kutscher, President
The Foundation of Thanatology
630 West 168th Street
New York, NY 10032
—MAXINE LAZARUS

FUNERALS

At various times in history society has been preoccupied with thoughts of death or has taken all possible evasive actions to avoid such thoughts. But no matter how people choose to think about death, certain realities demand attention. The human corpse is perhaps the most basic and compeling facet of this reality. Those expecting the imminent appearance of the Anti-Christ on the verge of the year 1000 AD could think about little except death and damnation. By contrast, in mid-twentieth-century America, health care professionals as well as laypeople often made elaborate efforts to avoid discussing or even thinking about death (Feifel, 1959). Although these societies differed greatly in their attitudes toward death as well as in many other ways, both had to confront the reality of the corpse. "This is a dead body. What should we do with it?"

Funeral photograph ca.1940. By the 1930s, professional photographers had developed several standard "shots" in which caskets and funeral symbols were displayed, with the face of the deceased now consigned to the background. Photo property of Jay Ruby, The Center for Visual Communication. Reprinted by permission.

The funeral, then, represents a near universal response to a universal situation. In the enormous variety of funeral practices (e.g., Habenstein & Lamers, 1974), those of one culture may seem bizarre, even incomprehensible, to people of another culture, but each affords the comfort of tradition in its own place. Striking as the surface differences may be, the funeral serves fundamentally similar purposes in all human societies. The Tibetan priests who preside over a sky burial to the accompaniment of bells, gongs, and prayer wheels seem to be doing something quite different from what was accomplished by the Russian specialists who installed the corpse of Lenin in a custom-made viewing structure. Kites and other birds of prey will quickly reduce the Tibetan corpse to

the purity of bone, while Lenin's preserved body is still on display. But both procedures served the same two basic functions: to make a final disposition of the body, and to do so through a process that expresses the society's needs, beliefs, and meanings.

The cliché "funerals are for the living" has reached the status of a supposed self-evident truth. Funerals certainly are for the living, but this statement passes too quickly over the deep concerns people may have for the dead. History and literature are replete with examples of sacrifices made and risks taken to see that a deceased loved one receive all the attention, ritual, and honors to which he or she is entitled. This theme is dominant in several Greek dramas that survive from the clas-

Anonymous deceased child, ca.1890. Funeral photographs at this time often represented a "last sleep" or an "almost still alive" theme with the deceased individual in familiar domestic surroundings. Photo property of Jay Ruby, The Center for Visual Communication. Reprinted by permission.

sical period. For example, *The Suppliants* by Euripedes opens with a group of bereaved mothers who have come to the Temple of Demeter at Eleusis. Aethra, sympathetic to their cause, asks for divine intervention: "so now their mothers would bury in the grave the dead, whom the spear hath slain, but the victors prevent them and will not allow them to take up the corpses, spurning Heaven's laws." The Chorus of Mothers, on their knees, add their plea: "and my old lips beseech thee . . . rescue from the slain my children's bodies, whose limbs, by death relaxed, are left a prey to savage mountain beasts, beholding the bitter tears which spring to my eyes and my old wrinkled skin torn by my hands; for what can I do else? who never laid out my children dead within my halls, nor now behold their tombs heaped up with earth . . . .so in my

sore distress I do beseech thee of my misery. Place in my hands my son's dead body that I may throw my arms about his hapless limbs" (Euripedes, 1971, p. 258).

This motive has not perished with the years. There was such distress when young soldiers died far from home during the War Between the States that a major national effort was mounted to bring the bodies home for burial. This effort led to the perfection of embalming techniques and encouraged the development of modern funeral directing services (See **Embalming**). Intensive efforts to bring the bodies of casualties home have been made by parties to armed conflicts around the world since then. Anxiety, rage, and a sense of unfinished business are often experienced by family members who have not had the opportunity to provide a suitable funeral for loved ones who have died away from home. Mourning and grief processes may be delayed, intensified, prolonged, and complicated when the need for a funeral process has not been met (See also **Grief: Missing in Action Families**). Even people anticipating a peaceful death may prearrange transportation for burial in a town that means home for them (See **Burial: "Going Home"**).

Symbolic Interactions Between the Living and the Dead

The funeral process enables the living to pursue a variety of symbolic interactions with the dead and this, in turn, often helps to channel interactions among the living as well.

A contemporary northern Mexican funeral provides one illustration of the way "that social relationships with the deceased continue, in a sense, even after one dies" (Osuna & Reynolds, 1970, p. 259). According both to Catholic belief and Mexican folk culture, the body of the deceased, in this instance Tia Elena, a 50-year-old woman, must be distinguished from her soul and person. "Nevertheless, the body remains *a symbol* of the deceased person. It is treated with respect . . . spoken of as 'she' . . . and it is even kissed as one might kiss a loved *person* farewell." Tia Elena's body was the center of attention throughout the ceremonial period following her death. Three peaks of emotional response were shown by her survivors, and all focused on the body: "when it arrived at the home, when it left the home following the wake, and when it was lowered into the grave." The immediate family was present at all these significant moments. It was their right and also their responsibility to express their love for the body that now was a symbol of their deceased family member.

> The wake itself may be described as a series of reunions--reunions among survivors and between survivors and the deceased. The coffin was "center stage." It was placed in a conspicuous place in the living room of the house in which the wake was held. Some attention was given to the proper positioning of the coffin since, with the hinged lid open, there was a natural "front" and "back." Chairs and sofas around the room were arranged to face the body. Persons who entered the living room were expected to face the body and not turn their backs to it. Voices were lowered as one approached and entered the living room. Throughout the wake people would socialize together, then slip in for a period of prayer, meditation, or recollection, then back to the kitchen chores, chatting, or sleeping, and, again, back to the body. . . . Thus, the body was treated with symbolic respect in some ways even greater than that accorded a living person. It, too, was a focal point for reunion (p. 260).

Respectful symbolic interactions with the body of Tia Elena continued throughout the night of the wake, during the next day's processions to the church and cemetery, and during the leavetaking ceremonies at the grave. Throughout this process there was also much discussion about the life of Tia Elena--how kind a person she had been, how well she looked after her family, and so forth. People also wanted to know if she had spoken any last words, expressed any last wishes, and how, in general, she had responded to the approach of death. These discussions took on the character of a selective recollection; that is, the survivors emphasized both the positive aspects of Tia Elena's personality and of her last days on earth. Furthermore, particular attention was given to her final wishes, which concerned some aspects of the funeral arrangements. Her wishes regarding

the distribution of her personal effects were also regarded as binding.

The expression of grief throughout the funeral process was somewhat different for men and women. The women were expected to weep, even to faint. A woman who could not cry might be considered cold and unfeeling. It was also acceptable but not required for men to weep. In this as well as in other Mexican and Mexican-American funeral processes that have been observed by outsiders, men are not considered any less manly or *macho* for expressing their deep feelings of loss at this time. Nevertheless, it was also acceptable for men to restrain themselves from weeping. The women mourners also differed from the men by wearing black or very dark clothing throughout the funeral ceremonies, a practice not followed by the men. Mexican and Mexican-American funerals do not all necessarily follow the specific ceremonies and traditions that were observed in this situation. However, Tia Elena's funeral process provides one clear and vivid example of the way in which survivors can continue their symbolic interactions with the deceased.

Another well-observed example has been found among the Melanesian people of New Guinea. The Kaliai comprise a small (approximately 1,000) and geographically isolated society. As with most people, the funeral ceremonies practiced by the Kaliai are intimately linked with their general beliefs concerning life and death (Counts, 1979). Bodily death is a natural and inevitable event, but it signals the beginning of a transition period between human life and the achievement of a new superhuman kind of existence. This transformation can take place only for those who have already reached a certain level of mental and social maturity. The passage from infancy and early childhood to full human (social) life is marked by the individual's ability to discuss his or her dream life. Those who die before they achieve this level of maturity are not accorded funerary rites, their bodies being simply exposed to the elements.

The major function served by the extended funeral/memorial process among the Kaliai is to help the deceased person become liberated from remaining ties to the living, and vice versa. When death can be foreseen, advance efforts will be made to lessen the obligations and debts that bind the individual to society. Both before and after death, these efforts primarily take the form of the exchange of wealth and material goods. Such exchanges are at the core of Kaliai social interaction during life, and so they continue after death until an acceptable balance has been achieved.

A "good death" is possible in Kaliai society, but it is a difficult and not very common outcome. This desirable goal does not involve either acceptance or seeking of death. A person threatened by illness, injury, or the hostility of others should attempt to stay alive by whatever means. However, when death is in clear prospect, its reality should be faced. Next, the dying person should take some initiative in severing his or her ties with society, thereby creating a friendly situation when the time comes for departure. "What militates against the achievement of a good death for nearly everyone is that the behavior required of every person passing through a normal life cycle in Kaliai society assures that at some point he or she will offend someone or something, either by a violation of rights, the causing of shame, or the arousal of envy sufficient to cause the other to kill the offender. Nearly everyone, then, dies before his time, being torn out of the web of relationships and leaving it to his survivors to finish the task of balancing the flow" (Counts, pp. 42–43).

As described by anthropologist David Counts, then, the extensive funeral ceremonies undertaken by the Kaliai are intended to reverse what has often been a lifelong pattern of discord and alienation and to do so mainly through the ritualistic exchange of material goods. Although markedly different from the northern Mexico funeral, the New Guinea ritual also demonstrates the importance of symbolic interactions between the living and the dead.

Orthodox Jews provide still another example. Burial arrangements must be prompt and simple. There is no place for showy and extravagant fripperies. Obeying their strict laws and customs, Orthodox Jews reject embalming and cremation (Goldberg, 1981–82). Affirming their faith in God through the Kaddish prayer, Orthodox Jews "sit *Shiva*" for seven days after the death. The family is united in grief. At the conclusion of this period, the mourners may return to their daily lives but continue to remember the dead in both ceremonial and personal ways.

The funerals of famous and powerful people generally produce a greater response from society. In the history of the United States dramatic examples include public response to funeral arrangements of leaders such as Abraham Lincoln, John F. Kennedy, and Martin Luther King, Jr., but also charismatic entertainers such as Rudolph Valentino and Elvis Presley.

But comparable magnitude does not necessarily mean comparable emotions and actions. Two significant deaths in the respective histories of Eastern and Western civilization illustrate how different may be the response of society to the death of a leader (Kastenbaum, 1986). Ch'in Shih-huan-ti, known as the first emperor of a united China, was one of the most powerful and innovative monarchs ever to rule on earth. The Great Wall was but one of his achievements. Lost for more than two thousand years, his great tomb was rediscovered in 1974 beneath a mound of earth in Shensi province. The remarkable life-sized terra cotta army found in his tomb quickly became a major international tourist attraction. Two points are significant about the funeral and entombment of Ch'in Shih-huan-ti. Having lived on a grand scale, Ch'in obviously thought that he should also die in a similar manner. However, it is almost certain that more than high self-regard was involved. His "power death" asserted dynastic claims. A monarch's achievement, no matter how stupendous, is always threatened by death. His funeral and tomb were probably intended to maintain an appearance of such unassailable might that his empire and his chosen successors could have no serious opposition. The other point is that it didn't work. Having made numerous enemies across the land, Ch'in's remains and his works were attacked with fierce determination soon after his death.

By contrast, the death of Prince Albert, consort to Queen Victoria, elicited a totally different reaction. Disliked and ridiculed by many during his life as a foreigner who had dared marry a Queen of England, Albert became an admired and beloved cult figure soon after his death. Many characteristics of more recent personal death-cult responses emerged upon Albert's death. Britishers in large numbers purchased Prince Albert statues, belt clasps, lamps, pencil cases, and other mementoes. There were reasons for this turnabout. The deep grief expressed by Queen Victoria confirmed the love she had felt for him, and public opinion, given a second chance, recognized that Albert had been a gifted person who was loyal to his adopted nation. Postmortem adulation included emulation of the Queen's mourning behavior and the creation of numerous statues and edifices dedicated to his memory (one notable example: London's Victoria and Albert Museum, among the great museums of the world). The funeral itself and the extensive memorialization process served the function of *symbolically incorporating* Albert into the British Empire. Not only was Albert, in death, an Englishman, but many took him as a prime embodiment of the self-images and aspirations of the Victorian Era.

Funerals Today

Funeral services remain important today for most families and most societies. However, there is also a pattern of conflict and controversy. The ancient and nearly universal process of observing funeral ceremonies has found opposition from those who see such behavior as inappropriate to contemporary beliefs and values, and also from those who have encountered sharp business practices or outright fraud in the arrangement of commercial funerals.

One current example of conflict can be found in mainland China. The Communist regime (especially under Mao Tse-Tung and Chou En-Lai) strongly discouraged the traditional practice of ground burial and all its accompanying ritual. Instead, Chinese were to cremate their dead and scatter the ashes. This new doctrine was supported by such actions as the construction of hundreds of crematoriums and the offering of "bargain" prices for cremation. This "modern" approach to body disposal became standard practice. Now, however, the old ways are returning. Taking advantage of the liberalization that followed the termination of the repressive

Cultural Revolution, some Chinese have become prosperous enough to afford tomb burial for themselves and their ancestors (Browning, 1988). Authorities are reported as being disturbed over the large acreage of valuable farmland that is being converted to burial space, as well as by the burgeoning demand for the limited supply of wood. Accompanying this revival of the ancient tradition is the reappearance of the "Feast of Hungry Ghosts," a holiday observance forbidden by the former regime. In this instance, then, the forces of pragmatic economic planning and modernism have been countered by the people's opportunity to restore a cherished tradition.

Controversy and conflict have taken a different form in North America. Here a focus of dissension has been what many have seen as the unacceptable expense and ostentation involved in funeral arrangements. These practices were held up to criticism and ridicule by Nancy Mitford (1963) in *The American Way of Death,* a book that attracted wide readership and discussion. Other books of a more scholarly nature (e.g., Bowman, 1959; Irion, 1966) also raised questions and concerns. Were Americans attempting to compete with each other by overspending on funerals? Were funeral directors taking advantage of the public? Were funerals even needed in today's world, or were they useless relics from our collective past?

Although these questions are still debated, some constructive patterns have emerged in recent years. Federal regulations in the United States now require funeral directors to make their prices readily available to all prospective customers. This disclosure regulation and other provisions give the consumer ready access to information needed in making decisions, although consumers must still be alert enough to take advantage of this opportunity. Furthermore, a number of human service organizations and consumer advocacy groups now provide information and guidance for those who would like some help in examining the available alternatives. Inexpensive funerals are available through local Memorial Society chapters, and useful guidebooks are in circulation (Lamont, 1954; *Manual of Simple Burial,* 1964).

The funeral industry itself has spoken out against those individuals and firms that have engaged in deceptive practices or applied undue pressure on family members. The National Funeral Directors Association and many of its members are aware of the standards that should be maintained and realize that the reputation of the entire industry is threatened whenever one funeral director engages in a shoddy practice. Moreover, there is a marked increase in the number of funeral directors who have educated themselves in such fields as counseling, psychology, and sociology and become sensitive to the needs of bereaved persons. Deceptive and fraudulent practices have not been eradicated, but the consumer now has an improved chance of finding funeral directors who will listen carefully to their needs and provide suitable arrangements.

Through some of their own sponsored research (e.g., Marks & Calder, 1982), funeral directors have become more aware of the public's expectations and wishes, as well as how funeral services are evaluated by family members. This is another encouraging sign that, as a whole, funeral directors are attempting to meet emerging needs in a responsible manner. Nevertheless, the future of funeral services will continue to depend much upon the way each of us chooses to think about life and death and how honestly and completely we choose to share these thoughts with those closest to us.

See also Burial: "Going Home"; Cemeteries; Cremation; Embalming; Grief; Grief: Missing in Action Families; Kaddish; National Funeral Directors Association; Survival Beliefs and Practices: Roman Catholic; Tombs.

—ROBERT KASTENBAUM

References

Bowman, L. (1959). *The American funeral: A study in guilt, extravagance, and sublimity.* Washington, DC: Public Affairs Press.

Browning, M. (1988). "Chinese desire for tomb burial takes good farmland out of use." *Arizona Republic,* July 3, p. AA10 (reprinted from *The Miami Herald*).

Counts, D.R. (1979). "The good death in Kaliai: Preparation for death in western New Britain." In R.A. Kalish (Ed.) *Death and dying: Views from many cultures.* Farmingdale, NY: Baywood, 39–44.

Euripides (1971). *The Suppliants.* Translated by E.P. Coleridge. In R.M. Hutchins (Ed.) *Great books of the Western world.* Chicago: Encyclopedia Britannica, Vol. 5, pp. 258–69.

Feifel, H. (Ed.) (1959). *The meaning of death.* New York: McGraw-Hill.

Goldberg, H.S. (1981–1982). "Funeral and bereavement rituals of Kota Indians and Orthodox Jews." *Omega, Journal of Death and Dying, 12*: 117–28.

Habenstein, R.W. & Lamers, W.M. (1974). *Funeral customs the world over.* 2nd rev. ed. Milwaukee: Bulfin.

Irion, P.E. (1966). *The funeral: Vestige or value?* New York: Abingdon Press.

Kastenbaum, R. (1986). *Death, society, and human experience.* Columbus, OH: Charles E. Merrill.

Lamont, C. (1954). *A humanist funeral service.* New York: Horizon Press.

Manual of simple burial (1964). Burnsville, NC: Celo Press.

Marks, A.S. & Calder, B.J. (1982). *Attitudes toward death and funerals.* Evansville, IL: Northwestern University, The Center for Marketing Sciences.

Mitford, N. (1963). *The American way of death.* New York: Simon & Schuster.

Osuna, P. & Reynolds, D.K. (1970). "A funeral in Mexico: Description and analysis." *Omega, Journal of Death and Dying, 1*: 249–70.

G

GRIEF

Grief can be defined as the highly personal and subjective set of responses that an individual makes to a real, perceived, or anticipated loss. Grief reactions occur in any loss situation, including divorce or separation as well as death. People grieve their own loss of health or function; loss of the life, health, function or relationship of others in which they have emotional investment (family, friends, national leaders, pets); loss of possessions; and loss of ideals, dreams, and hopes. Any of these losses can lead to grief whether they have already taken place or are impending or threatened.

Definitions

In recent years there have been attempts to distinguish the definition of "grief" from those of "mourning" and "bereavement." Bereavement can be defined as an objective state of loss, or a change of status resulting from loss. Bereavement, then, refers only to the basic fact of loss, while grief refers to the individual's response or feelings regarding that loss. One can grieve without having been bereaved, as, for example, in the case of anticipatory grief. Similarly, one can be bereaved yet not experience grief, as, for example, in situations in which the survivor has little or no emotional response to the death.

"Mourning" can be defined as the culturally patterned expressions or rituals that accompany loss and allow others to recognize that one has become bereaved. Wearing black and attending funerals are examples of mourning behaviors. Again, though, one can mourn without experiencing grief, or grieve without mourning. For example, a newly divorced person may experience a profound sense of grief, but there are few rituals or behaviors through which the feelings of loss can be expressed to others.

Although these distinct definitions of grief, mourning, and bereavement are becoming increasingly common and accepted by caregivers and researchers, there is still not a total consensus on their use. Particularly (but not exclusively) in older writings these terms may be used differently and even interchangeably. Freud (1917), for example, defines mourning as a normal reaction to loss.

Symptoms of Grief

The symptoms that individuals experience in grief can vary widely. Physical symptoms can include headaches, dizziness, exhaustion, muscular aches, menstrual irregularities, sexual impotency, loss of appetite, insomnia, feelings of tightness or hollowness, breathlessness, tremors and shakes, and oversensitivity to noise.

Bereaved people, particularly widows, do have a higher rate of mortality in the first year of loss (Rando, 1984). This may be a direct result of stress or changes in life-style and health attributable to the loss itself (although it can represent the effects of a shared lifestyle that caused the death of the partner). It is thus important that physical symptoms of grief be assessed and monitored by a physician who is alert to the survivor's loss and to the relationships between grief and illness.

Other grief symptoms are affective or emotional. Affective reactions can include anger, guilt, anxiety, a sense of helplessness, sadness, shock, yearning, numbness, and self-blame. Some bereaved experience a sense of relief or even a feeling of emancipation. This, however, may be followed by a sense of guilt. As in many situations of emotional crisis, contradictory feelings such as sadness and relief can be experienced at the same time.

Cognitive or mental symptoms of grief are also extensive. These include a sense of depersonalization, in which nothing seems real. There can also be an inability to concentrate, a sense of disbelief and confusion, an idealization of the deceased, a search for the meaning of life or death, dreams of the deceased, and a preoccupation with the image of the deceased. These cognitive symptoms can impair performance in work or school. A number of studies have shown that many bereaved persons may experience a vague sense of the deceased's continued presence or even fleeting auditory, visual, olfactory, or tactile hallucinatory experiences (e.g., Hoyt, 1980; Lindstrom, 1982). Most bereaved persons interpret such experiences positively as reassuring signs that the deceased person will be near them, or is happy and at peace, or that they themselves should continue with their lives. In some cases, however, experiences of "presence" are perceived negatively and inhibit the resolution of grief.

Behavioral symptoms of grief include crying, withdrawal, avoiding reminders of the deceased, seeking or carrying reminders of the deceased, overactivity, and a variety of changes in relationships with other people.

Grief may persist for a considerable time. It may take as long as three to five years to resolve a significant loss. Some recent research indicates that a continued sense of loss, an "empty space," can last indefinitely. Many bereaved people experience grief as a roller coaster series of highs and lows that tend to be intense at first and diminish over time. A wide range of intense symptoms are likely to be experienced in the first six to thirteen months, gradually diminishing thereafter. It is not uncommon for the bereaved person to experience painful episodes periodically— particularly at holidays, significant dates in the relationship, or at the anniversary of the death.

Each individual experiences grief as an unique reaction, varying in the intensity, pattern, time, and resolution of symptoms.

Resolution of Grief

Many factors influence the nature of a grief reaction and its resolution. These include:

1. The bereaved person's unique relationship with the deceased
2. The strength of the attachments
3. The degree of ambivalence and unfinished business in the relationship
4. The circumstances of death, including the length and nature of the illness, the preventability of the death, the conditions of the death (e.g., what happened at the time of death, where the bereaved was, etc.)
5. Reactions to previous loss
6. The personality and coping behaviors of the bereaved person
7. The bereaved person's ability to express emotions and seek and receive help
8. Social variables such as the strength and nature of the family system
9. The presence and nature of informal support systems, cultural and religious beliefs and practices
10. General health and life-style practices

The grief reaction of any given individual is highly personal and idiosyncratic. How people experience their loss and how they express (mourn) their loss in public is not a simple measure of their love and devotion to the deceased, but is the outcome of many interacting factors.

The ways in which bereaved people resolve their grief is also highly individual. Earlier observers attempted to look at the grief process as though it were a series of general stages beginning, for example, with shock and ending with recovery and resolution. However, more recent work has emphasized that the bereaved must complete certain tasks such as accepting the reality of the loss, experiencing and resolving the emotions associated with grief, readjusting to life without the deceased, withdrawing emotional energy from the deceased, and reinvesting in other and/or finding creative ways to retain the memory of the deceased (by dedicating oneself to fulfilling the deceased's ideals, for example), and perhaps reassessing and rebuilding the faith or philosophical system that had been challenged by the loss. The advantage of this kind of "task model" is its recognition that individuals may complete these tasks in different sequences and at different rates.

Over time, most bereaved people do resolve the loss, meaning that they reach a point in which they can remember the deceased without the extensive pain experienced earlier. Studies have generally shown that over 80 percent of bereaved persons resolve their losses without deleterious long-term effects. However, some bereaved people experience more complicated or atypical grief reactions (Rando, 1984; Worden, 1982).

These include chronic grief, in which the intensity does not diminish over time; exaggerated grief, in which certain symptoms, such as guilt or phobias, become highly intensified; delayed grief, in which grief expression is suppressed at the time of the loss and reappears later; and masked grief, in which the loss manifests itself in psychosomatic illness or maladaptive behaviors such as delinquency or substance abuse. Other long-term effects of unresolved grief can include mental or physical illness.

Assistance in Coping with Grief

There are many resources that can assist a person in coping with grief. Books that explain the grieving process or provide a first person account of grief can be helpful in cases of uncomplicated grief (e.g., Donnelly, 1987; Krementz, 1981; Loewinsohn, 1984; Schiff, 1987; Truman, 1987). Such resources can reassure bereaved people that their reactions are normal and understandable and remind them that grieving is a long process. Such books and articles can facilitate insight into one's own feelings and warn of times and circumstances (such as death anniversaries) that may be difficult, as well as suggest various coping strategies and provide hope of eventual resolution.

Others may find self-help groups, such as widows groups, or The Compassionate Friends, useful. These groups provide not only reassurance that grief is normal, but also a supportive environment in which individuals can express their feelings and rebuild the interactional networks that were disrupted by the loss. Individual grief-related counseling may be helpful to some people. Grief counselors seek to assist bereaved persons in completing the tasks of grieving. Counselors may help their bereaved clients explore what tasks are still uncompleted, what factors impede the resolution of these tasks, and what strategies might be used for this purpose. Parkes (1980) points out that self-help groups and counseling can be especially valuable for those who perceive that their family and friends are not supportive. For those who have more complicated or atypical grief reactions, it may be necessary to seek longer term therapy with a focus on identifying and resolving conflicts that have impeded the grieving process.

Some Studies and Theories

The phenomena of grief have long been recognized. Classical literature, including the Old and New Testaments, and the writings of Eastern and Western philosophers, are replete with observations on the nature of grief. Grief is also recognized in some of the classic writings in the behavioral and clinical sciences. One example has already been mentioned, Freud's (1917) essay, "On Mourning and Melancholia," in which he differentiated between normal and abnormal states of grief. In another significant contribution, Helene Deutsch (1937) commented on psychological factors in the absence of grief.

One of the most influential early studies of grief was Erich Lindemann's (1944) contribution, "Symptomatology and Management of Acute Grief." Lindemann studied people who had lost friends or relatives in Boston's Coconut Grove Fire (1942) and described their thoughts, feelings, and behaviors. This was one of the first empirically based studies that attempted to delineate the symptomatology and nature of normal grief. Another significant contribution to the understanding of grief is the work of C.M. Parkes on the process and recovery from grief as it had been experienced by samples of British widows.

Several theoretical models of the origin and nature of grief have been offered within the past thirty years. One of the most basic is the psychobiological perspective developed in the work of John Bowlby (1980). His theory emphasizes that attachment, or bonding, is an instinctual response found in many higher animals. When the object of that attachment was missing, certain behaviors were instinctual responses to the loss. These behaviors (crying, clinging, searching) were seen by Bowlby as biologically based responses that sought to restore the lost attachments and maintain the bond. When the object of attachment is permanently lost, as in death, these behaviors continue until the attachment is divested of emotional meaning and significance. A secondary purpose is also served by these behaviors, according to Bowlby. By expressing distress, they call upon the care, support, and protection of the larger social group. The psychobiological approach, then, sees grief as a natural, instinctive response to loss that continues until the bond is restored or the bereaved person is reconciled to the loss.

The medical model is another approach to grief. In this model, grief is perceived as a disease. Although this model builds upon the pioneer work of Lindemann, it is most clearly developed by George Engel (1961), who defines grief as "the characteristic response to the loss of a valued object, be it a loved person, a cherished possession, a job, status, home, country, an ideal, a part of the body, etc." Once this loss is experienced, according to Engel, uncomplicated grief runs a consistent course. This is thought to include an initial state of shock, an intermediate period in which the developing awareness of loss brings on a series of psychological, cognitive, affective, and behavioral symptoms, and a prolonged period of gradual recovery.

Engel insists that the process of grief has all the characteristics of a disease—suffering, impairment, predictable course, and symptomatology. The fact that grief may be modified by social and psychological variables such as the abruptness of the loss or the nature of the relationship is not unlike many other diseases which also are affected by external variables. Similarly, the fact that grief is universal and often does not require medical treatment is also characteristic of many other disease processes. And, as Engel notes, whether or not a condition requires medical attention is a social judgment that changes over time. Epilepsy, mental illness, and alcoholism are examples of conditions that have come to be recognized only recently as diseases. Finally, Engel reminds readers that grief, again like many other disease states, can have a normal, uncomplicated course of recovery, or can become complicated and lead to other pathological conditions, such as mental illness, or physical illnesses of a life-threatening nature.

Still another paradigm views grief as a psychological trauma brought about by the loss of a loved object. This model is historically the earliest, based upon the work of Freud who saw grief as a normal defense against the psychological trauma of loss. To Freud, grief is a crisis but does not necessarily require professional assistance. Left alone, the condition will improve over time. Freud (1917) made a marked distinction between the normal state of mourning and its pathological variant, melancholia. Others have since suggested that grief occurs along a continuum, moving from normal grief through pathological reactions and, in some cases, to full blown neuroses and psychosomatic reactions at the other extreme.

Since the mid-1970s, there has been increased research on many facets of grief (Raphael, 1983). Much of this research has attempted to delineate the particular problems that are posed for survivors by different types of loss (husband, wife, child, parent, sibling, lover, friend), and varying conditions of loss (e.g., sudden death, suicide, accidental death, violent death, chronic disease). Taken as a whole, this active field of research is a powerful reminder that every loss creates its own distinctive sets of difficulties, issues, and concerns for each survivor.

See also Anticipatory Grief; Compassionate Friends; Grief; Grief: Death of a Child; Grief: Missing in Action Families; Grief, Vicarious; Grief Counseling; Psalms of Lament; Sudden Infant Death Syndrome (SIDS).

—KENNETH J. DOKA

References

Bowlby, J. (1980). *Attachment and loss: Loss.* Vol. 3. New York: Basic Books.

Clayton, P.J. (1979). "The sequelae and nonsequelae of conjugal bereavement." *Psychiatry, 136*: 1530–34.

Deutsch, H. (1937). "Absence of grief." *Psychoanalytic Quarterly, 6*: 12–22.

Donnelly, K. (1987). *Recovering from the loss of a parent.* New York: Gamut Books.

Engel, G.L. (1961). "Is grief a disease? A challenge for medical research." *Psychosomatic Medicine, 23*: 18–22.

Freud, S. (1917/Reprint 1957). "Mourning and melancholia." Standard Edition Vol. 14. London: Hogarth Press.

Hoyt, M. (1980). "Clinical notes regarding the experiences of 'presences' in mourning." *Omega, Journal of Death and Dying, 11*: 105–11.

Krementz, J. (1981). *How it feels when a parent dies.* New York: Knopf.

Lindemann, E. (1944). "Symptomatology and management of acute grief." *American Journal of Psychiatry, 101*: 141–49.

Lindstrom, B. (1982). "Exploring paranormal experience of the bereaved." Presented at Fifth Annual Conference of the Forum for Death Education and Counseling, September, San Diego.

Loewinsohn, R. (1984). *Survival handbook for widows.* Washington, DC: AARP.

Parkes, C.M. (1972). *Bereavement: Studies of grief in adult life.* New York: International Universities Press.

Parkes, C.M. (1980). "Bereavement counseling: Does it work?" *British Medical Journal, 281*: 3–6.

Rando, T. (1984). *Grief, dying, and death: Clinical interventions for caregivers.* Champaign, IL: Research Press.

Raphael, B. (1983). *The anatomy of bereavement.* New York: Basic Books.

Schiff, H. (1987). *Bereaved parent.* New York: Crown.

Worden, J.W. (1982). *Grief counseling and grief therapy.* New York: Springer.

GRIEF: DEATH OF A CHILD

The death of a child is unlike any other loss known. Studies have documented that parental grief is particularly severe, complicated and long-lasting, with major and unparalleled symptom fluctuations occurring over time. The typical experience of parental grief after a child's death closely resembles what is considered to be "unresolved" or "abnormal" grief after the deaths of others.

With the death of their child, parents have lost some of their own most precious hopes, dreams, and expectations. They have lost parts of themselves, each other, their family, and their future. In many ways, the age of the deceased child is irrelevant to the parents' grief, although they will be influenced somewhat by the developmental issues prevailing in the relationship at the time of the child's death. Age may have some relevance when the child who dies is at one end or another of the age spectrum, that is when the death is a miscarriage, stillbirth, or infant death, or the death of an adult child. Nevertheless, research indicates that no matter what the age of the deceased, the parents still have lost their "baby."

The Parent-Child Bond

There is a unique relationship between parent and child. The parent-child bond is the most intense that life can generate psychologically, socially, or physically. This bond begins long before birth as the parents project a variety of conscious and unconscious feelings, expectations, hopes, and needs onto their child-to-be. Since the child is an extension of the parents both biologically and psychologically, their feelings about him or her are a mixture of feelings about themselves and significant others. The child may signify any number of positive or negative values, as someone who will need and love the parent, a proof of the parent's maturity, a source for parental sense of purpose and social immortality.

In no other role except that of parent are there so many responsibilities that are either inherently assumed or assigned by society. Parents are expected to be all-loving, all-good, all-concerned, totally selfless, and motivated solely by the child and his or her welfare. These expectations can never be completely fulfilled. Parents may be burdened by unachievable ideals that fail to allow for the normal feelings of ambivalence, frustration, and anger that are part of any close relationship. Lacking legitimization for these unacceptable feelings and believing that they should be able to love, nurture, and protect the child in all situations without limit, parents may be haunted with guilt whenever these expectations are unmet. Additionally, parents tend to assume the roles of protector, provider, and problem-solver, becoming accustomed to being in control of what happens to and for the child.

When a Child Dies

When a child dies, those aspects of the relationship between parent and child that most reveal its intimacy and uniqueness are also those that most intensify grief. The death of a child multiplies the losses to self usually felt after the death of any close person. This is true not only because of the numerous investments placed in the child, but because mourning for the child means mourning for the self as well, since parental attachment is built upon a mixture of love for the child and self-love.

With the death of a child, there is a sense that parents have failed to sustain the basic functions of parenthood: to protect and provide for the child who should survive beyond the parents' own lives. This sense of failure leads to a monumental assault on parental identity. Parents report feeling "mutilated" and "disabled" not only from the specific loss of the child, but also from the ripping asunder of their adult identity that centered around providing and caring for the child. When they cannot carry out their core functional roles, parents experience an oppressive sense of failure, a loss of power and ability, and a deep sense of having been violated. These are major blows to the self-esteem and identity that bring additional feelings of disillusionment, emptiness, and insecurity.

A crucial factor in parental grief is the unnaturalness of the child predeceasing its parents. The natural cycle of life, in which the old die first and are replaced by the young, has been violated. The very orderliness of the universe seems to be undermined when this expectation is upset (Gorer, 1965).

Grief reactions of bereaved parents include all of the responses commonly found in any bereavement. However, these responses are likely to be especially intense when it is a child who has died. Guilt appears to be the single most pervasive parental response to the death of a child. Although guilt often is felt in grief reactions in general, this feeling is especially intense in parents who have expected themselves to be able to protect their child in every respect. Although their expectations may have been unrealistic, the resulting guilt can be overwhelming. Other intensified responses often include extreme anger, profound depression, an intense search for meaning, excruciating pain and yearning over the separation, and special problems in identification with the deceased.

Society has great problems with child death since this represents our worst fears. Since child death is so anxiety-provoking, bereaved parents are likely to become the victims of ostracism, sometimes reporting that they feel like "social lepers." Inappropriate expectations are placed upon them to keep their grief and mourning within "normal" bounds. Often deprived of social support by those who do not understand the intensity and meaning of parental grief, they may experience disorganization and impairments in reality testing. Insensitive and hurtful responses from society only exacerbate the deprivation, stress, and anxiety of bereaved parents.

Impact on the Marriage

The death of a child strikes both partners in the marital dyad simultaneously and confronts them with overwhelming loss. Each partner's most therapeutic resource is taken away, as the person to whom each would normally turn for support is also deeply involved in grief. Feelings of incompetence or insecurity in the marital role can develop as grief-stimulated changes in each person lead to a changed marital relationship.

It is erroneous to assume that both partners have suffered the same loss and will deal with it in the same way because they have lost the same child. Actually, each partner has sustained a different loss and will have a unique grief experience because each has had a separate and distinct relationship with the child. Bereaved parents must recognize this fact and not expect their mates to be equally distressed about the same things or at the same times as they are. Problems develop when partners assume that each should grieve in the same fashion. Individual ways of coping with grief should be recognized and respected (Rando, 1988). Differences in the grief experience and ways of coping with it can place additional stress on the marriage. One partner may feel rejected by his or her mate, or feel that the spouse did not love the child as much. This kind of misinterpretation is less likely to arise if parents realize that their differences in grief and mourning do not mean a lack of love. It is important to assure each other of love and support despite apparent differences in response to the overwhelming grief. It is useful to grant each other a wide latitude for individual expression of grief in order to avoid unnecessary problems. It is also helpful to recognize that at certain times their grief experiences and emotional needs may be further apart than at other times. These differences seem to be especially pronounced within a period two to five years after the death of an infant (Fish, 1986).

Communication problems are not uncommon. Daily problems may not receive adequate attention because of the parents' preoccupation with death, the desire to protect one another, or the sense of being overwhelmed by grief. These ordinary problems of daily life can accumulate and lead to an explosion. The result may be even greater misunderstanding between the partners and feelings of helplessness in an already overstressed couple.

Grief can dramatically alter the couple's sexual relationship. Inhibition of sexual response and intimacy among bereaved parents may be the result of the fear of losing still other children, or guilt over experiencing pleasure. Sexual problems may also be symptomatic of the grief or depression experienced by one or both of the partners. While the intimacy of sexual contact may be comforting to one spouse, it may be precisely what the other cannot endure at that moment for fear of being vulnerable to other, less positive feelings, such as pain and grief. It is not unusual for the sexual relationship to be compromised by disinterest, depression, avoidance, or other grief-related responses for two years after the death.

Misinterpretation of data has lead to a myth about an abnormally high divorce rate. It is absolutely untrue that the death of a child must lead to divorce. Despite the fact that the death of a child does stress marriages, when divorce does occur it is usually the result of problems that existed prior to the death, and not a direct consequence of the death of the child.

Child death profoundly affects the family system as an entity. Role reassignments will be necessary and must be appropriate. Many serious problems develop when surviving or "replacement children" (Cain & Cain, 1964) are expected to fill the void and take over the roles and identities of deceased siblings. Bereaved parents often find some difficulty in parenting the remaining children. This can stem from deficiencies in parenting skills because of continued preoccupation with grief, feeling overwhelmed, a tendency to overprotect the other children, and insufficient understanding about children's grief.

Socioculturally, the dramatic effects of child loss in societies subject to war and famine cannot be minimized. It is probable that a society's chronic exposure to child loss has profound psychosocial, political, and economic effects, although little direct research has been done in this important area.

In conclusion, the available information indicates that parental bereavement cannot be understood adequately in terms of the general conceptualizations held for grief and mourning. The characteristics of the parent-child relationship and the unique factors involved in parental bereavement are precisely those that are most likely to intensify and complicate any individual's grief response (Rando, 1986). Consequently, a new model of parental mourning should be constructed that will take into consideration the particular difficulties inherent in mourning the loss of one's child, and new criteria must be established for the identification of pathology within parental bereavement.

See also Children, Dying; Children and Death; Children's Hospice International; Compassionate Friends; Grief; Hospice: Children.

—THERESE A. RANDO

References

Cain, A.C. & Cain, B.S. (1964). "On replacing a child." *Journal of the American Academy of Child Psychiatry, 3*: 443–56.

Fish, W. (1986). "Differences of grief intensity in bereaved parents." In T.A. Rando (Ed.) *Parental loss of a child.* Champaign, IL: Research Press, pp. 415–28.

Gorer, G. (1965). *Death, grief, and mourning.* London: Cresset Press.

Knapp, R. (1986). *Beyond endurance: When a child dies.* New York: Schocken Books.

Limbo, R. & Wheeler, S. (1986). *When a baby dies: A handbook for healing and helping.* La Crosse, WI: Resolve Through Sharing, La Crosse Lutheran Hospital/Gundersen Clinic.

Rando, T.A. (Ed.) (1986). *Parental loss of a child.* Champaign, IL: Research Press.

Rando, T.A. (1988). *Grieving: How to go on living when someone you love dies.* Lexington, MA: Lexington Books.

Schiff, H. (1977). *The bereaved parent.* New York: Crown Publishers.

GRIEF: MISSING IN ACTION FAMILIES

There is a special group of families who suffer from a type of bereavement that casts them into chronic unresolved grief. These are the wives, children, siblings, and parents of men who still remain missing in action (MIA) after the release of the American servicemen from Vietnam in 1973. According to figures issued in 1985 by the National League of Families of American Prisoners of War and Missing in Southeast Asia, 2,441 Americans remain missing and unaccounted for—1,797 in Vietnam, 556 in Laos, 82 in Cambodia, and 6 elsewhere. As of November 1, 1985, there had been 805 reported firsthand live sightings of American prisoners of war (POWS) in Indochina. Most of these reports (85 percent) are thought to involve individuals who have since left Indochina, men who have died, and possibly some fabricated reports. However, this does leave 119 men reportedly seen in the 805 live sightings whose current status remains unknown. This fact generates continuing ambiguity and nurtures the persistent hope that a missing family member may still be alive somewhere in Southeast Asia. The stress of these individuals' unresolved grief continues today, a quarter century after the conflict began in 1964.

An incident that occurred shortly after the return of the POWs in 1973 illustrates how all-encompassing the MIA situation had become. One MIA family member related a dream she had had. A real estate agent, she usually spent considerable time each day driving about in her automobile. In her dream, she was going about her job as usual. However, in the back of the station wagon was the body of her missing husband. Nonchalantly, she continued showing property to her clients as if there were nothing unusual about having her husband's body in the back seat. She explained, "That's precisely the way it is. I'm sure he's dead, and yet I can't bury him. He's always with me wherever I go" (Hunter, 1982). Examples such as this indicate that MIA family members are "the combat casualities who remain at home" (Hunter, 1980, 1983, 1984).

MIA families continue to grieve because there is no way their losses can become reality. They continue to wait and hope and pray for resolution. Stuck in an emotional limbo, not knowing for certain if their loved ones are alive or dead, they experience unresolved grief as a way of life. The stress for family members is both prolonged and indefinite. Moreover, the situation is ambiguous and without guidelines. It includes the threat of death or permanent loss of the family member, but without confirmation. This threat is ongoing; it does not end in an hour, a week, a month, or even a year. Despite the continuing passage of years, the families often cannot "accept" the loss of their missing members. Consequently, both chronic and intermittent feelings of helplessness, hopelessness, powerlessness, anger, guilt, and rage combine to interfere with the development of effective coping strategies within the family system.

Personnel missing in the Vietnam war remained listed as missing for an unprecedented length of time (average length of absence was five years), even when there was strong evidence that they probably had not survived. In the first months of the Vietnam conflict the decision was made at top levels not to change any statuses from MIA to presumptive findings of death until the war ended. The assumption at that time was that the war would end within six months to a year. The families of MIAs continued to receive full pay and allowances (even flight pay) of the missing men because changes in status were withheld. However, the war dragged on for nine long years, and the families waited. Although the policy of keeping men listed as MIA provided substantial increases in monetary benefits to the families, they paid a high emotional price in their inability to complete the grieving process.

The family is profoundly affected when any family member is lost, either temporarily or permanently. A primary emotion experienced by MIA parents and other family members, especially during the initial weeks, was fear. As time passed, feelings of isolation, alienation, anger, guilt, hostility, and depression also developed. These feelings were experienced in a type of emotional roller coaster pattern which finds family member reactions ranging from hope to despair, from rage to remorse (Figley, 1980). At the time of the plight of the waiting Iranian hostage families in 1980, one Vietnam era MIA family member, Foley (1980, p. 2) made the following observations based on her own personal experiences:

> The families of the hostages are probably experiencing all of Kubler-Ross's steps of the grief cycle, on a "temporary" basis. They are bouncing back and forth within that cycle. . . . They are experiencing a sense of helplessness; they cannot control their own lives. . . . Their once-secure family now rests on the whims or fickleness of captors who are highly suspect . . . They cannot take charge of the issue that has disrupted their lives; it is far too big. . . . Wives will experience intense fear for their husband's safety. They will also be angry, because they have been left alone, and then they will feel guilty because they are angry. . . . The final outcome is uncertain; the "limbo" could end tomorrow or next year. . . . Some wives may be able to reach decisions, based only on their husband's pre-stated wishes. . . . Others may be able to demonstrate more independence or autonomy. Some may be paralyzed.

The grief of MIA families cannot be successfully resolved in the same way as grief that is subsequent to confirmed losses. Only when the family has some confirmation of the death will they be able to come to the type of resolution that might be considered as definitive after a loss. In the absence of this, caregivers must be advised that even in the presence of positive, life-continuing actions, MIA family members always remain vulnerable to grief experiences and continue to "wait for news." To this vulnerability must be added the press of unresolved and unfinished business with regard to the missing loved one.

See also Grief; Grief Counseling.

—E.J. HUNTER

References

Figley, C.R. (Ed.) (1980). *Mobilization I: The Iranian crisis: Final report of the Task Force on Families of Catastrophe.* West Lafayette, IN: Purdue University.

Foley, B. (1980). "Reflections of an MIA wife." Paper presented at a meeting of the Task Force on Families of Catastrophe, February, Purdue University, West Lafayette, IN.

Hunter, E.J. (1980). "Combat casualties who remain at home." *Military Review, 60*: 28–36.

Hunter, E.J. (1982). "Marriage in limbo." *Naval Institute Proceedings, 108*: 27–32.

Hunter, E.J. (1983). "Captivity: The family in waiting." In C. Figley & M. McClubin (Eds.) *Stress and the family: Coping with catastrophe.* Vol. 2. New York: Brunner/Mazel, pp. 166–84.

Hunter, E.J. (1984). "Treating the military captive's family." In F. Kaslow & R. Ridenour (Eds.) *Treating the military family: Dynamics and treatment.* New York: Guilford, 35–46.

Hunter, E.J. (1986). "Missing in action." In T. Rando (Ed.) *Parental loss of a child.* Champaign IL: Research Press, 277–90.

National League of Families of American Prisoners of War and Missing in Southeast Asia. (1985). Newsletter, November 8.

Rando, T. (Ed.) (1986). *Parental loss of a child.* Champaign, IL: Research Press.

GRIEF, VICARIOUS

The sorrow and apprehension one feels for a loss suffered by another person has been described as vicarious grief (Kastenbaum, 1988). In both direct and vicarious grief there may be a sense of emptiness and constriction, along with difficulties in sleeping, loss of appetite, and an obsessional review of what happened and how it might have been avoided. It is not yet known if vicarious grief endures over extended periods of time, nor should this empathic response to another person's sorrow be considered as identical to a personal loss in every respect.

At present, the only available research-based report on vicarious grief derives from a study of elderly residents of adult communities in Arizona. This study was focused upon concepts of personal time (past, present, and future). The vicarious grief findings emerged unexpectedly during the course of semistructured in-depth interviews and were most frequent among women.

The following excerpt from an interview with a 63-year-old married woman conveys some of the mood and thought associated with vicarious grief. The interviewee is commenting on an elective abortion recently undergone by a young woman who was her friend and the granddaughter of one of her closest friends:

> She tries to make nothing of it. Like her mother. Like her mother does. But she hurts inside. Inside, she hurts inside . . . and I hurt for her. She acts like she doesn't feel anything . . . but I know she does, and it's how you feel coming out of anesthesia, but she hasn't come out yet. She'll hurt for herself when she realizes, she realizes . . . the child . . . there is no child and she is . . . um . . . the mother of a dead child . . . um . . . a dead child . . . and this will hurt her though she didn't think she wanted the child. What she did—the abortion—it doesn't matter I don't approve. Judge not that ye be not judged. But it hurts all the same. It hurts all the same though I could be the only one who feels it. . . . She will, too. You can't, um, you can't have a dead child and not feel it.

All the examples of vicarious grief found in this study were attributable to a recent death. Whether or not vicarious grief can also arise from other types of loss remains to be determined.

It is possible that some people are unusually sensitive to the sorrows experienced by others and that elderly women are among those most likely to resonate to these losses. Much remains to be learned about the frequency, dynamics, and implications of vicarious grief, but more attention to this neglected phenomenon may help us to an improved understanding of the human bond.

See also Grief; Old Age and Death.

—ROBERT KASTENBAUM

Reference

Kastenbaum, R. (1988). "Vicarious grief: An intergenerational phenomenon?" *Death Studies, 12,* 447–53.

GRIEF COUNSELING

Grief counseling is the intervention by human service professionals with bereaved individuals and families. A distinction is sometimes made between grief therapy and grief counseling, the former being reserved for those whose grief response is extreme enough to be called pathological. However, currently there is no agreement on the definition of pathology in grief, so we will consider counseling and therapy as on a continuum from simple education and support to the examination and reassessment of central dynamics and interaction patterns in the individual and in the family system.

Importance of Social Support

The most consistent finding of studies on the resolution of grief is that social support is the most important factor. A less adequately researched, but broadly shared consensus is that extreme difficulty in grief is grounded in pre-existing personality dynamics and not in issues immediately concerned with death.

Individuals with little social support, or with conflicted support networks may seek counseling as a dependable social support. In these instances, the counselor relies on the general supportive strategies of putting the individual in contact with similar others, providing opportunity to ventilate, expressing concern, "being there," and providing a philosophical or religious perspective. The counselor avoids the unhelpful strategies of giving advice, encouraging recovery, enforcing cheerfulness, and false identification (Lehman et al., 1986). If the goal of intervention is to resolve problems within the natural support system, then the techniques of family therapy are used to realign the family system to function without the missing member (Krell & Rabkin, 1979).

When the difficulty is within preexisting personality dynamics, the goal of intervention is to facilitate mourning. An assessment of the pre-existing dynamics will usually reveal the difficulty. In borderline personalities, for example, the difficulty in differentiating self from other makes it hard for the person to break the symbiosis in order to relinquish or reinternalize the deceased.

Goals of Intervention

Researchers disagree about the nature of resolution of mourning and therefore about the goal to which intervention should be directed. The majority of writers in the field see the function of mourning as allowing the individual to relinquish old roles, patterns of interaction, and sources of gratification that were once fulfilled by the person who died. Only when these are relinquished can new and satisfying roles, interactions, and sources of gratification evolve (Raphael, 1983, p. 57).

The goal of intervention within this understanding of the resolution of grief is to recognize behaviors or feelings aimed at interacting with the deceased and to redirect those behaviors and feelings toward objects in the present environment. This may be accomplished by attending to the tasks of grief which Worden (1982) has developed:

1. To increase the psychological reality of the loss

2. To help the counselee deal with both expressed and latent affect
3. To help the counselee overcome various impediments to readjustment after the loss
4. To encourage the counselee to make a healthy emotional withdrawal from the deceased and to feel comfortable reinvesting that emotion in another relationship

In some cases, where the loss seems a psychological irreality, intervention may use more active techniques such as recreating the loss by guided fantasy and then helping to relinquish the deceased by guided mourning (Mawson et al., 1981) or "regriefing" (Volkan, 1981).

Inner Representation of the Deceased

A minority of writers, largely psychoanalytic, claim that the resolution of mourning involves the inner representation of the deceased as well as adjusting to and bonding in a world without the deceased (Volkan, 1981). The inner representation is first those aspects of the self that were identified with the deceased, characterizations or thematic memories of the deceased, and emotional states connected with those characterizations or memories. Internalizations may take the form of introjection or identification. Introjection involves keeping the deceased as an entity frozen in the psyche. Identification involves a fusing of the representation of self with the inner representation of the deceased in order to enrich the ego. Introjections can be used as objects of solace (Horton, 1981).

The psychoanalytic group regards introjected inner representation of the deceased as pathological. Therefore, therapy from this perspective attempts to externalize the introjected inner representation of the deceased. In this way, it is thought, one can relinquish the inner bond with the deceased and enrich the ego through an identification process.

However, in his study of bereaved parents, Klass (1988) finds that introjections are widespread and that they are often very helpful in allowing the bereaved to live fully in their new world.

Therefore, an additional goal of intervention is to help the bereaved to reformulate the inner representation in a way that provides optimal functioning in a world permanently made poorer by the loss.

See also Compassionate Friends; Grief.

—DENNIS KLASS

References

Horton, P.C. (1981). *Solace: The missing dimension in psychiatry.* Chicago: University of Chicago Press.

Klass, D. (1988). *Parental grief.* New York: Springer.

Krell, R. & Rabkin, L. (1979). "The effects of sibling death on the surviving child: A family perspective." *Family Process 18*: 471–77.

Lehman, D.R., Ellard, J.H., & Wortman, C.B. (1986). "Social support for the bereaved: Recipients' and providers' perspectives on what is helpful." *Journal of Consulting and Clinical Psychology, 5*: 438–46.

Mawson, D., Marks, I.M., Ramm, L., & Stern, R. (1981). "Guided mourning for morbid grief: A controlled study." *British Journal of Psychiatry, 138*: 185–93.

Raphael, B. (1983). *The anatomy of bereavement.* New York: Basic Books.

Volkan, V. (1981). *Linking objects and linking phenomena: A study of the forms, symptoms, metapsychology, and therapy of complicated mourning.* New York: International Universities Press.

Worden, J.W. (1982). *Grief counseling and grief therapy: A handbook for the mental health practitioner.* New York: Springer.

H

HADES

Hades (literally, the invisible or unseen) has come to be regarded as almost a synonym for Hell: a place of fiery torment for damned or unfortunate souls. Earlier generations would express anger by inviting somebody to "Go to Hades!" or "Go to blazes" if they felt it improper to speak of Hell. Even this blurred concept of Hades has become diminished in more recent years with the reduced attention given to mythology and the classics by the educational system. Nevertheless, the Hades of Greek mythology remains not only an interesting but somewhat unsettled and mysterious concept.

At first, Hades was the name given to the god who ruled the "infernal regions." Later, this god (also known as Dis) became more definitively known as Pluto. Today, in a time when cartoon characters are more familiar than the gods of antiquity, it may be difficult to set aside the Disney version of Pluto and recall this wicked and daring son of Cronus/Saturn. Pluto was one of only three children to escape being devoured by his father who, not at all incidentally, was the incarnation of time. Himself representing the grave, Pluto stole the beautiful goddess Proserpine for his bride and carried her off to Hades. Eventually, the lord of the underworld's name stabilized as Pluto, and his realm became Hades.

The characteristics attributed to Hades vary from time to time and from one story to another within the panoply of Greco-Roman myth. A location for Hades is suggested by Virgil: near the volcanic Mount Vesuvius, where, as Bulfinch phrases it, "the whole country is cleft with chasms, from which sulphurous flames arise, while the ground is shaken with pent-up vapors, and mysterious sounds issue from the bowels of the earth." No life is found on the banks of its steamy waters or flying above its awesome terrain. (However, Hades is not always given such a precise location.) From such descriptions it is not difficult to see where the Hades/Hell comparisons draw their inspiration. However, Hades itself is not necessarily a place of perpetual fiery torment. The most alarming aspects of Hades are usually depicted as occupying its outer perimeter, the boundary one must cross over to enter. It was here that one might encounter Cerberus, the dog-monster whose three serpentine heads roared violence.

Within Hades, one might be subject to some species of torment or frustration, or find ease and repose. Furthermore, when the image of Hades is examined over the entire Greek mythology span, it often appears that "life" in Hades is neither torment nor blessing for most dwellers; rather, it is a somewhat dreary, boring form of subexistence. Although the more dramatic stories and descriptions are most likely to capture our imagination, some historians believe that, all in all, Hades was usually viewed by the ordinary person as an unpromising, unpleasant, but not absolutely horrendous destination. It will be kept in mind, of course, that Christian concepts of damnation, torment, and redemption were not part of the tradition in which the image of Hades arose so, strictly speaking, there was no need to equip Pluto's realm with excessive tortures for the average expectable soul.

Nevertheless, one can find examples of ingenious punishment in Hades. This is where Sisyphus, a king who angered the gods, was condemned to roll a boulder to the top of a hill, exerting every ounce of his strength—only to have the boulder tumble back down and his impossible task begin once again. Tantalus (whose plight has given us that valuable word, tantalize) seemingly was offered water for his great thirst and food for his great hunger, but never could he bring these tempting delights to his lips.

The memorable punishments were generally reserved for those who had fallen afoul of one or more gods. An ordinary mortal was not likely to be so ill-treated. When punishment—or simply a good fright—was required, Pluto would usually call upon The Furies—the unleashed, merciless, vengeful, usually hidden side of femininity.

In general, Hades had a less fearsome aspect than the Christian Hell it preceded. Rarely would a devout Christian feel relieved to enter the portals of Hell, but good Greek citizens knew they had the right to cross the border (assuming always proper burial and Charon's fee). Furthermore, in some versions, Hades had a region set aside for those in high favor. The Isles of the Blest, a version of paradise, were introduced into Greek thought during the Hellenistic period as a zone of Hades. By contrast, in Christian visions of the afterlife, heavenly and hellish venues are usually kept at a greater distance.

Sheol, the Hebrew word for the under or lower world, was translated as Hades in the Greek Old Testament. However, these two images, although similar in some respects, are not identical and interchangeable.

See also Charon; Styx.

—ROBERT KASTENBAUM

References

Anon. (1988). "Temple of doom." *Discover,* October, p. 6.
Bulfinch, T. (1855/Reprint 1977). *Bulfinch's mythology. (Part I).* New York: Avenel Books.
Garland, R. (1985). *The Greek way of death.* Ithaca, NY: Cornell University Press.
Knight, W.J. (1970). *Elysion: On ancient Greek and Roman beliefs concerning a life after death.* London: Rutledge & Kegan Paul.
Morford, M.P.O. & Lenardon, R.J. (1977). *Classical mythology.* New York: David McKay.

HEMLOCK SOCIETY

The Hemlock Society was founded in 1980 by Derek Humphry and Ann Wickett in advocacy of "the right to die." The Society is concerned with "active" euthanasia, also known as "mercy killing," and with "assisted suicide." A journalist, Humphry previously had been associated with the London-based Voluntary Euthanasia Society (also known as EXIT). Humphry had personal experience with the euthanasia issue when he helped his dying wife end her life (Humphry & Wickett, 1986). In collaboration with Ann Wickett, his second wife, Humphry established The Hemlock Society in Los Angeles. It is now an organization with national membership and recognition.

The Hemlock Society supports "the option of active voluntary euthanasia for the terminally ill." It attempts to promote tolerance of the right of terminally ill people to end their lives in a planned manner. However, the group "does not encourage suicide for any primary emotional, traumatic, or financial reasons in the absence of terminal illness. It approves of the work of those involved in suicide prevention." The manner and timing of death for the terminally ill person should be "an extremely personal decision," according to the Society, and "wherever possible taken in concert with family and friends." The Society does not attempt to impose its views on others or challenge religions and philosophies that oppose active euthanasia or assisted suicide. Its activities have included information development and dissemination, public discussions, consultation on living will legislation, and a publication program.

Among publications produced or promoted by the Hemlock Society are *Jean's Way* (Humphry & Wickett, 1978); *The Right to Die* (Humphry & Wickett, 1986); *Let Me Die Before I Wake* (Humphry,

1981); *Euthanasia Journal,* and *Hemlock Quarterly,* a newsletter distributed to members.

Further information can be obtained from:

Hemlock Society
PO Box 66218
Los Angeles, CA 90066–0218
Telephone (213) 391-1871

See also Euthanasia; *Euthanasia Review* (Journal); (The) Living Will; Suicide: Assisted.

—ROBERT KASTENBAUM

References

Humphry, D. (1981). *Let me die before I wake.* Los Angeles: The Hemlock Society.
Humphry, D. & Wickett, A. (1978). *Jean's way.* New York: Quartet Books.
Humphry, D. & Wickett, A. (1986). *The right to die.* New York: Harper & Row.
Johnson, G. (1987). *Voluntary euthanasia: A comprehensive bibliography.* Lake Bluff, IL: Quality Books.

HOSPICE: CHILDREN

Hospice principles and values are applicable to at least three situations involving children: (1) those who are incurably ill or dying; (2) those who are grieving over their own condition or the dying or death of a significant other person, and (3) adults who are grieving the dying or death of a child (Corr & Corr, 1985a–c). In each of these situations, the hospice philosophy emphasizes palliative care or the amelioration of sources of distress as a means to maximize quality in living.

Benefits of the Hospice Approach

Children who are coping with incurable illness or dying may benefit from a hospice approach through home care, home- or center-based respite care, or inpatient care. Extensive research led by Ida Martinson (1976) has demonstrated that home care for dying children is both desirable and feasible for those families who are able and who wish to exercise that option. As the original social institution in

which health and wellness are promoted in our society, the home is an appropriate context for many children and their families when there is no reasonable hope for cure and death is near. This may also be true when the side effects of curative interventions have come to be seen as outweighing the prospects for cure.

This does not constitute an argument in favor of abandoning children to die at home. On the contrary, enabling children who are near death to live their last days with quality at home is a demanding challenge. Professional expertise and human support must be made available in the home. Family strengths must be mobilized. All the needed social and health care resources available in the community must be well coordinated in order not to add to the burdens of dying children and their families. Hospice approaches introduce professional and other resources within the home setting to enhance quality in living, sustain effective parenting, and contribute to a sense of security.

Hospice staff and volunteers visit the home by invitation and intervene directly only when requested or required for the welfare of all concerned. The way in which these services are delivered depends upon the needs, resources, and circumstances of the local community. For example, services of this sort are provided by a hospice program in Louisville, Kentucky (Wheeler et al., 1985), by a hospital-based staff in Milwaukee (Lauer & Camitta, 1980), and by community caregivers with hospital coordination in Los Angeles (Martin, 1985).

Variety of Hospice Approaches

Depending upon its form, hospice respite care can be either a way of supplementing home care or a bridge between home and inpatient facilities. For example, in-home respite care sustains the family unit by providing time off for family caregivers to work, sleep, shop, and take care of needs that would otherwise go unsatisfied. Center-based respite care adds time out of the home in a suitable environment for the ill child. These two modes of hospice respite can be illustrated by the programs of Helen House in Oxford, England (Burne, 1982, 1984; Mother Frances Dominica, 1982), and that of Edmarc,

Inc., in Virginia (Cutchins & Mease, 1985).

Hospice approaches to inpatient care can be implemented in a variety of settings: a pediatric medical center, a general hospital, or a special purpose facility. Thus, Children's Hospital of Denver established a program of family-centered hospice care within its neonatal intensive care unit (Siegel, 1982; Whitfield et al., 1982), while St. Mary's Hospital for Children in Bayside, New York, added to its services a comprehensive pediatric hospice program and a ten-bed inpatient unit (Wilson, 1982). The structure or location of the program is less important than its holistic approach and its effectiveness in serving the needs of each child-and-family unit.

Care for grieving or bereaved children is well within the charter of adult hospice programs when the youngsters in question are the children, grandchildren, or other relatives of their adult patients. Extending this care to children and adults who are grieving or bereaved in relation to the illness or death of a child is simply an expansion of the circle of care. It reminds us that we have much still to learn about grief in childhood (Fleming, 1985) and in adolescence (Corr & McNeil, 1986), about parental bereavement (McGlowry et al., 1987; Miles, 1984), and about integrating with existing resources such as community self-help groups (Klass, 1985; Lattanzi, 1982).

Other valuable components of hospice care for situations involving children include advocacy, education, and research. A leader on a national and worldwide scale and a stimulus to others in these areas is Children's Hospice International, 1101 King Street, Suite 131, Alexandra, VA 22314, (703) 684-0330.

The application of hospice principles and values to situations involving children essentially represents an outlook, philosophy, or approach to care. As such, it is not the exclusive property of any particular type of program or group of caregivers. In fact, it may not be necessary to have a formal program of pediatric hospice care before beginning such work. In view of the small numbers and great diversity in child-and-family units who might require such care in any given locality, it does not seem likely that there will be many comprehensive programs of pediatric hospice care. Many pediatric caregivers in their present work may already be implementing hospice principles, while others might enter into such work either by reconsidering the nature or by expanding the scope of their current efforts. Doing so recognizes the needs and facilitates assistance for children and families who are coping with the difficult problems of dying, death, or bereavement. It also teaches important lessons about our own mortality and humanity, even as it helps to bring about a more caring community in the society as a whole (Mother Frances Dominica, 1987).

See also Children, Dying; Children and Death; Compassionate Friends; Hospice: Philosophy and Practice; Siblings of Dying Children.

—CHARLES A. CORR & DONNA M. CORR

References

Burne, S.R. (1982). "Helen House—a hospice for children." *Health Visitor, 55*: 544–55.

Burne, S.R. (1984). "A hospice for children in England." *Pediatrics, 73*: 97–98.

Corr, C.A. & Corr, D.M. (Eds.) (1985a). *Hospice approaches to pediatric care.* New York: Springer.

Corr, C.A. & Corr, D.M. (1985b). "Pediatric hospice care." *Pediatrics, 76*: 774–80.

Corr, C.A. & Corr, D.M. (1985c). "Situations involving children: A challenge for the hospice movement." *The Hospice Journal, 1*: 63–77.

Corr, C.A. & McNeil, J.M. (Eds.) (1986). *Adolescence and death.* New York: Springer.

Cutchins, R.C. & Mease, B.S. (1985). "Respite care and the dying child." In C.A. Corr & D.M. Corr (Eds.) *Hospice approaches to pediatric care.* New York: Springer, pp. 87–105.

Fleming, S.J. (1985). "Children's grief: Individual and family dynamics." In C.A. Corr & D.M. Corr (Eds.) *Hospice approaches to pediatric care.* New York: Springer, pp. 197–218.

Klass, D. (1985). "Self-help groups: Grieving parents and community resources." In C.A. Corr & D.M. Corr (Eds.) *Hospice approaches to pediatric care.* New York: Springer, pp. 241–60.

Lattanzi, M.E. (1982). "Hospice bereavement services: Creating networks of support." *Journal of Family and Community Health, 5*: 54–63.

Lauer, M.E. & Camitta, B.M. (1980). "Home care for dying children: A nursing model." *Journal of Pediatrics, 97*: 1032–35.

Martin, B.B. (1985). "Home care for terminally ill children and their families." In C.A. Corr & D.M. Corr (Eds.) *Hospice approaches to pediatric care.* New York: Springer, pp. 65–86.

Martinson, I.M. (1976). *Home care for the dying child: Professional and family perspectives.* New York: Appleton-Century-Crofts.

Martinson, I.M. (Ed.) (1978a). *Home care: A manual for implementation of home care for children dying of cancer.* Minneapolis: University of Minnesota School of Nursing.

Martinson, I.M. (1978b). "Alternative environments for care of the dying child: Hospice, hospital, or home." In O.J. Saher (Ed.) *The child and death.* St. Louis: C.B. Mosby, pp. 83–91.

Martinson, I.M. et al. (1977). "When the patient is dying: Home care for the child." *American Journal of Nursing, 77*: 1815–17.

Martinson, I.M. et al. (1978a). "Home care for children dying of cancer." *Pediatrics, 62*: 106–13.

Martinson, I.M. et al. (1978b). "Facilitating home care for children dying of cancer." *Cancer Nursing, 1*: 41–45.

McGlowry, S.G. et al. (1987). "The empty space phenomenon: The process of grief in the bereaved family." *Death Studies, 11*: 361–74.

Miles, M.S. (1984). "Helping adults mourn the death of a child." In H. Wass & C.A. Corr (Eds.) *Childhood and death.* Washington, DC: Hemisphere, pp. 219–41.

Moldow, D.G. & Martinson, I.M. (1980). "From research to reality—home care for the dying child." *MCN: The American Journal of Maternal Child Nursing, 51*: 159–66.

Mother Frances Dominica (1987). "Reflections on death in childhood." *British Medical Journal, 294*: 108–10.

Siegel, R. (1982). "A family-centered program of neonatal intensive care." *Health and Social Work, 7*: 50–58.

Wheeler, P.R. & Lange, N.F., with Bertolone, S.J. (1985). "Improving care for hospitalized terminally ill children: A practicable model." In C.A. Corr & D.M. Corr (Eds.) *Hospice approaches to pediatric care.* New York: Springer, pp. 43–60.

Whitfield, J.M. et al. (1982). "The application of hospice concepts to neonatal care." *American Journal of Diseases of Children, 136*: 421–24.

Wilson, D.C. (1982). "The viability of pediatric hospices: A case study." *Death Education, 6*: 205–12.

HOSPICE: PHILOSOPHY AND PRACTICE

Modern public health and medical advances have not been matched by equivalent progress in meeting the needs of the chronically ill and of the dying person. The research techniques and public health measures that served so well to eradicate such diseases as smallpox and polio are less effective when the target is not simply a microorganism but a complex of life-threatening conditions or chronic disease. The remarkable successes achieved in overcoming many infectious diseases led to the expectation that all ailments could be as well prevented or managed. Paradoxically, though, because many of the "easy" problems have been solved and because more people now live long enough to develop a variety of deteriorative conditions, physicians and nurses now face a higher proportion of "tough" cases. The elderly adult with cardiovascular insufficiency, emphysema, cancer, or Alzheimer's disease, for example, requires skillful, multifaceted, and continuing management.

Another major reason for the less adequate care often received by the chronically ill and the dying person is that health care professionals tend to be frustrated when they cannot restore a patient to health. The dying person not only represents the doctor's "failure," but reminds the doctor of personal mortality.

By the 1960s there was a growing awareness of the dying person's plight in the health care professions, behavioral and social sciences, and the general public. Criticism increased against "aggressive medicine" that added only to the discomfort of the dying person. "Death with dignity" became a powerful rallying call. According to the critics (and many of the researchers), the medical system was intensifying the distress of dying people and their families by ignoring their basic human needs while at the same time ex-

Dame Cicely Saunders, DBE., FRCP., FRCS., Chairman, St. Christopher's Hospice, Sydenham, England. Founder of St. Christopher's Hospice and leader of the international hospice care movement. Photo reprinted by permission of Dame Cicely Saunders.

posing them to painful and futile indignities. The time was ripe for an alternative approach—hospice.

Hospice Philosophy

The modern hospice descends from a tradition of Christian hospitality toward travelers and others needing shelter and comfort (See **Hospice Development in the United Kingdom**). This tradition renewed itself in the middle of the twentieth century with an emphasis on care of the dying person and his or her family. The pioneering work of Cicely Saunders and her supporters led to the establishment of model hospice programs in the United Kingdom. Those motivated to improve care of the dying person in North America drew upon both the philosophy and practical experience of the British movement.

The hospice philosophy is based upon respect for the individuality of the dying person and his or her friends and significant others. It is the person, not the disease, that is the focus. This is a meaningful departure from the ordinary medical practice of our times. Instead of being primarily the recipient of standardized procedures, each patient is regarded as the center of his or her unique life. Treatment planning therefore takes the patient's distinctive values, needs, fears, hopes, and expectations into account.

The patient and family unit are central to hospice philosophy. The patient's family members and significant others are seen not only as important sources of support to the patient but also as individuals who are themselves undergoing stress and who should be given sensitive attention. With this concept in mind, hospice programs attempt to form a partnership with those who constitute the natural support network for the dying patient. This approach contrasts with the bureaucratization and "medicalization" of care in which the patient is almost completely taken over by health care professionals and family members are given little opportunity to participate.

Another keystone of hospice philosophy is the emphasis on pain relief and symptom control. One might think that this is a very obvious objective that can be taken for granted in all medical settings. But it was the *lack* of adequate symptom relief in many settings that did much to stimulate the development of hospice programs. A surprisingly large number of physicians were deficient in providing pain relief either because of inadequate training in that area, a misplaced fear that a dying person would become a drug addict, or an overemphasis on futile treatment measures that increased rather than alleviated discomfort. The general reluctance to spend time with the dying patient also contributed to this situation. By contrast, the hospice philosophy is firm in its resolution to relieve the dying person from pain, nausea, and other sources of physical distress. Moreover, the intent is also to liberate the patient from *fear* of unbearable pain. Hospice specialists are well aware that fear and apprehension can be as disturbing as the actual presence of severe pain.

Overall, the hospice philosophy holds that patients, family, and staff all have legitimate needs and interests, and that the patient should have a sense of basic security and protection in his or her environment. This orientation leads to a number of more specific principles. For example, families should have the opportunity to discuss dying, death, and related needs with the staff and should have privacy with the dying person both while living and immediately after death (Kastenbaum, 1986).

It is also common for the hospice philosophy to emphasize the spiritual needs of patients, family, and staff (Saunders, 1967). Although spiritual needs are seldom defined in any precise way, this goal expresses the commitment of the hospice movement to each person as a unique and valuable being who cannot be reduced to a disease. The Christian tradition from which hospice developed is often still in evidence, although varying from one program to another. However, it is almost invariably the intent of hospice philosophy that all religious orientations are to be respected, as well as preferences for agnosticism or atheism. The hospice philosophy does not call for the imposition of any particular religious or spiritual values upon the dying person, but rather, calls for the continued opportunity to actualize such spiritual values as the patient may hold.

One further component of hospice philosophy is so basic that it sometimes has gone without saying: the services are to be offered in a professional, competent, and responsible manner. Goodwill is to be bolstered with up-to-date technical knowledge demonstrated by people who are well qualified for their assignments. Although the hospice philosophy differs from that of traditional medical care in many respects, it shares the concern for establishing and maintaining high standards of training and performance.

Hospice Practice

The first hospice organization in North America was established in New Haven, Connecticut, in 1974. Its first medical director was Dr. Sylvia Lack, who had previously served with St. Christopher's and St. Joseph's hospices in England. Hospice, Inc. differed in several ways from its UK models, especially in the fact that it had no residential beds of its own at first, providing home care service only. The first Canadian hospice followed the next year when Dr. Balfour M. Mount opened a palliative care unit (PCU) at the Royal Victoria Hospital (Montreal). This PCU, which became the model for others, had an inpatient unit, a home care service, and a within-hospital consultation service. Although these were the first official hospice establishments in North America, several existing facilities had long made an effort to provide special comfort to dying patients (a notable example is Home of the Holy Ghost, in Cambridge, Massachusetts).

There are now approximately 1,700 hospices in the United States. Some are freestanding organizations, others are special services offered by hospitals. Although this represents an impressive growth of the hospice movement in a short time, there are still serious challenges to its sustained viability. Funding was precarious at the start of the movement and remains a concern of many hospice organizations today. Limited financial support was offered (to three hospices) by the National Cancer Institute, followed by a large-scale demonstration project sponsored by the Health Care Financing Administration (See **National Hospice Study**). In a significant development, hospice care became reimbursable under Medicare (effective November 1983). Both hospice organizations and patients have to meet a set of regulations and standards for participation in this Medicare benefit. This financial support has helped to make the option of hospice care available to many patients and their families. However, it has not completely solved the financial problems involved; for example, some hospices do not qualify, some individuals do not qualify, and there are circumstances in which hospices can be liable for large necessary expenses that are not reimbursable. Virtually all hospice organizations must continue to seek additional financial support from the community.

Another major unresolved issue is the question of how and how well hospice will be integrated into the total health care system. This is an important question because it involves the type of cooperation hospice can expect on such matters as patient referral and continuity of care. It is obvious that much progress has been made in the integration of hospice with other health and social service organizations, but difficult problems still arise.

A full-service hospice that qualifies under The National Hospice Reimbursement Act must have the following configuration of personnel and services:

1. A governing body with clear authority and accountability
2. A medical director
3. An interdisciplinary team that includes (at the minimum) a physician, registered nurse, social worker, volunteers, and pastoral or other counselor
4. Continuity of care must be ensured at all times and wherever the patient may be located.
5. A plan of care must be established and maintained for each patient.
6. The quality of care must be evaluated on a continuing basis and effective actions taken to correct any problems that are identified.
7. The hospice must comply with all applicable licensing regulations in its locality.
8. The hospice must provide or take responsibility for all the core services required by the patient.
9. Essential hospice services must be available on a 24-hour basis every day.
10. An in-service training program must be in operation to maintain and improve the skills of staffs and volunteers

Those interested in making use of hospice services can expect these services and characteristics to exist for hospice organizations that have been approved by Medicare. Some hospices also meet these requirements but have chosen not to participate in Medicare, and other hospices provide useful services but do not encompass the entire scope required by Medicare.

A given hospice may or may not have its own inpatient residential facility. Some remain "hospices at home," providing support to family members and offering their expertise in the relief of pain and other symptoms. Hospices that do not have their own residential facility do have arrangements with one or more local hospitals. There is also an emerging emphasis on intermediary placements, settings that provide short-term care when for some reason neither the home nor the hospital is most appropriate at the moment.

Volunteers play a crucial role in hospice practice. Some volunteers interact directly with patients and families; others carry out a variety of useful services to help keep the organization going. It is not unusual for nurses and other professionally qualified individuals to volunteer their services to a hospice, although there is usually also a core paid staff. To become a hospice volunteer, one must be approved in a screening interview and then participate in a carefully structured course of training.

Hospice practice has influenced care in hospitals. Some hospital staff members have participated actively in hospice care, and physicians increasingly have turned to hospice experts and to their research literature for information on pain relief.

The availability of hospice care varies from place to place, and some patients and some families are not good candidates for this option. For example, it may be impractical for a patient who does not have a family member available to serve as primary caregiver (although sometimes a friend or neighbor may accept this role). Some patients and their families continue to choose traditional medical care for any of a number of reasons. This is consistent with the overall hospice philosophy that a person should be able to exercise choice on matters that so directly affect his or her well-being.

See also Children's Hospice International; Death Education; Dying; Hospice: Children; Hospice: Volunteers; Hospice Association of America; Hospice Development in the United Kingdom; *Hospice Journal: Physical, Psychosocial, and Pastoral Care of the Dying;* National Hospice Organization; National Hospice Study.

—ROBERT KASTENBAUM

References

Kastenbaum, R. (1986). *Death, society, and human experience.* 3rd ed. Columbus, OH: Charles E. Merrill.
Levy, M.H. (1987–1988). "Pain control research in the terminally ill." *Omega, Journal of Death and Dying, 18*: 265–80.

Mor, V. (1987). *Hospice care systems.* New York: Springer.

Mor, V., Greer, D.S., & Kastenbaum, R. (1988). *The hospice experiment.* Baltimore: The Johns Hopkins University Press.

Mount, B.M. (1976). "The problem of caring for the dying in a general hospital; the palliative care unit as a possible solution." *Canadian Medical Association Journal, 115*: 119–21.

National Hospice Organization. (1981). *Standards of a hospice program of care.* McLean, VA: National Hospice Organization.

Saunders, C. (1967). *The management of terminal disease.* London: Hospital Medical Publications.

Stoddard, S. (1978). *Hospice movement—a better way of caring for the dying.* New York: Stein & Day.

Twycross, R.G. (1984). *Pain relief and cancer.* Philadelphia: Saunders.

Zimmerman, J. (1981). *Hospice: Complete care for the terminally ill.* Baltimore: Urban & Schwarzenberg.

HOSPICE: VOLUNTEERS

Volunteers play a significant role in hospice care programs. Whether care is provided in a hospital, a nursing home, or the family residence, the volunteer represents the compassion and support of the community. The caregiving and befriending bond that is established between volunteers and patients and their families sets the hospice team apart from the more traditional type of health care agency. The volunteer may be said to be at the heart of the hospice concept, working alongside professionals from such fields as nursing, social work, administration, fiscal management, and the ministry.

The Volunteer in Action: Hospice of the Valley

The Hospice of the Valley (Phoenix, Arizona) typifies the hospice approach in the United States. A "hospice without walls," the Hospice of the Valley (HOV) provides a wide range of services for the terminally ill and their families in their own homes. Volunteers serve on the HOV Board of Directors and Advisory Board, while others provide guidance and direction and partipate in fundraising. Office volunteers relieve the professional staff of many time-consuming desk tasks, enabling them to work more directly in caregiving. The home care volunteer is the "tie that binds" the patient and family to hospice services from the time the referral is received until a year after the patient has died.

Home care volunteers come from a wide variety of occupations, levels of schooling, and socioeconomic conditions. Individuals in health-related fields often find the hospice volunteer training program to be a valuable refresher course. Family members, survivors, and their close friends relate their hospice training course to their own life experiences. Other individuals apply to become volunteers in order to increase their own knowledge and improve their skills in helping others. All prospective volunteers are interviewed by a hospice staff member. The applicant's motivation, life experiences, and existing level of knowledge and skills are taken into consideration. Attention is also given to the obligations and commitments that the prospective volunteer already has to meet. Although a very busy person might still find time to be a volunteer, HOV, like other hospices, does not want to deprive families of the time they need from a member who is also a prospective volunteer.

Religious orientation is another factor that is considered when interviewing prospective volunteers. Hospice does not exist to exert religious pressure of any kind upon the participating patients and families. Some volunteers may draw strength and inspiration from their own religious views, but hospice will not knowingly send out a person who is motivated to proselytize or attempt to change the religious orientation of others. Volunteers befriend and support patient and family; they are not there to change them. The volunteer director will be careful about accepting applicants who have a hidden agenda that could create problems for patients and families. A person who needs to work through his or her own unresolved grief, for example, would not be assigned to home care work, nor would those motivated chiefly by curiosity or the desire to practice their counseling skills.

HOV uses the following criteria for assessing potential home care volunteers. The volunteer

1. Must not have suffered a loss (bereavement) within the past year
2. Must be in agreement with the hospice concept and philosophy
3. Must be physically healthy
4. Must have a positive mental attitude
5. Must not be a zealot about their religion
6. Must be able to give the patient or family four hours a week
7. Must live within the HOV service area

The volunteer training course itself provides information on the philosophy, mission, and goals of hospice, as well as policies and procedures, legal aspects of being a volunteer, listening skills, spirituality, and such other relevant topics as AIDS, death, dying, and bereavement. The HOV training course also includes visiting a mortuary in case the volunteer needs to help the family in making decisions in this realm.

HOV volunteers give a minimum of four hours a week, although there are individual variations as the situation requires. Generally, the volunteer's assistance to the family continues for about a year after the patient's death.

Examples of Services

The following examples are typical of services provided by volunteers associated with the HOV and other hospice organizations.

- A new home care volunteer on her first case found that the patient and his wife were frightened and confused about all the legal papers they were being asked to sign. She spent many extra hours helping them through these immediate worries, and continued to support them through the entire course of their needs.
- One volunteer drove the survivor on a trip of several hours so she could see the marker on her husband's grave—and did it again when the widow again expressed this need.

- A patient expressed the desire to return to her home state in the midwest in order to die at home with a son and his family. The volunteer made the many arrangements that were necessary (including procurement of medical records), met the daughter-in-law at the airport when she came to accompany the patient, invited her to spend the night in her home, drove her and the patient to the airport, and saw them safely on the plane. The patient had two good days in her son's home, and died on the third day, her wishes fulfilled.
- An unmarried careerwoman accepted the case of a young woman with a four-year-old son. She listened carefully and encouraged the patient to make her own choices. Toward the end, the volunteer took the son along on her business trips so the patient could rest and be fresh for the child. The volunteer's whole family became involved in bringing food and babysitting.
- A local police officer had a secret fear of death from a brain tumor after a close friend of his had died this way. He volunteered to serve on a cancer case with a similar tumor and saw the patient through to the end, growing personally through the experience.

Additionally, volunteers often take their patients' families out to dinner or shopping, carry on a correspondence with survivors who have relocated outside the HOV service area, and provide many other services, some of them specific, to the needs of a particular patient and family. It is not only the home care volunteer who provides valuable services. Others help to keep office records up to date, assist with correspondence, prepare training materials, enter data on computer, and perform a variety of other tasks that contribute significantly to the ability of hospice to function effectively.

Whether the hospice volunteer engages in direct contact with patients and families or provides supportive services in other ways, he or she is an indispensable part of a community-based effort to help people end their lives in the surroundings of their choice and in the company of those who are dearest to them.

See also Hospice: Philosophy and Practice.

—JULIA WILLIS

HOSPICE ASSOCIATION OF AMERICA

The Hospice Association of America (HAA) was founded in 1986 with support from the National Association for Home Care and the Association of Cancer Care Centers. Its purposes are to advance the cause of hospice care through licensure, legislation, and information; to increase access to hospice care; and to serve as a voice for hospice at the federal and state levels. There are both hospice and individual memberships in HAA.

Further information and a copy of the newsletter, *Hospice Forum,* can be obtained from:

Pat Jones, Executive Director
Hospice Association of America
214 Massachusetts Avenue, N.E.
Suite 240
Washington, DC 20002
(202) 547-5263

—JOAN LOWELL

HOSPICE DEVELOPMENT IN THE UNITED KINGDOM

Early History

To weary medieval pilgrims the word *hospice* meant sanctuary, a safe place for spiritual and physical refreshment. Hospitality to those far from home was a tangible expression of Christian charity and moral obligation. The medieval hospice was an all-purpose religious unit that looked after the sick, the pauper, the orphan, and the disabled as well as the pilgrim. The medical relief offered was, of course, limited to the crude and primitive techniques of that time.

Blacaders, an establishment in Glasgow, Scotland, illustrates the functions carried out by hospice operators in the past

(Durkan, 1962). There the hospice keeper, a resident layman, and his wife cared well for the visitors. The pilgrims were fed good meals, bedded comfortably, and—in biblical tradition—had their feet washed in a huge cauldron. Documentation from the sixteenth and seventeenth centuries suggests that there were at least a thousand religious houses providing these comforting functions in Scotland and England alone (Cowan & Easso, 1976; Manning, 1984). The term *hospice* gradually came to be associated with the care that these religious orders provided for the sick and dying, although this was but one aspect of the services offered.

By the nineteenth century, these institutions provided an alternative both to the charitable hospitals, which excluded the "incurables," and to the workhouse infirmary, which provided shelter for the destitute.

Origins of the Modern Hospice

The inauguration of Our Lady's Hospice in Dublin in 1879 under the direction of Sister Mary Aitkenhead opened a new chapter in hospice care. A more precise role was established in providing care for patients and families of patients who faced advanced cancer and other mortal illnesses. The Dublin-based Irish Sisters of Charity believed that hospice care was principally for patients with advanced malignant cancer. This view continued to be influential and was adopted by St. Joseph's Hospice, Hackney, London, when it opened in 1905. The hospices of the nineteenth century were still basically religious institutions that provided nursing care and were not integrated well either with medical practice or scientific scrutiny. They did, however, offer loving care for the dying within the framework of a shared Christian tradition.

This pattern continued after World War II when the National Health Service was introduced in the United Kingdom in 1948. Existing charitable institutions were linked with the established state-financed hospitals, thus providing a comprehensive health care program for all.

The hospice movement has grown considerably since that time. This growth has been stimulated by a remarkable awakening of interest in terminal care and by the initiative of a small number of individuals and agencies who form the core of what has become known as the modern hospice movement.

The first of these teacher-physicians to come to prominence was Dr. Cicely Saunders who, as medical officer at St. Joseph's Hospice, observed that pain control could be improved if the frequency and quantity of dosage were detailed, planned, and given before the patient's need arose (Saunders, 1967). This strategy helped to relieve not only the pain but also the anxiety a patient might feel at the prospect of pain. In her seminal book, *On death and dying* (1969), the psychiatrist Elisabeth Kubler-Ross outlined the psychological overlay to both pain and suffering. The skilled use of palliative treatment of all types together with personalized care of patients and support for their relatives were advocated as requisites of care and became the hallmark of the modern hospice movement.

The association between hospice care and cancer continued to be evinced. Specialized nursing homes were established by the Marie Curie Memorial Foundation to provide residential care both for seriously ill and for convalescent cases. Another important resource for cancer patients in the United Kingdom is the Cancer Relief Macmillan Fund, founded in 1911 by a Scotsman, Douglas Macmillan, at a time when the cancer mortality rate was doubling. Begun as the National Society for Cancer Relief, its initial preoccupation was with disseminating information on cancer. By 1924, as it was becoming clear that the amount of treatment and care did not meet the increasing demands, the organization became a charity to promote benevolent care. By the time of Macmillan's death in 1969, attitudes toward care of the terminally ill had changed in the light of Cicely Saunders' work. The Macmillan Fund took on a larger role, building care homes and training nurses. Thirteen continuous care homes were built in the 1970s and a nursing service was initiated in 1975 that has already created more than three hundred fully trained Macmillan nurses. The current expressed aim of the Fund is "to see a Macmillan nurse working in every health district in the country."

Current Hospice Care in the United Kingdom

There are now more than 100 in-patient units in the United Kingdom and the Republic of Ireland, and more than 170 home care services, with others being planned. Following the success of the new methods of palliative care pioneered at St. Christopher's Hospice, joint projects were begun by the National Society for Cancer Relief in the early 1970s, whereby capital grants were given to establish in-patient units built within National Health Service hospital grounds with the local Health Authority taking over the financial responsibility for the operating costs. As Cicely Saunders (1987) has written: "'Hospice' is now an internationally accepted term referring to care by a multi-disciplinary team for patients and families facing advanced cancer or other mortal illness. Experienced symptom control and understanding of the support needed for patient and families to find their own strength is backed by teaching and appropriate research."

The aim of a hospice is to care for terminally ill patients and their families. This includes both the drug control of symptoms and the support and counseling of patients and their families and supporters as death approaches. All the patient's problems are carefully assessed, in their physical, psychological, and social aspects. This combination of skill, symptom control, compassion, and an appropriate environment was found to be a prescription that could transform the last few weeks of the terminally ill patient's life from traumatic to bearable with relative comfort and dignity. In the United Kingdom, palliative medicine is now officially recognized as a subspecialty of medicine.

Types and Availability of Hospice Care

Hospice care has developed in several different ways that are appropriate to the varying needs of particular patients and families.

The *independent freestanding hospice* relies mainly on voluntary financial support by the public, with varying amounts of statutory support. Often in the United Kingdom contractual arrangements exist with the National Health Service through local health authorities. Some buildings are constructed as freestanding hospices, while others are inherited or purchased with a view to conversion. The Marie Curie Memorial Foundation and the Sue Ryder charities administer freestanding homes and receive income from the National Health Service as well as voluntary contributions. The Macmillan Continuing Care Homes operate facilities on the grounds of NHS hospitals, and continuing care units have also been opened as hospital adjuncts.

The *home care team* is the hospice component that serves the needs of many patients who wish to remain at home with their families, supported by their own family doctors. As well as providing emotional support to the whole family, the hospice home care team of skilled nurses and physicians will support the patient's own primary care team and advise on the relief of pain and other distressing symptoms. Most home care teams in the United Kingdom are supported or organized by the Macmillan Continuing Care Service. There is also substantial support from the Marie Curie Memorial Foundation and the NHS.

There are also *hospital support teams* that operate within general hospitals and offer advisory services to other medical units. Most of these teams take referrals only within their own institution, but some also accept patients from the community. The first hospital support team in the United Kingdom was established at St. Thomas's Hospital (London) by Dr. Thelma Bates. Variation in funding of these teams is dependent on particular staffing and management circumstances.

Not all of the services described above are available in all areas of the United Kingdom. Many patients who are in the final stages of their illness are looked after instead by the National Health Service. The style of hospice care also varies across the country. For example, in some surprisingly large areas only one solitary nurse who is attached to an area nursing team assists those in need of hospice care. At the other extreme, a comparatively small geographically delineated area may be served by several hospices. This proliferation of hospices is most commonly seen in the southeast of England. Some hospices have fully trained medical and nursing staff who are expert in palliative oncological techniques and closely linked with other areas of modern hospital practice. However, other units take a more informal approach, believing that this allays anxiety and helps in the befriending process that is such an essential feature of palliative care.

Furthering Hospice Ideals

In the ideal situation, a hospice should attempt to provide an integrated system of care that includes a home care service, a pain control or palliative care unit, a day ward, an in-patient service, and a resource and equipment center. Additionally, there should be a twenty-four-hour telephone hotline. This can be operated effectively by trained volunteers with recourse to immediate professional advice in difficult cases. Such a service often develops support and counseling functions as well, links patients and their families and supporters with hospice, and acts as liaison with the primary care team.

Hospices also can play important roles in the education of medical and nursing students and postgraduate doctors of all types. Furthermore, at every stage of hospice development, attempts should be made to engage the support and approval of the local medical, nursing, and lay community. Experience in the United Kingdom has demonstrated the value of involving professional and lay members of the community in all hospice initiatives from the very beginning. This involvement tends to overcome any initial misgivings, resulting in a general and enthusiastic response from all sections of the community it proposes to serve.

In recent years two agencies have emerged which are helping to promote hospice ideals. The Hospice Information Service was initiated by St. Christopher's Hospice in 1977. First developed as a means of identifying and locating in-patient units, home care teams, and hospital symptom control teams throughout the country, the service has since become an information exchange and communication network for the hospice movement throughout the United Kingdom. Help the Hospices was founded in 1984 as a national charity dedicated to the better care of the dying, whether in hospices, hospitals, or at home. This charity is active in the fields of education and communication and offers a large number of fellowships, courses, and conferences for health care professionals, administrators, fundraisers, and volunteers.

As for the way ahead, it seems likely to be a closer collaboration and integretion between hospices and the NHS at policy, planning, and funding levels. The hope is to form an integrated system of care so that a more harmonious match of services may be achieved in which hospital, hospice, and home are seen as strands in a seamless robe of care.

See also Children's Hospice International; Dying; Hospice: Children; Hospice: Philosophy and Practice; Hospice: Volunteers.

—ANNE J.J. GILMORE, M.D.

References

Cancer Relief Macmillan Fund (1986). *To mark the 75th anniversary.* London: Cancer Relief Macmillan Fund.

Cowan, I.B. & Easson, D.E. (1976). *Medieval religious houses, Scotland.* London: Longman.

Department of Health and Social Security (1987). *Achieving a balance: Plan for action.* London: Department of Health and Social Security.

Directory of Hospice Services in the United Kingdom and the Republic of Ireland (1987). Sydenham, Kent: St. Christopher's Hospice Information Service.

Durkan, J. (1962). *Essays on the Scottish Reformation.* Glasgow: J.S. Burns.

Help the Hospices (1987). *Progress report 1984-1987.* London: Help the Hospices.

Kubler-Ross. E. (1969). *On death and dying.* New York: Macmillan.

Manning, M. (1984). *The hospice alternative.* London: Souvenir Press.

Marie Curie Memorial Foundation (1985). *A brief history 1948-1984.* London: The Marie Curie Memorial Foundation.

Saunders, C. (1967). *The management of terminal disease.* London: Hospital Medical Publications.

Sue Ryder Foundation (1987). *Remembrance summer.* Sudbury, Suffolk: Sue Ryder Foundation.

(THE) HOSPICE JOURNAL: PHYSICAL, PSYCHOSOCIAL, AND PASTORAL CARE OF THE DYING

The Hospice Journal is a peer-reviewed scholarly journal that encourages submissions from all disciplines associated with terminal care. Articles may be research studies, program evaluations, reviews of related research, theoretical papers, or reports of advances and innovations in clinical practice.

Haworth Press and Editor David Dush began the organization of *The Hospice Journal* in 1983, with the support of Central Michigan University and Midland-Gladwin Community Mental Health. Its fifty-member editorial advisory board of leading professionals in terminal care and related fields serve as the primary reviewers. Additionally, the journal is organized around associated editors with major responsibility for several key disciplines: William Lamers, Jr. (medicine), Madalon O'Rawe Amenta and Barbara Petrosino (nursing), Howard Bell and Allan Reed (pastoral care), Lenora Finn Paradis (medical sociology), Dan Toal (pharmacy), Catherine Corboda (social work), and David Dush (clinical psychology).

The Hospice Journal began publication in 1985. It became the official journal of the National Hospice Organization in 1986. NHO members now receive the journal as a benefit of membership. In addition to its regular, diverse mix of clinical and research articles, the journal has enlisted the help of guest editors for special issues on topics such as psychosocial assessment, hospice nursing, bereavement care, and staff stress and burnout.

Information for Contributors

Manuscripts should be submitted in triplicate to:

Dr. David M. Dush, Editor
Midland-Gladwin Community Mental Health
3611 N. Saginaw Road
Midland, MI 48640

More detailed instructions are given in the back of each issue. Papers may be prepared in either AMA or APA style. The review process generally requires 60 to 90 days. The most common reasons for manuscript rejection are (a) an advocacy rather than scholarly tone, (b) failure to recognize methodological limitations of the study, (c) failure to adequately integrate the paper with existing literature in terminal care and related fields, and (d) insufficient depth. The writer should assume that the readership consists of professionals from multiple disciplines who are already experienced and sophisticated in terminal care.

Subscription and business correspondence should be directed to:

Haworth Press
12 West 32nd Street
New York, NY 10001

Inquiries regarding membership in the National Hospice Organization should be directed to:

National Hospice Organization
1901 North Fort Meyer Drive
Suite 902
Arlington, VA 22209

See also National Hospice Organization.

—DAVID M. DUSH

HUMOR AND THE FEAR OF DEATH

Humor can help to transcend fear of death and lead to personal growth and enjoyment of life. The function of humor and comedy is to reveal the secrets of human nature that arouse the most fear and dread. Death, then, is certainly one of those topics.

When used to express our common humanity, humor is on the side of life and survival. An example is found in *A Death of One's Own* (1978), Gerda Lerner's moving memoir of the struggles of her husband Carl, and indeed of the entire family, to cope with the brain tumor that eventually ended his life. When Carl was scheduled to

undergo brain surgery, the doctor told him the following story:

A man went to a bar and asked for the usual. The bartender brought him a double martini. The man gulped it down and asked for another. Same routine. After the third round the customer heaved a deep sigh. "Feeling better?" the bartender asked sympathetically. The man nodded. The bartender went on. "Had a hard day? How's the brain surgery going, Doc?" "Not bad," the man said.

Mrs. Lerner was at first upset with the doctor for telling such a joke at such a time. "But Carl was laughing uproariously with real enjoyment," she reported, "and before I knew it I was laughing too. . . . In the months to come we would increasingly find sentimentality, pity, or a tragic stance unbearable and ludicrous. We had, without knowing, shaped our attitude that day" (Lerner, p. 28).

What made the difference was the interaction between doctor, patient, and patient's wife. The doctor was willing to risk telling a joke at a time when the patient might have been feeling downcast, and Carl was receptive, showing an ability to laugh at a life-threatening condition. He could do so because the joke humanized the medical profession and the doctor-patient relationship while acknowledging the possible inadequacies of the healing arts. As a result, Carl felt less alone. Rather than assuming the role of the dying man who has been separated from the living, Carl could see himself as still being part of life and society.

Humor can also help those who are afraid of the unknowable and the terrifying. An example was Walter P., a 71-year-old man who had developed a severe agitated depression following a moderately severe heart attack. He responded very well to medication and supportive therapy for himself and his wife. But then a close friend died suddenly, also of a heart attack. Mr. P.'s symptom's returned. With the help of his wife he was able to acknowledge that the friend's death had frightened him. I was reminded of a story which I shared with them.

A 95-year-old man with a very bad heart condition bought a lottery ticket—and won five million dollars. His family was afraid to tell him the news for fear that the shock would be too much for him; so they asked the family physician to notify him gently. The doctor came to visit the old man and asked, "What would you do if you won five million dollars?" "I would give half of it to you," said the old man. And the doctor dropped dead.

Both Mr. and Mrs. P. laughed heartily, then he commented, "Gee, antidepressant medication does work!" I chose to see laughter as the antidepressant, but whether the effect was brought about by laughter, medication, or other sources of strength and support, there has been no major reappearance of Mr. P.'s symptoms in the succeeding three years. In part, I believe he recovered because we all laughed together at death anxiety.

Not all expressions of humor have such fortunate outcomes. George T., for example, was a successful and seemingly well-functioning business executive. He told the following story:

A man called a funeral parlor to arrange for the funeral of his deceased wife. "But I buried your wife two years ago," protested the funeral director. "Since then I had remarried," explained the man, "and this is for my second wife." "Oh, I didn't know you had married again—congratulations!"

This joke was told by a man who, not incidentally, had in fact married a second time. But within a month of telling the story, he was dead. There had been a fierce quarrel with his wife. She walked out of the apartment at the height of the argument. Filled with rage and having no outlet, he jumped from his twelfth story window. When his wife reached the street, he was already on the ground to greet her.

I had loved this man, as had many other of his friends. The death occurred over twenty-five years ago. My subsequent work in suicide prevention was my way of working out my own grief, and a response to the thought, "If only I had known . . . I might have been able to help you." I believe the joke and its underlying message—a plea for dealing with his death wishes—was not heard for what it was because it had not been shared in a sufficiently caring or healing context.

Not all situations resemble the two that have just been described. The meaning of humor varies from person to person, with even the same story having a variety of possible responses. Because humor is not always a simple matter, it is useful to consider some observations made by a variety of perceptive writers.

Theoretical Background

The following reflections are based primarily upon the psychoanalytic writings of Freud (1953, 1957, 1960), Kris (1952), and Zwerling (1955); the philosophical theories of Susanne Langer (1948); the social psychological studies reported by Goldstein and McGhee (1972); and literary theories of comedy as described by Milburn (1966).

The messages concealed in humor often are not heard because a different language is involved, the same as that found in dreams and close to that of poetry. It is based upon what Freud called the primary process, a form of communication that is as different from ordinary discourse as religion is from science. One must therefore learn to understand and then translate the underlying meanings, as Freud (1960) did in his classic analysis of jokes (or wit) and the unconscious.

Jokes flourish in a playful atmosphere and themselves contribute to such playfulness because they represent the mind's relaxation of its usual adherence to logic and reality. Through humor, thoughts that are ordinarily forbidden become socially acceptable. These usually hidden parts of ourselves are also those that make us most anxious, such as concern about the inevitability of death.

To laugh at what makes us anxious is a form of mastery. Through laughter, therefore, we are enabled to transcend and, in a sense, overcome death. That is probably why jokes told by older people, those who have come to terms with life and death, are often so much more genuinely humorous and good natured as compared with the tense, fear-ridden stories of the young.

A 90-year-old man told the story of another elderly gentleman who underwent an operation:

From the recovery room the old man was wheeled down to his hospital room, where his wife and a nurse were waiting. Meanwhile, a fire had broken out in the adjoining room, and the nurse pulled down the blinds. "Why did you do that?" asked the wife. "I didn't want your husband to wake up and think the operation was a failure," explained the nurse.

This allusion to the fires of hell conveys the 90-year-old joke-teller's covert expression of thanks that he is still alive. There is also good-natured laughter at the fears of death and what awaits us beyond, a suggestion that our worries are unnecessary.

By contrast, jokes told by the young express less pleasure and greater anxiety associated with sexually related topics. Compare the stories told by the elderly with the following riddles told by the young. (Unfortunately, the most revealing examples are too raw and offensive to be printed here.) The following was told by a 14-year-old boy.

Q: Why did Billy the Kid have notches on his gun?
A: Termites.

The castration imagery, the fear of damage or being damaged, as seen in the image of the termites, and the fear of being found wanting are all prominent in this example. This riddle suggests that the threshold of sexual life was being approached in a state of doubt and apprehension.

Girls are also vulnerable to such anxieties, but usually in a sex role linked manner. A 15-year-old girl told this one:

Q: What's the difference between a ping pong ball and a dead baby?
A: : You can't eat a ping pong ball.

Such "sick" jokes are told for their shock value. "Dead baby" jokes are primarily told by adolescent girls, in my experience collecting jokes. They reflect the fear of many young women that they will not be able to fulfill their role as mothers and give birth to normal children. It is significant that sex plays such a major role in the death jokes of these teenagers. Death itself can be a symbol of castration anxiety, impotence, and fears of failure as a man or woman.

In the jokes of elderly adults, on the other hand, there is often a more kindly and relaxed attitude toward both sex and death, consistent with the words Maurice Chevalier sang, "I'm so glad I'm not young any more."

A Survey of Death Themes Touched by Humor

Although much has been written about humor, very little has been published specifically on humor and death. This survey, therefore, focuses upon the raw material: examples drawn from joke books and a variety of other written sources, as well as those related by friends, colleagues, patients, and others. Because this material is so voluminous it is possible to present only an example or so of each facet of the death theme.

The Definition of Death. Death was once a simple matter to define: it was the complete and total cessation of all vital functions. Today, however, modern medicine possesses the Frankenstein-like ability to keep hearts pumping, blood circulating, and vital organs functioning while at the same time the individual is "brain dead" and in a persistent vegetative state. The definition of death has thus become more uncertain.

Nevertheless, death is still conceived of in Western society as something completely removed from life. That is why the pseudoepigram, "Death is nature's way of telling us to slow down," is so absurd. It seems to deny death while, through the technique of a conversion into the opposite, the saying reminds us of death's complete finality. A joke with a similar theme is part of Irish folklore, although I heard it from a Jewish man:

A friend came to view Callahan's body in the funeral parlor. He said to Mrs. Callahan, "Look at the beautiful smile on his face." "Yes," she replied. "He died in his sleep. He doesn't know he's dead yet."

Again, through a conversion into the opposite, this story is a reminder that death is a totally "other" state. A dead man cannot smile because he thinks he's alive, for with death there is no knowledge of life or death. However, this joke also refers to the truth that there is something inconceivable and unbelievable about death. There are many people who believe that the boundaries between life and death are fluid and not completely final. This view can be seen in the accounts of people who were revived after a cardiac arrest and felt they had died and returned to the living (See **Near-Death Experiences**).

The Definition of Dying

> Mr. Jones was lying in bed very ill, when he smelled some delicious food his wife was cooking. He called to his daughter and said, "Could you ask mother if I could have a plate of that delicious meat?" The daughter left, and returned shortly. "Mom says you can't have it. We're saving it for the wake."

Being terminally ill is not only a biological fact, says this story. It is also a social and psychological state in which others may no longer consider you part of life. In this story, too, the removal from the living is symbolized as oral deprivation, with death as the ultimate anorexia.

But the nearness of death can also be seen as an invitation to oral self-indulgence and the overcoming of fear.

> A prisoner about to be executed was told that for his last meal he could have anything he wanted to eat. "I want some mushrooms," he said. "I've always been afraid to eat them."

Death as a Wish. Death wishes are ubiquitous and probably universal. They are expressions of anger, frustration, and helplessness. Fortunately, they are usually relatively short-lived and not to be taken literally.

> One summer night, an elderly couple were sitting on their front porch and looking at the cemetery across the way. The woman said sadly, "Every time I think of our beautiful daughter laying there in the cemetery, I want to cry." "I feel the same way," said her husband. "Sometimes I even wish she was dead."

This joke plays with death as a fact (lying, "laying," in the cemetery) and an expression of disapproval for their daughter's sexual promiscuity (she even gets laid in the cemetery). The technique is based upon the double meaning of the word "laying."

Death as a Metaphor. A person in error may be described as "dead wrong." An even more relevant example is the frequent complaint that analyzing a joke "kills" it. But a metaphor can be used to deceive as well as to clarify.

> Freud [1960] told the story of the marriage broker who informed the prospective bridegroom that the girl's father was no longer living. After the marriage, the groom found out that her father was alive and in prison. He protested, but the businessman replied, "What did I tell you? You can't call that living!"

Death as a Family Matter. Marital conflicts provide one ready source of death jokes.

> A man who worked nights suspected his wife of being unfaithful. One night he left work early and, arriving home at two in the morning, found his best friend's car outside. He rushed into the house and into his wife's bedroom. She was awake, lying in bed naked, but reading a book. The husband searched everywhere but could not find a man. Finally, he went berserk, threw the TV out the window, then turned to the kitchen where he smashed all the plates and threw the refrigerator out the window. At the end of this performance, he shot himself. Arriving in heaven, he saw his friend, also waiting for admission. "What are you doing here?" asked his friend. The man described what happened, then asked—"but what are you doing here?" "I was in the refrigerator," explained his friend.

This story is a good example of the suicidal situation, including a marital crisis, accumulating stress, decompensating defenses, and impulsivity (or "temporary insanity"). Marital problems and their repetition are also revealed in homicide jokes.

> "My life has been a very hard one," said a man at a bar to the man next to him. "I've been widowed three times. The first two died of eating poisoned mushrooms, and the third from a concussion." "A concussion?" said the other man, "how did that happen?" "She wouldn't eat the mushrooms," explained the widower.

Unfortunately, these tragedies are not confined to jokes; rather such hostile forms of humor remind us that society includes "death-carriers," people who destroy those who come close to them.

Sex Leads to Death. A familiar example is that of the 86-year-old man who married a 19-year-old woman. The family doctor warned him that too much sex could be fatal. "Well," shrugged the old man philosophically, "If she dies, she dies."

The young wife's threatened death in this case is more an affirmation of the old man's virility. In an allusive manner, then, sex is presented as the life force, the opposite of death. A somewhat similar message underlies the story of a couple who had not missed a night of sex during their thirty years of marriage.

> The wife did not feel well one day, and was told by her doctor that she must have complete rest for six months, including complete sexual abstinence, or she would not live. The couple moved to separate bedrooms. After three months, however, the husband could stand it no longer, and left his room to go to hers. At the same time, she left her bedroom. "I was just coming to you to die," she said. "I'm glad," he replied, "because I was just going to your room to kill you."

The doctor in this story warned that sex leads to death, an idea that has been expressed more than once in our culture. But to this couple sex was life and an affirmation of their love and relationship. That they both left their rooms simultaneously suggested some kind of special communication between them.

Sex Conquers Death. According to many jokes, the opposite of death is not life, but sex.

> There was an old couple who had been married for over fifty years. The wife became very ill and finally was on her deathbed. As the end came near she said to her husband, "I'm dying, but before I go make love to me just once more, in memory of our life together." The husband complied. In fact, he made love to her more passionately and tenderly than ever before. And lo and behold, a miracle happened. The wife renewed her will to live and became well again. "I'm alive," she said, "and I owe it all to you, because you made such beautiful love to me." Her husband was silent for a long time, and finally said, "I was just thinking; I could have saved Mama."

This joke has had other punchlines. The requirement seems to be that the life-saving powers of sex are put to some scandalous or unlikely use.

Execution or the Death Penalty as a Form of Homicide. By a conversion into the opposite, the following story implies that a civilization that is built upon legalized murder contains serious flaws and is not truly civilized.

> A shipwrecked mariner floated on a raft for days, until the current finally carried him to a strange shore. As he drew nearer he saw some men erecting a gallows. The sailor fell on his knees in gratitude and cried out, "Thank God, I have reached a civilized country!"

The Doctor as Both Rescuer and Bringer of Death. As the saying goes, "The patient was at death's door, but the doctor pulled him through." There are also stories in which funeral directors express their gratitude to the medical profession for providing them with so many customers, or in which relatives who were heirs thank physicians for their new-found wealth. Doctors are thus placed upon a pedestal so that they can be knocked down.

The responsibilities of medicine arouse great concern in doctors still in training or about to begin their practice. One medical student told the following story:

> A man died and had great difficulty being accepted into Heaven because they had no record of him there. Finally, St. Peter said, "You must have had a lousy doctor. You're not due here for another three years."

The identification of the student, of course, was with the suspected "lousy doctor."

> A worried patient shared his concerns with the doctor: "I've heard of cases where the doctor has treated someone for pneumonia and he died of typhoid fever." The doctor was highly offended. "Ridiculous," he replied. "When I treat a patient for pneumonia, he dies of pneumonia."

This depiction of the physician is part of a larger topic, that of the helper or rescuer of whatever background.

Death as the Result of the Destructive Wishes of Others. The following chilling story presents suicide as a response to the lack of love and caring, as well as domination by self-serving needs. It is in the tradition of criticizing man's inhumanity to man—or woman—in general.

> "I think I'm pregnant," said the girl to her boyfriend. "What are you going to do?" he asked. "I'm going to kill myself!" she replied emotionally. "You are a good sport!" he replied gratefully.

Jokes also can suggest an appropriate response to destructive messages.

> A man loved to go to the zoo and tease the animals. One day he went to the orangutan cage and began making gestures, but everything he did was imitated by the ape. Finally, the man simply scratched his head—and the orangutan went crazy, tore the bars apart, and attacked his visitor. The zookeeper visited him in the hospital, and the man told him what happened. The zookeeper explained, "You should know that in orangutan, scratching your head means 'go to hell'." After the man recovered he returned to the zoo with two sets of barber supplies, including a soap mug, brush, and razor. He gave one to the ape, who took it, and the man started making gestures. Again, the ape imitated him. Finally, the man lathered his face, and the ape did the same. The man then pretended to cut his throat. And the orangutan scratched his head.

This story is a prototype of the response of the invitation to suicide. If followed, it offers one possible antidote to all the destructive interactions to which vulnerable people are subjected.

Life is Better than Death. Asked how he felt about turning 80, Maurice Chevalier replied, "I feel fine about it, considering the alternative." There is the following story as well.

> A weary old man was walking up a steep hill, carrying a heavy load of wood. Finally he could stand it no longer. He threw down his burden and, raising his hands to Heaven, called out, "I want the Angel of Death to come and take me!" At once, the Angel of Death appeared before him. "You called?" "Yes," replied the old man quickly. "Will you help me get this load back on my shoulders?"

Conclusion

Death, directly or in disguise, is a prominent theme in humor, and in some creative persons the problem of death is the motivating force in the production of humor. For all of us, humor may be one of the best available and healthful prescriptions for the enjoyment and enrichment of life.

See also Brain Death; Death Fears and Anxiety; Death Themes Through History; Near-Death Experiences.

—JOSEPH RICHMAN

References

Freud, S. (1901/Reprint 1953). *The interpretation of dreams.* Standard edition. Vol. 5. London: Hogart.

Freud, S. (1905/Reprint 1960). *Jokes and their relationship to the unconscious.* Standard edition. Vol. 8. London: Hogart.

Freud, S. (1915/Reprint 1957). *Thoughts for the times on war and death.* Standard edition. Vol. 14. London: Hogart.

Goldstein, J.H. & McGhree, P.E. (1972). *The psychology of humor.* New York: Academic Press.

Kris, E. (1952). *Psychoanalytic explorations in art.* New York: International Universities Press.

Langner, S. (1948). *Philosophy in a new key.* New York: New American Library.

Lerner, G. (1978). *A death of one's own.* New York: Simon & Schuster.

Richman, J. (1977). "The foolishness of age and the wisdom of jokes." *The Gerontologist, 17*: 210–19.

Zwerling, I. (1955). "The favorite joke in diagnostic and therapeutic interviewing." *Psychoanalytic Quarterly, 24*: 104–15.

I

INTERNATIONAL ASSOCIATION FOR NEAR-DEATH STUDIES (IANDS)

The International Association for Near-Death Studies (IANDS) is a world-wide organization of scientists, scholars, those who have had near-death experiences, and the general public, dedicated to the exploration of near-death experiences (NDEs) and their implications. IANDS was incorporated as a nonprofit educational organization in 1981 under the leadership of Raymond Moody, Kenneth Ring, Bruce Greyson, Michael Sabom, and John Audette. Its purpose is to encourage the study of the NDE. Further, IANDS hopes to increase understanding of near-death and other transformative experiences, and to assist their integration into the lives of individuals and society, in the belief that in those areas of scholarship where science and spiritual traditions meet, the potential of human consciousness may be most fully realized.

IANDS' objectives are to encourage and support research into NDEs and related phenomena; to disseminate knowledge concerning NDEs and their implications; to promote the utilization of near-death research by health care and counseling professionals; to form local chapters of near-death experiencers and interested others; to sponsor symposiums and conferences on NDEs and related phenomena; and to maintain a library and archives of near-death-related material.

Activities include publication of the quarterly academic *Journal of Near-Death Studies (Anabiosis)* and of *Revitalized Signs,* a quarterly newsletter of general interest; the sponsorship of research conferences and workshops for professional and lay audiences; offering supportive services to near-death experiencers, their families, and professionals working with them; and providing reliable information through its printed materials, media work, audiovisual archives, and speakers' bureau. "Friends of IANDS" exist in many cities as support groups for those who have had near-death experiences and other interested persons.

IANDS is governed by a board of directors consisting of researchers, clinicians, near-death experiencers, and interested members of the general public. Membership in IANDS is open to all persons, lay or professional, who have an interest in NDEs and related phenomena. There are two principal membership categories: general members receive the quarterly newsletter and discounted admission to sponsored conferences; research members receive the same plus the quarterly *Journal of Near-Death Studies.*

For more information, write to:

IANDS
Department of Psychiatry
University of Connecticut Health Center
Farmington, CT 06032

See also Near-Death Experiences.

—BRUCE GREYSON

INTERNATIONAL CLASSIFICATION OF DISEASES (ICD)

A standard categorization system for causes of death (the ICD) exists so that information concerning the changing configuration of causes of death within a nation and differences in the distribution of causes of death across societies can be obtained. The international classification system has evolved gradually over the last century. The current Ninth Revision of the ICD went into effect in 1979. Since 1946 the World Health Organization has been responsible for the ICD, which is revised every ten years.

Causes of death are distributed throughout seventeen broad categories in the Ninth Edition of the ICD. Sixteen of these categories deal with various illnesses and diseases, the other category is for external causes of death, such as accidents. The seventeen categories are (1) infectious and parasitic diseases; (2) neoplasms; (3) endocrine, nutritional, and metabolic diseases and immunity disorders; (4) diseases of the blood and blood-forming organs; (5) mental disorders; (6) diseases of the nervous system and sense organs; (7) diseases of the circulatory system; (8) diseases of the respiratory system; (9) diseases of the digestive system; (10) diseases of the genito-urinary tract; (11) complications of pregnancy, childbearing, and the puerperium; (12) diseases of the skin and subcutaneous tissue; (13) diseases of the musculoskeletal system and connective tissue; (14) congenital anomalies; (15) certain conditions originating in the perinatal period; (16) symptoms, signs, and ill-defined conditions; and (17) external causes of injury and poisoning.

Within each broad category are several more specific classes that are further divided into particular diseases, disease sites, or conditions. For example, diseases of the circulatory system are divided into ischemic (coronary) heart disease and cerebrovascular diseases, among others, which are further broken down into more detailed causes. External causes are divided into accidents (further broken down by type), suicides (detailing various methods), and homicides.

Use of ICD Data

In theory, the ICD is a useful tool in the analysis of trends and differentials in causes of death and in the assessment of progress in overcoming life-threatening diseases and conditions. In practice, there are a number of limitations. Four of the most significant limitations are:

1. Cross-national comparisons are affected by variations in data quality. These variations result from differences in the diagnostic skill and type of training of the certifying medical attendant or coroner, in the accuracy of the diagnosis recorded on the death certificate, and in the accurate coding of the information. A high proportion of deaths classified in the vague category "symptoms, signs, and ill-defined conditions" can serve as an indicator of poor data quality.

2. Trend analysis is affected by changes over time in the ICD categories themselves. For example, the large apparent decline in the U.S. standardized mortality rate for "bronchitis, emphysema and asthma" between 1968 and 1978 is artificial, being simply the result of changes in classification between the seventh and eighth revisions of the ICD.

3. The ICD categories are based on a single cause of death. This is the "underlying" cause that is deemed by the medical examiner to have generated the sequelae leading to death. For populations in developed societies, where most deaths occur at old age and where multiple factors are often involved, a classification system based on a single cause of death can lead to data distortions.

4. The Ninth Revision does not contain categories for new diseases such as AIDS, or diseases that had been largely neglected, such as Alzheimer's.

See also Acquired Immune Deficiency Syndrome (AIDS); Causes of Death; Mortality Rate.

—ELLEN GEE

References

Israel, R.A. (1978). "The International Classification of Diseases: Two hundred years of development." *Public Health Reports, 93*: 150–52.

Office of Population Censuses and Surveys (1982). *Mortality statistics: Comparison of the Eighth and Ninth Revisions of the International Classification of Diseases.* London: Office of Population Censuses and Surveys.

INTERNATIONAL WORK GROUP ON DEATH, DYING, AND BEREAVEMENT

The International Work Group on Death, Dying, and Bereavement (IWG) is composed of clinicians, researchers, and teachers dedicated to the development of knowledge and services for those who are confronted by death, dying, and bereavement. The organization sees itself as a catalyst and seeks to spread its own work as well as the work of others. The IWG was founded at a meeting of interested persons in 1974 at Columbia University (New York City) as an outgrowth of Ars Moriendi, a group of Philadelphia-area physicians and other caregivers interested in the terminally ill. The IWG was incorporated in the State of Pennsylvania in 1979.

The IWG meets every eighteen months for the purpose of facilitating informal interaction among its members as well as developing standards of care. In 1978 the "Assumptions and Principles for Standards of Care for the Terminally Ill" was published; in 1981 the "Assumptions and Principles Regarding Bereavement" and in 1987 the "Assumptions and Principles Concerning the Care of the Dying and Bereaved in Developing Countries" were published. "Assumptions and Principles of Spiritual Care" is in draft form. "Assumptions and Principles for the Care of the Patient with AIDS," "Assumptions and Principles for Education about Death, Dying, and Bereavement," and "Assumptions and Principles Concerning Symptom Control" are in various stages of development.

Membership is by invitation. Presently there are members in eight countries: Canada, Israel, Japan, Norway, Sweden, South Africa, the United Kingdom, and the United States. To find out more about the IWG, contact:

The International Work Group on
  Death, Dying and Bereavement
c/o Dr. John D. Morgan, Secretary
King's College
266 Epworth Avenue
London, Ontario, Canada N6A 2M3
(519) 432-7946; (519) 433-3491.

—JOHN D. MORGAN

J

JONESTOWN

There were signs of impending danger on the morning of Saturday, November, 18, 1978. Some members of the community established in Guyana by followers of the Reverend Jim Jones were desperately attempting to leave. Later there were rumors that Jones had ordered the assassination of those who were perceived as unsympathetic to his Peoples Temple Mission. By the end of that day, a reported 883 men, women, and children lay dead, victims of mass suicide and murder. Several journalists and a United States congressman had also been killed. The Peoples Temple Mission no longer existed.

The Jonestown massacre remains both a human tragedy and a disturbing example of how destructive forces can emerge from group behavior that started with peaceful and constructive motives.

Jim Jones and the Peoples Temple

Born in 1931 in a small farming community by the Indiana-Ohio border, Jim Jones reacted against the racial prejudice that dominated at the time. After several failed efforts to establish a racially integrated congregation, Jones, at age 25, started his own church, the Peoples Temple, in Indianapolis. He and his wife, who were both white, adopted black, white, and Asian children to demonstrate the sincerity of their beliefs. Jones was described at this time as having a magnetic personality and the ability to inspire others. Another side of his personality had also been observed,

however. The young minister insisted on intense discipline and allegiance from his followers and showed domineering and paranoid tendencies. There was a basis in reality for some fear and distrust: Jones had long been harassed and taunted for his liberal views on racial relations.

Jones attracted additional attention and supporters with his faith-healing claims and demonstrations. These activities were criticized by some authorities and health care professionals on the grounds that people with cancer and other serious ills were relying completely on Jones and failing to seek proper medical care. A number of official inquiries were started in response to various concerns about the claims and activities associated with Jones's Temple, but none were pursued to conclusion. However, there were other problems. Jones and his venture remained financially insecure. He also appeared to be troubled by the fact that racial tensions were still very much in evidence despite all his efforts.

Jones relocated of the Temple to Redwood Valley, a small town in an agricultural area 125 miles north of San Francisco, where he worked hard to gain the trust and approval of the community. "The Mendocino County folk remember Jones as appealing but eccentric—nice, pleasant, doing good turns whenever he could, but a little strange in his ways" (Kilduff & Javers, 1978, p. 30). His reception in the community was mixed, however, and there was also dissension within the Temple as some members became troubled over certain aspects of Jones's behavior, including his increased interest in talking about sex. Jones soon made himself known in San Francisco and Los Angeles with dramatic faith-healing meetings. Again, some of his claims and actions were criticized by the press (he claimed to have restored more than forty dead people to life and he traveled with heavily armed bodyguards).

In 1972 he moved his Temple to San Francisco and attempted to draw support primarily from the Bay Area's black community. Critics saw this as a move to increase his political strength and thought some of his actions were far removed from his proclaimed intentions of brotherly love. Nevertheless, Jones became increasingly successful, established another Temple in Los Angeles, started publishing a newspaper, and went on the air with a weekly radio series.

By 1977 Jones was a very well-known figure in California. His Temple appeared to be flourishing, yet there were continuing allegations of fraud, oppression, and sex scandals. Some former members of the Temple, expressing fears about reprisal, began to tell about Jones's alleged double standards of behavior and morality, financial demands upon his followers, and his self-appointed right to take any woman who appealed to him. It was claimed that Jones would "rave for hours" about his sexual prowess and try to persuade his followers that he was "the only legitimate object of sexual desire." According to *San Francisco Chronicle* reporters Marshall Kilduff and Ron Javers: "Jones found sex a useful tool for controlling his Temple parishioners. Couples who thought of themselves as good Christians found, after engaging in adulterous and homosexual conduct, that they were liable to blackmail and subject to intense guilt. But to married couples Jones would often have another form of advice: abstention. Couples were forced apart and told not to engage in sexual intercourse because it was evil" (p. 55). Meanwhile, Jones had become dependent on drugs and was seldom seen without dark glasses.

Conflicting reports about Jones and his Temple were proving difficult to evaluate and place in balance. It was within this context that it was learned that one of the Temple's projects was the establishment of a new community in the undeveloped countryside of Guyana. Temple money was being invested in this plan, usually through cash transfers by courier. Jones himself then turned over the daily operations of his San Francisco Temple to subordinates and led his cult to Jonestown. It is thought that Jones was prompted to this move by the increasing difficulties he was experiencing, including criminal investigation and media criticism as well as internal dissension.

The settlement itself was in the largely uninhabited northwestern portion of Guyana, an English-speaking South American nation with a largely black population. Guyana welcomed the prospect of a thriving settlement near its Venezuelan border. Jonestown had its preliminary beginnings in 1973, but there were still only fifteen Temple members working to clear the land in 1975, and only about seventy residents by May 1976.

The Suicide/Massacre

Many of Jones's San Francisco followers accompanied him to Guyana. Discipline was strict and punitive, including electric shocks for children who wet their beds. Workdays often extended from 6 a.m. to 10 p.m. and all were obliged to follow every rule set down by Jones. Along with the harsh conditions at Jonestown there were difficulties back in San Francisco, where relatives who inquired at the Temple were given no information on the whereabouts and condition of their family members who might or might not have gone to Jonestown (the move having been conducted with some secrecy). A public relations campaign attempted to convey the picture of Jonestown as a model community where people were enjoying healthy and positive lives. Meanwhile, Jones placed severe pressure on those in Guyana to remain with the settlement no matter how they disliked it. Several people attempted to visit Jonestown and make firsthand observations, but were harassed by those close to Jones.

Perhaps the first indication of the impending catastrophe was included in a letter from Jones to all U.S. senators and congressmen in which he complained of interference and harassment by American government agencies: "I can say without hesitation that we are devoted to a decision that it is better even to die than to be constantly harassed from one continent to the next."

U.S. Congressman Leo Ryan of California decided that the reports circulating about Jonestown and the possible mistreatment of its residents required his personal attention. A National Broadcasting Company camera crew received permission to accompany him to Guyana, as did several newspapermen. Attempts were made by the government of Guyana to discourage the visit, but Ryan and the media people held firm to their intentions. Ryan assured the reporters, "Trust us. We'll walk you through." In retrospect, it appears that the congressman and the reporters were all aware that there could be personal dangers involved, but each thought that the other would serve as a safety-assuring escort. Who would attack a U.S. congressman? Who would attack accredited newspaper and television reporters?

The visiting delegation was delayed by Guyanese officials before gaining reluctant permission to proceed to Jonestown. Ryan had indicated that he would be delighted to find that the unfavorable reports had been erroneous and that Jonestown was, in fact, the thriving, successful settlement that had been painted by the Peoples Temple.

When their plane landed on the jungle airstrip, the visitors were faced by a 30-gauge shotgun pointed at their faces by a Guyanese police officer who said he was acting under instructions from Jones. After a period of conversation and negotiation, however, they were trucked to the settlement. To the American visitors, Jones appeared to be in an unstable condition, unhealthy and sweating. One of the eyewitnesses thought at the time that "I was looking at a man in decay." They were given dinner (which they ate while wondering if Jones had chosen that occasion to poison them), and treated to a performance by "an excellent rock band" and other entertainers from the Jonestown settlement. It was the visitors' impression that the cult members in attendance were under orders to look cheerful and enthuasiastic. Congressman Ryan said a few pleasant words and received a prolonged, standing, shouting ovation. He then made it clear that he was visiting in the capacity of conducting a congressional inquiry, and the Temple members contin-

ued to indicate that all was well with them. But one woman approached a reporter in the dark and slipped him a note with several signatures on it and the request: "Please help us get out of Jonestown."

Before the evening was over, the visitors had received other information indicating that conditions were far from ideal. A Guyanese policeman told of a small black box in which those who disobeyed Jones's rules were held captive—without light or air. This report was consistent with other rumors that had been circulating. Additional pieces of negative information were also passed along to the visitors as opportunities presented themselves. On the following day, the visitors were given a tightly controlled tour of the settlement, watched carefully so they could not break away to explore for themselves. It was evident, however, living conditions were primitive, and many of the residents fearful. Even as some of the old women living in barracks assured the visitors that they were "living in paradise," their anxiety and terror could be seen.

A turning point came when one old woman told a reporter and the congressman that she wanted to leave the settlement. Becoming agitated, Jones tried to talk the woman out of her request: "The old woman would have none of it. She stared ahead, her hands squeezed together in her lap, and she didn't reply. Jones seemed to be growing more desperate. Sweat broke out on his forehead. . . . At this point we noted several more people were getting up courage to say they wanted to go" (Kilduff & Javers, p. 159). The list grew to twenty people who were willing to defy Jones and ask for deliverance from Jonestown. This posed a logistical problem as the plane held only eighteen passengers; two trips would be needed, and Congressman Ryan decided he would go on the second flight. Meanwhile, it had become clear that Jones had styled himself as father to his "subjects." His conversation was rational at times, but he swung increasingly into a vehement and hysterical mood in which he expressed belief in a conspiracy against Jonestown, and accused some Temple members of lying to him. Jones became further upset when he realized how many people had signed up to leave him. He told the reporters that he wanted to hug them all before they left.

Violence erupted at the airstrip as the visitors and the defecting cult members prepared to leave. First, a young man rushed out of the crowd and attempted to stab Congressman Ryan. The assailant was himself wounded as others intervened and disarmed him, and Ryan, covered with his attacker's blood, entered the plane where other passengers were already waiting. Another man then approached and asked to be taken aboard. The other passengers were very upset by this and urged that he not be included. They are quoted as saying, "He is one of his (Jones's) lieutenants. He is one of the higher-ups. He'll kill us, he'll kill us all." However, the visitors allowed him aboard, taking the view that everybody had a right to leave if he so chose. By this time there were two planes waiting to take off, a second plane having been chartered to provide enough space for those who wanted to leave.

Although efforts were made to take off immediately, it was already too late. Several armed men jumped off a dump truck and started firing. Congressman Ryan was among the first to be killed. NBC reporter Don Harris and photographer Greg Robinson also were shot to death by the opening rounds. Cameraman Bob Brown continued to photograph the scene until his head was blown apart. A woman sitting in the plane, Patricia Parks, was also killed by a shotgun blast. Among the seriously injured was another journalist, Steve Sung; the congressman's aide, Jackie Speier; and Anthony Katsaris, a man who had come to Guyana to learn about the situation of his daughter, a member and possibly a captive of the cult. The death squad shot out one of the engines of one plane, then left. For some hours afterward there were fears that the killers would return to murder those who had not been able to escape with the other plane.

This attack on the unarmed visitors was prelude to the mass suicide and massacre that followed at Jonestown. Two American lawyers at the settlement ("protected" by one of the airstrip assailants) heard one of the gunmen declare "We're gonna commit revolutionary suicide." The lawyers decided to escape through the jun-

gle. As they left, "They heard Jones's voice cry, 'Mother mother mother mother!' This was followed by what sounded . . . like three shots" (Reiterman & Jacobs, 1982, p. 542). The lawyers kept running.

The next lethal episode occurred a few hours later in the Guyana city of Georgetown, where cult member Sharon Amos apparently misinterpreted the approach of a police car as confirmation of her fear that the "white night" of destruction was at hand. She and three of her children were found dead, their throats slit. There is more than one version of this incident, which might possibly have involved murder as well as suicide.

The final scene occurred later that same afternoon. First, syringes were filled with cyanide and squirted into the mouths of the babies. The Jonestown children were then lined up in the central pavilion and given cups of Kool-Aid to which cyanide had also been added. The adults were then summoned to take the lethal drink. Armed guards stood ready to shoot any who would not obey. Over the loudspeaker system, Jones said: "There is great dignity in dying. It is a great demonstration for everybody to die." Most of the men, women, and children in camp died within five minutes, many with their arms around each other. A few escaped or were not present at the time. Jones himself was found dead with a bullet in his right temple.

The Peoples Temple members who had remained in San Francisco were shocked by news of the tragedy, as were former members. Many had friends or relatives among the dead.

Lessons from Jonestown

The first reaction of shock and horror has subsided over time, but Jonestown has taken its place in public consciousness as a massive example of self-destructive group behavior. Many commentators have hoped to draw constructive lessons from this painful event. It must be acknowledged, however, that no completely adequate and convincing explanation has emerged. Nevertheless, there are several remembrances of the Jonestown tragedy that might well be kept in mind:

1. A person can exercise charismatic leadership qualities despite having dangerous and unstable elements in his or her personality.
2. Life-affirming beliefs and practices (such as developing a sense of community and overcoming the barriers of racial prejudice) can be linked perilously with strong self-destructive tendencies.
3. The hazard of allowing one person to make rules and decisions on the behalf of others with near-absolute authority has again been demonstrated.
4. Fear and apprehension on the part of all the people involved probably contributed significantly to failures in communication, misinterpretations of intention, and the final episodes of violence, murder, and suicide.
5. Murder and suicide can all too easily be promoted as though merely political actions or as demonstrations of "dignity" and meaning—even though the actual outcome is the death of individuals who might otherwise have enjoyed active, meaningful, and socially useful lives.

Traditional sociological and psychiatric formulations of suicide fall short of explaining what occurred in Jonestown, with its distinctive circumstances and its mixture of murder and self-destruction. Improved understanding is needed of group behavior, especially groups that see themselves as threatened by outsiders. Although the conditions that led up to the Jonestown tragedy were unique, there can be no assurance that similar episodes might not occur when people grow increasingly desperate within a climate of fear and mistrust.

See also Death System; Suicide.

—ROBERT KASTENBAUM

References

Kilduff, M. & Javers, R. (1978). *The suicide cult.* New York: Bantam.
Rieterman, T. & Jacobs, J. (1982). *Raven: The untold story of the Rev. Jim Jones and his people.* New York: E.P. Dutton.

JOURNAL OF NEAR-DEATH STUDIES (ANABIOSIS)

The scholarly journal that is the official organ of the International Association for Near-Death Studies was begun in 1981. Originally published semi-annually under the name *Anabiosis* (Greek for 'restoration to life from a death-like condition'), the journal expanded to quarterly publication and its current name in 1987.

The *Journal of Near-Death Studies (Anabiosis)* publishes original articles on near-death experiences (NDEs), their empirical effects and theoretical implications, and on such related phenomena as out-of-body experiences, deathbed visions, experiences of dying persons, comparable experiences occurring under other circumstances, and the implications of such phenomena.

An international editorial board of physicians, psychiatrists, psychologists, nurses, sociologists, anthropologists, philosophers, theologians, and parapsychologists select articles that include empirical studies, scientific and philosophical perspectives, theoretical and conceptual formulations, and cross-cultural and clinical studies. A typical issue of the journal includes five manuscripts plus book reviews. The range of material published is suggested through a sampling of titles such as "NDEs and the Mind-Body Problem"; "Are NDEs Evidence of Survival?"; "Why Birth Models Cannot Explain NDEs"; "Clinical Approaches to the NDE"; "NDEs and Attitude Change"; "A Multivariate Method for the Classification of Pre-Existing Near-Death Conditions"; and "Pathophysiology of Stress-Induced Limbic Lobe Dysfunction: A Hypothesis for NDEs."

Information for Contributors

Manuscripts should be submitted in triplicate, APA style, to:

Bruce Greyson, Editor
Journal of Near-Death Studies (Anabiosis)
Department of Psychiatry
University of Connecticut Health Center
Farmington, CT 06032

Subscription and Business Information

The journal is sent to all Research Members of the International Association for Near-Death Studies. Nonmembers may subscribe by writing to the publisher:

Human Sciences Press
72 Fifth Avenue
New York, NY 10011–8004

See also International Association for Near-Death Studies (IANDS); Near-Death Experiences.

—BRUCE GREYSON

(THE) JOURNAL OF PSYCHOSOCIAL ONCOLOGY

The Journal of Psychosocial Oncology, published quarterly since 1983, was developed to meet the needs of health professionals in oncology for clinical and research information in the rapidly developing field of psychosocial oncology. Thus, the aim of the journal is to provide a forum for the dissemination of such knowledge and to facilitate the exchange of ideas.

Manuscripts are reviewed by members of an international editorial board representing the many different fields that comprise psychosocial oncology, such as education, epidemiology, health advocacy, medical oncology, neurology, nursing, nutrition, pastoral counseling, physical therapy, psychiatry, psychology, public health, social work, sociology, and surgical oncology.

A typical issue contains seven to nine clinical, research, and review articles, several book reviews, abstracts, and a bibliography of articles on related topics. The section "Perspectives" provides a vehicle for discussions of current ethical and philosophical topics relevant to oncology. Another, "Research Issues in Psychosocial Oncology," addresses the development, design, and methodology of psychosocial research as well as research concepts for clinicians. Pilot studies on topics not previously studied also are published occa-sionally. Finally, a few issues have been devoted entirely or in part to conference proceedings or to topics of special interest.

The following is a representative sample of articles: "The Emotional Impact of Recurrent Cancer," "How Adults with Late-Stage Cancer Experience Personal Control," "Development of a Scale for Assessing Sexual Function After Treatment for Gynecologic Cancer," "Sources of Work Stress for Hospice Staff," "Helping Children Communicate About Serious Illness and Death," "An Examination of the Concrete Service Needs of Advanced Cancer Patients," "Suicide and Cancer. Part I. Medical and Care Factors in Suicides by Cancer Patients in Sweden, 1973–1976," "Gay Grief: An Examination of Its Uniqueness Brought to Light by the AIDS Crisis," "Conflicts in Cancer Care: The Role of Moral Reflection," and "Quality of Life Among Survivors of Childhood Cancer: A Critical Review and Implications for Intervention."

Information for Contributors

Manuscripts should be submitted in triplicate to:

Grace H. Christ, Editor
Memorial Sloan-Kettering Cancer
 Center
1275 York Avenue
New York, NY 10021

Abstracts of 100 to 150 words are required. Specific instructions for the preparation of manuscripts appear opposite the table of contents. Books for review should be submitted to Lois Weinstein, Book Review Editor and Associate Director, Memorial Sloan-Kettering Cancer Center. Submitted manuscripts are acknowledged immediately. The review process usually takes sixty days.

Subscription and Business Information

The Haworth Press, Inc.
75 Griswold Street
Binghamton, NY 13904

—GRACE H. CHRIST

K

KADDISH

The Kaddish, one of the best-known prayers of the Jewish faith, is recited after the death of a loved one. The meaning of the prayer and its place in Jewish life are not limited to situations of loss and mourning, however, nor does the prayer itself directly speak of death.

The Kaddish is a declaration of faith in which God is praised with full depth of feeling. It is a part of the traditional Jewish liturgy, recited at the conclusion of other major prayers, and also at the end of the worship service. It is also recited on other solemn occasions, such as the completion of a period of Talmudic study, burial, and services and remembrances specific to mourning.

A transliteration of the Kaddish has been provided by Rabbi Maurice Lamm (1969):

Mourner: Yisgadal v'yiskadash shmai raba. Magnified and sanctified be His great name.
Congregation: Amen.
Mourner: B'olmo deev'ro chir'usai, In this world which he has created in accordance with His will, *v'yamlich malchusai, b'chayechon u'vyomechon,* may He establish his kingdom during your lifetime, *u'vychayai d'chol bais Yisroel,* and during the life of all the House of Israel *ba'agolah u'vizman koriv, v'imru amen.* Speedily and let us say, Amen.
Congregation: (Repeats verse.)
Mourner: *Yisborach v'yishtabach v'yispa-er v'yisromam* Blessed, praised, glorified and exalted; *v'yishnasai v'yishadar v'yisaleh v'yis-halal,* extolled,

honored, magnified and lauded, *shemei d'Kudsha, b'rich Hu.* Be the name of the Holy one, blessed be He.
Congregation: *B'rich Hu.* Blessed be He.
Mourner: *L'aila min kol birchasa v'shirasa, tushbechasa v'nechamasa,* He is greater than all blessing, hymns, praises and consolation, *da'amiron b'olmo; v'imru, Amen,* which can be uttered in this world, and let us say, Amen.
Congregation: Amen.
Mourner: *Osah shalom bimeromav, Hu ya-aseh shalom,* He who makes peace in the heavens, may He make peace, *alenu v'al Kol yisroel; v'imru amen.* For us and for all Israel; and let us say, Amen.
Congregation: Amen.

This ancient prayer has several alternative forms, the Mourner's Kaddish being the version recited by bereaved persons. Despite its silence on the fate of the dead, the Kaddish offers consolation to the bereaved. As Lamm observes: "this beautiful litany begins with the admission that the world that is known only to Him, the Omniscient Creator of the universe, remains mysterious and paradoxical to man. It ends with an impassioned hope, expressed in the words of the friends of Job as they sought to comfort him . . . that He who is sufficiently mighty to make peace among the celestial bodies may also bring peace to all mankind" (Lamm, p. 154). The prayer also links the bereaved person with the history of the Jewish people as it seeks consolation for the destruction of their ancient temple. Lamm also points out that the consolation offered through recitation of the Kaddish is strengthened by the fact that it is a prayer to be offered in the company of others, many of whom are usually themselves mourners. One therefore recognizes that others have also suffered pain and loss, "that death is a natural, if often untimely, end to all life."

Traditionally, the son of the deceased has the obligation to say Kaddish; others may also choose to do so. The Kaddish is said twice a day for the first eleven months after the death of a loved one. Thereafter it is said on days of fasting and rejoicing. There are several other traditions that may be followed depending upon the survivor's pattern of religious observances.

There is still another and rather unusual form of consolation embodied in the Kaddish. God Himself has suffered a loss when one individual life perishes. When the human mourner magnifies the name of the Lord (*Yamllich malchusai*) through the Kaddish, this expresses a shared grief: God and human both mourn and offer consolation to each other.

In addition to the Kaddish there are other Jewish prayers through which sorrow and praise are combined. An important example is the Memorial Prayer, which concludes (in the version for women): "May the Lord of Mercy bring her under the cover of His wings forever, and may her soul be bound up in the bond of eternal life. May the Lord be her possession, and may she rest in peace. Amen." The Memorial Prayer differs from the Kaddish by offering a prayer specifically on behalf of the dead.

See also Survival Beliefs and Practices: Jewish.

—ROBERT KASTENBAUM

Reference

Lamm, M. (1969). *The Jewish way in death and mourning.* New York: Jonathan David.

L

LIFE AFTER DEATH?

In this age of science, death is still a mystery left to our ever-changing belief systems. Dante, the towering genius of his time, describes his beliefs in *Convito*: "I say, that of all idiocies, that is most stupid, most vile, and most damnable which holds that after this life there is no other." However, people have also been criticized for holding to a belief in afterlife, especially as this view has come under attack in the modern era. The fact is that a large majority of Americans (73 percent) do affirm such a belief (National Opinion Research Center, 1986).

But the strength of conviction in both camps appears to be weak. When death comes to oneself or immediate family, many want to know, rather than to depend on belief alone. For these people, empirical information might be of some interest. Relevant literature can be found under such headings as survival, psychical research, and parapsychology.

Studies of Apparitions ("Ghosts")

Phenomena suggestive of afterlife have been reported throughout the history of various cultures; for example, Plato, in *The Republic,* described out-of-body journeys of a soldier, Er, who was thought to have been killed in action. Pliny the Younger described a ghost case in Athens.

Well-organized, systematic studies of apparitions started after the Society for Psychical Research (SPR) was founded in England in 1882. The SPR was soon joined in this quest by the American Society for Psychical Research (ASPR) and by smaller research groups and individual investigators in continental Europe. Scholarly journals were established to publish ongoing research as well as theoretical speculation and fierce debates. The basic idea of these efforts was to apply scientific method to data collection, evaluation, and interpretation of psychic phenomena—an area which nineteenth-century materialistic sciences had ignored up to that time.

Apparition experience was one of the first phenomena studied. In a pioneering survey, 17,000 respondents were contacted. This "census of hallucinations," as it was called, netted many apparition experiences as well as other phenomena that were purely psychological. Reports were analyzed and published in two major works: Gurney et al. (1886) and Myers (1903). Several other collections appeared later, such as those by Bennett (1939), Green & McCreedy (1975), Jacobson (1973), and Jaffee (1979).

An apparition experience is awareness of the presence of a personal being whose physical body is not in the area of the experiencer, provided the experiencer is sane and in a normal waking state of consciousness. In contrast to extrasensory perception (ESP) of a distant event, the apparition is felt to be in the immediate vicinity of the experiencer. Unlike daydreams, apparitions are experienced as part of the immediate real world and cannot be readily created, altered, or terminated at will, except by physical actions such as closing the eyes, running away, or hiding under bedcovers. (For a detailed conceptualization, see Osis, 1986.)

Methods for researching apparition experiences were largely developed by the SPR and have now reached a high level of efficiency. Modern advances in psychology, psychiatry, sociology, and forensic sciences are incorporated, as well as techniques of qualitative and quantitative investigation. Mere hallucinations, hypnogogic and hypnopampic imagery, mistaken identity, illusory reshaping of normal stimuli, deliberate hoaxes, and chance coincidences have had to be identified and sifted off in the process of serious research. Journalistic books usually bypass methodological rigors and can be misleading as to actual observations.

Apparitions are experienced in many ways. "Seeing" is the most frequent sense modality that furnishes this experience. The apparition might look so lifelike that it is mistaken for a flesh-and-bones person—only sudden vanishing gives away its ghostly nature. Sometimes, however, the images represent only parts of the body, or appear as vague and misty outlines. They might portray the dead, the living, or unidentifiable strangers. Sounds, such as steps approaching and doors opening, are often heard. Touch, smell, and temperature sensations may be reported, but sometimes the experience is of a "felt presence" without any specific sensory qualities. Apparitions usually are of short duration, less than a minute. They can be a once in a lifetime experience, or recurrent.

Not all apparitions are of interest for the afterlife issue. Many have been traced to various different roots. Some were thought to be hallucinations whose cognitive content was derived from a telepathic message which is then projected out like a mental slide, retrocognition or sudden glance of events in time long past (e.g., D-Day in Normandy, or a scene from Marie Antoinette's time). If a mother sees her son walking through the kitchen with drenched clothes at the time he was drowned, that experience could hardly be separable from her own ESP projection of her son's image in the kitchen. But if neighbors see him entering the kitchen door at the same time, that would be of interest.

ESP, like our other thoughts and feelings, is a private experience that is directly observable only by the experiencer. Some apparition phenomena, however, have been collectively experienced by several persons. About one-third of those apparition experiences where more than one person was present, awake, and in a position to see, were collective (Hart, 1959). Often, animals also react: dogs growl, cats bristle. In haunted houses, phenomena may be reported as occurring repeatedly over the years to the distress of the family and surprise of visitors. For example, in a house near Pittsburgh, sixteen witnesses have reported observations of some ghostly phenomena over a period of twenty years. The exact nature of stimuli in collective cases is still unknown, but apparitions that are collectively seen do suggest a disembodied agency. Numerous attempts have been made to explain them, such as by the super ESP hypothesis. However, these explanations have been severely criticized (Gauld, 1982), because ESP of the magnitude and reliability needed to account for the observed phenomena has not been found.

Usually an apparition appears to perform physical actions, such as opening doors, but nothing is later found to have been moved. The noises of opening and closing doors turn out to be an imitation of the sounds of real events. On rare occasions, however, physical objects are affected: lights or gadgets are switched on or off, locked doors are reported opening, and so on. L.E. Rhine (1957) advances an explanation that does not presume a discarnate agency. She claims that psychic forces (psychokinesis, PK) of the observer could do the same as the ostensible ghost. The formidable burden of this hypothesis is to explain why such a mighty psychokinetic effect occurs at the moment of an apparition experience to people who have never exerted such an effect before or after in their lives.

In two-thirds of poltergeist (literally, 'noisy ghost') cases, a living agent has been identified. However, such cases are very rare in comparison with the frequency of reported hauntings, and the patterns of both phenomena differ markedly. Poltergeist phenomena are linked to persons who must be present for the effects to occur.

Furthermore, the time sequences and movements of objects seem to be different (and much more destructive). Apparition cases that involve physical action are very unnerving to the experients because they cannot be readily explained away as hallucinations and, instead, forcefully suggest an external agency. It would be a strange hallucination, indeed, that could open windows, say, in a mental hospital.

Out-of-Body Experiences

The out-of-body experience (OBE) is another phenomena which, in its best examples, seems to suggest something akin to short-term disembodied existence. The main characteristic of OBE is the experiencer's feeling that his or her other viewpoint and center of perception are located somewhere outside the body, at the ceiling, for instance. Some researchers also include a state of intense attention deployment, such as the feeling of being right on the stage when one is absorbed in watching a play. C.T. Tart (1977) has attempted to sharpen the criteria delineating "discrete OBE states." The literature on OBE is less extensive than on apparition experiences. As with apparition experiences, only some types of OBE could be considered suggestive for disembodied existence, namely those in which the experience is not completely private, but accessible also to observers and registering instruments. There are cases on record where one or two external observers "see" the person experiencing an OBE as an apparition at the same time as the person experiences himself as visiting the observers. It is more impressive if the "visit" is not announced beforehand but comes as a surprise.

In very rare cases animals also have been reported to react to the OBE apparition. Only experiments with gifted subjects have been suggestive. In one experiment, a kitten in the laboratory was measurably quieter at randomly selected intervals when its master made OBE "visits." In another experiment, strain gauge measures in the projection area gave some indications of OBE presence. Experiments with unselected subjects usually give no indications suggesting that anything "goes out" during OBE.

Parapsychological phenomena have also been reported to occur in states near death (See **Near-Death Experiences**). These may have indirect bearing on the survival hypothesis because they shed some light on spontaneous OBEs. One cross-cultural study was designed to contrast the phenomena according to a model of postmortem survival versus a model of death as extinction (Osis & Haraldsson, 1977, 1986). Not only the experiences of revived patients but also those who actually were dying were sampled in the United States and in northern India. The reported data fit the survival model much more consistently than they do the extinction counterpart.

Messages Ostensibly from the Dead

Messages interpreted as coming from the dead are reported in many cultures. They captured the interest of Western intellectuals in the heyday of spiritualism from the middle of the nineteenth century to the first decade of the twentieth century. Scholars struggled to develop methods for separating the ostensibly real from chance coincidences, believers' excessive claims, and the often fraudulent practices of mediums. William James, the great thinker in American psychology at the time, discovered a psychic genius, Eleanora Piper, who was extensively studied by scholars in the United States and England. The literature is too voluminous and complex to be abstracted here (e.g., Myers, 1903; Hart, 1959; Gauld, 1982). Many luminaries have been impressed by the emerging evidence for the survival hypothesis. For example, a past president of the American Psychological Association, Gardner Murphy, wrote (1961, p. 273), "Where, then, do I stand? To this the reply is: what happens when an irresistible force strikes an immovable object?" As a psychologist of his day he could not accommodate the pressure of evidence and remained "unmovable" until his death—so far as I know. His *Challenge of Psychical Research* (1961) provides an excellent description of that "irresistible force."

Messages coming in dreams are sometimes suggestive. For example, J.L. Chaffin (Anon, 1927) appeared to his disinherited son, giving clues for finding a second will.

Following the dream message, the will was found and recognized by the court, restoring the inheritance to the dreamer. Most clearly identifiable messages come from specially gifted psychics such as L. Piper, G.O. Leonard, and E.J. Garrett. While some psychics have claimed to identify the sources of their information as coming from spirits of the deceased, it soon becomes clear that they may give the wrong address. Without being aware of it, psychics incorporate in their message bits of information that have come from their living informants, the persons seeking to communicate with beloved dead. It has been argued that if messages from the dead are to be verifiable, they have to be checked either with a living person, records, or objects. Psychics can also access these "living" sources by their ESP—without requiring any information obtained from the dead. This, roughly, is the super ESP hypothesis. The best mediumistic data are hardly interpretable in this way. ESP from this-world sources was indeed available but it had to be pieced together from various obscure documents found in different places. Gauld's *Mediumship and survival* (1982) provides the best contemporary overview.

Reincarnation Memories

Reincarnation is a long-standing belief held mostly by people in India and Buddhist countries. Scientific studies of the phenomena pointing to reincarnation have been conducted in recent years by Ian Stevenson, a well-known psychiatrist at the University of Virginia, and his collaborators. Stevenson took a hard look at the claims of hypnotic age regression to previous lives and found nearly all of them unimpressive. But he was intrigued by cases in which pre-school children seem to remember having been somebody else from a distant location and family. He developed a network of informants in India, Burma, Sri Lanka, Lebanon, Turkey, and among the Alaskan Indians, to lead him to cases he could investigate. Stevenson has developed efficient methods for interviewing the child, his or her family, and other witnesses, as well as for locating and interviewing the alleged family of previous incarnation. Normal sources of os-

tensible past life memories are considered and possible selfish motives weighed. Sometimes Stevenson has been able to take the child to the family of previous life to see if he or she would identify persons, places, and possessions. Stevenson carefully evaluates his data and presents alternative explanations. Most impressive are the very detailed descriptions and analyses of forty individual cases published in four volumes with a total of 1,439 pages: *Cases of the Reincarnation Type, 1975–1983*. Stevenson also presents various quantitative analyses of more than 1,000 cases in his files. Stevenson's overview (1987) gives enough information for most readers.

His findings indicate that a large sample of children did give verifiable information about their ostensible previous lives: names of family members, locations, descriptions of houses, objects, and cause of death. Errors also abound. Some children exhibit behavior consistent with previous family and alien to present family, such as an Indian child preferring the food of a different caste. Phobias and preferences for clothing also seem to come from remembered past lives. Previous lives ending in violent death seem to be more frequently remembered than others.

Stevenson also found birthmarks in some cases that coincided with the location and shape of fatal wounds in a previous life. Birthmarks were photographed and, whenever possible, checked against autopsy reports and other medical records.

In his cautious style, Stevenson (1987, p. 260) concludes: "Although the study of children who claim to remember previous lives has convinced me that some of them may indeed have been reincarnated, it has also made me certain that we know almost nothing about reincarnation."

Conclusions

Evidence for possible survival of bodily death comes mainly from research on the following phenomena: apparition experiences collectively perceived, some types of out-of-body experiences, certain aspects of near-death experiences, selected communication ostensibly coming from the dead, and reincarnation memories. Assessments of the evidence vary greatly among researchers, ranging from those who find no acceptable evidence for survival (Siegel, 1980) to those who find certainty (Hart, 1959). The researcher's own philosophical outlook seems to have a strong influence on the conclusions that are reached. Most researchers take a position somewhere in the middle, and various theories of survival are presented by Thouless (1984). Apparently, the evidence is not yet strong enough to sway scholars whose philosophy has no place for disembodied existence.

Most Americans, regardless of their age or level of education, say they believe in life after death. When death approaches us or our dear ones, the research findings mentioned above might be useful to these believers and, possibly, to some others, especially if they themselves have experienced phenomena suggestive of afterlife. Of course, when counseling, one's own opinions and beliefs should be given less emphasis than the background, ideas, and feelings of the client.

See also Near-Death Experience: Scale; Near-Death Experiences; Psychopomp; and various entries for Survival Beliefs and Practices.

—KARLIS OSIS

References

Anon. (1927) "Case of the will of Mr. James L. Chaffin." *Proceedings of the Society for Psychical Research, 36*: 517–24.

Bennett, E. (1939). *Apparitions and haunted houses: A survey of evidence.* London: Faber & Faber.

Gauld, A. (1977). "Discarnate survival." In B. Wolman (Ed.) *Handbook of parapsychology.* New York: Van Nostrand, Reinhold, pp. 577–630.

Gauld, A. (1982). *Mediumship and survival: A century of investigation.* London: Heinemann.

Green, C. & McCreery, C. (1975). *Apparitions.* London: Hamish Hamilton.

Gurney, E., Myers, F.W.H., & Podmore, F. (1886). *Phantasms of the living.* 2 vols. London: Trubner.

Hart, H. (1959). *The enigma of survival.* Springfield, IL: Charles C. Thomas.

Jacobson, N.O. (1973). *Life without death?* New York: Dell.

Jaffe, A. (1979). *Apparitions: An archetypal approach to death, dreams, and ghosts.* Irving, TX: Spring.

Kastenbaum, R. (1979). "Death through the retroscopic lens." In R. Kastenbaum (Ed.) *Between life and death.* New York: Springer, pp. 156–84.

Kastenbaum, R. (1984). *Is there life after death?* New York: Prentice-Hall.

Landau, L. (1963). "An unusual out-of-body experience." *Journal of Society for Psychical Research, 42*: 126–28.

Morris, R.L., Harrary, S.B., Janis, J., Hartwell, J., & Roll, R.W. (1978) "Studies in communication during out-of-body experiences." *Journal of American Society of Psychical Research, 72*: 1–22.

Murphy, G. (1961). *Challenge of psychical research.* New York: Harper & Row.

Myers, F.W.H. (1903/Reprint 1954). *Human personality and its survival of bodily death.* 2 vols. London: Longman, Green.

Osis, K. (1986). "Apparitions old and new." In K.R. Rao (Ed.) *Case studies in parapsychology: Papers presented in honor of Dr. Louise E. Rhine.* Jefferson, NC: McFarland, pp. 74–86.

Osis, K. & Haraldsson, E. (1986). *At the hour of death.* Rev. ed. New York: Hastings House.

Osis, K. & McCormick, D. (1980). "Kinetic effects at the ostensible location of out-of-body projection during perceptual testing." *Journal of American Society for Psychical Research, 74*: 319–29.

Rhine, L.E. (1957). "Hallucinatory psi experiences: The initiative of the percipient in hallucinations of the living, the dying, and the dead." *Journal of Parapsychology, 21*: 13–46.

Rhine, L.E. (1977). "Research methods with spontaneous cases." In B. Wolman (Ed.) *Handbook of parapsychology.* New York: Van Nostrand, Reinhold, pp. 59–80.

Siegel, R.K. (1980). "The psychology of life after death." *American Psychologist, 35*: 911–31.

Stevenson, I. (1975–1983). *Cases of the reincarnation type.* 4 vols. Charlottesville, VA: University Press of Virginia.

Stevenson, I. (1987). *Children who remember previous lives.* Charlottesville: University Press of Virginia.

Tart, C.T. (1977). *Psi: Scientific studies of the psychic realm.* New York: E.P. Dutton.

Thouless, R.H. (1984). "Do we survive bodily death?" *Proceedings of the Society for Psychical Research, 57*: 1–52.

(THE) LIVING WILL

The living will (termed a "will" because it sets forth an individual's wishes, and "living" because it takes effect prior to death) is one of a number of documents commonly known as advance directives. Such forms enable individuals, while still competent, to state the type of medical care they wish to receive or to refuse should they become incompetent and unable to participate in treatment decisions.

The living will serves two important functions. By clearly indicating a patient's preferences regarding certain medical procedures or measures, it guides the treatment decisions made by the patient's loved ones and health care providers. This ensures respect for the patient's autonomy even if the patient becomes mentally incompetent or unable to communicate. In addition, it documents in a legally accepted fashion a patient's instructions regarding the withholding or withdrawing of life-sustaining treatment. This documentation provides certainty to judges, in the unfortunate event that a court is called upon to see that a patient's wishes are honored. It also protects health care providers and institutions that follow the patient's directions.

Since its inception in 1968, the living will has been distributed nationwide. Thirty-eight states and the District of Columbia have passed legislation that specifically upholds the living will. Even in those states that do not have living will legislation, the document is judicially and professionally accepted as a legally enforceable instrument that embodies a patient's preferences about life-sustaining treatment. Indeed, the concept of the living will is now endorsed by many hospital and medical groups, members of the bar, and organizations that work with patients who are terminally ill.

The living will may be simple or complex, depending on the individual's wishes and needs. It commonly expresses the patient's general wishes about life-sustaining treatment and instructions about particular therapies such as cardiopulmonary resuscitation, artificial respiration, artificial nutrition and hydration, and the use of antibiotics or pain medication. Although some people still use language regarding "extraordinary" or 'heroic" measures, the prevailing wisdom dictates that a patient indicates his or her own wishes about specific treatments in addition to any preference about "extraordinary care."

Copies of the living will may be obtained by contacting:

Concern for Dying
Room 831
250 West 57th Street
New York, NY 10107

The current version of the living will, given below, may also be reproduced. Concern for Dying provides documents applicable for those states that have living will legislation as well as for those states that do not.

My Living Will
To My Family, My Physician, My Lawyer and All Others Whom It May Concern

Death is as much a reality as birth, growth, maturity, and old age—it is the one certainty of life. If the time comes when I can no longer take part in decisions for my own future, let this statement stand as an expression of my wishes and directions, while I am still of sound mind.

If at such a time the situation should arise in which there is no reasonable expectation of my recovery from extreme physical or mental disability, I direct that I be allowed to die and not be kept alive by medications, artificial means or "heroic measures." I do, however, ask that medication be mercifully administered to me to alleviate suffering even though this may shorten my remaining life.

This statement is made after careful consideration and is in accordance with my strong convictions and beliefs. I want the wishes and directions here expressed carried out to the extent permitted by law. Insofar as they are not legally enforceable, I hope that those to whom this Will is addressed will regard themselves as morally bound by these provisions.

DURABLE POWER OF ATTORNEY
(optional)

I hereby designate _____
to serve as my attorney-in-fact for the purpose of making medical treatment

decisions. This power of attorney shall remain effective in the event that I become incompetent or otherwise unable to make such decisions for myself.

Signed _____

Optional Notarization: Date _____

"Sworn and subscribed to Witness _____

before me this _____ day Address ___

of _____ , 19 _____ ," Witness ___

Notary Public Seal Address_____

Copies of this request have been given to _____

_____

(Optional) My Living Will is registered with Concern for Dying (No. _____).

In completing a living will, one may also add other specific statements in the space between the introductory text and the signature. Several possible additions are described by Concern for Dying (1986).

See also Concern for Dying.

—GILES SCOFIELD

References

Alexander, G.J. (1988). *Writing a living will.* New York: Praeger.

Concern for Dying (1986). *The living will and other advance directives.* New York: Concern for Dying.

LULLABIES OF DEATH

Through the centuries in many lands children have been put to bed with sleep songs or lullabies. These soothing songs were passed from generation to generation until, in modern times, they have become less common. Traditional lullabies are gradually disappearing as the urban way of life with television and other technology introduces many discontinuities into the ties that bind generations together.

Surprising though it may seem, a number of traditional lullabies contain themes of death and violence. A recent study (Achté et al., in press) has explored such lullabies in twenty-four nations. Particularly rich material was found in the Finnish tradition. Some of the old songs reflect the fatalistic belief that it is best for the child to die and pass from this troubled world. The mother's own sense of exhaustion and pessimism is also expressed in some of these songs as she wishes her child a better life than her own (that is, a quick death). The difficult life that often awaited a little girl was given particular attention in lullabies.

One of the best known Finnish lullabies is titled, "Tuuti las Tuonelaan" ('Rock the Child to Tuonela,' the land of death). The traditional lyrics are:

> Rock the child to Tuonela
> To the chamber of the church
> There's a hut there with a roof of turf
> A fine place for a sandy field

Old Finnish lullabies often describe the grave as a cozy and protective place in which a small child is able to rest comfortably. One of the variant lullabies, "Rock the Child into the Ground," is gloomy. This song tells of an open grave that awaits the child while church bells call upon him to die. It is probable that songs of this kind originate in the history of high infant mortality not only in Finland but through much of the world throughout history. "Nuku, nuku nurmilintu" ('Sleep, sleep, grass bird') is brighter in tone, referring to the child as a bird who is told to build a nest in a tree or on the ground. Bird symbols clearly refer to the ancient beliefs concerning the shape of the soul as a bird (Rowland, 1978).

The lullaby may also contain a more direct threat of death, such as "Tule surma sarvinesi" ('Come, Death, with your horns'). It is probable that such songs originated in situations in which the childminder has been disturbed by crying and by the continuing demands of the baby or young child. In some versions, the singer promises to reward Death with a pair of socks or shoes for taking the child away. In the pessimistic Finnish lullabies, the child is either being soothed into the sleep of death, or the singer is waiting for Death to come and free him or her of the child.

Death may be portrayed as either admittance to a happier realm or simply a harsh exit from life. In Finland today, the deeply pessimistic lullabies of the past are seldom if ever sung, while more optimistic variations of the old songs and some new, brighter, sleep songs have appeared in their place.

Estonian lullabies have much in common with the old Finnish songs, but typically emphasize funerals; they describe how a child is taken into the churchyard and what happens next:

> Come, come to death
> swing to the churchyard
> legs first, head last
> arms crossed upon your breast.

And, again:

> Today Vanyushka will die
> the funeral will be held tomorrow
> we shall bury Vanya
> and toll the big bell.

One of the most popular Danish lullabies deals with the death of the day, and asks the child to go to sleep with it. The ancient analogy between death (*Thanatos* in Greek mythology) and sleep (*Hypnos*) seems to be represented here.

Threat songs have been relatively common in some Western European countries. A French lullaby, for example, threatens that a wolf will come and eat the child up if he does not go to sleep, while a German lullaby poses the gentler threat that two sheep will come and nibble on his toes (Daiken, 1959). It is not unusual for the lullaby to mention a death threat that is dismissed as soon as it is uttered or that allows the child to escape the danger in the course of the song.

Slavic lullabies include numerous examples of the "falling cradle" theme (Spitz, 1979). In a well-known example, the string breaks and the cradle falls into a ravine:

> I don't mourn the new cradle
> I mourn only the little child
> For I can build a cradle in a day or two
> But I cannot raise a child in a whole
>   year
> If the child dies
> The mother will not forget him

Spitz (1979) points out that threats have always been common in the discipline of children in Russia, perhaps accounting for the high frequency of death threats in traditional lullabies (again, these threats are often revoked by the time the song has ended).

English-speaking countries seem to have employed the falling cradle theme as a way of expressing and resolving parental ambivalence toward the child. Resentment or hatred are sometimes transformed again into love by the final couplet:

> Mother will catch baby
> cradle and all

Violent themes are found in many Spanish lullabies, some of which tell stories of warfare:

> Mambru's gone to war
> I don't know when he'll come back
> Do re mi, do re fa....
> Mambru, now dead in the war
> They take him to be buried
> With four officers
> And a sacristan
> Do re mi, do re fa

Interestingly, no lullabies describing the death of children, death threats, or violence are reported from present-day Israel, Egypt, Saudi Arabia, or Turkey. In Turkey, however, children daily hear the melancholy songs about broken hearts, loneliness, and death that adults often favor.

A Perspective on Lullabies of Death

Lullabies originated during the centuries that most people lived in agricultural communities, did hard work, and battled against the forces of nature. Famine was an ever-present threat, and epidemics killed many people, especially young children. Misery and the prospect of violent death were also intensified by recurrent wars. Infant mortality continued high at the turn of the twentieth century, making the death of a child a very real threat. It is possible that as the mother fears the loss of her child, she takes the initiative by singing a funeral lullaby, thus mourning the death in an anticipatory manner. Some of the songs may also have been influenced by the Christian belief that the surest way of getting to heaven is to die innocent, that is, very young.

A woman's life was especially difficult at that time. Some mothers may have felt that death offered the only release from a joyless life and continuous labor. The mother's own depression and frustration may have been crucial factors in the origins of lullabies with death themes. Perhaps overworked and depressed mothers transferred their own death wishes to the child. In the background, however, one usually finds a firm belief in a happier life after death.

Lullabies with themes of death are part of a disappearing culture. Infant mortality rates have now been reduced markedly as compared with former times, and the status of women in general has also undergone a fundamental change. Perhaps the altered conditions of life are responsible for the newer type of lullaby, as in the recent Finnish song about a nice little boy called Nukku-Matti (Sleep Matthew) who comes to take the child out for a car ride or to entertain him during the night with games and songs.

See also Children and Death; Personifications of Death; *Tuonela.*

—KALLE ACHTÉ

References

Achté, K., Fagerstrom, R., Pentikainen, J., & Farberow, N.L. (In Press). "Themes of death and violence in lullabies of different countries." *Omega, Journal of Death and Dying.*

Daiken, L. (1959). *The lullaby book.* London: E. Ward.

Rowland, B. (1978). *Birds with human souls.* Knoxville, TN: University of Tennessee Press.

Spitz, S.A. (1979). "Social and psychological themes in East Slavic folk lullabies." *Slavic and East European Journal, 23*: 14–24.

M

MAKE-A-WISH FOUNDATION

The Make-A-Wish Foundation was founded in central and southern Arizona in 1980 with the purpose of granting the favorite wish of a terminally ill child. The founding chapter has now granted such wishes for hundreds of Arizona children. Inspired by this example, local chapters of the Make-A-Wish Foundation now operate in thirty-eight states, and also in Australia, Canada, England, and New Zealand.

The first "make-a-wish" child was a terminally ill boy who wanted to be a policeman. Officers from the Arizona Department of Public Safety had a police uniform made for him—complete with helmet and badge—and gave him a ride in their helicopter. The child's delight with this experience led other compassionate people to build upon this example and establish the Make-A-Wish Foundation.

The founding chapter's Fact Sheet points out that it hopes not only to help the terminally ill child, but also to "provide the family with some special memories, instead of the final images of hospitals, doctors, pain and stress. During a time of heart-wrenching turmoil for a family, a 'wish' provides a welcome respite—a time of normalcy and just plain fun." The entire family unit is emphasized in the process of granting the wish of its terminally ill child: "The family is never separated during the wish, because an ill child is as much a loved brother or sister as a son or daughter."

The Foundation will consider the wish of any terminally ill child under the age of 18. Perhaps the most popular wish has been for a trip to Disneyland, but many other requests have been made and fulfilled. The Foundation covers all expenses involved, including, where appropriate, lodging and salary lost as a result of parents' days off work.

The Make-A-Wish Foundation is funded entirely by contributions made by the public. In addition to financial contributions, some individuals and corporations support the Foundation by donating hotel rooms, meals, use of a car, etc. There are also periodic fundraising events developed by community groups.

For further information, the reader may want to contact the nearest local chapter of the Make-A-Wish Foundation. Inquiries are also welcome at the national headquarters. Phone (602) 240-6600 or write to:

Make-A-Wish Foundation of America
2600 North Central Avenue, Suite 936
Phoenix, AZ 85004

See also Children, Dying; Children and Death; Children's Hospice International; Grief: Death of a Child.
—ROBERT KASTENBAUM

MEMENTO MORI

"Remember: you must die!" and "Remember your death!" are two functional translations of the Latin phrase, *memento mori*. But who would need—or desire—such a reminder? Are we not all clearly aware of our mortality? The reminder might seem both superfluous and intrusive. Upon a little reflection, however, it can be recognized that both individual and society often deny death. The common assumption is that there will be a tomorrow and we will be there to enjoy (or complain about) it. By and large, we do not appreciate having this illusion of continuity disturbed. How people respond when their personal mortality is brought forcibly to their attention is explored by Muriel Spark in her absorbing novel, *Memento Mori* (1958). Without divulging too much of the plot, it can be said that each character behaves in character when death's warning bell sounds.

History is rich with examples of memento mori. Some take the form of objects associated with death. As Carla Gottlieb (1959) observes:

> Some of the traditional symbols for death are the scythe and hourglass borrowed from the god Chronos (Time), the bow and arrow borrowed from the god Eros (Love), the inverted torch, and the sword. Skulls and bones are other obvious references to death. Such memento mori—to give them their official title—have been employed widely by artists. Yet the purpose for which they were shown has varied with the age concerned (p. 160).

In ancient Egypt and Rome, for example, miniature coffins might be passed among the guests as an invitation to enjoy this present moment of their fleeting existence. Small wooden mummy figures have survived from the Egyptian dynasties, having, in a sense, outlived those who they reminded of death many centuries ago. There is reason to believe that these sobering reminders often were presented with a leavening sense of humor. Frederick Parkes Weber (1910/1971) tells of the Roman host who remarked how sad it was to think that wine should have a longer life than human beings as he played with a small, jointed toy skeleton. Perhaps the most common appearance of memento mori in the ancient civilizations of the Western world was as an intensifier for enjoying the good life in the here-and-now. There is evidence that these symbols served to acknowledge that the good times do not last forever. Occasionally a voice arose to urge a "quick remembrance of death" as a spur to living a moral and responsible life, as when Seneca urged that each day be treated as though it might be the last

In the Christian era memento mori took on an increasingly moral and severe tone—with some bizarre flourishes as well. Reminders of death were now pressed into the service of persuading people to follow the commandments of scripture and church. (The pagan Seneca was eventually called upon as still another authority for this view.) The spirit of memento mori reached a peak of expressive intensity in the late Middle Ages. As early as the eleventh century there were signs of a heightened sense of individuality—and, with this, a heightened fear of death. This could be seen in the design of tombs, which now began to serve as a memento mori. The Black Death and other catastrophies that devastated much of the world during the fourteenth century had profound effects on all facets of society (Kastenbaum, 1976). Memento mori dominated the artistic response. Death became an obsessively popular figure for artists, sculptors, poets, and craftsmen; death-head rings, for example, could be found on the fingers of prostitutes and priests. In general, this emergence of memento mori as a leading expressive theme took the form of "morbid preoccupation with the physical miseries of the human condition" (Boyle & Morriss, 1987).

Some of the most extreme depictions—such as distinguished bishops portrayed with worms invading their decaying flesh—may remind contemporary moviegoers of the most gory late night horror films. This comparison must end, however, with the superficial similarities. The memento mori of the late Middle Ages grew out of humankind's very direct and recent encounters with death in a particularly merciless and overpowering form. Peculiar as this response may appear to the twentieth-century reader, it did represent an attempt to develop a new relationship with God and create a stronger society. Little of this character can be seen in the exploitation films that treat mutilation and death in a pornographic vein.

The memento mori had its highest artistic expression between the fifteenth and seventeenth centuries. A significant example is "The Triumph of Death" by Peter

"Knight, Death and Devil," an engraving by Albrecht Dürer, Nuremberg, 1513. The proud and the powerful must be reminded that they also face the prospect of death. Reprinted, by permission, from Ernst & Johanna Lehner, *Picture Book of Devils, Demons and Witchcraft*, frontispiece. © 1971 by Dover Publications, Inc.

Brueghel the Elder (1525–1569), in which Death rides on a

> lean, phantom-like horse, at the head of a ghastly, horrible company of armed skeletons, bringing destruction to the living. In the foreground on the left the vanity of worldly possessions is represented by a purple-robed king falling down whilst his hoarded treasures are being seized by a skeleton in armour. On the right a group of men and women, in the midst of their feasting and merrymaking, are being scared by the approach of the skeleton-soldiers of Death. In a conspicuous part of the foreground is the death-cart rolling along collecting the victims. In the landscape of the background are representations of shipwreck, accidental deaths by sea and land, executions by hanging, capitations, etc. (Weber, 1910/1971, p. 135).

A similar theme by a medieval French artist is depicted on the jacket of Barbara W. Tuchman's stimulating examination of the fourteenth century, *A Distant Mirror* (1978).

From the historical standpoint, exploration of the memento mori theme should also take into account its close relationship with the *Ars moriendi* tradition and the Dance of Death. From a contemporary standpoint, we might understand our own symbols (such as the skull and crossbones) more thoroughly by recognizing how many of them owe their origin to humankind's earlier encounters with death. And, since history is still being made today, we might observe how our own special death-related concerns —AIDS is the example that cannot be overlooked—eventually give rise to new memento mori symbols.

See also Acquired Immune Deficiency Syndrome (AIDS); *Ars Moriendi*; Dance of Death (*Danse Macabre*); Tombs.

—ROBERT KASTENBAUM

References

Aries, P. (1981). *The hour of our death.* New York: Alfred A. Knopf.

Beaty, N.L. (1970). *The craft of dying.* New Haven, CT: Yale University Press.

Boyle, J.M. & Morriss, J.E. (1987). *The mirror of time.* New York: Greenwood.

Gottlieb, G. (1959). "Modern art and death." In H. Feifel (Ed.) *The meaning of death.* New York: McGraw-Hill, 157–88.

Kastenbaum, R. & Aisenberg, R.B. (1976). *The psychology of death.* New York: Springer, 1976.

Spark, M. (1958). *Memento mori.* Cleveland, OH: Meridian.

Tuchman, B.W. (1978). *A distant mirror.* New York: Alfred A. Knopf.

Weber, F.P. (1910/Reprint 1971). *Aspects of death and correlated aspects of life in art, epigram, and poetry.* College Park, MD: McGrath.

MORS

Her face was seldom portrayed, nor were temples dedicated to her, or sacrifices offered. Today her very name has sunk into such obscurity that it is seldom mentioned when the gods of antiquity are reviewed. Nevertheless, Mors was worshipped by the ancients and often sung about by their poets. This female deity, remembered today mostly from Roman verse, was a reigning personification of death. It was Mors—pale, wan, emaciated—who set the snares of Death to catch doomed mortals. "The poets describe her as ravenous, treacherous, and furious, and as roving about open-mouthed and ready to swallow up all who came in her way," observes the classical scholar, M.A. Dwight (1864). She was imagined as a black-robed, dark-winged figure who might, like an enormous bird of prey, hover above her intended victim until the moment came to seize it. In Dwight's judgment, she was not honored with temples and sacrifices "because Death is inexorable, inaccessible to entreaties, and unmoved by prayers and offerings."

Death in the form of this deadly female hunter is a striking figure to contemplate, especially when we consider that most contemporary personifications portray Death as masculine, if a sex is specified, and that, in fact, women much more often than men provide care and comfort to the terminally ill. Mors seems to represent, then, the type of very powerful female deity who laid claim to human imagination before God the Father became the dominant image, and also to embody a perception of femininity radically different from the sweet innocence that requires constant protection from the male.

See also Personifications of Death.

—ROBERT KASTENBAUM

Reference

Dwight, M.A. (1864). *Grecian and Roman mythology.* New York: A.S. Barnes & Burr.

MORTALITY RATE

A mortality rate measures the frequency of deaths occurring at a given time in a population (or subpopulation), relative to the size of the population. Usually the mortality rate encompasses a one-year period. There is no "one" mortality rate. Instead, there are many types of mortality rates that differ in degree of refinement and in the aspect of mortality that is of primary concern. Three mortality rates are used commonly: the crude death rate, the age standardized mortality rate, and age-sex-specific mortality rates.

Three Types of Mortality Rates

The crude death rate (CDR) is also known as the general death rate, the total death rate, and, most simply, as the death rate. The CDR is the total number of deaths in a year divided by the average total population in that year. The CDR is expressed as a rate per 1,000 population. It is a crude measure in that it does not take into account population compositional variables such as sex, race, and, particularly, age, that are associated with the likelihood of dying. For example, many Third World countries have lower levels of the CDR than industrialized nations although, at all ages, their mortality is higher. Their lower CDRs are a function of their younger age compositions; that is, they have proportionately fewer people in the older age groups where the risk of dying is high. Although CDRs are reported frequently because of their ease in computation and their minimal raw data requirements, any mortality comparisons based on the CDR should be viewed with caution.

Similar in appearance to the CDR is the age-standardized (or age-adjusted) mortality rate (ASMR). This is a single mortality index that is expressed as a rate per 1,000 population annually. However, the ASMR is unaffected by age compositional differences. It is a hypothetical rate, based on the assumption that age composition has remained constant over time in one population or is constant across populations. By convention, the U.S. population in 1940 is the "standard" used. ASMRs presented in the last column of Table 3, are superior to the CDR in that any differences or changes in mortality level are not attributable to differences or changes in age structure.

In order to take into account differential mortality by age, sex, or other important variables, mortality rates can also be computed for specific subpopulations. Age-sex-specific mortality rates are one major example. They can be thought of as "mini" CDRs, calculated separately for each sex and for specified age groups (usually five- or ten-year clusters). As presented in Table 3 for the United States from 1900 to 1983, age-sex-specific mortality rates provide rich information on mortality trends and patterns.

Life Expectancy

Often, mortality is measured in terms of life expectancy, most commonly life expectancy at birth (although gerontologists are concerned with life expectancy at older ages as well). Statistics on life expectancy are derived from a mathematical model known as the life table. Age-sex-specific mortality rates are the raw material for the construction of life tables. However, mortality rates and life expectancy differ conceptually. While mortality rates assess the frequency of deaths occurring annually in a population, life expectancy figures estimate the number of years that persons of a given age and sex can expect to live. Life expectancy figures are more intuitively understandable than mortality rates; however, care must be taken with their interpretation. Life expectancy at birth for females in the United States approximates 79 years at the present time. But this figure does not mean that women in the United States can expect to live 79 years. What it does indicate is that if all females born this year had the same risks of dying throughout their lives as those indicated by current

TABLE 1: Age-sex-specific mortality rates and age standardized mortality rates, United States, 1900–1983. (Per 1,000 population. "All" takes as its standard the 1940 U.S. population.)

Sex	Age											
	-1	1–4	5–14	15–24	25–34	35–44	45–54	55–64	65–74	75–84	85+	ALL
Male												
1983	12.1	0.6	0.3	1.4	1.7	2.7	6.9	17.3	38.9	85.4	170.8	7.2
1980	14.3	0.7	0.4	1.7	2.0	3.0	7.7	18.2	41.1	88.2	188.8	7.8
1970	24.1	0.9	0.5	1.9	2.2	4.0	9.6	22.8	48.7	100.1	178.2	9.3
1960	30.6	1.2	0.6	1.5	1.9	3.7	9.9	23.1	49.1	101.8	211.9	9.5
1950	37.3	1.5	0.7	1.7	2.2	4.3	10.7	24.0	49.3	104.3	216.4	10.0
1940	61.9	3.1	1.2	2.3	3.4	5.9	12.5	26.1	54.6	121.3	246.4	12.1
1930	77.0	6.0	1.9	3.5	4.9	7.5	13.6	26.6	55.8	119.1	236.7	13.5
1920	103.6	10.3	2.8	4.8	6.4	8.2	12.6	24.6	54.5	122.1	253.0	14.7
1910	145.5	14.6	3.0	4.8	6.9	10.0	15.2	28.7	58.3	127.4	255.8	16.9
1900	179.1	20.5	3.8	5.9	8.2	10.7	15.7	28.7	59.3	128.3	268.8	18.6
Female												
1983	9.9	0.4	0.2	0.5	0.7	1.4	3.9	9.2	20.9	52.0	140.1	4.1
1980	11.4	0.5	0.2	0.6	0.8	1.6	4.1	9.3	21.4	54.4	147.5	4.3
1970	18.6	0.8	0.3	0.7	1.0	2.3	5.2	11.0	25.8	66.8	155.2	5.3
1960	23.2	1.0	0.4	0.6	1.1	2.3	5.3	12.0	28.7	76.3	190.1	5.9
1950	28.5	1.3	0.5	0.9	1.4	2.9	6.4	14.0	33.3	84.0	191.9	6.9
1940	47.7	2.7	0.9	1.8	2.7	4.5	8.6	18.0	42.2	103.7	227.6	9.4
1930	60.7	5.2	1.5	3.2	4.4	6.1	10.6	21.2	46.8	106.6	221.4	11.3
1920	80.7	9.5	2.5	5.0	7.1	8.0	11.7	22.4	50.5	115.9	255.7	13.8
1910	117.6	13.4	2.9	4.2	6.1	7.9	12.1	23.7	52.4	117.4	246.0	14.6
1900	154.4	19.1	3.9	5.8	8.2	9.8	14.2	25.8	56.3	118.8	255.2	17.0

Sources: *Historical Statistics of the United States, Colonial Times to 1970* (1975). Washington, DC: U.S. Bureau of the Census; *Vital Statistics of the United States, 1983* (*Volume II—Mortality, Part A*) (1987). Washington, DC: U.S. Department of Health and Human Services.

age-specific mortality rates, then their average age at death would be 79 years. Life expectancy figures provide a useful summary index of mortality level as long as one is aware of their hypothetical nature.

Mortality Rates for Special Purposes

There are numerous other mortality rates. Some focus on particular age groups, as does the infant mortality rate—the number of deaths to children under the age of one per 1,000 live births per annum. Others are analogous to age-sex-specific mortality rates but are calculated for other variables (race, marital status) and may also include age and sex. Cause-specific mortality rates assess the number of deaths attributable to specific causes, relative to the population annually. These vary from crude measures such as the number of heart disease deaths per 1,000 annually to refined measures; for example, the number of heart disease deaths to persons of a given sex and age group.

As with CDRs, crude cause-specific mortality rates should be accepted cautiously. They fail to take into account population composition variables, particularly age, that are closely associated with the risk of dying from specific causes.

Age, Sex, and Mortality

The age pattern of mortality differs according to mortality level. When mortality is high, the age curve of mortality is U-shaped. As mortality levels decline, deaths are increasingly postponed until older ages, and the curve takes on a J-shape. Recent U.S. data (see Table 1) display the J-shaped curve that is typical of economically developed countries. Relatively high mortality rates occur in the first year of life. They are followed by a sharp decline for other childhood ages and gradual increases so that mortality rates exceeding those of infancy are reached at ages 45–54 (men) and 65–74 (women), after which sharp increases occur.

Mortality rates have declined substantially in this century for all ages and for both sexes, as shown in Table 1. Factors contributing to the overall decline include both social reform and medical intervention. The trend of mortality decline varies by age and sex. The age groups experiencing the largest declines are infants and young children. Most of these declines occurred early in this century; more than 75 percent of the entire reduction in mortality rates for children was accomplished by 1950. In contrast, major mortality reductions for older age groups (65+) have been more recent, with substantial declines commencing after 1960. (A notable exception are men 65+, who have experienced no improvement in mortality rate since 1970.)

Women have experienced a larger mortality reduction than men, a trend that has been observed in all developed countries. In 1900, the male ASMR (18.6) exceeded the comparable female rate (17.0) only slightly, a ratio of 1.09. Female rates have declined more substantially than male rates at all ages with the result that the sex differential in ASMRs in 1983 was 1.76. Sex differences in the amount of mortality decline are noteworthy among the older age groups. Women aged 65+ experienced declines in mortality in excess of 50 percent; their male counterparts witnessed decreases of approximately one-third. Overall, the increase in the sex differential in mortality paralleling socioeconomic development appears related to (1) declines in maternal mortality; (2) improvements in the control of infectious diseases, to which women were traditionally more susceptible; (3) the development of early detection techniques for a number of "female" cancers; and (4) lifestyle differences that have become increasingly important as the traditional takers-of-life, such as contagious and infectious diseases, have been overcome to a large extent.

See also Causes of Death.

—ELLEN GEE

References

Preston, S.H. (1976). *Mortality patterns in national populations.* New York: Academic Press.

Shyrock, H.S., Siegel, J.S., & Associates (1980). *The methods and materials of demography.* 3rd printing. Washington, DC: U.S. Department of Commerce.

United Nations (1982). *Levels and trends of mortality since 1950.* New York: U.N. Department of International Economic and Social Affairs.

MURDER

"Thou shalt not kill" is an injunction that has been disobeyed frequently throughout human history. We have destroyed our own kind in combat, through massacre of civilians, and by abandonment of infants and others who were unable to care for themselves. Regimes have killed by legal executions, by covert operations including assassination, and, occasionally, by impulse. Failures in the management of food, transportation, manufacturing, energy sources, waste disposal, and other activities have also resulted in deaths that arguably could be described as killings, if usually unintentional. It is obvious that killing must be considered as a function that occurs within all societies (See **Death System**).

Murder is generally regarded as an individual form of killing—one person the aggressor, the other the victim. Those who have studied murder closely, however, often conclude that these acts cannot be separated from the nature of the sociocultural circumstances in which they occur. It is always an individual who dies, and the murderer—when apprehended and convicted—is also an individual. However, the killing itself may have been influenced strongly by a variety of social forces including, for example, racial tensions, the drug culture with its financial incentives and risks, the ready availability of firearms, and so on. It would be mistaken to conclude that such factors "cause" only one killing but equally naive to regard murder as a simple expression of an individual's anger and brutality.

Murder: The Current Situation

Murder is usually defined as the intentional and unlawful killing of a person. *Homicide*, a word often used interchangeably, also refers to the act of killing a person but does not necessarily presume "malice aforethought." A person may be judged to have committed "justifiable homicide" in defending himself or herself against a life-threatening attack. The charge may be "negligent homicide" if a person is thought to be responsible for a fatal accident. Both murder and homicide are distinguished from the killing of another person by accident or negligence.

The United States has one of the highest murder rates in the world. Only in Northern Ireland can a higher murder rate be found, but most of the killings in that troubled land are related to the bitter long-time struggle between political-religious factions. Murder rates are about four times higher in the United States than in neighboring Canada, and eight times higher than those reported for France and the Federal Republic of Germany. England, the Netherlands, Norway, and Switzerland have only about one-tenth the murder rate characteristic of the United States. International data summarized by Foster et al. (1987) reveal a murder rate of 7.9 per 100,000 in the population for the United States. Other than Northern Ireland (whose rate fluctuates markedly from one year to another), no other nation for whom reliable data are available has a rate that exceeds 3. This high rate represents actually a decline. As recently as 1982, the U.S. murder rate was 13.8. (It is possible that some higher murder rates would come to light if reliable information were available from all nations, including those with major civil unrest and disturbances, but there is no doubt that, among its closest peers in the international community, the United States must be regarded as the realm most beset by murder or homicide.)

Who are the victims? And who are their killers? The following conclusions can be drawn from statistical information.

1. Most murder victims are men (about 3 of 4).
2. Most killers are men. A man is the murderer in about 9 of 10 cases in which a woman is a victim and in about 8 of 10 cases in which a man is victim.
3. By far the greatest number of murders are committed by killers who are of the same race as the victim (94 percent among blacks, 88 percent among whites).
4. About 3 of 5 murders involve people who know each other, such as relatives, lovers, friends, neighbors, or colleagues. It is possible that this is an underestimate of the number of victims who know their killers, because the relationship between killer and victim remains undetermined in many cases. A stranger is most likely to kill another stranger while engaged in a criminal activity.
5. Murders are more common in the large cities (populations of 250,000+) than in smaller cities and rural areas. The largest cities (populations of a million or more) have been experiencing especially high murder rates—about three times greater than the national average.
6. The southern states continue to have the highest murder rates, about twice that of the next highest, the western region. ("Southernness" is associated with the homicide rate but not with the suicide rate; Lester, 1986–87.)
7. Firearms are the weapons most commonly used to commit murder in the United States, being involved in about 3 of 5 killings, and handguns are by far the most frequently used type of firearm in murders (about 4 of 5 gun-related murders). Knives and other cutting or stabbing instruments are the next most frequent method used in murders, followed by the use of physical force by hitting, pushing, and kicking.

The Gun Control Controversy

The fact that many murders, as well as numerous accidents, involve the use of handguns has elicited efforts to subject possession of such weapons to more regulation and restraint. There is strong opposition to control measures, however, and the issue has become divisive and "politically sensitive." Organizations leading the campaign to control guns include:

Handgun Control, Inc.
810 18th Street, N.W.
Washington, DC 20006

National Coalition to Ban Handguns
100 Maryland Avenue, N.E.
Washington, DC 20002

National Council for Responsible
   Firearms Policy
1028 Connecticut Avenue, N.W.
Washington, DC 20036

Mustering the opposition to handgun control are organizations such as the following:

National Rifle Association
1600 Rhode Island Avenue, N.W.
Washington, DC 20036

Citizens' Committee for the Right to
   Keep and Bear Arms
The James Madison Building
12500 N.E. Tenth Place
Bellevue, WA 98005

Gun Owners of America
951 Arden Way
Sacramento, CA 93815

All the above organizations provide informational materials and speaker lists to those who want to become more acquainted with their positions.

The Second Amendment of the Bill of Rights of the U.S. Constitution states: "A well regulated militia being necessary to the security of a free State, the right of the people to keep and bear arms shall not be infringed." Not everybody agrees on precisely how this statement should be interpreted. Does it refer to individual rights, or to the existence of a standing "well regulated militia"? Does "shall not be infringed" mean that everybody, including the convicted felon, the emotionally disturbed, the child, has the right to carry about any and all firearms on any and all occasions? Some of these differences are expressed in state constitutions. The Bill of Rights language is repeated or slightly paraphased in the consitutions of Alaska, Rhode Island, and a number of other states. However, some states add that "military power shall always be held in an exact subordination to the civil authority and be governed by it" (e.g., Massachusetts). Significantly, the "shall not be infringed" provision has not stood in the way of certain added restrictions. The Louisiana constitution, for example, states that this provision "shall not prevent the passage of laws to prohibit the carrying of weapons concealed to the person." Texas adds that "the Legislature shall have power, by law, to regulate the wearing of arms, with a view to prevent crime," and Washington makes it clear that "nothing in this section shall be construed as authorizing individuals or corporations to organize, maintain, or employ an armed body of men."

These and similar provisions in state constitutions help to put the assertions of gun control advocates and opponents in perspective; despite the "shall not be infringed" provision, legislative bodies have in fact placed some restrictions on the right to bear arms.

Attempts to introduce any further regulation and control measures—including, for example, waiting periods before a handgun can be sold—have been met by resolute opposition. Those opposed to gun control measures have other arguments in addition to the constitutional right to bear arms. Perhaps the most often articulated arguments are: (1) Law-abiding people will have less opportunity to defend their lives and property if "only the bad guys" have the guns; (2) "Guns don't kill people—people kill people"; a determined killer will find some means even if guns are not available; and (3) Many people own guns for purposes of hunting, target shooting, and collecting, and their right to enjoy these activities would be unfairly restricted. Opponents also observe that, in practice, it might be very difficult to restrain the possession of guns no matter what laws are passed.

Gun control advocates include many law enforcement agencies that have concluded from their experience that handguns in the possession of the general public are perhaps more a menace than a protection. Many tragic accidents have resulted from children and careless adults making use of handguns. Other advocates point out that murder rates are much lower in nations that have strict gun control laws. Witnesses have testified that "guns in the home do not prevent lawlessness, violence and death; they cause it. For every intruder stopped by a homeowner with a gun, there are four accidents in the home" (Representative Fauntroy, cited by Foster et al., 1987, p. 100). Advocates also state that they do not intend to restrict the lawful use of firearms by sportsmen and collectors but only to reduce the number of handguns loose in our society. Efforts to pass gun control legislation continue to meet with stiff opposition and to be among the most divisive issues in American life.

Attitudes Toward Murder

American society has long had ambivalent attitudes toward murder. The public has almost invariably expressed sorrow and anger when a person's life has been taken by an act of violence. Murder is condemned by religious and humanistic principles. Additionally, certain types of murder, such as the wild and random attacks of an emotionally disturbed person, have generated anxiety.

Nevertheless, murder is also a favorite topic of media reportage and the stock subject of many television programs and movies. The fact that "Murder, She Wrote" continues to be one of the most popular television programs would not surprise those who know that murder, presented as mystery, drama, or comedy, was also a staple of American entertainment in the days of radio, as well as in books and stage plays. The same society, then, the same individuals who are alarmed by "real murder," may find this act of violence to their liking when it is safely esconced in a book or movie.

Ambivalence toward murder may be part of a deeper human conflict between impulses toward love and creativity on the one hand, and violence and destruction on the other. This conflict was examined by Freud (1920) (See **Death Instinct.**) Although this theory as such has not been widely accepted, many other observers have called attention to the complexity of our attitudes toward murder. Houts (1970), for example, suggests that victims have at times "invited" the violence. Wertham (1966) describes some of the ways in which the mass media's fascination with violence and murder can lead impressionable individuals to commit such crimes in real life. In a milestone report, the *National Commission on the Causes and Prevention of Violence* (Graham & Gurr, 1969), many contributing causes were identified. These included, among other factors, racial discrimination and tensions, the effects of overcrowding, and the "frontier" tradition that has led some Americans to feel that violence is an acceptable solution to many problems.

Uncovering the psychological and social influences on murder is not the same as condoning violence or releasing killers from responsibility for their crimes. For example, a recent study (Humphrey & Palmer, 1986–87) has found that, in comparison to other people, murderers had more stressful life events (such as death of a loved one) prior to committing their crimes. Findings of this kind remind us that murderers, too, are people, and that their crimes must be seen in relationship to their entire lives. How society can most clearly understand and most effectively prevent murder remains one of the great challenges of our time.

See also Death Instinct; Death Penalty; Death System; Suicide.

—ROBERT KASTENBAUM

References

Foster, C.D., Siegel, M.A., Plesser, D.R., & Jacobs, N.R. (1987). *Gun control.* Plano, TX: Information Aids, Inc.

Freud, S. (1920). *Beyond the pleasure principle.* Vol. 28 in *Collected Works.* New York: W. W. Norton.

Graham, H.D. & Gurr, T.D. (1969). *Violence in America.* New York: Signet Books.

Houts, M. (1970). *They asked for death.* New York: Cowles.

Humphrey, J.A. & Palmer, S. (1986–1987). "Stressful life events and criminal homicide." *Omega, Journal of Dying and Death, 17:* 299–308.

Lester, D. (1986–1987). "Southern subculture, personal violence (suicide and homicide) and firearms." *Omega, Journal of Death and Dying, 17:* 183–86.

Wertham, F. (1966). *A sign for Cain.* New York: Macmillan.

N

NATIONAL FUNERAL DIRECTORS ASSOCIATION

Unlike most other organizations that deal with death-related issues, the National Funeral Directors Association (NFDA) has been on the American scene for more than a hundred years. By 1879 many funeral directors across the nation were expressing an interest in developing improved communications with each other and advancing their field through collaborative efforts. Leadership for this movement was provided by funeral directors in Michigan who first formed a state association and then planned a national meeting in Rochester, New York, in 1882 that marked the official beginnings of the NFDA (Lamers, 1981).

The Association proved useful both immediately and over the long term. In the early years of the NFDA, America was still attempting to recover from the painful losses and divisiveness of the War Between the States. Funeral directors had taken on a heavy burden under difficult circumstances during the war and now needed to adapt themselves to the new demands of a rapidly expanding industrial society. The NFDA became a resource for helping disseminate technical and scientific information to keep funeral practices up to date and responsive to emerging needs. It also served, as it does now, to establish and maintain standards of ethical behavior and carry out a variety of functions related to the responsibilities of the funeral director.

The NFDA holds regular annual meetings throughout the nation and encourages meetings and activities at the local level. A number of research and educational activities of potential interest and benefit to the general public have been sponsored by the NFDA.

Anyone with an interest in funeral-related problems and questions is welcome to request information from the NFDA. Staff are available to answer questions on such topics as death, grief, bereavement, and final disposition. There is also a unit known as FSCAP (Funeral Service Consumer Arbitration Program), an independent panel "designed to resolve disagreements between consumers and funeral directors through binding arbitration. The panel is composed of consumer professionals and exists to assist consumers with legitimate complaints" (NFDA, 1987).

Readers may also find various NFDA publications of interest. A number of brochures are available on such topics as anatomical gifts, embalming, cremation, funeral costs, death away from home, and "funeral etiquette."

For information, write or call:

The National Funeral Directors
   Association
11121 West Oklahoma Avenue
Milwaukee, WI 53202
(414) 541–2500.

See also Burial: "Going Home"; Cremation; Funerals; Uniform Anatomical Act.

—ROBERT KASTENBAUM

References

Lamers, W.M. (1981). *A centurama of conventions.* Milwaukee: National Funeral Directors Association.

National Funeral Directors Association (1987). *About life: Contemporary American Funeral Service.*

NATIONAL HOSPICE ORGANIZATION

Founded in 1977, the National Hospice Organization (NHO) is a non-profit membership organization devoted to promoting and maintaining quality care for the terminally ill and their families. NHO has described itself as "dedicated to integrating hospice in the United States health care system. As the representative of hospice providers and caregivers, NHO actively addresses areas of concern to established and newly forming hospices including: standards criteria, research and evaluation, reimbursement, licensure, professional liaison, ethics, public information, legislation affecting hospice, and education" (NHO, no date).

NHO publications and surveys provide useful and up-to-date information on many aspects of hospice functioning. These publications include *The Hospice Journal,* and an annual *Guide to the Nation's Hospices.* NHO data are generally considered the most accurate available on such topics as the number of hospices in operation in the U.S. (approximately 1,700 at the time of writing) and the number of patients served (more than 100,000 a year).

Information about NHO can be obtained from:

National Hospice Organization
1901 North Fort Myer Drive
Suite 307
Arlington, VA 22209
(703) 243–5900

The role of the NHO in the U.S. health care system is touched upon by Mor (1987) in his comprehensive review of available data on hospice care.

See also Children's Hospice International; Hospice: Children; Hospice: Philosophy and Practice; *(The) Hospice Journal: Physical, Psychosocial, and Pastoral Care of the Dying;* National Hospice Study.

—ROBERT KASTENBAUM

References

Mor, V. (1987). *Hospice care systems.* New York: Springer.

National Hospice Organization (n.d.). *About hospice* (brochure). Arlington, VA: NHO.

NATIONAL HOSPICE STUDY

In 1978 the U.S. Health Care Financing Administration invited existing hospice programs to apply for participation in a Hospice Demonstration Program in which hospice services were to be Medicare-reimbursed. Twenty-six hospice programs were selected from a nationwide applicant pool of 233. In order to assess the policy implications of Medicare reimbursement for this new system of care, Brown University was chosen to conduct an independent evaluation of the cost effectiveness and quality of hospice services in terms of patient and family outcomes. Complete details of the research design and analysis plan have been published elsewhere (Greer et al., 1983). Evaluators at Brown University selected fourteen hospice sites comparable in size and program content to the demonstration sites, but which were not reimbursed by Medicare, as well as fourteen conventional oncological care settings to afford a comparison between outcomes in hospice and conventional care. Participating hospices were classified as hospital- or home care-based, depending on whether or not the hospice offered in-patient services. Data collection began in September 1981 and continued until March 1983. The major findings of the National Hospice Study are summarized below. (For a more complete discussion of findings, see Greer & Mor, 1986; Greer et al., 1986; and Mor et al., 1988.)

Hospice patients received substantially more care at home and were in the hospital for fewer days in the last month of life than were hospital-based hospice or patients receiving conventional care. Those served in any type of hospice were significantly less likely to receive diagnostic testing to intensive therapy such as surgery, chemotherapy, radiation therapy, transfusions, and intravenous therapy than were conventional care patients.

Quality-of-life domains examined included performance status, pain and other symptoms, satisfaction with care, and social involvement. In general, quality of life was comparable among patients in both types of hospices and in conventional care. Small but statistically significant differences favoring hospital-based hospices were observed in pain, other symptoms, and satisfaction with care. All hospice patients were more likely to die at home. Families provided more direct care help to hospice patients than to conventional care patients. There was no evidence that patients in hospice experienced any negative consequences attributable to hospice care either in terms of survival or the provision of medical interventions for palliation (Greer et al., 1986; Mor et al., 1988; Morris et al., 1986).

The level of secondary morbidity (illness, incapacity) experienced by family caregivers following patient death was less than anticipated, with hospitalization rates lower than the age-sex adjusted national norms and physician use rates not substantially higher than the national norms. No differences by setting were observed with respect to these outcomes. However, the extra caregiving burden of families in home care hospices was reflected in higher reported levels of stress and social disruption, based on information collected during a bereavement interview (Mor et al., 1986; Greer et al., 1986).

Results with respect to cost savings attributable to hospice are mixed. Home care hospices save money relative to conventional care by substituting care at home for hospital care. These savings occur primarily in the last months of life and are sufficient to offset higher costs incurred by patients served by hospice longer than two months. Hospital-based hospices add home care to already high in-patient use; however, they consume very low levels of in-patient ancillary services, yielding low per-diem hospitalization costs relative to con-

ventional care patients. Hospital-based hospices in the study thus yielded costs comparable to conventional care over the last year of life (Mor & Kidder, 1985; Birnbaum & Kidder, 1984).

National Hospice Study results thus indicate that hospice, particularly the home care model, is a less costly means of caring for terminally ill patients, most noticeably in the last months of life. Since hospice apparently has no negative effects and costs no more than conventional care, from a social policy perspective it is a viable alternative for those patients and families who prefer a palliative, nontechnological approach to terminal care (Mor, 1985; Mor et al., 1988).

See also Hospice: Philosophy and Practice; Hospice Development in the United Kingdom.

—VINCENT MOR, DAVID S. GREER & SUSAN MASTERSON-ALLEN

References

Birnbaum, H. & Kidder, D. (1984). "What does hospice cost?" *Journal of the American Public Health Association, 74*: 689–97.

Greer, D.S. & Mor, V. (1985). "How Medicare is altering the hospice movement." *Hastings Center Report, 15*: 5–10.

Greer, D.S. & Mor, V. (1986). "An overview of National Hospice Study findings." *Journal of Chronic Diseases, 39*: 5–7.

Greer, D.S., Mor, V., Morris, J.N., Sherwood, S., Kidder, D., & Birnbaum, H. (1986). "An alternative in terminal care: Results of the National Hospice Study." *Journal of Chronic Diseases, 39*: 9–26.

Greer, D.S., Mor, V., Sherwood, S., Morris, J.N., & Birnbaum, H. (1983). "National Hospice Study analysis plan." *Journal of Chronic Diseases, 36*: 737–80.

Mor, V. (1985). "Commentary: Results of hospice evaluations: A view from the National Hospice Study." *Quality of care for the terminally ill: An examination of the issues,* a special publication of the *Quality Review Bulletin,* pp. 80–85.

Mor, V., Greer, D.S., & Kastenbaum, R. (Eds.) (1988). *The hospice experiment.* Baltimore: The Johns Hopkins University Press.

Mor, V. & Kidder, D. (1985). "Cost savings in hospice: Final results of the National Hospice Study." *Health Services Research, 20*: 407–22.

Mor, V., McHorney, C., & Sherwood, S. (1986). "Secondary morbidity among recently bereaved." *American Journal of Psychiatry, 143*: 158–63.

Morris, J.N., Mor, V., Goldberg, R.J., Sherwood, S., Greer, D.S., & Hiris, J. (1986). "The effect of treatment setting and patient characteristics on pain in terminal cancer patients: A report from the National Hospice Study." *Journal of Chronic Diseases, 39*: 27–35.

NATIONAL INSTITUTE FOR JEWISH HOSPICE

The National Institute for Jewish Hospice (NIJH) was conceived in July 1985, opened its office at Cedars-Sinai Medical Center in Los Angeles in September of that year, and was incorporated as a legal entity in January 1986. Its founder and first president is the author of this article.

The idea of a Jewish-oriented hospice program developed from the realization that there was no strategy of care specifically concerned with the spiritual and ethnic aspects of the dying Jewish person. The hospice idea draws the focus of care to the whole person rather than only to his or her purely physical aspects. This or her approach implies that different people trigger different treatment strategies and that unique components require unique care. The spiritual component--a person's view of the meaning of life, his or her place in the world, his or her concept of what death means, his or her view of life after death, and the religious interpretation of his or her condition—is a major component of the human personality, whether for the negative or positive.

However, the hospice idea had not reached the consciousness of the general Jewish population, who assumed it represented a Christian attitude of resignation in the face of death. Jews, by contrast, traditionally have assumed that they were expected to "rage against the dying of the light." The Jewish community was not prepared for the hospice idea, and the hospice establishment was not prepared for the Jewish idea.

NIJH takes as its scope the Jewish community in the United States, Canada, and Israel. The range of its mission is illustrated by its early programs. One of these is a mail education program that has raised the consciousness of the Jewish community to Jewish hospice. Educational materials are sent to a million Jewish households every year; 26,000 had become members by January 1988. NIJH has also initiated a Central Telephone Network, anchored by a toll-free number. This Network provides information and counsel for the terminally ill, their families, and health care professionals. It is based on exhaustive research into all Jewish care facilities and professionals who relate to the terminally ill. Specially trained volunteers operate the program.

NIJH has recently published a series of booklets covering many aspects of terminal care. NIJH is now making itself ready to produce professional quality video training tapes in the Jewish care of Jewish patients for professionals and volunteers. A research program is also being planned with a consortium of schools, led by the Albert Einstein School of Medicine, Ferkauf Graduate School of Psychology, the Rabbinical School of Yeshiva University and other rabbinical seminaries, the Wurzweiler School of Social Work, and the Cardozo School of Law. NIJH also publishes a quarterly bulletin, *The Jewish Hospice Times,* that reports on its activities.

NIJH is led by a board of governors that includes presidential appointees, congressmen, novelists, and bank presidents. The professional advisory board was first chaired by Dr. Herman Feifel, and includes twelve scholars who have published in this field, including Norman Cousins.

See also Hospice: Philosophy and Practice; Survival Beliefs and Practices: Jewish.

—MAURICE LAMM

NEAR-DEATH EXPERIENCE: SCALE

The Near-Death Experience (NDE) Scale is a reliable, valid, and easily administered sixteen-item questionnaire for the quantification of a NDE. It was developed by Greyson (1983) to provide a screening instrument for the clinical assessment of NDEs and the investigation of their possible causes and effects. The sixteen items are grouped into four psychologically meaningful clusters, based on empirical inter-item correlations:

1. A *Cognitive Component* that includes time distortion, thought acceleration, life review, and sudden understanding.
2. An *Affective Component,* comprising feelings of peace, joy, and cosmic unity, and an experience of a brilliant light.
3. A *Paranormal Component,* including enhanced vision and hearing, apparent extrasensory perception, precognitive vision, and an out-of-body experience.
4. A *Transcendental Component,* comprising encounters with an apparently unearthly realm, a mystical being, visible spirits, and a barrier or point of no return.

Scores on the NDE Scale range from 0 to 32, with a mean score of 15 among near-death experiencers. The Scale has documented internal consistency (alpha=.88), split-half reliability (r=.92), and test-retest reliability (r=.92). NDE Scale scores are highly correlated with Ring's Weighted Core Experience Index (WCEI) (r=.90), an earlier instrument that had been used to measure NDEs but which proved to have weak discriminative validity. NDE Scale scores are not significantly correlated with age, gender, elapsed time since the NDE, or conditions of the close brush with death. Scores are normally distributed among persons who have had NDEs, with 68 percent of scores falling within one standard deviation of the mean.

Clinicians may use the NDE Scale to differentiate NDEs from organic brain syndromes and nonspecific stress responses following close brushes with death. For research purposes, the NDE and its components may be used to discriminate among individuals who vary in the type and degree of NDE reported. The NDE Scale can be administered as a self-scoring questionnaire or as an interviewer-rated instrument, with comparable results.

See also Near-Death Experiences.

—BRUCE GREYSON

References

Greyson, B. (1983). "The Near-Death Experience Scale: Construction, reliability, and validity." *Journal of Nervous and Mental Disease, 171*: 369–75.
Greyson, B. (1985). "A typology of near-death experiences." *American Journal of Psychiatry, 142*: 967–69.

NEAR-DEATH EXPERIENCES

The systematic scientific study of what today are called near-death experiences is a very recent undertaking, having its modern origin in the mid-1970s. However, accounts can be found in literature and historical documents dating back hundreds of years. A small number of such cases were collected by interested investigators beginning in the late nineteenth century. The principal impetus for modern studies was the publication in 1975 of the book, *Life After Life,* by psychiatrist Raymond A. Moody, Jr. This slender volume, which quickly became a best-seller in the United States and Western Europe, introduced millions of persons to the concept of the near-death experience, an expression used by Moody to refer to a common pattern of subjective experience that many persons who nearly die or survive a brief episode of clinical death claim to have undergone. It should be noted, however, that although Moody's book indisputably represents the emergence of the NDE as a compelling phenomenon, earlier observations by other physicians such as Elisabeth Kubler-Ross (who contributed the forward to the book) and Russell Noyes, Jr. (1972), had already provided strong support for Moody's own formulation of the NDE as well as for his anecdotal findings.

Moody's conceptualization of the NDE is based upon his detailed interviews of fifty persons who reported to him that they had some kind of a conscious experience while they were on the threshold of apparent imminent biological death. (This selection of fifty cases, however, was from a total sample of 150.) Moody observed that fifteen "elements" tended to occur in these NDE narratives. It is in fact this pattern of recurring features that has come to define the NDE (or the "core NDE" as it is sometimes called). Virtually all NDE researchers have followed Moody's lead in providing composite descriptions of the NDE in which many of the elements he identified duly make their appearance. The following paragraph presents a composite summary of a typical NDE (one with most of the facets Moody noted).

A Typical NDE. An individual brought to the brink of death by, for example, a cardiac arrest begins to feel dissociated from his body. He then is aware that he can actually see his physical body down below, surrounded by a medical team, while he himself seems to be floating above the body, feeling very detached and extremely comfortable and having no pain whatsoever. His vision is extremely acute and his mind is functioning in a hyperlucid fashion. That scene disappears as he finds himself being drawn into a darkness and he begins to move through this darkness, which appears more and more like a tunnel, at a tremendous rate of speed. He notices at the end of the tunnel an incredibly radiant golden-white light that draws him like a magnet. He feels a sense of overwhelming peace, well-being, and absolute total love. Universal knowledge pours into him from a limitless source. Suddenly, his entire life unfolds before him in a million vivid visual images and he reviews his life without judgment but with deep compassion and understanding. At the same time, a voice telepathically communicates to him that he has a choice to make—to go further into this experience or return to physical life. In an instant, the individual realizes that he has to return—usually for the sake of others—and with that decision, he is abruptly "back" inside his physical body. All the pain is there again with the return to the physical world, but the reality of his experience—in no way like a dream or hallucination—remains an abiding, if often troubling and perplexing memory of his experience of dying.

Needless to say, there are many variations around this basic NDE theme and many NDEs will be more fragmentary than the illustration just provided. However, the many studies of the NDE phenomenon that Moody's book helped to launch have, on the whole, amply

authenticated both his data and his description of the core NDE. At this point, then, we are in a position to summarize what is known about this phenomenon.

Frequency. Does the NDE invariably occur when there is a near-death crisis? In terms of self-report (which is the usual basis for inferring an NDE), the answer appears to be decidedly in the negative. Indeed, most studies that have addressed this question find that the NDE occurs in a minority of all instances involving a near-death episode. Nevertheless, the proportion of cases in which an NDE is subsequently reported is not small. At this time, the evidence suggests that a core NDE will be found in approximately one of every three near-death cases studied.

Incidence. The NDE is a surprisingly widespread phenomenon in modern times, owing mainly to the development of effective techniques of resuscitation. According to a Gallup poll, there may be as many as eight million adult Americans who have already experienced an NDE in connection with a near-death event. (In any case, NDE researchers have collectively studied many thousands of such experiences.) No reliable estimate is currently available for the number of persons in the world who may have survived an NDE, but it seems reasonable to assume that there must be many millions who have and, because of modern cardiopulmonary resuscitation measures, many more who will.

Varieties of NDEs. Although most NDEs reported conform by and large to the Moody model, some do not. There have been, for example, occasional accounts of negative (though not necessarily hellish) NDEs and some idiosyncratic experiences that violate the usual NDE framework. No researcher has yet made a careful study of such anomalous NDEs, perhaps because the paucity of these cases makes this kind of investigation quite difficult, so this matter remains to be explored.

Mode of Near-Death Onset. Does the way in which one nearly dies affect the nature of the NDE? Although there appears to be some variation in this respect, the bulk of the accumulated evidence on this point suggests that once one crosses the threshold into clinical death, the experience is largely invariant regardless of the condition that has brought one close to death. Classical NDEs have been recounted, for example, not just by persons who have nearly died because of illness or surgical interventions, but also by survivors of accidents, suicide attempts, and intentional killing (combat veterans).

Individual Differences. Are there any personal or demographic correlates of NDEs? Despite a persistent search for such factors, the results so far suggest that the NDE is not conditioned by variables of this kind. For example, the nature and incidence of NDEs appear to be independent of demographic factors. There are no clearly established personality correlates of NDEs, though some work on cognitive style and on childhood experiences seems promising at the present time. Preexisting religious beliefs and affiliation do not affect the likelihood of NDEs; atheists, for instance, are just as likely to have an NDE as the devoutly religious. Prior information about NDEs has no effect on their reported occurrence; indeed, if anything, those unfamiliar with NDEs seem somewhat more likely to relate them.

Cross-Cultural Studies. Almost all of the research on NDEs has been conducted in the United States and in Western Europe, and in those regions most of the cases studied fit the Moody model quite well. In countries whose cultural traditions and religious belief systems are quite different from those of the West, research on NDEs has thus far been too fragmentary and inconclusive to support any firm generalizations. Sometimes NDE accounts appear to correlate well with the basic features of the type most commonly found in the West, but often there are clear culturally determined overlays evident. Any given experience appears to be an amalgam composed of the individual's personal background, his or her cultural frame of reference, and a universal archetypal patterning of death-and-rebirth motifs. In any case, the extent to which the NDE may be invariant across contemporary cultures cannot be determined at the present time—but the historical and cross-cultural data we do have suggest that the modern NDE does not necessarily constitute a universal prototype for the experience of dying, despite its pervasive occurrence in the West.

Aftereffects of NDEs. Although the short-term aftermath of the NDE can be difficult for the survivor (and the survivor's family), the long-term effects of the experience often prove to be very salutary indeed—at least from the perspective of the experiencer. Typical aftereffects include (1) permanent and significant reduction, if not elimination, of the fear of death; (2) deepened conviction in some form of life after death; (3) increased appreciation for life; (4) increased feelings of self-worth; (5) heightened concern and love for others; (6) decreased interest in material things for their own sake; (7) an increase in spirituality (but not necessarily religiousness); (8) an awakening or enhancement of psychic sensitivities. Most experiencers appear to feel a deep sense of gratitude for their experience despite (or perhaps in some cases because of) the sometimes poignant dislocations it can engender in their lives.

Interpretations of NDEs. From the beginnings of modern research on the NDE, there has been unabating controversy over how to interpret the NDE. Not a few critics have tended to explain it in reductive physiological terms (e.g., as a response to cerebral anoxia or massive endorphin release); others have seen it as a psychodynamically understandable response to the threat of physical death; still others have preferred to conceive of it as an expression of a "higher state" of (spiritual) consciousness which the onset of death evokes. Some, like Moody himself, confess their continuing perplexity in the face of such a complex and enigmatic phenomenon, or simply take an "agnostic" position. The passage of time and the accumulation of more data have seemingly done little to clarify the matter, and the mystery of just what the NDE is remains unsolved.

Summary. Though the mystery about the NDE itself lingers, the fact of its existence has been established beyond any reasonable doubt. The NDE is a remarkably robust phenomenon, seemingly "ecumenical" (a random variable) and questionably widespread in its dispersion. In contrast to the early days of anecdotal reports of NDEs, recent scientific investigations have provided ample documentation that these experiences do indeed occur. Not only are these very real experiences to the percipients, but they are undeniably real in their effects, which have also been carefully delineated. Because of this, health care professionals who may have occasion to work with NDE survivors or with dying persons should familiarize themselves with the nature and dynamics of NDEs as well as with their aftereffects. The clinical (and spiritual) implications of the NDE constitute a treasure trove of insights for those counseling the dying or those who have survived an NDE. Finally, the NDE is not merely a fascinating clinical phenomenon that accompanies the passage into death; it is also a cultural phenomenon of modern life, having found its way into our journalism and literature as well as onto our television and movie screens. The popular acceptance of the NDE is not necessarily conducive to its professional legitimization (in fact, in some quarters it may militate against it), but it does make the NDE increasingly difficult to dismiss. Accordingly, it seems safe to conclude that the NDE is no passing fad but is a salient fact of our time and perhaps, from now on, for all time.

See also International Association for Near-Death Studies (IANDS); *Journal of Near-Death Studies (Anabiosis);* Near-Death Experience: Scale.

—KENNETH RING

References

Gallop, G., Jr., (1982). *Adventures in immortality.* New York: McGraw-Hill.
Greyson, B. & Flynn, C.P. (Eds.) (1984). *The near-death experience.* Springfield, IL: Charles C. Thomas.
Moody, R.A. (1975). *Life after life.* Atlanta: Mockingbird Books.
Noyes, R., Jr., (1972). "The experience of dying." *Psychiatry, 35*: 174–84.
Ring, K. (1984). *Heading toward Omega.* New York: William Morrow.
Sabom, M. (1982). *Recollections of death.* New York: Harper & Row.
Zaleski, C. (1987). *Otherworld journeys.* New York: Oxford University Press.

NECROMANCY

From the Greek *nekros* ("a dead body") and *manteia* ("divination"). Necromancy is the process of raising a corpse from the grave through magical powers. This, at least, is the illusion that a necromancer attempts to produce. There are three common features that can be observed in most reports of necromancy: (1) the conjurer is usually a woman; (2) the spirit of the dead person returns for only a short period of time; and (3) the spirit returns for the purpose of giving a judgment, providing or receiving information, and, less often, carrying out an action. The conjurer usually claims the power to bid the spirit's attendance but does not necessarily claim to control how the spirit will respond. It is the visiting spirit, then, who passes judgment on the living or reveals a secret. Nevertheless, the necromancer may in some circumstances claim the ability to lure or oblige the spirit to accede to the wishes of the person who is paying the fee for this performance. Often considered part of the repertoire of a witch or warlock, necromancy may also be carried out to serve the conjurer's own motives, perhaps most frequently, revenge.

Necromancy can be practiced upon the corpses of those who have recently died, but also upon a more or less standard list of eminent spirits. In so-called black magic rituals, the conjurer was most likely to call upon a famous and particularly powerful spirit. Part of the necromancer's craft was to know which spirit to call upon for the particular situation, even for the particular day of the week. Furthermore, one would select the time, day, and reigning spirit to conform to the specific purpose of the conjuration. If one is interested in obtaining treasures, for example, it would be appropriate to wait until the eleventh hour of a Sunday evening and then, having prepared the correct magic circle, summon the spirit known as Surgat with words of this nature:

> I conjure thee, O Surgat, by all the names which are written in this book, to present thyself here before me, promptly and without delay, being ready to obey me in all things, or, failing this, to des-

patch me a Spirit with a stone which shall make me invisible to every one whensoever I carry it! And I conjure thee to be submitted in thine own person, or in the person of him or of those whom thou shalt send me, to do and accomplish my will and all that I shall command, without harm to me or to any one, so soon as I make known my intent (quoted from medieval sources by Waite, 1961, pp. 294–95).

The cautionary phrase, "without harm to me or to any one," must always be included, for rather obvious reasons. The conjuration may then continue at some length. Blasphemy is often involved as the name of Jesus or God is invoked to suit the conjurer's purpose; for example, "I warn thee by the other Sacred Names of the most great Creator, which are or shall hereafter be communicated to thee; hearken forthwith and immediately to my words, observe them inviolably, as sentences of the last dreadful day of judgment, which thou must obey inviolately, nor think to repulse me because I am a sinner, for therein shalt thou repulse the commands of the Most High God." In the medieval belief system, necromancy was one of the "black arts" (owing in part to a mistaken connection between the words denoting death/dead and the color black). Christian elements were introduced into "diabolical" rites, much against the teachings of the Church.

It is a more arduous procedure to recruit the spirits of real people. The necromancer must be at the churchyard or tomb precisely at midnight to perform a painstaking ritual that requires the physical presence of the corpse. Preferably, the corpse itself is present, but, if necessary, the conjurer and his or her assistant insert a tube into the grave for "communication" with the corpse. The necromantic ritual requires certain props that have became famous in their own right, such as the magic wand. The conjurer invokes Christian theology to threaten the perhaps reluctant spirit; for example, "By the virtue of the Holy Resurrection, and the torments of the damned, I conjure and exorcise thee, Spirit of (deceased person), to answer my liege demands, being obedient unto these sacred ceremonies on pain of everlasting torment and distress. . . . Arise, arise, I charge and command thee!"

Attendants at the successful necromantic ritual claim to see the apparition or ghost and hear it answer the questions put to it. The necromancer's task is said to be much more difficult when the deceased spirit is that of a suicide. The careless, unskilled, or unlucky necromancer fears being destroyed if he or she makes an error.

Although necromancy has been strenuously opposed by organized religion through the centuries, it must be recalled that examples are to be found in the Scriptures. An interesting example appears in I Samuel. One evening Saul disguised himself (in mourning clothes) and, with two companions, approached a necromancer: "Divine now for me with necromancy, and conjure up for me whom I shall tell you." This request troubled the woman because Saul had banished the necromancers from his land. After promising that no harm would come to her, Saul asked to have Samuel raised from the dead. The necromancer reported that she could see an old man rising from the grave, wrapped in a cloak. Saul bowed and prostrated himself. He heard Samuel ask why he had been summoned. Saul spoke of his great distress that God had turned away from him and the Philistines had gained the upper hand. What was he to do? Samuel explained that Saul had brought the crisis upon himself by not obeying the Lord's commands to their fullest. David would now possess the kingdom. The interview ended with Saul terror-stricken.

Rosenberg (1984) points out that there has long been controversy over the nature of this alleged encounter with the spirit of Samuel. Some commentators believe that Saul was duped by an old trick (a concealed confederate of the conjurer impersonates the deceased person while the highly emotional visitor is vulnerable to the force of suggestion). Others hold that Saul was too well versed in the magical practices of his time to fall for such a ruse. Still another view is that a demon possessed Samuel's body and spoke for him. In any event, the idea of raising the dead to serve the purposes of the living has been with us for a long time and has appeared in many contexts, including the most significant sacred writings.

Necromancy has an important commonality with the "Spiritism" or "Spiritualism" that developed during the nineteenth century, replete with seances and mediums—here, too, contacts with the dead were made or alleged. The procedures, purposes, and contexts differed appreciably, however, and require separate examination.

See also Life After Death?

—ROBERT KASTENBAUM

References

Rosenberg, A.J. (1984). *The book of Samuel 1.* New York: The Judaica Press.

Waite, A.E. (1961). *The book of ceremonial magic.* New Hyde Park, NY: University Books.

NECROPHILIA

From the Greek words *nekros* ("dead body") and *philo* ("a loving or fond attitude"). The term *necrophilia* is most often encountered as a psychiatric expression for pathological attachment to dead bodies. Some clinicians believe there is an association between necrophilia and such other tendencies as voyeurism, coprolalia (using scatological language for sexual gratification), and, in men, the fear of intimate relationships with women. There have been few systematic studies of necrophilia, and caution should be exercised to distinguish this phenomenon from intense but temporary attachments to the corpse of loved ones that may occur during the course of bereavement and under other special circumstances.

See also Grief.

—ROBERT KASTENBAUM

References

Brill, A.A. (1941). "Necrophilia." *Journal of Criminal Psychopathology, 2*: 433–43.

Stoller, R.J. (1975). "Gender identity." In A.M. Freedman, H.I. Kaplan, & B.J. Sadock (Eds.) *Comprehensive textbook of psychiatry.* 2nd ed. Baltimore: Williams & Wilkins.

NECROPHOBIA

Pathological fear of the dead (*nekros* + *phobia*, "fear") is distinguished in its scope and intensity from the more common aversion to contact with dead bodies that many people express. In necrophobia, alarm at actual or prospective contact with a dead body can produce an anxiety attack with a variety of psychophysiological disturbances (nausea, dizziness, chills), as well as impulsive actions. As with any other phobia, fear of dead bodies becomes a problem when major areas of one's life are affected and normal functioning and relationships are endangered by dread of possible contact with the feared object.

Necrophobia is to be distinguished from thanatophobia, the fear of death in its more general aspects. An individual may have an intense fear of personal death, for example, but not necessarily show an extreme reaction to dead bodies. Necrophobia may be intensified by some cultural belief systems; in fact, what seems necrophobic to one ethnic group may seem quite normal to another. The meaning of the dead body to the survivors has been studied and discussed to some extent, but only limited attention has been given to the origins, consequences, and possible modification of necrophobia. It is probable that with the increasingly pervasive influence of the medical care system, fewer people now have direct experiences with dead bodies in contemporary society. The possible impact of this trend on necrophobia and other attitudes remains to be determined.

See also Death Fears and Anxiety.

—ROBERT KASTENBAUM

References

Channon, L.D. (1984). "Death and the preclinical medical student. 1. Experiences with death." *Death Education, 4*: 231–36.

Mandelbaum, D.G. (1959). "Social uses of funeral rites." In H. Feifel (Ed.) *The meaning of death.* New York: McGraw-Hill.

Noll, C.T. (1981). "Grief and bereavement in the military." In O.S. Margolis et al. (Eds.) *Acute grief.* New York: Columbia University Press.

Raphael, B. (1982). *The anatomy of bereavement.* New York: Basic Books.

O

OLD AGE AND DEATH

Many people dislike the terms *old* and *old age*. This is an understandable reaction because of modern society's tendency to equate *old* with *useless, worn out, undesirable* and other adjectives describing negative qualities. Although a number of alternative terms are used today, none have escaped disapproval and criticism. *Aged* and *geriatric* are often regarded as even more unacceptable than *old,* while *elderly, senior adult,* and *senior citizen* seem to be verbal flourishes that have not won a secure place in everyday usage. There is also widespread resistance to being classified as a *retiree,* a term that misrepresents the active life-style of many "not-exactly-young" adults.

This difficulty is not likely to be resolved as long as *old* continues to carry a burden of negative social stereotypes: the underlying problem remains no matter what word is selected. But there is another significant reason for resistance. When all people of a particular age are lumped into the same category there is a danger of overemphasizing this one similarity and neglecting the many individual differences. The unwary person may even conclude that age explains or causes the observed characteristics, instead of providing only a criterion for establishing the population under study. If, for example, an 80-year-old woman cries when her favorite cat dies, does this response really have anything to do with old age or is it, rather, a basic human response to loss?

Despite these difficulties, there is often good reason for studying the age-related aspects of human behavior and experience. The young child, the adolescent, and the octogenarian differ appreciably in their life histories and current biosocial situation. Care will be taken to avoid an overemphasis on chronological age, which by itself provides only a limited basis for prediction and no persuasive explanation of individual behavior and experience. We will use *old,* the simplest and most direct term, and will distinguish, when appropriate between the "young-old" (approximately 65+) and the "old-old" (80+).

Is Death "Natural" for Old People?

One of the most striking assumptions about old age is that death is somehow a natural outcome, or even a fulfillment. By contrast, this assumption is almost never made about childhood or adolescence. There is an obvious link between old age and death, of course. Those of us who do not die young will die old. This association has become strengthened by the marked increase in life expectancy during the twentieth century. Infants and children have been the prime beneficiaries of advances in public health, preventive medicine, and antibiotics. It is not surprising, then, that, more than ever, death should be viewed as something that happens "naturally" to old people.

However, the situation is not as simple or rational as it may appear. There is a persistent tendency in our society to use "natural death for old people" as a psychological maneuver. If old people "specialize in death," then younger people can keep their own anxieties in the closet. We may grieve over the death of an old man or woman, but there is also the (perhaps hidden) reassurance that Death is "going by the book," harvesting the old and sparing the young (Kastenbaum, 1975). This theme has even been enshrined in popular theories of human development. Erik H. Erikson's (1968) epigenetic theory, for example, is typical in its emphasis on facing death ("integration vs. despair") as the major developmental task for the old person. In fact, children and adolescents often show more concern about death than do old people (See **Death Anxiety and Fears**). However, many social scientists as well as laypeople continue to assume that the death theme is dominant in old age. Many people find it less painful to think about the death of old people, as compared with the young, and this psychic ease translates readily into the belief that death is "natural" for old people. There is also a secondary advantage in viewing old people as living in the shadow of death and, presumably, preoccupied by this fact. Seen as "disengaging" from society and awaiting their deaths (Cumming & Henry, 1961), old people can then be more readily shunted aside, segregated, and removed as competitors for resources and power.

Gadow (1987) points out that "The consequences of accepting a natural connection between death and age are troubling. Designating death in late age as more natural than earlier death may not mean forcing elderly patients to die by denying them care, but it may encourage them, through the governing ethos, to regard their own deaths as natural and so to refuse care." She also takes note of Burt's (1986) conclusion that "The right to die becomes transformed into the obligation to die, by which elderly people are persuaded to join as agents in their own social devaluation and, consequently, in their own physical destruction."

There are not one but three different meanings commonly given to "natural death," according to Gadow. Sometimes this term signifies only that death is inevitable. However, the inevitability of death as an outcome of a particular disease or injury has changed markedly over the centuries and is still changing. Because people now survive many conditions that in the past would have ended in inevitable, natural death, we now tend to "place death in what we consider its normal position, at the close of a long life." Yet many old people today grow older still, and it has become increasingly possible to prevent or ameliorate life-threatening problems even among quite aged adults. This makes "the natural time for death" something that is subject to negotiation. "Death at 90," writes Gadow, "may become as preventable as death in infancy. The claim that death is natural after a long life assumes the possibility of agreement on 'long enough,' and that agreement is not yet available." Gadow concludes that "how long a life is long enough" is a determination that cannot be made for the human species in general but only on a person-by-person basis, taking into account the individual's own personal criteria for fulfillment.

The second common meaning is that a death is "natural" and therefore "acceptable" when it resembles "the model of death in nature." People may speak poetically about the supposed beauty of death in nature, but Gadow asks, "Where is the death in nature that we would wish for ourselves at any age?" In "nature," the fawn is fed to the wolf, and the foot to gangrene. From the anthropomorphic standpoint, death in nature is "violent and unappealing." Gadow holds that "Nature itself provides us with no humanly ideal manner of dying." Furthermore, the place of death in the ecology of nature does not translate well to the lives of individual men and women. "Nature produces a virtual infinity of life forms, but only as long as none of the lives lasts indefinitely, usurping the place of its successor. . . . The only sense of natural death that can be wrested from nature itself is that the old die for the sake of the young." In human society, however, a very old man or woman may have a uniquely valuable contribution to make to the young and may foster rather than obstruct the development of new generations.

The other common usage is that a "natural" death is orderly and peaceful. There is no violence, no messiness, but simply the conclusion of a biological process. Aging, therefore, can be seen as the most appropriate biological model for death—a natural process that reaches its natural conclusion. This is a convenient view, as Gadow observes, because it provides a scientific-sounding reinforcement for the idea of a "good death." Among many difficulties with this concept, however, is the equating of aging with dying, an attitude that can undermine the value and neglect the individuality of an old person's life. "But aging is more than the process of cells dying, just as death is more than the sum of their dying." This pseudobiological idea of natural death leaves out too much of human experience and is itself only an idea whose origins, motivating forces, and limits must also be examined.

All three common usages of "natural" death assume a "realm that transcends human ambiguities and artifice." This would make nature itself a deity that "rescues us from the maze of human relativity." Gadow argues that the conception of a separate natural realm is itself a human contrivance. She offers an alternative approach. Death is either "natural" or "unnatural" depending upon the individual's own personal meanings. "Because the essence of human experience is the personal, not the general, the meaning of natural death cannot be framed in general terms, such as peaceful death, dying without apparatus, or death after 90. Natural in human terms can be defined only by the individual."

From a philosophical standpoint, these considerations force us to go beyond the assumption that death is somehow "natural" to old people and search instead for a way to understand all deaths at any age, especially as events that are meaningful to us as individuals and as a society. From a very practical standpoint, the emphasis on death as natural to old age is contributing to pressures for limiting medical and other services for people beyond a particular age cut-off. One influential proposal calls for the exclusion of life-extending treatments to old people, thereby saving money that would otherwise be wasted (Callahan, 1987). Such plans are more likely to have a favorable reception on the part of decision-makers when in the prevailing attitude the notions "old," "natural," and "death" seem to fit smoothly together.

Attitudes Toward Death Among Older Adults

Attitudes often grow out of experiences. Kalish (1985, p. 154) summarizes some of the experiences that tend to be more common for older adults:

> For the most part, older people have had many more death-related experiences than younger people. They have virtually always experienced the deaths of both parents; they have experienced the deaths of more family members and friends; they have attended more funerals and visited more people who were dying; and they are more likely to have had one or more personal encounters with their own possible death and are more likely to be suffering from a life-threatening health condition.

In all these ways, death tends to become more salient to older people, more a part of their everyday lives and thoughts. However, the sense of being closer to death does not necessarily lead to heightened anxiety. Studies reviewed by Kalish indicate that older men and women were somewhat more likely to think and talk about death but less frightened by the topic, as compared with younger adults. This pattern suggests that death has become a "thinkable" aspect of life to older people. Mortality is a fact of life that can no longer be dismissed or evaded, however, this recognition lacks some of the sting it carries for younger people.

One factor contributing to this difference is the feeling among many younger people that they have yet to enjoy the relationships, adventures, and achievements that would make their lives complete—death, then, is a threat to the future self. By comparison, older people are somewhat more likely to feel that they stand on the other side of time, having aleady had an active and eventful life. This attitude does not mean that older adults feel ready for death or indifferent to the end of their lives, but rather that death has a different aspect and meaning to them than would have been the case in their youth. Another likely factor, already mentioned, is that older adults are more apt to suffer from chronic and life-threatening conditions. This direct awareness of physical vulnerability pierces the illusion of indestructability that often shields young people. The person who at 20 sometimes felt "I'm going to live forever!" is more inclined, sixty years later, to feel thankful for every day of reasonably good health.

Nevertheless, there are many individual differences in the attitudes held by older adults. Some men and women have been tormented by fears of death throughout their lives. These fears may continue into old age. One 87-year-old widow, for example, had episodes of panic in which she would tremble, hyperventilate, and cry out for help. "I'm dying! Stay with me! I'm dying!" Although highly distressing both to herself and other residents and staff in the geriatric facility, these episodes did not have much relationship to her age as such. She had experienced numerous panic attacks of this kind throughout her life. Her acute fear of dying had developed during her childhood when first her mother, and then her caregiving aunt, died. Situations that renewed the old woman's fears of separation and abandonment were also likely to precipitate a panic attack in which the fear of death was paramount.

A richly detailed study in Holland (Munnichs, 1966) was among the first to reveal how many different orientations toward death are held by older people. Although most respondents expressed a predominantly positive attitude toward dying and death, there were others who were still using evasive strategies. Interesting differences were found among both those who accepted and those who continued to evade death. Furthermore, there was a pattern of attitudinal change within this sample of older adults. The "young-old" tended to think more about death and to be working actively to answer the question, "What should death mean to me at this time in my life?" The "old-old," by contrast, usually seemed to have taken their "final stand" and therefore did not have to give as much thought and energy to this topic.

Dying in Old Age

What is the experience of dying—as distinguished from attitudes toward death—in older people? One valuable source of information comes from an intensive study of 120 men and women who lived and eventually died in a geriatric hospital (Weisman & Kastenbaum, 1968; Kastenbaum & Weisman, 1970). Most of these people remained alert and responsive until the very end of their lives, or until they lapsed into a coma soon before death. This meant that they could interact with family and staff members, express their wishes and needs, and experience affection and support. Some patients slipped in and out of contact, usually becoming responsive when a family member or familiar staff person sought their attention. Few of the dying old men and women expressed a fear of dying either in word or behavior. Several had often talked about death apprehensively before the onset of terminal illness but seemed to accept it when the time actually came. A few patients were agitated in the last days of their lives, with or without expressing fears of death. These were people who had previously shown a pattern of defective reality-testing, in some cases including frank psychosis.

There were two primary patterns of adaptation observed among these old men and women as they became aware of impending death. Some explicitly acknowledged that the end was near. These people then withdrew from their previous activities and social interactions and quietly awaited their deaths. Others, however, kept themselves busy, engaged in as many activities as their energies permitted, and continued to make plans for the future. Although less likely to talk about dying and death, they were usually able to speak about it when the occasion seemed appropriate. For example, one woman met her doctor in the hospital's activity area after he had failed to find her on the ward: "I'm playing bingo today! You tell Death he can just come and find me if he's got a mind to!"

Those patients who did want to talk about death often encountered difficulty in finding somebody to listen. At that time (the late 1960s), few allied health professionals had received training in coping with dying and death. Most hospital personnel attempted to change the subject, minimize the illness, provide hasty and ill-founded support, and otherwise avoid entering into a real conversation (Kastenbaum, 1967). Fortunately, this situation has improved considerably, although the dying person, young or old, may still encounter health care workers who are unable to listen and respond to death-oriented comments.

There are also some research findings to indicate that behavioral and mental changes may occur relatively early in the dying process, even before it is clear from a medical standpoint that the person does not have long to live (see, e.g., Lieberman, 1965). In general, these signs take the form of decreased energy, emotional withdrawal, simplified perceptions, and difficulty in coping with complex problems.

Today, many older people receive hospice care during their final illnesses. Studies indicate that pain and other symptoms can be well controlled during the dying process and, furthermore, that they can enjoy the security and comfort of remaining at home with their loved ones during at least part of this time. It is also encouraging to learn that many older people have also proven to be effective caregivers when given appropriate support from a hospice organization.

See also Adolescence and Death; Appropriate Death; Autopsy, Psychological; Causes of Death; Children and Death; Death Anxiety: Measures; Dying; Grief, Vicarious; National Hospice Study; Personifications of Death; Suicide: Aged Adults.

—ROBERT KASTENBAUM

References

Burt, R.A. (1986). "Legal reform and aging: Current issues, troubling trends." In T.R. Cole & S.A. Gadow (Eds.) *What does it mean to grow old? Reflections from the humanities.* Durham, NC: Duke University Press, 120–29.

Callahan, D. (1987). *Setting limits.* New York: Simon & Schuster.

Cumming, E.M. & Henry, W.E. (1961). *Growing old.* New York: Basic Books.

Erikson, E.H. (1968). *Identity: Youth and crisis.* New York: W.W. Norton.

Gadow, S.A. (1987). "Death and age: A natural connection?" *Generations, 11*: 14–18.

Kalish, R.A. (1985). "The social context of death and dying." In R.H. Binstock & E. Shanas (Eds.) *Handbook of aging and the social sciences.* New York: Van Nostrand Reinhold.

Kastenbaum, R. (1967). "Multiple perspectives on a geriatric 'Death Valley.'" *Community Mental Health Journal, 3*: 21–29.

Kastenbaum, R. (1975). "Is death a life crisis? On the confrontation with death in theory and practice." In N. Datan & L.H. Ginsberg (Eds.) *Life-span developmental psychology.* New York: Academic Press, 19–50.

Kastenbaum, R. (1987). "When a long life ends: The search for meaning." *Generations, 11*: 9–14.

Kastenbaum, R. & Weisman, A.D. (1970). "The psychological autopsy as a research procedure in gerontology." In D.P. Kent, R. Kastenbaum, & S. Sherwood (Eds.) *Research, action, and planning for the aged.* New York: Behavioral Publications, 210–17.

Lieberman, M. (1965). "Psychological correlates of impending death: Some preliminary observations." *Journal of Gerontology, 20*: 181–90.

Moss, M., Lesher, E.L., & Moss, S.Z. (1986–1987). "Impact of the death of an adult child on elderly parents: Some observations." *Omega, Journal of Death and Dying, 17*: 209–19.

Munnichs, J. (1966). *Old age and finitude.* Basel: Karger.

Weisman, A.D. & Kastenbaum, R. (1968). *The psychological autopsy: A study of the terminal phase of life.* New York: Behavioral Publications.

OMEGA, JOURNAL OF DEATH AND DYING

This scholarly journal has been published quarterly since 1970. Manuscripts are reviewed by members of an international editorial board and by other contributors to the field. *Omega* publishes original manuscripts on such topics as grief, bereavement, suicide, terminal care, definitions and attitudes toward death, and sociocultural meanings of death. Both the contributors and the readership reflect the universal nature of the subject-matter: anthropologists, educators, historians, nurses, philosophers, psychologists, psychiatrists, psychotherapists, sociologists, social workers, theologians.

A typical issue of *Omega* includes seven or eight articles on a diversity of death-related topics, as well as book and film reviews. Most articles present new empirical material. Historical perspectives, critical reviews, case studies, and personal experiences are also published. An occasional issue will be devoted largely or entirely to a particular topic. The range of material published in *Omega* can be suggested through a sampling of titles: "Parental Death in Childhood and Loneliness in Young Adults," "An Empirical Search for Stages of Widowhood," "Consideration of Physiologic Mechanisms in Animal Models of 'Sudden Death,'" "Death and Ritual on the Gallows: Public Executions in the Australian Penal Colonies," "Returning Home: The Interstate Transportation of Human Remains," "Stress Encountered by Significant Others of Cancer Patients Receiving Chemotherapy," and "A Tale of Two Bridges: Comparative Suicide Incidence on the Golden Gate and San Francisco-Oakland Bay Bridges."

Information for Contributors

Manuscripts are to be submitted in triplicate to:

Robert Kastenbaum, Editor
Adult Development and Aging Program
West Hall
Arizona State University
Tempe, AZ 85281

Abstracts of 100 to 150 words are required. Specific instructions on preparation of manuscripts are given on the inside back cover of the journal and may also be obtained by writing to *Omega*. Submitted manuscripts are acknowledged immediately. This is a peer-refereed journal. The review process usually results in a decision within sixty days. *Omega* is open to a variety of material and welcomes innovative and controversial contributions.

Subscription and Business Information

Baywood Publishing Company, Inc.
26 Austin Avenue
Amityville, NY 11701

—ROBERT KASTENBAUM

P

PERSONIFICATIONS OF DEATH

A formless, dark entity may be the most well-known death image. The crossing of the river Jordan or Styx, sleep, the ace of spades, a black swan, a skull, a broken column, a black hand with a thumb pointing down, a weeping willow, or an empty bench have also symbolized death. However, no image has provided so rich or historically important a channel for the expression of emotional and intellectual orientations toward life and death as the personification (Aries, 1974). Representations of death as a person have appeared among many peoples at many times, providing an essential bond between history and biology.

In the period of middle childhood (approximately years 6 through 8), death personifications often make their first appearance. Death may be imagined as a scary, frightening, dangerous, unfeeling, unhearing ghost, ugly monster, or skeleton. This frightening being is associated with carrying off the old and the ill, but not usually the children themselves or their parents. Personifications play a major role in how adults conceive of death as well, if usually somewhat below the surface of consciousness. Kastenbaum and Aisenberg (1972, 1977) report that death is most often seen as a male by North American men and women. These researchers found four major types of death personifications: the "gay deceiver," "gentle comforter," "macabre," and "automaton." The gay deceiver is a combination of an ego ideal and a con man: poised, sophisticated, attractive, and hedonistic. The gentle comforter is an adult, often of advanced age, who is seen as wise and noble. The macabre is a horrible, disfigured, and decaying figure. The automaton, not found as frequently in subsequent studies, looks like an ordinary person but has a mechanical, unfeeling approach to his lethal work. Death personifications have also been noted in the fantasies and dreams of terminally ill persons. Such "deathbed visions" have provided the basis for an improved awareness of the dying person's complex perspective on death (Osis & Haroldsson, 1977).

Theorists, therapists, and researchers have suggested that personifying death is one of the most ancient and durable methods for coping with death-related anxiety and fears. Studies of the nature of the relationship between personifications and death anxiety have shown that these images can either heighten or reduce anxiety. Lonetto and Templer (1986) have found that those who give macabre-type personifications tend to have higher levels of anxiety. By contrast, those who favor gentle comforter or gay deceiver personifications usually have lower levels of death-related anxiety and fears. Furthermore, when death is seen as a spiritual light, a vivid pattern of colors, or as a great openness, there is also a tendency to have a relatively low level of death anxiety.

These studies have also indicated that personifications of death have undergone a shift from the macabre figure to less-frightening perceptions of death. There is no doubt that personifications of death contain useful information about the process of symbolization and our conceptual relationship to the meaning and purpose of life. In the future, the extent to which personifications can be therapeutic deserves much fuller exploration.

See also Death Fears and Anxiety; Mors; Psychopomp; Styx.

—RICHARD LONETTO

References

Aries, P. (1974). *Western attitudes toward death from the Middle Ages to the present.* Baltimore: The Johns Hopkins University Press.

Kastenbaum, R. & Aisenberg, R.B. (1972, 1977). *The psychology of death.* New York: Springer.

Lonetto, R. (1980). *Children's conceptions of death.* New York: Springer.

Lonetto, R. & Templer, D.I. (1986). *Death anxiety.* New York: Hemisphere.

Osis, K. & Haroldsson, E. (1977). *At the hour of death.* New York: Parapsychology Foundation.

PROLONGATION OF LIFE

Since ancient times, humans have attempted to defy their own mortality and the aging process by a variety of means. For the most part, these attempts have ended in failure, if not disaster. Perhaps the first to suffer from his attempts to combat mortality was Aesculapius, the Greek god of healing and medicine. He was so skillful at healing people that he himself was put to death by Zeus out of fear that Aesculapius would make humans immortal and transform them into gods.

Attempts to resist age and death can be classified into three general categories (Parker & Gerjuoy, 1979). The immortalist approach attempts to extend the maximum upper limit of the lifespan by altering the basic processes that result in old age and death. The incrementalist approach includes interventions that extend and improve the quality of life by treating the diseases and avoiding the circumstances (accidents, wars) that are responsible for deaths, but without necessarily extending the upper limit of the lifespan. The meliorist approach simply tries to improve the quality of life without extending the length of life.

Changes in Life-Style

Shunamatism. This approach is based upon the ancient notion that the body is imbued with a vital factor or life force whose depletion results in death. There have been several methods of attempting to replenish this life force. The association between this life force and body heat has led people to recommend the consumption of foods that were considered "hot," and using other means of maintaining a "warm, youthful" body. One notable method based upon this line of reasoning is called Shunamatism and is based upon a passage from I Kings (Chapter 1) in the Old Testament (American Standard Version). King David had become very old and his bedcovers were no longer able to keep him warm at night.

1. Now king David was old and stricken in years; and they covered him with clothes, but he gat no heat.
2. Wherefore his servants said unto him, let there be sought for my lord the king a young virgin: and let her stand before the king and let her cherish him, and let her lie in thy bosom, that my lord the king may get heat.
3. So they sought for a fair damsel throughout all the borders of Is-ra-el, and found Abi-shag the Shu'nam-mite, and brought her to the king.

A similar practice was known in medieval Europe, where a common treatment for the pains of old age was to sleep between two young people of unspecified sex. Similar therapies were practiced by the Romans and have also been reported from northern India.

Although it is clear that David (I Kings 1, 4) did not have sexual intercourse with his young bedmate, opinion on the importance of sex in this cure was divided. The Arabian physician Avicenna thought that sex was an important part of the treatment, but others such as Roger Bacon, Franciscan friar, physician, and mathematician of the thirteenth century, believed it was not necessary. Bacon justified the concepts underlying this practice by reasoning "If disease is contagious, why not vitality?" For Bacon, simple proximity was enough to permit the transfer of vitality from the young to the old. In fact, Bacon did not believe that human company was essential; he suggested that a warm puppy would be sufficient.

Recent research has shown that mated rats live longer than rats kept celibate and that men in their 50s with younger wives have lower mortality rates than those with wives older than themselves. However, in the case of humans, this difference in longevity may be explained by the premarital selection of younger wives by healthier men.

Exercise. The physicians of classical Greece and Rome believed that exercise (along with diet) was a prime method for treating the disabilities of old age. Recent studies suggest that regular exercise can prevent and reverse some, although not all of the physical decline in later life (Stones & Kozma, 1985).

The beneficial effects of exercise on fitness, reaction time, cognitive performance, and sense of well-being have been documented. Regular exercise may also reduce vulnerability to several life-threatening diseases related to cardiovascular functioning. In order to achieve these effects, the exercises must be aerobic, increasing the capacity of the lungs to absorb oxygen and the capacity of the heart to deliver oxygen throughout the body. In general, exercise is not an immortalist intervention because it does not extend the maximum lifespan. It is, however, an effective incrementalist intervention.

Changes in Diet

Dietary Restrictions. In the seventeenth century, a Venetian nobleman, Luigi Cornero, wrote a book on what is currently called "successful aging" before he died at the age of 99 (Cornero, 1979). One of Cornero's strongest recommendations was for dietary restriction: "The food that a man leaves does him more good than what he has eaten." Current research suggests that undereating prolongs life in laboratory animals. It was discovered that rats given only the daily minimum essential vitamins, minerals, and proteins lived as much as twice as long as those that had been allowed to eat ad libitum. The implications of these findings for humans, however, are not well developed. The animal research demonstrated that restrictions on diet are most effective when started fairly early in life, and it is unlikely that underfeeding children will become an accepted method of achieving longevity. Nevertheless, epidemiological studies indicate that life expectancy is greatly reduced in persons who are overweight. Actuarial data indicate that underweight people can expect to live 15–20 percent longer than people who are overweight. Although it is still not clear how dietary restriction can best be applied to humans, this general approach holds considerable potential as an incrementalist intervention.

Dietary Supplements

Antioxidants. One of the changes that occurs as a person grows old involves damage to the genes that control biochemical processes in the cells. Although many factors contribute to this damage, the presence of a class of chemicals called "free radicals" has received much attention from researchers interested in modifying degenerative processes. Because free radicals have an unpaired electron, they have a strong tendency to combine with and damage molecules that are involved in cell maintenance and repair. The accumulation of such damage and the consequent decreases in functioning are considered by some biologists to be the fundamental cause of aging.

Several substances called "antioxidants" or "free radical scavengers" can neutralize free radicals and reduce the damage they cause. Antioxidants are created naturally in the body, but certain substances that may also be included in the diet are also antioxidants. Common substances such as the food preservative BHT, vitamins C and E, and ethyl alcohol possess these properties. Despite evidence that some of these substances may extend the life of some laboratory animals, there is no evidence that they have any beneficial effect when they are included in the diet of humans.

Vitamins. Claims that vitamins increase health and prolong life have been based upon several lines of reasoning, including their usefulness as free radical scavengers. One of the most influential proponents of large doses of vitamin C and other vitamins has been Linus Pauling. Dr. Pauling points out that in human evolutionary history, our ancestors consumed considerable quantities of vitamin C in their diet and consequently our bodies have lost the ability to manufacture it. The diet of many people today contains an insufficient amount of this vitamin for normal functioning, according to Dr. Pauling, who therefore recommends massive vitamin C supplements. In general, however, research has not confirmed the effectiveness or usefulness of megadoses of vitamin C or any other vitamin (such as E or B5) for increasing life expectancy.

Yogurt. The Nobel Prize winning Russian biologist Eli Metchnikoff speculated that old age resulted from slow poisoning of the body by a toxin created by bacteria in the intestine. He proposed that one method of eliminating this toxin-producing bacteria was to displace it by eating yogurt, because this food contains a nontoxin-producing bacterium. In support of his ideas Metchnikoff pointed out that Bulgarians, who eat large quantities of yogurt, are very long-lived. Metchnikoff's theory also led to a series of surgical operations on elderly people in which yards of bowel were removed to prevent the formation of this toxin. In fact, one Montreal surgeon in the 1920s who performed this operation extensively called it "intestinal spring cleaning."

Metchnikoff's toxin has never been identified, and his theory remains totally without scientific support. Even though there is also no indication that Bulgarians live longer than anyone else, yogurt is still associated in the public mind with health and longevity.

Alcohol. Since ancient times, alcohol in the form of wine has been recommended as a medicine to reduce suffering, diminish the ravages of old age, and prolong life. When Arnaud de Villeneuve invented cognac in the thirteenth century, he was convinced that he had discovered the miraculous *aqua vita* that alchemists had been seeking for centuries in their efforts to prolong life. In the centuries that followed, it became apparent that alcohol in the concentrated form that was produced by de Villineuve's distillation was not the benefit to the health of mankind that he had proposed. It is clear that alcohol abuse is one of the surest means of increasing the probability of an early death. However, it also has been clearly demonstrated that consumption of beer and wine in moderation can improve sleep, feelings of well-being, and possibly even cognitive functioning in elderly people (Mishara & Kastenbaum, 1980).

Despite the well-documented dangers of alcohol abuse, moderate consumption does not have negative effects on longevity. In fact, persons who abstain totally from drinking have slightly shorter average lifespans than those who drink occasionally. This, however, does not necessarily mean that alcohol prolongs life. Nondrinkers are a relatively small minority group in North America and may have a slightly shorter life expectancy because of other behaviors or characteristics that are more common among abstainers than drinkers.

Treatment with Plants and Animals. Various substances derived from plants and animals have been claimed to possess the power of increasing longevity and causing a rejuvenative effect. In many cases these powers have been ascribed on the basis of the sympathetic magic principle: things that are similar in appearance will influence each other. The orchid is one such plant. Its flower resembles the scrotum, a symbol of regeneration of life and vitality. Another is the root of the mandrake. This plant has a taproot that often has one major division and, consequently, it often resembles the human form. In addition to being associated with rejuvenation of elderly people (See Genesis 40: 14–16), the mandrake has a long history of use as an aphrodisiac, as do many other alleged rejuvenants.

Another putative rejuvenator is the drug *soma,* praised in the hymns of the Sanskrit Rig Veda. Soma has now been identified as the *Amanita muscaria* mushroom. According to legend, soma achieved rejuvenation not by stopping or reversing the aging process but by causing a complete rebirth of the individual from his or her own body.

Medical and Technical Interventions

Hormone Therapy. Some people have believed that the decline in old age that precedes death is associated, at least in men, with a diminished sexual interest and capacity. This is thought to be coincident with a decline in sex hormones. Replenishment of sex hormones might then be expected to restore not only sexual capacity but also youth. In 1889 the French physician, C.E. Brown-Sequard, at the age of 72, claimed that he had succeeded in rejuvenating himself by self-injecting an extract of dog's testicles. Despite the rejection of this claim by the medical community and his death a few years later, Brown-Sequard's ideas were adopted by a few opportunistic doctors in the early twentieth century who performed testicle transplants on elderly males seeking rejuvenation. There is no evidence that this sort of hormone therapy had any beneficial effects. In fact, the treatments created new problems for some recipients, who acquired syphilis when given testicles taken from infected monkeys.

Paul Niehan's Cell Therapy. Dr. Paul Niehans developed a therapy based upon the belief that aging was a result of a weakening of body organs. These weakened organs could be restored, he proposed, by injecting cells from the organs of healthy animals. Treatment at Niehan's clinic required an initial analysis of the urine to determine which organs were not functioning properly. In the treatment phase, the organs identified as deficient were removed from the embryo of a sheep, ground up, and injected into the patient.

Niehans was well connected socially (his mother was an illegitimate daughter of Fredric III of Germany), and his clinic attracted many rich and powerful people. Among these clients were Pope Pius XII, Somerset Maugham, and Winston Churchill. Consequently, his theory and techniques achieved some prominence. In its day, cell therapy achieved some scientific credibility, but it is no longer accepted. Nevertheless, cell therapy is still practiced in Switzerland and some other countries. Curiously, the technique, although variously accepted and rejected, does not seem to have received a thorough scientific evaluation.

Gerovital. In the 1930s and 1940s, a Romanian physician, Anna Aslan, experimented with injections of procaine hydrochloride in the treatment of both vascular and arthritic diseases of the limbs. Dr. Aslan found that this treatment also seemed to reverse many age-related symptoms of a general nature. She refined her treatment, and it is now given by intramuscular injection under the name Gerovital H_3, or GH_3. A course of twelve injections is given eight times a year, and this must be repeated every year. It has been claimed that this drug, similar to the commonly used local anesthetic whose proprietary name is Novocain, when given in this manner, produces miraculous effects on elderly people. Many individuals have flocked to European clinics to receive the treatment. To date, however, careful clinical trials in the United States have not confirmed the claimed age-reversal effect. It has been shown, though, the drug may have antidepressant properties and therefore may relieve depression, contributing in this way to an improved sense of well-being. Even this finding, however, is disputed.

Cooling. One class of theories holds that aging is a result of metabolic processes. It was noted around the turn of the century that most animal species consume a constant number of calories for every gram of their body weight over their lifespan. It would seem to follow that if the metabolic rate of an organism could be slowed, then the lifespan might be extended accordingly. Research has shown this to be true in species like fruit flies and fish that do not maintain a constant body temperature. One study of fish showed that a decrease of 5–6 degrees centigrade increased lifespan by 75–100 percent, and that cooling was more effective in the second half of life than in early life. It is also known that mammals whose temperature is lowered during hibernation live longer than those that do not hibernate.

Although it appears as though the mechanism by which cooling increases lifespan is metabolic, there is another possibility. Cooling reduces the immune system response and therefore its beneficial effects in some circumstances may take the form of decreasing autoimmune diseases.

It is not yet evident how these findings can be applied usefully to humans. Lowered body temperature cannot be achieved by lowering the temperature of the environment; this usually increases metabolic rate and stresses the body. However, it is possible to use certain drugs to reduce body temperature. Gerontologist Alex Comfort has pointed out that a significant effect on lifespan might be achieved if a person's body temperature could be lowered by only 1 to 2 degrees centigrade during sleep at night.

Conclusions

Despite several thousands of years of preoccupation by many of the most gifted and observant physicians and scientists in the world, no miraculous way has been found to prolong life (Gruman, 1966; Harrington, 1969). The immortalist interventions with the greatest promise appear to be undereating without undernutrition, and cooling. Regular aerobic exercise has been established as an effective incrementalist and meliorist intervention. Technical and medical interventions that have claimed some initial success either have not withstood extended testing or remain untried in humans.

There is, however, no compelling theoretical reason why aging might not be stopped or reversed. At least one gerontologist does not fear the fate of Aesculapius; Alex Comfort has claimed that if the scientific and medical resources of the United States were mobilized, aging could be conquered within ten years.

See also Causes of Death; Old Age and Death.

—BRIAN L. MISHARA & WILLIAM A. McKIM

References

Cornero, L. (1664/Reprint 1979). "The art of living long." New York: Arno Press.

Gruman, G.J. (1966). "A history of ideas about the prolongation of life. The evolution of prolongevity hypotheses to 1800." *Transactions of the American Philosophical Society, 56*, Part 9.

Harrington, A. (1969). *The immortalist.* New York: Random House.

McKim, W.A. & Mishara, B.L. (1987). *Drugs and aging.* Toronto: Butterworth.

Mishara, B.L. & Kastenbaum, R. (1980). *Alcohol and old age.* New York: Grune & Stratton.

Parker, J. & Gerjuoy, H. (1979). "Life-span extension: The state of the art." In R.M. Veach (Ed.) *Life span: Values and life extending technology.* San Francisco: Harper & Row.

Stones, J.M. & Kozma, A. (1985). "Physical performance." In N. Charness (Ed.) *Aging and human performance.* New York: John Wiley & Sons, Ltd.

PSALMS OF LAMENT

Anger, despair, grief, anxiety, loneliness, and a sense of helplessness are among the feelings that have been observed as part of the dying experience. Nevertheless, many terminally ill people find it difficult to vent such intense emotions. They may fear that expressing feelings of this kind would drive away the people they most love and need. Furthermore, some people have a long-standing habit of keeping a tight rein on their emotions. Others think it would violate their religious principles to express intense negative emotions precisely when their faith is being put to its ultimate test—especially when some of these feelings are directed at God.

Yet it is in the ancient text of the Book of Psalms (Old Testament) that a model is given for bringing to speech the desperate cry of the human heart when life begins to disintegrate into death. Psalms of lament, personal and communal, constitute approximately one-third of the Psalter. These poetic utterances address human speech or song to God. Lament psalms or psalms of complaint, therefore, articulate some of the deepest, most distressed emotions known to the human spirit.

The language of lament moves "the awareness and imagination of the speaker away from life well-ordered into an arena of terror, raggedness, and hurt. In some sense this speech is a visceral release of the realities and imagination that have been censored" (Brueggemann, 1984, p. 53). Most of the Psalms progress from complaint to praise, as if the last word to God dare not be a negative word. "These poignant human outcries express a faith that dares to question and even to wrestle with God in situations of suffering and distress. Perhaps there is something therapeutic in prayer of this kind" (Anderson, 1983, pp. 103–04).

Psalm 88 is the one psalm of lament that has no word of hope or praise from beginning to end and is the most discouraged and forlorn. Other personal lament psalms are 6, 13, 22, 35, 38, 42, 43, 102, and 143. In addition, there is a large group of psalms in which a negative petition in the lament of the individual is a modified complaint against God. These include such requests as "Be not silent, O God of my praise!" "Do not cast me away." A negative petition of this kind stands in the place of lament in Psalms 26, 27, 28, 35, 38, 55, 69, 71, 102, and 143 (Westermann, 1981). A problematic aspect of these laments is their frequent reference to enemies and the vindictive attitude toward them. A constructive way to deal with this problem is to think of "enemies" as anything that threatens one's safety and well-being, and to remember that God, in the view of the writer, is able to hear and deal with any expression we are able to voice.

Psalm 13 is a good example of the personal lament Psalm:

How long, O Lord? Wilt thou forget me forever?
How long wilt thou hide thy face from me?
How long must I bear pain in my soul, and have sorrow in my heart all the day?
How long shall my enemy be exalted over me?
Consider and answer me, O Lord my God;
lighten my eyes, lest I sleep the sleep of death;
lest my enemy say, "I have prevailed over him";
lest my foes rejoice because I am shaken.
But I have trusted in thy steadfast love; my heart shall rejoice in thy salvation.
I will sing to the Lord, because he has dealt bountifully with me.

Psalms such as these may be of comfort to some people facing death, both encouraging the expression of their own feelings and confirming their faith.

See also Deathbed Scenes; Dying; Grief.

—GERALD Q. ROSEBERRY

References

Anderson, B.W. (1983). *Out of the depths: The Psalms speak for us today.* Rev. ed. Philadelphia: Westminster Press.
Brueggemann, W. (1984). *The message of the Psalms.* Minneapolis: Augsburg Publishing House.
The Holy Bible. Revised Standard Version (1962). Cleveland: World.
Westerman, C. (1981). *Praise and lament in the Psalms.* Atlanta: John Knox Press.

PSYCHOPOMP

The psychopomp is a messenger for the gods of ancient religions who assists and comforts souls as they depart from their bodily abode and journey to the next world. *Pompos* is a Greek term denoting a guide or leader. The psychopomp may be a god, such as Hermes (Greek), or a fabulous creature such as a soul-bird (Egyptian) or winged lion (Babylonian). Contemporary versions of the belief that the dying person may be contacted by some type of spirit figure have been documented. Osis and Haraldsson (1986) report the results of a cross-national study of "deathbed visions" in which some dying people appeared to be interacting with spirit figures or apparitions. Deceased parents and spouses were among the most frequent deathbed figures observed. Nevertheless, there were also a variety of other escort figures, such as a taxi driver who took a dying woman to "beautiful, endless gardens" and a cow that led an Indian woman to the next life. The experience of perceived contact with a deathbed figure often was reported in a coherent and alert manner. It was not unusual for the dying person to achieve a more serene state of mind after the experience. Aries (1981) and Meyer-Baer (1970) examine some historical facets of the psychopomp or escort (for an evaluation of the available data, see Kastenbaum, 1984).

See also Deathbed Scenes; Dying; Life After Death?; Personifications of Death.

—ROBERT KASTENBAUM

References

Aries, P. (1981). *The hour of our death.* New York: Alfred A. Knopf.

Kastenbaum, R. (1984). *Is there life after death?* Englewood Cliffs, NJ: Prentice-Hall.

Meyer-Baer, K. (1970). *Music of the spheres and the dance of death.* Princeton: Princeton University Press.

Osis, K. & Haraldsson, E. (1986). *At the hour of death.* Rev. ed. New York: Hastings House.

R

RIGOR MORTIS

The body undergoes a continuing series of changes after death. Perhaps the most often mentioned change is the postmortem stiffening that is known as rigor mortis. This reaction occurs first in the involuntary muscles (such as the heart and other internal organs) and then progresses to the head, neck, trunk, and, finally, the extremities. It has been found that rigor mortis results from the cessation of glycogen synthesis, which, in turn, deprives body tissues of adenosine triphosphate (ATP). Muscles contract and, locked in this position, immobilize the joints. Rigor mortis usually can be observed within two to four hours after death, but the timing is affected by the amount of ATP in the muscles at the moment of death. For example, a person who engaged in strenuous muscular activity immediately before death may have incurred an "oxygen debt" that diminished ATP and glycogen. Rigor mortis is likely to appear more rapidly in such a situation (Evans, 1963). Unusual environmental conditions can also affect the timing of rigor mortis; for example, very low temperatures tend to retard the appearance of rigor mortis.

Several other terms are also employed to describe postmortem conditions. The fall in body temperature after death is known as *algor mortis*. This is primarily a result of the cessation of blood circulation and hypothalamic function. Ordinarily, body temperature will decline about two degrees Fahrenheit per hour until room temperature is reached. *Livor mortis* is a term applied to skin discolorations that appear as red blood cells break down (Kneisel & Ames, 1986). Postmortem staining usually begins shortly after death and is completed within about eight hours (Pryce & Ross, 1963).

It may be useful to recognize that these and a number of other physical reactions are predictable and characteristic postmortem changes. For example, a layperson may fear that reddish-bluish spots on the skin mean that the person had been bruised and mistreated while still alive, when, in fact, these are normal changes after death. Experts are aware of exceptions to the general rule that can be important in determining causes of death in difficult or ambiguous cases. For example, a rise instead of a fall in body temperature after death can occur after strychnine poisoning (but also for several other conditions).

Some of the more spectacular "ghost stories" of past generations may have been stimulated by a postmortem phenomenon that is seldom seen in our own time. "Old stories, often retold, linger on in oral tradition telling of the glowing of exhumed human remains, the awe-inspiring sight sometimes being accompanied by equally mysterious events such as the tolling of invisible bells and the calling of ghostly voices" (Evans, 1963, p. 11). It is now known that this type of glow is produced by luminous bacteria—not by the dead bodies themselves, nor by spectral visitors. This phenomenon occurred especially in forests and in other conditions in which dampness encouraged the growth of wood fungi and has been eliminated by contemporary funeral and cemetery practices.

Understandably, many people feel uncomfortable when confronted with—or even thinking about—the physical changes that occur after death. Physicians, nurses, funeral directors, and others have learned to understand and accept these changes in order to perform their services in an effective and responsible manner. As death has become less of a taboo topic in society, more people have proven themselves able to accept both the reality of postmortem physical changes and the unique personality and value of the individual.

See also Brain Death; Cemeteries; Funerals.

—ROBERT KASTENBAUM

References

Evans, W.E.D. (1963). *The chemistry of death.* Springfield, IL: C.C. Thomas.

Kneisel, C.R. & Ames, S.W. (1986). *Adult health nursing: A biopsychosocial approach.* Menlo Park, CA: Addison-Wesley.

Pryce, D.M. & Ross, C.F. (1963). *Ross's postmortem appearances.* London: Oxford University Press.

S

SIBLINGS OF DYING CHILDREN

Houses of Chronic Sorrow

The siblings of terminally ill children live in houses of chronic sorrow. The signs of illness, sorrow, and death are everywhere, whether or not given voice. The signs are there on parents' faces, in the hushed conversations, in irritability and outbursts of anger. Schedules are often interrupted. Plans and even life-style change. Most noticeably, the signs of death are on the ill sibling's face. "He can't do much anymore. He has trouble breathing. He just lies there."

The healthy sibling finds himself in a situation quite unlike his peers, often quite unlike what he has known before. In the last weeks and months of the ill child's life and for a long time afterward, the well sibling's role in the family changes. He often finds himself in the role of caretaker for the ill child or consoler and "parent" of the parent. Healthy siblings are at risk of becoming nonpersons—there, but largely ignored.

There are many sources of confusion for well siblings, including mercurial shifts in their parents' emotions, contradictory information coming their way, changing and contradictory expectations for their own behavior. They often report feeling alone, betrayed, unsupported, rejected, and neglected. At times, however, they also feel overprotected by their parents. Healthy siblings are also in conflict with themselves over the amount of attention the termi-

nally ill child receives. As one brother said, "It is tough. She (the boy's ill sister) gets the extra attention, but she has to have the attention so she'll live. My mother tries to make up for it, but she can't."

Just as the well child experiences increasing difficulty in getting from his parents what he once did, so, too, does he experience difficulty in getting what he once did from his ill sibling. The relationship cannot proceed as usual. In consequence, the well child is often without a companion. Communication is sometimes distorted. Mutual aid declines. Using the sibling as a means toward self-definition becomes problematic. Add to this configuration feelings of jealousy, rivalry, ambivalence, and guilt, and it is not surprising that many clinicians and researchers have found maladaptive behaviors in the siblings of terminally ill and deceased children. These behaviors include: sleep disorders, rebelliousness, poor school performance, school phobia, withdrawal from family and peers, regression, exaggerated independence, "little adult behaviors," physical complaints, fear of minor illness, loss of appetite or overeating, depression, timidity, idealization, over-solicitation or overt hostility toward the ill sibling, and preoccupation with the deceased. Much needs to be learned about the incidence, prevalence, and duration of these behaviors as well as the factors that contribute to their development.

The healthy sibling's reaction to the news of his sibling's death provides important clues to what the child is thinking and feeling. For example, it is not unusual to hear statements such as: "Now I can have his toys," "I wanted my own room, anyway," or "He was so much better than me." Rooted in these responses are feelings of anger, jealousy, sadness, and loss. The feelings are often ambivalent and may have existed prior to the child's illness and death. The work of John Bowlby (1980) demonstrated that even very young children can experience a deep sense of loss and engage in mourning behaviors.

Parental Response

The bereaved child's needs are great, but often the people to whom he looks for support and comfort—the parents—are too caught up in their own grief to give the surviving children what they need. It is important to help the parent help the child, for it is to the parent that the child looks for reassurance and with the parent that the child wants to reestablish a secure relationship.

Parents should be helped to understand how necessary it is for them to talk to the surviving child or children about what has happened. Silence breeds confusion and resentment. It is important to take one's cues from the child. These cues are often difficult to interpret because the child's thinking may be far more complex than he can put into words. Sensitive parents will share information and answer questions in ways that can be understood.

It is important to reassure the child that he is not responsible for his sibling's death, and that he will be protected and not deserted. Parents should neither idealize nor cease talking about the deceased child. The surviving child may also need help working through his identification with the deceased.

Parents should be aware that their tragedy is not the same as the child's, and that the child's reactions will not be the same either. The child may be sad one moment and out playing the next. The impact and meaning of the child's death also changes over time. For the surviving sibling, there may be a period of intense longing, searching, and discussion of the deceased. This may be followed by a period during which nothing at all is said and, in turn, by another period of detailed questioning about the circumstances of death (which, unfortunately, parents may find annoying or offensive).

One talk is not enough. As the child grows up, he will need to integrate memories in different ways at different times. It takes time to integrate and respond to the powerful and disturbing experience of sibling death. No one can, nor should one even try, to "fix" a child's grief. It is his own, and he must work through it. And it is in the working through of grief that adults can and should offer support.

See also Children, Dying; Children and Death; Grief: Death of a Child.

—MYRA BLUEBOND-LANGNER

References

Bowlby, J. (1980). *Attachment and loss. Vol. 2: Loss.* New York: Basic Books.

Burton, L. (1975). *The family life of sick children.* London: Routledge, Kegan Paul.

Koocher, G.P. (1974). "Talking with children about death." *American Journal of Orthopsychiatry, 44:* 404–11.

Lindsay, M. & MacCarthy, D. (1974). "Caring for the brother and sister of a dying child." In L. Burton (Ed.) *Care of the child facing death.* London: Routledge, Kegan Paul, 189–206.

Rosen, H. (1986). *Unspoken grief: Coping with childhood sibling loss.* Lexington, MA: D.C. Heath.

Spinetta, J. (1981). "The sibling of the child with cancer." In J.J. Spinetta & P. Deasy-Spinetta (Eds.) *Living with childhood cancer.* St. Louis: C.V. Mosby, 234–52.

SOCRATES' DEATH

Most philosophers are known by their ideas and books. Socrates of Athens (circa 470–399 BC) wrote no books and his thoughts have survived only in the dialogues of his disciple, Plato, and, to a lesser extent, several theater pieces by Xenophon and Aristophanes. Those who expect philosophers to be solemn and venerated figures have only to read Aristophones' *Clouds* to find that this father of philosophy was considered by his contemporaries to be well suited for comedy. The enduring appeal of Socrates perhaps owes as much to his "gadfly" life-style and the dramatic circumstances surrounding his death as to his specific contributions to philosophy.

There is no question, however, that Socrates occupies a unique position in Western thought. In fact, all other philosophers of antiquity are classified as either pre- or post-Socratic. Introductory students today still are exposed to the "Socratic method," which is essentially a way of educing knowledge that individuals already possess without knowing that they do. This was a technique by which Socrates attempted to demonstrate that the most important ideas (such as truth, beauty, justice) are already in our minds. The task of education, on this view, is to educe—to draw out our intrinsic knowledge so we can apply it more adequately to our lives. His method also includes a probing and incisive cross-examination style that many a lawyer would envy.

An important corollary for Socrates was the injunction, "Know thyself." There is nothing more essential for a person to know than his or her own mind or soul. For these and other reasons, Socrates has remained an inspiration for those who would include the human mind itself as the primary challenge to be conquered by intellectual activity. Freud's creation of psychoanalysis is one significant example of a modern approach that owes much to Socrates (who, in one of his theatrical representations, actually employed the "free association" method that Freud reinvented more than two thousand years later).

Condemned to Death

Socrates was well known but not necessarily well liked in his own time. He held some beliefs that were unpopular. Although Athenian democracy differed considerably from modern democracy, it did express respect for the right of the individual citizen to participate in decision-making and rule. Socrates enjoyed criticizing this system, holding that the rule of the many could never be as wise and effective as the rule of an elite few who were really qualified for this responsibility.

Irksome views of this kind could be tolerated by the Athenians of his day. However, Socrates "spent his days in the highly unpopular but thoroughly successful task of proving to the Athenians their ignorance of things about which they thought they were well informed" (Jones, 1952, p. 93). Combining "an intensely realistic and down-to-earth common sense with a passionate mysticism," Socrates was more than most of his fellow citizens could contend with. But there were some who did take heartily to this eccentric and iconoclastic fellow: "bright young men who enjoyed watching him trap their elders in contradictions" (Jones, p. 95). It is probable that had he not attracted such a following among the youth, Athenian officialdom would have continued to shake their heads, shrug their shoulders, and reluctantly tolerate this annoying personage who had, after all, served as a brave and loyal soldier in his youth.

Finally, formal charges were brought against Socrates. He was accused of impiety and several other counts. Our knowledge of his trial and death is based upon descriptions given by Plato in his dialogues, *Apology, Crito,* and *Phaedo.* Many historians believe that Socrates could have won acquittal or been dismissed without punishment if he had admitted to at least a little wrongdoing, said he was sorry about it, and perhaps mentioned the wife and children that he had to look after. The establishment seemed to want Socrates to back down a little and thereby make him something less of a nuisance in the future.

Socrates had no intention of doing so. He used the trial as an opportunity to confront his accusers with their own ignorance and malice. If you convict me, he told the court, it will be not because of the evidence, which contains "hardly a breath of truth," but because of the "great hatred . . . in the minds of many persons." He complimented his accusers in the efforts they had made to present so false a picture of him that "I, for my part, almost forgot my own identity."

Even the prospect of a death sentence did not deter him: "To fear death, gentlemen, is nothing else than to think one is wise when one is not; for it is thinking one knows what one does not know. For no one knows whether death be not even the greatest of blessing to man, but they fear it as if they knew that it is the greatest of evils." He added that he surely would have been put to death long ago had he ventured into politics and raised his unsettling questions. Perhaps the closest he came to asking anything of the court was his request, "Do not be angry with me for speaking the truth." However, he immediately placed himself in peril again by adding, "The fact is that no man will save his life who nobly opposes you or any other populace and prevents many unjust and illegal things from happening in the state." He was found guilty and condemned to death.

Why Not Escape?

In prison awaiting his execution, Socrates had the companionship of Plato and other friends and disciples. They knew that it was possible to arrange for his escape and safe passage. Although the verdict had been pronounced, Athens was not really thirsty for the blood of this 70-year-old "character"; it might be just as well to let him get away and become somebody else's problem.

Socrates rejected this plan. Although he considered himself innocent of the charges, he chose to accept his execution. Why would a man turn down the opportunity to save his life, especially when the rescue operation was relatively risk free and harmless to others? Socrates seemed to be a man who was completely "at one with himself" (Kidd, 1967). His life and his philosophy were inseparable. And if this strong sense of unity led to the rational conclusion that death was the appropriate choice, then his life must follow the dictates of his philosophy. Apart from his specific reasons, then, Socrates in choosing death affirmed that a person should live out his philosophical beliefs despite temptations to waver and gain some temporary benefit.

But Socrates also had his more specific reasons and these he shared with his companions (as recounted in Plato's *Phaedo*). True to his customary style, Socrates developed his reasons through dialogue, often turning matters around so that he was questioning his disciples about their beliefs rather than replying directly to their questions. Although the dialogue occurs in prison and in near proximity to his death, Socrates continues to tease and jab at the concerns expressed by his disciples. It is obvious that the Socrates described in *Phaedo* took pleasure in continuing to persuade and outmaneuver his disciples. The dialogue by no means restricts itself to the immediate circumstances but ranges into such topics as the type of knowledge people might have before they are born.

Socrates challenges his friends to convince him by rational argument that he should evade his impending execution. The fact that some people think he should escape, observes Socrates, has no real bearing on the matter, for "most excellent friend, we must not consider at all what the many will say of us, but what he who knows about right and wrong . . . will say." And Socrates knows—his friends reluctantly agree—that it is wrong to violate the agreements one has made. Although the state judged him wrongly, still one must obey the laws. Private persons must not overturn the laws that govern all, or the entire state may be destroyed.

Nevertheless, one might be tempted to escape out of fear of death. Socrates, as in his speech in court, observes that we do not really know what death is or means. In fact, over the course of his long life, he has found ever more clearly that he has very little certain knowledge of anything—even why one and one must make two! Taking a position that might be described as "radical ignorance," Socrates impressed upon his companions the view that we actually have but a limited and undependable grasp on the everyday world around us, even the way our own mind, bones, and muscles function. How, then, can we presume to judge death so harshly?

Socrates allows that there is reason to believe that the soul is imperishable and immortal. If this is actually the case, then there is nothing to fear in death. One could expect a continued development of the higher parts of one's nature. Death should be considered a glorious venture. But even should he be mistaken about the immortality of the soul, there would still be nothing to fear. Wicked people should then have the least to fear because they have "a good bargain in dying . . . happily quit not only of their own body, but of their own evil." Whether or not there be immortal life after death, the good person obviously has nothing to fear after drawing his last breath on earth.

When Crito asked how they should bury him, Socrates replied, "In any way that you like; but you must get hold of me, and take care that I do not run away from you." This teasing response was followed by a more serious request that his other companions see to it that Crito did not give way to grief, but, rather, take comfort that the right thing had been done.

A Cup of Hemlock

After the leisurely dialogue, Socrates indicated he was ready for the cup of hemlock that would provide his exit from this life. First, however, he bathed himself "in order that the women may not have the trouble of washing my body after I am dead."

The last moments of Socrates' life constitute one of the few detailed examples of a deathbed scene to come down to us from such a great distance in time. Socrates spoke kindly of the jailer who brought him the cup of hemlock and "cheerfully drank off the poison." At this point, his friends could no longer restrain their sorrow, and began to weep openly. Socrates, however, remained calm. He wondered about this "strange outcry. . . . (for) I have been told that a man should die in peace. Be quiet then, and have patience."

Socrates then walked about until his legs began to fail. He then lay on his back, according to directions given by the jailer, and looked at his feet and legs. He demonstrated to his friends that his legs had become cold and stiff and that this numbness was moving upward through his body. When the poison reaches his heart, that would be the end, he said. And then his last words: "Crito, I owe a cock to Asclepius; will you remember to pay the debt?" Crito asked if there was anything else they should do, but Socrates' eyes were fixed in death.

A Model Death?

How should a person die? Death-avoidant patterns are common in many contemporary societies, including the United States. Until recently (See **Hospice: Philosophy and Practice; Stages of Dying**), the dying person has been isolated from society both physically and symbolically. One

consequence has been the paucity of "good examples" of ways in which people meet their death. The recently initiated study of deathbed scenes suggests that more people are familiar with seriously flawed manufactured versions of the last moments than they are with actual examples of real people meeting their real deaths.

The death of Socrates is one of the relatively few deathbed scenes that has become well known to a large number of people. One does not have to agree with Socrates' choice to find it illuminating and challenging. One does not even have to assume that Plato's description is an entirely faithful account, although there is no compelling reason for doubting it either. It is likely that the death of Socrates—along with the crucifixion of Christ and a very few other powerful examples--will long continue to draw the interest of thoughtful people.

Among recent commentaries, perhaps the one that Socrates would have found most interesting is I.F. Stone's *The Trial of Socrates* (1988). Stone's major contribution is the effort he makes to locate Socrates within his own time and traditions, to see him more in terms of the way he might have struck his own contemporaries. Stone concludes that Socrates resolutely sought his own death and managed to maneuver Athens into passing sentence on him. It is possible to read Socrates' death somewhat differently if Stone's position is accepted, though Stone himself takes little note of Socrates' last moments.

See also Appropriate Death; Deathbed Scenes; Dying; Hospice: Philosophy and Practice; Stages of Dying; Tame Death.

—ROBERT KASTENBAUM

References

Jones, W.T. (1952). *A history of Western philosophy.* New York: Harcourt, Brace.

Kidd, I.G. (1967). "Socrates." In P. Edwards (Ed.) *The encyclopedia of philosophy.* Vols. 7 and 8. New York: Macmillan, pp. 480–86.

Plato. *Dialogues.* (Many editions available.)

Stone, I.F. (1988). *The trial of Socrates.* Boston: Little, Brown.

STAGES OF DYING

The lectures, workshops, and writings of psychiatrist Elisabeth Kubler-Ross have introduced many health care professionals as well as members of the general public to issues concerning the dying person. Others (e.g., minister Edgar A. Jackson, psychologist Lawrence LeShan, psychiatrist Avery D. Weisman) had been providing sensitive and competent care for people with life-threatening conditions, but Kubler-Ross was the first to draw widespread attention to their neglected needs. A charismatic and seemingly tireless lecturer, she did much to break down the social and emotional walls that society had erected between itself and the dying person.

The Five Stages

During the 1970s, no concept in the area of dying and death was more familiar than the "stages of dying" discussed by Kubler-Ross in her first book (1969) and her many lectures. This concept continues to be restated in text books and other secondary publications and has been taken by many as fact. It is unfortunate that Kubler-Ross's message of compassion and understanding for the dying person has been somewhat overshadowed by the prominence given to the stage theory by those eager for a simple guide to complex and sometimes disturbing phenomena.

The five stages—denial, anger, bargaining, depression, acceptance—proposed by Kubler-Ross refer to the dying person's mental and emotional response to his or her condition. The sequence of denial, anger, bargaining, depression, and acceptance is said to begin when the person becomes aware that death is in prospect. Although distress and disturbance are present, the stages are not considered to be pathological and do not mean that there is anything abnormal about the individual's personality and coping mechanisms. Rather, the stages represent successive ways of attempting to deal with a major life crisis.

Denial is said to be the first response to information indicating that one has a terminal illness. This response can take many specific forms, but underlying them all is the attempt to negate, refute, or escape from the "death sentence" that seems to have been passed. The denial response is fueled by a rush of anxiety, usually brief. Therefore, when we see a terminally ill person exhibiting denial accompanied by an attitude of shock and psychological numbness, it is reasonable to expect that this psychological response will soon give way to other stages in which the reality of impending death is faced with increasing directness.

The second stage, *anger*, is often difficult for family, friends, and professional caregivers. "Why me?" is a characteristic response of the dying person. Rage and resentment may be focused on a specific target, or the individual may strike out at anybody who happens to be available. It is not unusual for people to become angry at God during this stage. Knowing that this is a normal stage of reaction to dying can help others realize that they are not really being attacked for personal reasons, and that this type of behavior, stimulated by fear and frustration, will disappear as the next stage begins.

In the middle stage, *bargaining*, the terminally ill person attempts to make some kind of private "deal" with fate. This can take place mostly within the person's own thoughts and feelings, as in promising God to become a better person if allowed to live just long enough to see a child graduate from high school. The bargaining can also take place with other people: "Promise you will do this, and I will do that." By this point in the dying process, the individual clearly recognizes his or her situation but still has some things to try in the hope of modifying the outcome.

As the illness progresses, the dying person experiences increasing direct evidence that death is in prospect. Fatigue, loss of function, and other symptoms show that even bargaining is not likely to be successful any more. This is the stage known as *depression*. Although the person's physical status contributes much to this stage, there may also be feelings of guilt and unworthiness, along with the surfacing of explicit fears of dying. Pervaded by a sense of great loss, the person may become sorrowful, withdrawn, and less responsive.

The final stage involves the end of the struggle, the letting go. Although known as *acceptance*, it is not necessarily a happy or serene condition. As Kubler-Ross has written (1969, p. 100), "It is almost void of feelings. It is as if the pain had gone, the struggle is over, and there comes a time for the 'final rest before the long journey' as one patient phrased it."

The stages are not quite as inexorable or rigid as it might seem from this summary, because the person may experience "hope" at various points in time. Even amid depression, for example, there may be a flickering of hope and a lifting of spirits.

Evaluation of the Stage Theory

The Kubler-Ross stage theory is valuable in several ways:

1. It describes a variety of mental, emotional, and behavioral responses to dying that can, in fact, be seen in a number of people.
2. It conveys the realization that people may have a number of different thoughts and feelings throughout the course of a final illness.
3. It offers an alternative to the assumption that it is somehow "abnormal" to have strong emotional reactions during the dying process.
4. It focuses on the human (as distinguished from the biomedical) side of dying and can encourage the sensitive and receptive person to become a better listener, companion, and helper.

However, there are also serious flaws and limitations. Some of these problems center on the theory and its evidential status, while other problems have been created by the naive ways in which the theory all too often has been applied. Included among the problems are the following:

Lack of confirmation. The stage theory has not been confirmed as fact. Although all the phenomena (e.g., denial, bargaining) are shown by some people during the dying process (as well as in other situations), there is not a universal fixed sequence that moves from the first to the last of the described stages. For example, one of the few actual controlled studies on denial found that denial increased rather than di-minished over time (Breznitz, 1983). There is no evidence for any universal sequence of stages. The information provided by Kubler-Ross in her first book was adequate for a humanistic presentation to a general readership. However, neither in *On Death and Dying* (1969) nor elsewhere has she (or others) presented the kind of information needed for scientific evaluation. There is not even evidence that any one person moved through the five stages.

Problems. The stage theory has inadvertently led to numerous problems.

1. Neglect of factors directly related to the specific illness from which the person is suffering.
2. Neglect of the way in which the treatment process affects a person's thoughts, feelings, and actions during the dying process.
3. Neglect of preexisting personality factors and individual differences.
4. Neglect of ethnic and religious factors that can have a strong bearing on a person's response to crisis.
5. Neglect of socioenvironmental factors (e.g., the patient may not really be in stage 2, anger, but, rather, have a good reason to be angry with poor communication and inadequate treatment).
6. Abuse of the stage theory by attempting to force dying people to move from one stage to the next, treating the theory as though prescriptive rather than descriptive.
7. Use of the stage theory by caregivers as a shield against examining their own assumptions and feelings, as well as to protect themselves from intimate encounters with the terminally ill individuals with whom they come into contact.

Premature, uncritical acceptance of the stage theory had a stultifying effect on research and fresh observation; too many assumed that "the five stages" were all anybody needed to know.

Kubler-Ross has made an enduring contribution by calling attention to the human needs of terminally ill people and by inspiring many to accept the challenge of caregiving. The stage theory still has some value as a general orientation but does not provide an adequate account of the dying process, certainly not the simple formula that some people would like to have when they interact with a terminally ill person.

See also Awareness of Dying; Dying.

—ROBERT KASTENBAUM

References

Breznitz, S. (Ed.) (1983). *The denial of stress.* New York: International Universities Press.

Kastenbaum, R. (1986). *Death, society, and human experience.* 3rd ed. Columbus, OH: Charles E. Merrill, pp. 110–13.

Kubler-Ross, E. (1969). *On death and dying.* New York: Macmillan.

STILLBIRTH

Approximately one in every one hundred babies in the United States is stillborn, according to the National Center for Health Statistics (1985). By medical definition, a baby is stillborn if he or she dies after the twentieth week of gestation. The logic of this definition is that babies are able to survive outside the mother's body after twenty weeks. The death of a baby before twenty weeks is termed a miscarriage or abortion.

Difficulty in Determining Cause

Autopsies are often performed to determine the cause or causes of stillbirth. However, Kirk (1984) points out that, "It is . . . important not to attach too much hope to the autopsy as a means of explaining everything." The cause of a particular stillbirth often remains in doubt, in spite of recent advances in genetics and medical sciences' ability to classify fetal abnormality. Kirk cites a recent study of 243 stillbirths in Finland in which medical investigators could not find a cause for fully 43 percent of the deaths.

Anoxia (the lack of oxygen) is one of the most common causes of stillbirth (Borg & Lasker, 1981). A baby depends upon a continuous supply of oxygen and food from the mother through the placenta and umbilical cord. If these do not function properly, complications can occur. Physi-

cians believe that sometimes a properly functioning umbilical cord can be compressed before or during delivery. Compression may occur if the cord enters the birth canal before the child does. The cord also may wrap around the infant's neck, cutting off oxygen.

Several problems with the placenta can result in stillbirth. The placenta sometimes separates prematurely from the uterus, or it may be implanted too low in the uterus and tear off late in pregnancy. Babies more than two weeks past due may not receive adequate nourishment from the placenta.

Various maternal conditions may contribute to the baby's death. Toxemia, high blood pressure, and diabetes all affect the flow of blood to the infant. Furthermore, if the mother's water breaks too early, the baby loses its protection from infections. The baby may have serious problems or abnormalities that lead to death. To add to all of these possible complications, labor itself is a punishing experience for mother and child (not to mention the father). The stress of labor and delivery apparently can sometimes kill an otherwise healthy baby.

Stillbirth and Family Crisis

Even if an obstetrician can list the cause of death as placental failure or preterm delivery, this explanation may leave a great deal of uncertainty in parents' minds. "Why did my baby die?" is a question science strives to answer. But for many parents it is, first and foremost, a theological question. Other related theological questions are: "Why did this happen to me and to my baby?" "What kind of world am I living in?" "What kind of God would kill babies?" There are, of course, no definitive answers to these theological questions although they have been examined repeatedly (e.g., DeFrain et al., 1978, 1982, 1986; Klass, 1986–87; Rando, 1986).

The stillbirth of a baby precipitates a major crisis in the lives of virtually all families. A recent interview and questionnaire study was conducted of 350 stillbirth parents (80% mothers; 20% fathers) in every region of the United States. The researchers (DeFrain et al., 1986) came to the following conclusions:

1. Shock, blame, guilt, and emotional hardship are so common among parents after a stillbirth as to be called almost normal behavior in a crisis of this magnitude. The emotions do not seem to follow any particular pattern. Rather, parents flow in and out of emotionally difficult times, depending upon their general state of physical health and the specific situation. For example, many years after a stillbirth a parent could easily lose control on the anniversary of the baby's birth and death, or an article in a magazine or a billboard with a baby's photograph can bring up old memories so readily that the parent will react as if the death happened "just yesterday."

2. Seeing the stillborn baby is important to most parents. Hospitals who give parents the opportunity to see, touch, and hold the baby are reacting in a sensitive and responsible manner. Also useful are birth certificates, photographs, and footprinting for these babies. In the words of one father, "It's not much, but it's all we have of her."

3. Autopsies were helpful for about half of the parents in the study who had them performed. The other half felt the autopsy was not particularly helpful, because the results seemed to be inconclusive.

4. Funerals or other memorial services are generally helpful for parents. The public event allows friends to show support for the bereaved family and helps make the death "real" for all concerned. Down through the centuries, stillbirth has been essentially an invisible death, few people having seen the baby. It is especially difficult for relatives and family friends to remember the baby actually lived, and for everybody concerned to come to grips with an essentially invisible death.

5. Irrational thoughts and feelings of momentary "craziness" are common among stillbirth parents:
   a. Many (65%) of the mothers and of the fathers (51%) in the study reported "irrational thoughts" after the death. For example, a parent might believe the baby was stolen by the doctor and sold on the black market. Parents have reported trying to dig up the baby's grave to rescue the infant who they imagined to be still alive in the coffin. Blaming others is extremely common among parents, many of whom regret what they have later come to realize was irrational bitterness toward medical personnel who they first thought contributed to the baby's death. (This is not to say, of course, that professionals never make mistakes.)
   b. Some mothers (24%) and fathers (18%) reported that they moved from their home or community in an effort to escape the pain of the baby's death; many cannot bear to go in the infant's room or, because of guilt and sorrow, do not wish to see relatives, neighbors, and friends.
   c. Some mothers (9%) and fathers (7%) reported having seriously considered divorce as a result of the stillbirth. Actual divorce was reported by a smaller number of parents (mothers, 1.5%; fathers, 3%).
   d. Alcohol or other drug use began or increased among family members as a direct result of the stillbirth, according to 13% of the mothers and 7% of the fathers.
   e. Suicide was "seriously considered" by some mothers (28%) and fathers (17%) as a direct result of the stillbirth.

6. The parents reported an almost unlimited number of practical ways that people can offer support to bereaved stillbirth families. These included simply being there and listening; sending cards and letters; calling on the telephone; bringing food; doing housework; caring for the surviving children; sharing one's own grief for the baby's death, and sharing one's own experiences of death and loss (in a noncompetitive way, of course); remembering the baby and the baby's name just as one would remember the family's living children (for the baby, deceased or not, is part of that family forever); letting the parents grieve, no matter how many months and years

have passed; not running away from families when they are gripped by crisis; and touching the bereaved with "one's eyes, one's arms, and one's heart."

7. The husbands in the study responded, on the surface, somewhat differently to the death of the baby. The men in general tended to be a bit more stoic than the women, but this sex difference can be easily overemphasized. In some families the mother was the "strong and silent one," and the father "the emotional one." Beneath the surface, deep down, mothers and fathers in the study were very similar: both sexes were terribly stricken by grief.

8. Husbands reported that they took about three years on average to regain the level of personal happiness they felt before the baby's death. This figure is only an average. There was a great deal of variation among parents. And it must be pointed out that if the average "recovery" time for fathers is three years, then half will recover before three years have elapsed, and half will require more than three years. Wives, similarly, also took about three years to "recover," though in reality parents never truly recover; life is never again quite the same. By way of comparison, the researchers had found in earlier studies that "recovery" after the death of a child due to Sudden Infant Death Syndrome (SIDS) also takes about three years for fathers and three years for mothers (DeFrain et al., 1982). A study of miscarriage is currently underway.

9. The individual, the marriage, and the family will never be the same after a stillbirth has occurred. A very small percentage of parents eventually commit suicide. Another small percentage sink into bitterness and despair over a period of many years. The researchers estimate that for many stillbirth parents the death will be seen in the long run as an irreparable and devastating event but one that did have some major, beneficial consequences. These people will conclude that life is a precious gift, that we must cherish our lives and the lives of our loved ones on a moment-by-moment basis, for life hangs on an extremely slender thread. Also, many parents report after a stillbirth that their belief in God, goodness in the world, or human kindness has expanded. This insight often is felt to be a result of the stillbirth experience. Finally, many parents report that their sense of self-esteem has increased as a result of the death and the crisis it precipitated. "I found out I am a survivor," is how one parent described it. "I have been to hell and back."

10. Support groups are important sources of comfort and understanding for many parents who have experienced a stillbirth, although the researchers found that only 21% who were aware of a support group in their community actually attended. The researchers encourage SIDS groups and other neonatal grief support organizations to welcome stillbirth parents into their groups, because stillbirth is clearly as devastating to families as any other type of infant death. Stillbirth is much more common than SIDS and other neonatal death, and support groups would increase dramatically in political and social influence by making every effort to open their arms to a wide variety of bereaved parents. The researchers predicted that their current study of miscarriage will show clearly that this, also, is a major crisis for many families, and that these people should also be welcomed into the support organizations.

Some people believe that infant death is more devastating than stillbirth, and that stillbirth is more devastating to families than miscarriage. This belief has no basis in fact, and causes many parents of stillborn children a good deal of unnecessary heartache and anger.

See also Grief: Death of a Child; Sudden Infant Death Syndrome (SIDS).

—JOHN DeFRAIN, LEONA MARTENS, JAN STORK, & WARREN STORK

References

Borg, S. & Lasker, J. (1981). *When pregnancy fails: Families coping with miscarriage, stillbirth, and infant death.* Boston: Beacon Press.

DeFrain, J. & Ernst, L. (1978). "Psychological effects of Sudden Infant Death Syndrome on surviving family members." *Journal of Family Practice, 6:* 985–89.

DeFrain, J., Martens, L., Stork, J., & Stork, W. (1986). *Stillborn: The invisible death.* Lexington, MA: Lexington Books.

DeFrain, J., Taylor, J., & Ernst, L. (1982). *Coping with sudden infant death.* Lexington, MA: Lexington Books.

Kirk, E.P. (1984). "Psychological effects and management of perinatal loss." *American Journal of Obstetrics and Gynecology, 149.*

Klass, D. (1986–1987). "Marriage and divorce among bereaved parents in a self-help group." *Omega, Journal of Death and Dying, 17:* 237–49.

National Center for Health Statistics (1985). Infant mortality tables. In *Statistical abstract of the United States.* 105th ed. Washington, DC: U.S. Department of Health and Human Services.

Rando, T. (1986). *Parental loss of a child.* Champaign, IL: Research Press.

STYX

It is across this body of water (usually described as a river, but sometimes as a lake) that the souls of the deceased crossed to the lower world in Greek mythology. Dark and deep beyond fathoming, this body of water entwines itself seven (or nine) times around Hades, serving as the main boundary between the living and the dead. Old Charon with his long pole and small boat stands ready to transport the dead across the Styx if they have been properly buried and have remembered to bring along his fee. The Styx was important for other reasons as well; the gods themselves were forced to tell the truth when they swore by the Styx, and one might also be annointed in and protected by these waters under rare circumstances. Despite these positive values, the Styx remained a foreboding image, as indicated by its derivation from the Greek verb signifying "to have".

See also Charon; Hades.

—ROBERT KASTENBAUM

References

Dwight, M.A. (1864). *Grecian and Roman mythology.* New York: Barnes & Burr.

Moncrief, A.R.H. (1934). *Classic myth and legend.* New York: William H. Wise.

Morford, M.P.O. & Lenardon, R.J. (1977). *Classical mythology.* New York: David McKay.

SUDDEN INFANT DEATH SYNDROME (SIDS)

One minute there is life, the next minute death. Suddenly and unexpectedly, a baby is dead and a family is forced into the painful realization of the fragility of a human life. Sudden Infant Death Syndrome (SIDS) was recognized and defined in 1970 as "The sudden death of any infant or young child, which is unexpected by history, and in which a thorough postmortem fails to demonstrate an adequate cause of death" (Bergman & Beckwith, 1970, p. 18). This continues to be the working definition for a medical puzzle that accounts for approximately two deaths per thousand live births each year in the United States. SIDS remains the leading cause of death for infants between one month and one year of age (Merritt & Valdes-Dapena, 1984).

Sudden infant deaths have been attributed variously to smothering, infection, immunologic incompetence, allergy, nutritional deficiencies, genetic predisposition, endocrine abnormalities, developmental disorders, homeostatic decompensation, metabolic abnormalities, toxins, and environmental exposure. Research continues to examine the many possible causes that have been identified in the hope of contributing to prevention. In recent years much research has focused on apnea (periods of time during which breathing does not occur) and its possible connection to SIDS. A consensus development conference sponsored by the National Institutes of Health in 1986 concluded that the home monitoring techniques to detect apnea had not proven effective. SIDS rates did not decline perceptibly in several communities in which home monitoring had been maintained for a decade or more (National Institutes of Health, 1987). It has also been found that pneumocardiograms are not predictive of SIDS, and that there is little relationship between pertussis immunization and SIDS (Frenkel, 1986). A recent study (Gilbert & Moss, 1987) offers more positive findings that abnormal levels of fetal hemoglobin may serve as a diagnostic marker for SIDS risk, but more research is necessary to confirm these results.

Despite increased knowledge and surveillance, the SIDS rate has remained relatively constant since the early 1970s. During this same period of time, however, there has been a significant decrease in all other causes of infant mortality in the United States (Southall et al., 1986). The hoped-for research and prevention breakthrough has yet to be made.

Family Grief

SIDS leaves families with little comfort except the reassurance that no one could have predicted the death. The unfulfilled potential the infant represented is a severe intensifier of the grief experienced by the parents. Infants have a functional role in the family, almost from conception. The birth of a child demands response and adaptation from the family--and sudden death completely disorganizes this adaptational process. Research confirms that unanticipated death results in more complicated bereavement reactions (Parkes & Weiss, 1983). Several other factors combine to exacerbate the grief response following a SIDS death.

The family faces not only their own grief about the finality of death, but sometimes public suspicions that child abuse or neglect was involved. Furthermore, all too frequently a SIDS death is not socially validated in the same way as other deaths. Others often fail to recognize that the family's attachment to the child who died was strong and deep, despite the brevity of the child's life. Parents may be thoughtlessly told that they are lucky they didn't have the baby long enough to become too attached, or that they are young and can have other children. Such responses invalidate the loss and inhibit the mourning that must occur. The family must make the difficult adjustment over time that their dreams, hopes, and expectations for that child will never be fulfilled.

Basically, all SIDS families should be regarded as mourners of a sudden, unanticipated death, and treated with strategies appropriate to the resolution of this type of grief. They need confirmation of the death through funeral and mourning rituals, and also repeated opportunities to talk about the loss. Social support is indispensable to validate the child's brief existence and to comfort the family.

Therapeutic intervention with SIDS families is recommended and has been shown to have a beneficial effect. Three specific goals for intervention are: (1) to reduce parental guilt by countering inaccurate and self-blaming explanations; (2) to encourage expression and acceptance of the emotions of grief; and (3) to support parents in coping with such problems as false accusations, health and economic difficulties, and plans for the future.

See also Anticipatory Grief; Compassionate Friends; Grief; Grief: Death of a Child.

—JACQUE TAYLOR

References

Bergman, A.B. & Beckwith, J.B. (Eds.) (1970). *Proceedings of the Second International Conference on Causes of Sudden Infant Death.* Seattle: University of Washington.

Frenkel, L. (1986). "Pertussis immunization and crib death." *Pediatric Annual, 15*: 452–54.

Giullian, G.G., Gilbert, E.F., and Moss, R.L. (1987). Elevated Fetal hemoglobin levels in Sudden Infant Death Syndrome. *New England Journal of Medicine, 18*: 316–21.

Merritt, T.A. & Valdes-Dapena, M. (1984). "SIDS research update." *Pediatric Annual, 13*, no. 3.

National Institutes of Health (1987). *Infantile apnea and home monitoring.* NIH publication no. 87–2905, Bethesda, MD.

Parkes, C.M. & Weiss, R.S. (1983). *Recovery from bereavement.* New York: Basic Books.

Southall, D.P., Richards, J.M., Stebbens, V., Wilson, A.J., Taylor, V., & Alexander, J.R. (1986). "Cardiorespiratory function in 16 full term infants with sudden infant death syndrome." *Pediatrics, 78*: 787–96.

SUICIDE

Suicide, the act of killing oneself, has always been a part of human behavior, as evidenced by many myths, fairy tales, sagas, and historical documents. However, the use of the word *suicide* to identify this act has been in existence for a comparatively short time. According to the *Oxford English Dictionary*, the word *suicide* first appeared in the English language in 1651. It was derived from the Latin *suicidium*, a combination of the pronoun for "self" and the verb to kill. Other Latin expressions had been used, previously, such as, *sibi mortem consciscere* ("to cause one's own death"), *vim sibi inferre* ("to inflict violence on oneself"), and *sua manu cadere* ("to fall by one's own hand").

For many years suicide was thought to be a form of behavior that did not appear until civilization and its relatively structured societies had developed. However, investigators have also found suicide in numerous tribal societies scattered throughout the world. This does not necessarily mean that suicide is universal, however. In a few isolated parts of the world there are people among whom suicide appears to have been unknown, such as the Andaman Islanders, the Yahgans of Tierra del Fuego, and some Aborigine tribes.

In general, suicides are either institutional, personal, or both. Institutional or social suicide is self-inflicted death that society expects from the individual in return for the privilege of membership. Personal suicide is the result of cultural and individual motives, such as escape from disgrace, expiation of guilt, cowardice, or loss of a loved one.

Attitudes toward suicide varied considerably among some of the early great cultures and religions. Suicide in ancient Egypt was viewed as a neutral event because death was merely the passage from one form of existence to another. It was simply a means of avoiding unnecessary pain, dishonor, injustice, or abandonment, or an expression of a general mistrust of the world. The dead were considered to have the same physical and emotional needs as the living.

Suicide was relatively infrequent among ancient Hebrews as a result of their strong feeling that the world was good because God had made it so especially for them, his chosen people. There was a clear prohibition against suicide. It was considered an affront to end life before death was normally supposed to occur. However, exceptions were acknowledged, such as apostasy, expiation of serious sin, and the ignominy of capture and disgrace in war. Suicide is not condemned in the Old Testament, and is factually reported in five major instances: Samson pulled the pillars of a Philistine temple away and brought it crashing down on his captors and himself (Judges 16: 28–31); Abimelech ordered his own soldier to kill him after he had received a mortal wound from a stone thrown by a woman (Judges 9: 54); Ahitophel hanged himself after failure of his conspiracy to overthrow King David (II Samuel 17: 23); and Saul and his armor bearer killed themselves after the defeat of the Israeli army in a battle with the Philistines on Mount Gilboa (I Samuel 31:4; II Samuel 1:6; I Chronicles 10:4). Likewise, in the New Testament, the self-hangings of Judas Iscariot (Matthew 17:5) and of his jailer (Acts 16:27) are reported factually and without condemnation.

The most spectacular mass suicide (although not necessarily the largest in terms of sheer numbers) occurred among the Jewish Zealots at Masada in AD 74. Almost the entire group—960 people—killed themselves rather than surrender to the Romans who had laid siege for over three years. This number was almost matched by the mass suicide of 911 persons in Jonestown, Guyana, on November 18, 1978, at the instigation of their leader, Jim Jones. However, reports also exist of the suicides of thousands of Indians enslaved by Spaniards in Central America, and of suicide epidemics involving large numbers in Russia and France that probably exceeded the two mass suicide events noted above.

Suicide among the Greeks and Romans varied widely with respect to tolerance and legal restrictions. Both Aristotle and Plato condemned suicide, although the latter made some exceptions. The Epicureans and Stoics considered suicide as an appropriate escape from the sufferings of physical illness and emotional frustration. A readily accepted motivation for suicide was maintaining one's honor (such as to avoid breaking an oath or promise), to protect one's virtue, to avoid capture and humiliation, or when faced with unrequited love or the death of a loved one.

Probably the best-known suicide death of any among the Greeks is that of Socrates, who chose to die rather than to recant his teachings. He was provided with hemlock, which had just been introduced as the official drug of execution. Despite choosing suicide, Socrates is on record as disapproving it: "man is situated in this life as if he were on a post or station which he must not quit without leave." Seneca approved of suicide as a way of escaping intolerable suffering, while Epicetetus went even further and urged suicide so long as there was "a good reason" for so ending one's life.

The Romans maintained a generally permissive attitude toward suicide, although the government officially opposed it. Suicide was primarily for economic reasons, as when soldiers or slaves killed themselves and were considered to be deserters, thereby depriving their masters of property.

In the early Christian era, suicide was not only tolerated but approved by the church. As a result, the church fostered martyrdom, leading to accounts of sects such as the Donatists and the Circumcelliones jumping off cliffs in great numbers in order to hasten to a life that promised much greater rewards than the one being lived on earth. Faced with the loss of so many of its members, the church came out strongly against suicide in the fourth century when St. Augustine set forth a new position in his book, *The City of God.* St. Augustine stated that suicide violated the sixth commandment, "Thou shalt not kill," that it precluded the possibility of penance, and that it presumed a right which belonged only to the church and state.

A number of councils in the ensuing centuries extended the church's condemnation and increased the penalties against suicide by denying both funeral rights and the saying of mass for the deceased. Those who died by their own hands were not allowed burial in church cemeteries. Eventually, the custom arose of desecrating the bodies of suicides and burying the mutilated remains at a crossroads. This custom continued for many hundreds of years, not ending until 1823.

Thomas Aquinas summarized the position of the church in the thirteenth century in *Summa Theologica,* arguing that suicide was contrary to man's natural inclinations, that it was a presumption of a right that man does not have, and that it was up to God to decide when a person should die.

In oriental and Far Eastern religions there are a variety of attitudes toward suicide. In Japan, *sepuki* became the highly formalized ritual through which suicide was performed by warriors and noblemen to escape from disgrace and expiate mistake or crime. This practice has become more popularly known as *hara kiri,* the result of reversing the two characters that originally meant "cutting of the stomach." Hinduism approved of suicide only in special cases, especially in its requirement for *sati,* a ritual sacrifice of the widow by self-immolation after the death of her husband. Brahmanism fostered suicide through its teachings of the denial of the flesh and its efforts to divorce the body from the soul. Mohammedism condemned suicide severely, declaring that it was a distortion of the divine will and an attempt to escape a fate determined by Allah.

During the Renaissance and the Reformation, radical changes began to appear in the attitudes of the general public toward suicide. Lutheranism shifted religion from its previous course of absolutism and obedience toward a path of personal inquiry and responsibility. The Industrial Revolution transformed the way of life. Poverty became stigmatized; goodness was made equivalent to prosperity, and economic failure equivalent to sinfulness. Life became more transient and death was seen as an escape. The rise of Calvinism at this time with its exaltation of God also made the individual person appear less important.

The writings of prominent philosophers of this period started to reflect the changes in attitudes toward suicide. Absolute condemnation gradually disappeared. Suicide was more often acccepted under specific conditions, such as terminal illness and extraordinary pain. Opposition to the severe penalties began to appear. John Donne's *Biathanatos* (1644) defended suicide, asserting that the mercy of God was great enough to forgive it. Hume's *Essay on Suicide* (1783) made suicide more tolerable by lowering its rank as a sin, if indeed it was one. Merian (1763) proposed suicide as an emotional illness, not as a crime. This laid the groundwork for the Catholic Church's eventual adoption of the phrase, "suicide while of unsound mind," and making it possible to circumvent many of the now unpopular penalties against suicide, such as denial of certain funeral and cemetery privileges when the deceased had died of suicide.

In the eighteenth and nineteenth centuries the spread of capitalism produced an increasing degree of individualism and urbanization. The increased isolation and detachment was accompanied by a rise in suicide. Furthermore, as suicide became more identified with insanity, it became disgraceful, especially among middle class urban families.

Statistical and large-scale sociological studies began to appear in the late nineteenth century. The prominent Italian sociologist Morselli (1881) concluded that suicide was the result of a struggle for life produced especially by the development of civilization and by the free discussion and individual thought favored by Protestantism. Masaryk (1881) in Czechoslovakia attributed suicide to the same factors but added that these produced a lessening of moral principles and a loss of the meaning of life that led to increased suicide. This last thought was restated by William James in an 1897 essay, "Is Life Worth Living?"; James believed it was essentially a loss of faith that led to suicide.

The most prominent names at the end of the nineteenth and the early twentieth centuries were Emile Durkheim in France and Sigmund Freud in Austria. Durkheim's epic study, *Le Suicide* (1897) concluded that suicide resulted from a social organization that reflected the extremes of two basic characteristics: regulation and integration. Low regulation produced anomic suicides and high regulation produced fatalistic suicides. Poor or little

social integration was characterized by egoistic suicides, while overintegration led to altruistic suicide.

Freud's studies of personality and the unconscious led to an understanding of the dynamics contributing to suicide. His first formulations (1917) were developed from his studies of melancholia and depression; he saw suicide as retroflex rage acted out against the self after the loss of an incorporated love object. Freud later (1922) proposed that suicide derives more directly from the death instinct (*Thanatos*) which exists alongside the life instinct (*Eros*). These two instincts were said to be in constant conflict with each other. Under extremely stressful conditions, the death instinct could become dominant. This would markedly increase the potential for self-destructive behavior.

Karl Menninger (1938) further developed the concept of the role of the death instinct in suicide by hypothesizing three elements: the wish to kill, the wish to be killed, and the wish to die. Menninger was the first to relate suicide to the more indirect forms of self-destruction that emerged in the form of life-threatening, life-negating, and life-injurious behaviors, a concept extended by Farberow (1981) through his research into various forms of indirect self-destructive behaviors. Stengel (1971) strongly cautioned that attempted suicide and completed suicide could not directly be compared to each other because of the vast differences in their overlapping populations and the often marked differences in their purposes and objectives.

In the early years of the twentieth century, efforts to determine the relationships between suicide and physiological or neurological conditions were conducted by physicians, primarily through medical autopsies. In general, these were unsuccessful. Scientific efforts to understand and prevent suicide concentrated primarily on sociological investigations of demographic and epidemiologic relationships, and psychological investigations of individual and interpersonal characteristics.

The modern era in the development of suicide prevention studies and intervention activities developed in the decade after World War II with the establishment of a suicide prevention center in Vienna by Caritas, an organization supported by the Catholic Church. Erwin Ringel directed the Vienna center, which was followed by Reverend Chad Varah's establishment of the Samaritans in London. The establishment of the Los Angeles Suicide Prevention Center in 1958 by Norman L. Farberow and Edwin S. Shneidman ushered in the era of suicide prevention in the United States. Further impetus to suicide prevention worldwide was provided by the establishment of the International Association of Suicide Prevention (1960) by Ringel, and the founding of the American Association of Suicidology (1967) by Shneidman. Since then, national associations have also been established in France and West Germany, and have either recently been established or are in their early stages in Canada, Austria, Yugoslavia, the Netherlands, Belgium, and Japan.

By 1987 there were 169 suicide prevention centers and crisis intervention centers (which include suicide prevention) operative in the United States. Of these, thirty-seven had been certified by the American Association of Suicidology, indicating that they have met its rigorous requirements and standards. In addition, suicide intervention services have been incorporated into community mental health services and into many of the independent psychiatric and psychological service centers that function autonomously in the United States. A number of suicide prevention and crisis intervention centers function similarly in Canada. The Suicide Information and Education Center in Calgary, Alberta, under the leadership of Bryan Tanney, has become the primary source of information and bibliography throughout North America. Scattered suicide prevention centers can also be found in Tokyo, Mexico City, São Paulo, Rio de Janeiro, Caracas, and Buenos Aires.

In Europe most of the suicide prevention centers have been developed by two organizations. The Samaritans, under the leadership of the Reverend Chad Varah, are active in England, some parts of Europe, and scattered cities throughout the world, such as Boston, Singapore, and Hong Kong. The International Federation of Telephone Emergency Services has established church-sponsored suicide prevention services throughout much of central Europe and Scandinavia.

Most suicide prevention centers function primarily as diagnostic and emergency telephone counseling services. The primary objective is to help the person through the immediate suicidal emergency and, when necessary, to refer the caller to resources in the community such as social services, long-term psychological care, hospitalization, or all three. A few centers have added ongoing and face-to-face services for their callers with the provision of individual and group therapy, as well as ancillary services such as rape counseling, runaway centers, adolescent and teen lines, elderly counseling services, drug and alcohol abuse counseling, groups for survivors of suicide, and other similar services.

At present, the greatest activity in suicide prevention is found in efforts to discover biological markers related to depression and suicide, providing help for significant others who are bereft by the suicide of a loved one, meeting the challenge of an elevated suicide rate among adolescents and youth, and bracing for the inevitable rise in suicides as the number of AIDS cases inexorably increases.

See also American Association of Suicidology; Autopsy, Psychological; *Biathanatos*; Death Instinct; Jonestown; Suicide: Indirect; *Suicide and Life-Threatening Behavior* (Journal).

—NORMAN L. FARBEROW

References

Aquinas, T. (1947, Reprint of 1st ed.). *Summa theologiae*. New York: Benziger Brothers.

Donne, J. (1644/Reprint 1977). *Biathanatos*. New York: Arno Press.

Durkheim, E. (1891/Reprint 1951). *Le suicide*. Paris: Librairie Felix Alcon; *Suicide*. Translated by G. Simpson. New York: Free Press.

Farberow, N.L. (Ed.) (1981). *The many faces of suicide*. New York: McGraw-Hill.

Freud, S. (1917/Reprint 1950). *Mourning and melancholia*. In S. Freud, *Collected papers*. Vol. 4. London: Hogarth Press.

Freud, S. (1922/Reprint 1950). *Beyond the pleasure principle*. London: Hogarth Press.

Hume, D. (1783/Reprint 1929). *An essay on suicide*. Yellow Springs, OH: Kahoc.

James, W. (1897/Reprint 1927). "Is life worth living?" In *The will to believe*. New York: Longman, Green.

Masaryk, T.G. (1881/Reprint 1970). *Suicide and the meaning of civilization.* Chicago: University of Chicago Press.

Menninger, K.A. (1938). *Man against himself.* New York: Harcourt, Brace

Merian (1763). "Sur la crainte de la mort, sur la mepris de la mort, sur le suicide, memoire." In *Histoire de l'Academie Royale des Sciences et Belles-Lettres de Berlin,* Vol. 19, pp. 385, 392, 403.

Morselli, H. (1881). *Suicide, an essay on comparative moral statistics.* New York: D. Appleton.

Stengel, E. (1971). *Suicide and attempted suicide.* Middlesex: Penguin Books.

SUICIDE: AGED ADULTS

Suicide is a significant problem among the old. The people most at risk for suicide are those 65 and older. Compared with younger adults, the old openly communicate their suicidal intent less frequently, use more violent and lethal means, and less often attempt suicide as a means of gaining attention (the so-called cry for help). All of these factors increase the risk of suicidal death among the old. The suicide rate of the old (65+) is approximately 50 percent higher than that of the young. The U.S. statistics for 1983 are typical. For the population in general (all ages), the suicide rate was 12.3 per 100,000. Those aged 65 and over, however, had a completed suicide rate of 20.3 (National Center for Health Statistics, 1988), as compared with 11.9 for those between the ages of 15 and 24. Elderly white men continued to have the highest suicide rate of all, 43.2. Thus, the highest rates of suicide by age are found not among the young, as many in our society believe, but among the elderly. This fact has been true ever since official suicide data have been recorded by the U.S. government; similar statistics can be found in most other nations as well (Shulman, 1978).

A recent national study of suicide in long-term care facilities has found that the rate of overt suicide among the institutionalized elderly is 15.8 per 100,000, as compared with the rate of 19.2 for elderly people who live in the community (Osgood & Brant, 1987). However, a different picture emerged when deaths from overt suicide were combined with intentional life-threatening behaviors, sometimes known also as forms of indirect suicide. Refusing to eat or drink, refusing medications, and eating foreign, inedible objects were among the life-threatening behaviors included. The combination of both direct and indirect self-destructive behaviors produced a calculated rate of 94.9 per 100,000—more than four times higher than the currently reported rate of suicide for the community elderly.

The rate of suicide has fluctuated over the past several decades. Between 1950 and 1980 the national suicide rate for older people declined 26 percent. Possible reasons suggested for the decline include improved government services and programs for the elderly, improved economic status and a higher standard of living attributed to Social Security and increased pension plans, improvements in antidepressant medications, and better health care. However, over the past few years there has been a steady rise in suicide rate for those 65 and over (U.S. Bureau of the Census, 1988). The rate increased from 17.1 in 1981 to 18.3 in 1982 and 20.3 in 1985. Explanations for the recent and continuing rise are primarily economic, emphasizing the negative impact of recent cuts in federal programs such as Medicare and Medicaid, as well as food stamps, along with reductions in medical services on the state level. This reduction of assistance has led many elderly men and women to fear for their futures and, in some cases, has encouraged thoughts of suicide. Many researchers warn that there is a potential new wave of suicides coming as the "babyboomers" born between 1946 and 1966 move into the twenty-first century, bringing with them all the unique economic, social, and psychological problems of their generation.

High-Risk Groups

Some older groups are at high risk. White men and the very old (75+) are the groups at highest risk. The National Center for Health Statistics (1985) reports that in 1981 there were 28.4 reported suicides for every 100,000 men from 65 to 74 years of age. The rate escalated to 41.4 among men

75–84. For men over 85, the figure rose to 50.1. Male rates of suicide increase throughout the adult years until reaching a peak in old age. By contrast, female rates increase until middle age (mid-40s to mid-50s) and decline thereafter. Female suicide rates are generally lower than those for males at all ages, and this is particularly so in old age. Investigations of both completed and attempted suicide have shown that relatively more men, as a group, use violent and lethal methods such as firearms, hanging, and jumping. Women more often prefer less violent techniques such as poisoning and suffocation (McIntosh & Santos, 1985–86).

There are also clear differences in the pattern of suicide rates between whites and nonwhites in the United States. Whites show a continuing increase in suicide rates with age. Nonwhites are most vulnerable to suicide in young adulthood (generally in the 20s or early 30s), and decline thereafter. Nonwhite elderly suicide rates are relatively low, and have been so for many years. Specific racial/ethnic group differences can also be found (McIntosh, 1985).

The unmarried elderly are more likely than the married to commit suicide. Elderly widowers are the most vulnerable. The elderly male widower is often isolated emotionally and socially, with fewer relatives and kin living nearby. Interacting less with family and friends, the elderly widower is also less involved in formal organizations and the community. Elderly people who live in low-income transient urban areas in central cities have a higher suicide risk than those residing in rural areas. In general, the elderly people are also at greater risk if they live alone.

Suicide rates calculated for the institutionalized elderly (Osgood & Brant, 1987) revealed higher rates for men than for women, and for whites as compared with nonwhites. Osgood et al. (1988–1989) found that in the institutionalized elderly population, men are more likely to engage in overt suicidal behavior such as wrist slashing and hanging. The "old-old" (75+) are more likely than the "young-old" (60–74) or those under 60 to engage in indirect life-threatening behaviors, and are the most likely to die as a result of their suicidal actions.

Precipitating Factors and Warning Signs

As Barter (1969) has noted: "A precipitating cause may be less obvious and the suicide may appear to be a reaction to a total life situation more than to any single event." Many older persons lose vital social roles in the world of work, family, politics, and community, with concomitant loss of income, power, status, and prestige. In addition to social losses, the elderly may suffer impaired vision, hearing, and mobility, financial restrictions, memory deficit, and many other types of loss. These increase stress at a time in life when the individual may be least able to resist and cope. Feelings of loneliness, depression, and despair result. Some older persons experience a deep sense of emptiness and meaninglessness, losing the motivation for both work and play. Those who have suffered severe loss and are socially and emotionally isolated often feel rejected and dejected, unwanted, unneeded, and unloved. Their self-esteem suffers, and they view themselves as inadequate and inferior.

Depression, the most common functional psychiatric disorder of late life, underlies two-thirds of the suicides among elderly adults. Two major factors have been recognized as contributing to depression and suicide among the aged: helplessness and hopelessness. Helplessness is a psychological state in which individuals feel themselves unable to control significant life events. The aged are susceptible to a sense of helplessness because they have often experienced severe loss of control and of life roles. Suicide among the aged is often a desperate response to hopeless and intolerable life situations. Suicide notes written by the elderly reveal a sense of hopelessness and psychological exhaustion. Other factors that increase vulnerability to suicide, many of them secondary to depression, include alcoholism and bereavement.

In the elderly, depression often manifests itself in physical complaints, including fatigue, headaches, muscle pain, increased heart rate, constipation, eating and sleeping disorders, and other bodily concerns. Depressed elderly people are anxious, preoccupied with physical symptoms, tired, withdrawn, apathetic, inert, and disinterested in their surroundings.

Unfortunately, visiting a physician does not necessarily reduce suicide potential. More than 75 percent of the elderly who commit suicide see a physician shortly before the act. The important role that physicians could play in preventing elderly suicide thus cannot be overemphasized. Physicians and others who are in a position to help the suicidal elderly should become alert to depression in their patients or clients. A suicidal person may give verbal or behavioral clues. Direct statements such as "I'm going to kill myself," or "Soon you won't have me around to worry about" should always be taken seriously. Behavioral clues to look for include purchasing a gun, stockpiling pills, making or changing a will, seeking advice on donating a body to a medical school, taking out insurance or changing beneficiaries, making funeral plans, giving away money or possessions, scheduling an appointment with the doctor for no apparent physical cause or shortly after an earlier visit, and changes in behavior such as shouting or screaming on the part of an individual who is usually quiet and reserved. Withdrawal behavior exhibited by a person who is usually outgoing and friendly can also signify a potential suicide attempt. These behavior changes do not necessarily mean that the individual has become suicidal, but all warrant close attention.

Accurate diagnosis and treatment of depression in the elderly is a key factor in suicide prevention. Pharmacological intervention with tricyclics or monamine oxidase inhibitors, and electroconvulsive therapy have all proven effective in relieving late life depression. Pet therapy, reminiscence and life review therapy, creative arts therapy (dance, drama, music, art), and other supportive therapies are also useful in alleviating depression in the elderly (Osgood, 1985). Active outreach and education of service providers, older adults, and the public also are necessary components of any large-scale effort to prevent suicide among older adults.

See also Old Age and Death; Suicide; Suicide: Black; Suicide: Youth.

—NANCY J. OSGOOD

References

Barter, J.T. (1969). "Self destructive behavior in adolescents and adults: Similarities and differences." In U.S. Department of Health, Education, and Welfare, *Suicide among American Indians: Two workshops.* PHS Publication No. 1903. Washington, DC: U.S. Government Printing Office.

McIntosh, J.L. (1985). *Suicide among minority elderly.* Presented at the annual meeting of the Gerontological Society of America, New Orleans, November.

McIntosh, J.L. & Santos, J.F. (1985–1986). "Methods of suicide by age: Sex and race differences among the young and old." *International Journal of Aging and Human Development, 22*: 123–39.

National Center for Health Statistics (1988). "Advance report of final mortality statistics, 1985." *NCHS Monthly Vital Statistics Report, 34* (6, Supplement 2).

Osgood, N.J. (1985). *Suicide in the elderly: A practitioner's guide to diagnosis and mental health intervention.* Rockville, MD: Aspen.

Osgood, N.J. (1987). "Suicide and the elderly." *Generations,* Spring: 472–51.

Osgood, N.J. & Brant, B.A. (1987). "Suicidal behavior in long-term care facilities: A preliminary report on an ongoing study." Virginia Commonwealth University, Richmond.

Osgood, N.J., Brant, B.A., & Lipman, A. (1988–1989). "Patterns of suicidal behavior in long-term care facilities: A preliminary report." *Omega, Journal of Death and Dying, 19*:69–78.

Osgood, N.J. & McIntosh, J.L. (1987). *Suicide and the elderly: An annotated bibliography and review.* Westport, CT: Greenwood.

Shulman, K. (1978). "Suicide and parasuicide in old age: A review." *Age and aging. 7*: 201–09.

U.S. Bureau of the Census. (1988). *Statistical Abstracts for the United States 1988.* 108th ed. Washington, DC: U.S. Department of Commerce.

SUICIDE: ASIAN-AMERICAN

Few attempts have been made to study suicide among Asian-Americans. However, some data do exist for those of Chinese, Japanese, and Filipino ancestry. Chinese and Japanese Americans had the highest suicide rates of any U.S. racial/ethnic grouping in the early 1950s, but by the 1970s and 1980s the rates for both groups had declined dramatically. By the 1979–81 period, Americans of Chinese and Japanese descent had suicide rates below that of the population in general. Meanwhile, the rate for Filipino-Americans had dropped to become the lowest observed for any racial/ethnic group: 3.6 per 100,000 (as compared with 12.9 for whites). Men were at higher risk for suicide than women in all three of these Asian-American groups, but this gap was smaller among Chinese-Americans than in any other U.S. ethnic/racial group for which information is available.

Age patterns for suicide among Asian-American groups are similar to those found for whites and the nation as a whole. The rate of completed suicide increases over the adult years and reaches its peak in old age. Unlike the rest of the U.S., however, Asian-Americans did not show an increase in youth suicide since the 1950s.

The decline in overall suicide rates for Asian-Americans since the 1950s is especially marked among the elderly. The previous high risk status of elderly Asian-Americans is thought to have been a consequence of the stress experienced by sojourner male populations who came to the United States to amass wealth and then to return home to their families. Little attempt was made toward acculturation, and these men often found themselves isolated in a society whose values and customs differed significantly from their own. Stress, loneliness, and depression may have contributed to their suicidal tendencies in old age. It is likely, however, that this historical explanation applies more accurately to Chinese-Americans than to other Asian-American populations. There remains the clear need to recognize specific ethnic group differences within the general Asian-American spectrum.

A distinctive aspect of Asian-American suicide is the method most frequently employed. Suicidal Asian-Americans of both sexes most commonly take their lives by hanging, while firearms are most extensively used by virtually all other U.S. ethnic/racial groups. Over time, however, the use of firearms has increased

among Asian-Americans, as it has throughout the United States in general.

See also Suicide.

—JOHN L. McINTOSH

References

McIntosh, J.L. (1980). "A study of suicide among United States racial minorities based on official statistics: The influence of age, sex, and other variables." Unpublished Ph.D. Dissertation, University of Notre Dame. *Dissertation Abstracts International*, 41: 1135B. University Microfilms No. 8020965.

McIntosh, J.L. (1985a). *Research on suicide: A bibliography.* Westport, CT: Greenwood.

McIntosh, J.L. (1985b) "Suicide among minority elderly." Presented at annual meeting of the Gerontological Society of America, New Orleans, November.

McIntosh, J.L. & Santos, J.F. (1981). "Suicide among minority elderly: A preliminary investigation." *Suicide and Life-Threatening Behavior, 11:* 151–66.

Mcintosh, J.L. & Santos, J.F. (1982). "Changing patterns in methods of suicide by race and sex." *Suicide and Life-Threatening Behavior, 12:* 221–33.

SUICIDE: ASSISTED

Assisted suicide, also sometimes referred to as "mercy killing," is "any conduct which is intended to or which tends to encourage the suicide of another" (Garbesi, 1984). Unlike euthanasia, in which the individual may not be in a position to provide informed consent, assisted suicide does imply the consent of and, in many cases, the request of the victim. Mixing a poison cocktail and leaving it by a relative's bedside, placing a lethal dose of drugs within the reach of a loved one, and shooting a friend who requests it are all examples of assisted suicide.

There is a critical difference in the legal status of suicide and assisted suicide. As the willful taking of one's own life, suicide formerly was condemned as a sin and a crime. As late as the nineteenth century, suicide victims were refused Christian burial, and severe penalties were imposed on their families. Since the 1960s, however, suicide has not been a crime in most states. Assisted suicide, on the other hand, is a crime in all states. It is explicitly prohibited by twenty-three states, and generally interpreted as an act of homicide by other states. As the law stands, a person assisting another to take his or her own life is exposed to a charge of murder, attempted murder, or manslaughter, all of which carry a maximum sentence of life in prison. The first prosecution for assisted suicide was that of Frank Roberts, who in 1920 received life imprisonment for assisting his terminally ill wife to commit suicide.

Advances in medical technology have allowed growing numbers of people to survive serious illness and have greatly increased the chance of a lingering period of severely reduced, even vegetative, existence prior to death. Although a cultural taboo against the taking of human life has existed for 4,000 years, today there are many calls for the "right to die" and "death with dignity." Assisted suicide has recently come to the forefront as a key legal, religious, and ethical issue. The 1980s have witnessed a rapidly growing number of cases of assisted suicide, the most famous of which is that of Roswell Gilbert. This 76-year-old man was convicted of murder and sentenced to 25 years in prison after shooting his wife of 51 years, who had been suffering from progressive dementia with no hope of recovery. Although most individuals who have assisted the suicide of a friend or loved one have received minimal sentences, the Gilbert case and others like it have elicited public outcries for "justice."

Advocates of "rational suicide" and the "right to die" include many who are members of the **Hemlock Society**, a California-based organization of 13,000 members which publishes a how-to manual to guide those seeking "self-deliverance." Changes are sought in existing laws. Some proponents of legalizing assisted suicide argue that "mercy killing" should be a defense to homicide. Others advocate making assisted suicide a special crime that carries a maximum sentence of two years in prison. In West Germany, the Netherlands, Switzerland, and some other nations, the law is more lenient than in the United States. Americans Against Humane Suffering, a California-based political group, is currently trying to have laws passed that would legalize assisted suicide in special cases. A Humane and Dignified Death Act, proposed in California, would permit a dying person to request the physician to end his or her life by administering a lethal injection.

In the United States, Fletcher (1967) has been an influential advocate of the view that the legal right to death control is similar to the legal right to birth control. Some libertarians argue for a constitutional right to death that corresponds to the constitutional right to life. Others point out that we "put sick dogs and cats to death," showing more humane treatment of animals in pain than of suffering people. Roman (1980) proposed the creation of an Exit House or other special place to assist those who wish to die. Arguing just as strongly against legalizing assisted suicide are religious leaders, "pro-life" groups, and others who claim that the sanctity of human life should be the guiding principle of an ethical society. Still others invoke the image of the "slippery slope" and the specter of Nazi Germany, suggesting that if we as a society legalize assisted suicide in *any* situation, then we may be taking the first step to the senseless killing of many individuals. There are also assertions that legalized killing in whatever form for whatever reason will result in the breakdown of social cohesion and social obligations and responsibilities, destroying the moral fiber of the country. Finally, many concerned people advocate more research into effective painkillers and humane care of the dying as promising far better solutions to the problems of human suffering than does assisted suicide.

See also Euthanasia; Hemlock Society; Suicide.

—NANCY J. OSGOOD

References

Battin, M.P. (1982). *Ethical issues in suicide.* Englewood Cliffs, NJ: Prentice-Hall.

Battin, M.P. & Maris, R.W. (Eds.) (1983). *Suicide and ethics.* New York: Human Sciences Press.

Fletcher, J. (1967). *Moral responsibility: Situation ethics at work.* Philadelphia: Westminster Press.

Humphry, D. (1986). *Let me die before I wake.* Los Angeles: Hemlock Society.

Humphry, D. (Ed.) (1986). *Compassionate crimes, broken taboos.* Los Angeles: Hemlock Society.

Roman, J. (1980). *Exit house: Choosing suicide as an alternative.* New York: Seaview Books.

SUICIDE: BLACK

Suicide rates for black Americans are among the lowest observed in the United States. For 1979–81 the rate for blacks was 5.7 per 100,000, as compared to 12.9 for whites. Only the rate for Filipino-Americans (3.6) was lower than that for blacks among those racial/ethnic groups for whom data were available. Young men represent the highest risk group for suicide among blacks. Although there has been a proportionate increase in their suicide rates in recent years, black women still have virtually the lowest rate recorded in the United States. The suicide rate for blacks reaches its age peak in young adulthood and declines thereafter. This pattern is true as well for Native Americans and Hispanics but not for whites, whose suicide rate continues to increase throughout the adult years. Young black men are at approximately the same level of risk as are their white counterparts. Elderly blacks, on the other hand, are at low risk of suicide, especially when compared to their white counterparts, who comprise the nation's highest risk group.

In addition to the strong supports of family and church in the black community, it is thought by some observers that the relatively low black suicide rates may be related to the scarcity of competitive employment and achievement opportunities in U.S. society. As the theory goes, attainment of status in a highly competitive and insecure field generates high stress levels and increases suicidal potential. It is predicted that as more blacks do achieve success in such fields, their suicide rates will increase. This, it should be noted, remains a theory.

Explanations for the high suicide rates among young black men have emphasized the psychological impact of discrimination and the gap between the aspirations and expectations on the one hand, and the difficulties in finding employment and other opportunities on the other. At the other end of the age spectrum, the low suicide rates for black elderly have been explained by the scaling down of aspirations after midlife that allow for coping with difficult conditions, the recognition that personal economic problems may reflect the lack of opportunity more than a lack of personal skill and worth, and the satisfactions of meaningful involvement in church activities. It is also clear that aged blacks are the resourceful survivors from a cohort or generation that has experienced many challenges to its well-being.

See also Suicide; Suicide: Youth.

—JOHN L. McINTOSH

References

Davis, R. (1979). "Black suicide in the seventies: Current trends." *Suicide and Life-Threatening Behavior, 9*: 131–40.

Howze, B. (1977). "Suicide: Special reference to black women." *Journal of Non-White Concerns in Personnel & Guidance, 5*: 65–72.

Kirk, A.R. (1966). "Destructive behaviors among members of the black community with a special focus on males: Causes and methods of intervention." *Journal of Multicultural Counseling and Development, 14*: 3–9.

McIntosh, J.L. (1985a). *Research on suicide: A bibliography.* Westport, CT: Greenwood.

McIntosh, J.L. (1985b). "Suicide among minority elderly." Presented at annual meeting of the Gerontological Society of America, New Orleans, November.

McIntosh, J.L. & Santos, J.F. (1981). "Suicide among minority elderly: A preliminary investigation." *Suicide and Life-Threatening Behavior, 11*: 151–66.

SUICIDE: HISPANIC

National data are currently unavailable for suicide among Hispanic Americans, and few investigations exist for this ethnic minority group. However, compilations of data for cities and states that contain sizeable numbers of Hispanics consistently suggest that Hispanic suicide rates are lower than for whites and the nation as a whole. A study of Hispanic suicide in 10 states (McIntosh, 1987) found that the 1979–1981 rate was 7.5 per 100,000, compared to 12.9 for whites as a whole. This rate was slightly higher than that for blacks (5.7), but lower than for Americans of Chinese (8.3) and Japanese (9.1) ancestry, as well as Native Americans (13.6). For Hispanics as well as blacks and Native Americans, suicide occurs most frequently among young adults. This is in contrast with the pattern for whites, in which the rate increases to a peak in old age. Suicide rates for Hispanics peak in young adulthood and are lower among the elderly. Hispanic men are much more likely to commit suicide than are women—a finding that is true of most other populations as well.

The limited data available suggest that there is some variation in suicide risk by specific subgroups of Hispanics (Mexican-American, Cuban, Puerto Rican) as well as by region of residence in the United States. Family cohesion and support and the strong role of Roman Catholicism have been advanced to explain the low rates of suicide observed for Hispanics in the United States. Much remains to be learned about the conditions and dynamics of suicide among Hispanic Americans, this large and diverse population whose aspirations and problems have yet to be given systematic consideration.

See also Suicide; Suicide: Youth.

—JOHN L. McINTOSH

References

Hoppe, S.K. & Martin, H.W. (1986). "Patterns of suicide among Mexican Americans and Anglos, 1960–1980." *Social Psychiatry, 21*: 83–88.

McIntosh, J.L. (1985). *Research on suicide: A bibliography.* Westport, CT: Greenwood.

McIntosh, J.L. (1987). "Hispanic suicide in ten U.S. states." Paper presented at the joint meeting of the American Association of Suicidology and the International Association for Suicide Prevention, San Francisco, May.

Smith, J.C., Mercy, J.A., & Warren, C.W. (1985). "Comparison of suicides among Anglos and Hispanics in five southwestern states." *Suicide and Life-Threatening Behavior, 15*: 14–26.

SUICIDE: INDIRECT

Direct and overt suicide attempts are not the only means of increasing the probability of a premature death. Many human behaviors that are seldom considered as suicidal nevertheless do result in a foreshortened life. These indirect means of increasing the possibility of one's own early death have been considered from a variety of perspectives. Sigmund Freud set the groundwork for later psychoanalytic conceptualizations of indirect suicide in his theory of thanatos, an unconscious death instinct (Freud, 1920/1955). Karl A. Menninger (1938) elaborated upon the concept of the death instinct as a constantly changing unconscious driving force that may produce self-injurious or self-limiting behaviors. The concept of an unconsciously motivated self-injury was further developed by Edwin Shneidman (1968) in his description of "subintentional death." He and Norman Farberow (1980) emphasize the distinction between direct suicidal behavior, in which the intention is to die, to gamble with death, or to hurt oneself, and subintentional death, where self-injury is not a conscious goal. Avery D. Weisman and Thomas Hackett (1961) found similar ideas useful in describing life-threatening behaviors.

Robert Kastenbaum and Brian L. Mishara described self-injurious behaviors as a means of achieving premature death. Their approach places less emphasis upon the motivations for self-destruction, whether conscious or unconscious, noting that it is often very difficult to establish the specific reasons for a complex human action. Instead, attention is directed to the actual or potential effect of a particular set of actions upon the individual's continued existence. Behaviors that have been studied within the perspective of indirect suicide include alcoholism, smoking, reckless driving, masochistic sexual perversions, noncompliance with medical treatment, compulsive addictive behaviors, extreme overeating, self-mutilation, gambling, delinquency and criminal offenses, and even altruistic interventions in violent criminal events, as well as needless risk taking in recreational and occupational pursuits

(Farberow, 1980). It has been found that self-injurious behavior occurs frequently among institutionalized elderly people, and can be related to the quality of the institutional environment.

The study of indirect suicidal behaviors is complicated by the fact that the same action may have different meanings and serve different purposes at different times in a person's life. For example, smoking may begin in adolescence as a response to peer pressure and the need for acceptance. Later, smoking may be relied upon as a means of coping with stress and start to reveal the overtones of a subtle self-destructive tendency. A person suffering from emphysema, often caused by prolonged smoking, may choose to continue this habit in order to bring about an end to a painful life. Society also may encourage certain types of life-threatening behaviors, such as risk-taking sports.

Fortunately, there is also a complementary category of behaviors that tend to prolong life, such as regular exercise and sound nutritional habits. Both classes of behavior operate in a subtle and complex manner over a long period of time and both may be represented in the lives of the same people.

See also Death Instinct; Suicide.

—BRIAN L. MISHARA

References

Farberow, N.L. (1980). *The many faces of suicide.* New York: McGraw-Hill.

Freud, S. (1920/Reprint 1955). *Beyond the pleasure principle.* Standard edition. London: Hogarth.

Kastenbaum, R. & Mishara, B.L. (1971). "Premature death and self-injurious behavior in old age." *Geriatrics, 26*: 70–81.

Menninger, K.A. (1938). *Man against himself.* New York: Harcourt, Brace.

Mishara, B.L. & Kastenbaum, R. (1973). "Self-injurious behavior and environmental change in the institutionalized elderly." *International Journal of Aging and Human Development, 4*: 133–45.

Shneidman, E.S. (1966). "Orientations toward death, a vital aspect of the study of lives." *International Journal of Psychiatry, 2*: 167–200.

Weisman, A.D. & Hackett, T.P. (1961). "Prediliction to death." *Psychosomatic Medicine, 22*: 232–55.

SUICIDE: NATIVE AMERICAN

Native Americans (American Indians) exhibit the highest suicide rate of any ethnic/racial grouping, including whites. For example, the rate for Native Americans was 13.6 per 100,000 for 1979–81, while that for whites was 12.9. However, marked differences exist among tribes, some showing extremely high and others extremely low suicide rates. A major distinction between Native American and white suicide is the pattern by age. Among whites and for the United States as a whole, the suicide rate increases with advancing age and peaks in old age. By contrast, among Native Americans suicide occurs predominately among the young. Suicide rates reach their peak in early adulthood (prior to age 35), and decline thereafter. Suicide rates among elderly Native Americans are relatively low. Native American suicide occurs at much higher levels among males (as for the nation as a whole and for whites). Alcohol is often involved in Native American suicide, more frequently than for other groups. Most suicides among Native American males involve the use of firearms; Native American females often employ firearms as well but are as likely to use solid or liquid poisons.

Explanations for high male youth suicide rates have focused on a sense of "marginality," the feeling that one does not quite belong to either the Native American culture or the surrounding mainstream society. High suicide risk arises when this feeling is intensified by other factors such as high unemployment and alcohol ingestion. On the other hand, the low rates of suicide among elderly Native Americans have been explained by their survivor status (they are a selective, nonsuicidal sample of their original cohort or generation), freedom from acculturation problems faced by the young, and a long-term adaptation to the harsh conditions of their life so that old age does not require critical new adaptations.

See also Suicide; Suicide: Youth.

—JOHN L. McINTOSH

References

McIntosh, J.L. (1983–1984). "Suicide among Native Americans: Further tribal data and considerations." *Omega, Journal of Death and Dying, 14*: 215–29.

McIntosh, J.L. (1985). *Research on suicide: A bibliography.* Westport, CT: Greenwood.

McIntosh, J.L. & Santos, J.F. (1980–1981). "Suicide among Native Americans: A compilation of findings." *Omega, Journal of Death and Dying, 11*: 303–16.

McIntosh, J.L. & Santos, J.F. (1981). "Suicide among minority elderly: A preliminary investigation." *Suicide and Life-Threatening Behavior, 11*: 151–66.

SUICIDE: YOUTH

Rates and Demographics

The rise in suicide rates for youth (ages 15–24) has been a cause of serious alarm for the public health and mental health communities of the United States. The suicide rate rose from 4.5 per 100,000 in 1950 to a high of 13.3 in 1977. This was an increase of 196%, or nearly triple the previous rates. Those in the 20–24 age range contribute more than twice the rate of those 15–19 (18.6 vs. 8.9 respectively in 1977). Since 1977 the rate for the 20–24 year old age group has declined (14.8 in 1963, a decrease of 26%), while the 15–19 age group has remained practically the same at the rate of 8.7, a decrease of 2%.

In both age groups it is the male who contributes most to death by suicide. In the 20–24 age group, the rate for males rises from 9.3 per 100,000 in 1950 to 29.9 in 1977, an increase of 222%. This rate drops to 24.3% in 1983, a decrease of 23%. The males in the 15 to 19 age group rise from a rate of 3.5 in 1950 to 14.2 in 1977, an increase of 306%, and then stay at practically the same level, 14. It is apparent that although they contribute far fewer in number to the suicide statistics, it is the younger males, 15–19, who have shown the greatest proportionate increase in rate and that this trend has continued into the 1980s.

Females in these two age groups have shown a parallel but smaller increase in suicide rate over the past three decades. Among the 20–24 age group the rate for females increased from 3.3 per 100,000 in 1950 to 7.3 in 1977, an increase of 121%, and then dropped to 5.2 in 1983, a decrease of 40%. Among the 15–19 age group, the rate increased from 1.8 in 1950 to 3.4 in 1977, or 89%. It then dropped very slightly to 3.2 in 1983, a decrease of 6%.

It is apparent that the increase in youth suicide has been primarily due to an increase in the rate of suicide for young males. In 1950 the ratio of male to female suicides in the 20–24 age group was 2.8; by 1983 it was 4.7. In the 15–19 age group the ratio was 1.9 in 1950 and grew to 4.4 in 1983. Furthermore, most (90%) of the young male suicide victims were white. Young white male suicide rates increased much more sharply from 1950 to 1980 than those of black and other males (224% vs. 160% respectively). The rate for black and other males continued to be lower than that for white males in 1980 (13.7 vs. 21.4).

The most frequent method of suicide for males in the 15–24 age group is firearms, with hanging next most common. Firearms as a method increased from 52% in 1970 to 64% in 1980, while the use of poisoning decreased in the same period from 14% to 5%. For females, the changes have been even more dramatic. In the 15–24 age group, the major method of suicide changed between 1970 and 1980 from drugs to firearms. The use of drugs to commit suicide declined from 42% to 20%, while the use of firearms increased from 32% to 53%.

Other Nations

The rise in the suicide rate for youth has not been limited to the United States. Canada, for example, showed a very similar pattern in its suicide rates of youth 15–24, with a peak in 1977 of 17.4 per 100,000 (up 205% from 2.5 in 1965), and with a slight drop in rate to 16.2 in 1981. Again, it was mostly the males whose rates went up, a rise of 219% from 9.0 in 1965 to 28.7 in 1977, and then a slight drop, 6%, to 27.2 in 1981. The females showed a similar increase of 187% during that same period, but their rates were considerably lower to start with, peaking at 6.6 in 1979, and dropping to 4.9 in 1981.

The suicide rate of Austria's young reached its highest point of 20.5 per 100,000 in 1981, a rise of 72% from 11.9 in 1965. Again, it was the males who contributed most to this rate, reaching 33.6 in 1981, an 80% increase over the rate of 18.7 in 1965. The young females in Austria had also increased their suicide rate from 4.9 in 1965 to 10.5 in 1981, a rise of 114%.

In Finland, the rate for youth suicide (15–24) reached the highest level of any reported for European countries. The highest Finnish rate of 26.1 was reported in 1975, up 178% from 9.4 in 1965. The rate then declined to 23.6 in 1980. The rate for males in this age group soared to 45.8 in 1975, an increase of 211% from the rate of 14.7 in 1965, before falling back slightly to 37.5 in 1980. The female rate increased from 3.9 in 1965 to 9.1 in 1974, a rise of 133%. France, West Germany, and Sweden tend to show, with variations, a rise to high rates in the 1970s and a much smaller drop-off in the early 1980s.

In the Far East, the pattern was somewhat different. In Japan, the suicide rates for young males rose early in the 1970s to 19.9 in 1973, stayed practically the same throughout the decade, and then decreased to 14.5 in 1982. The rate for females peaked in 1974 at 13.3 and then dropped gradually to 6.5 in 1982. By contrast, the rate for Australia's young males reached its highest level in 1979 with 18.1 and remained high into 1980 with a rate of 17.6. The rate for young females reached its highest level of 6.4 in 1973 and then showed a downward trend to 4.5 in 1980.

Not all countries have shown this pattern of high rates during the 1970s with a dropping off in the late 70s and early 80s. In England, for example, the young males show practically no change from a rate of 6.3 in 1965 to a rate of 2.0 in 1982. Asian nations such as Thailand, Singapore, and others report rates that are entirely idiosyncratic.

Suicide Attempts: Prevalence and Characteristics

The data reported above refer only to suicide deaths and do not include information relating to other aspects of suicidal behavior such as attempts and other self-destructive behavior. Information on these subjects is difficult to obtain in most nations, including the United States, because information on such behavior is not routinely collected as official data. The available information generally comes from studies of selected groups in specific locations and settings, such as communities, hospitals, and out-patient populations. The extent of the problem is indicated, however, by reports that the number of suicide attempts may be anywhere from 50 to 100 times as frequent as suicide deaths.

One estimate of the prevalence of suicide behavior was obtained in a recent (1986) statewide study in California of the older adolescent (ages 16–19). Males and females in this age group were asked how frequently suicidal behavior occurred among their friends and acquaintances. Sixty percent of the adolescents reported that they knew of such behavior (suicidal thoughts or attempts) among their friends; 41% indicated that they themselves had engaged in such behavior. In this latter group, 65% were females, 35% males. A committed suicide among their families was reported by 10% of the respondents.

In comparison to the group of students who had not reported suicidal behavior or thoughts, the suicidal group reported more intense periods of persistent depression, more sleep and weight problems, and more frequent feelings of hopelessness and helplessness—two of the most significant signs for potential suicide. Socially, the suicidal group reported a greater tendency to be a loner and to be disappointed by other people. They also felt less likely to be loved in their family. Drugs and alcohol were also used more frequently by the suicidal group.

The situations reported by the suicidal adolescents as most likely to lead them to feel like killing themselves were problems at home (58%), school pressures (35%), sweetheart problems (22%), and a "tough life" (20%). They listed the major causes of youth suicide today as family problems and pressures by parents, sweetheart problems, and school difficulties. While drug and alcohol abuse were reported, it was more often considered to be a parallel symptom of the problems experienced by the young person, rather than the directly contributing or primary cause.

Both the suicidal and nonsuicidal young people stated that what was needed to stop young people from deliberately killing or hurting themselves was to make them feel loved, get them to counseling, give them more education, find someone for them to talk to, and talk to them.

High Risk Groups and Warning Signs

Identification and assessment are key elements in preventing the suicide of young persons. Although there are no indications of a specific "suicidal type," there are a number of characteristics that have been identified in people with high risk. The probability of suicidal behavior in stress situations is high, for example, for those young persons with a history of one or more prior suicide attempts. The risk is further increased if the problems that led to the original suicide attempt or behavior have not changed and there has been no help in dealing with those problems. Other high-risk groups include teenagers in difficulty with the law, with parents, or with peers, and those who feel unable to live up to what others expect of them. The groups of abused, molested, or neglected children may develop feelings of shame and guilt, accompanied by low self-esteem. These negative feelings leave them open to developing a sense of worthlessness and inadequacy.

Learning-disabled students frequently go through school feeling alienated, different from, and less capable than their peers. An opposite way of behaving may be to develop extremely high standards and demand perfectionism in their school performance and school activities. For such persons, any small failure becomes intolerable and total. Other possible ways of handling feelings of inadequacy include unnecessary risk-taking, especially in high-risk sports and hobbies in the effort to win approval and admiration.

Insufficient attention has been paid to the severe problems experienced by homosexual adolescents who struggle with a socially unacceptable sexual identity as they realize differences between themselves and their peers. The difficulty can be deepened by the fact that at the same time they often lose the support of their families who may be unable to accept this variation in terms of their own expectations.

Losses of significant others are difficult for people of any age, and especially so with tenuously adjusted youths. Suicide risk is increased by recent losses such as death or divorce of parents, breaking up with a boyfriend or girlfriend, loss of status by receiving a bad grade, and similar events. These may result in strong feelings of undeserved guilt, unbearable grief, or fear of mental illness.

It is rare that any single traumatic or crisis event will precipitate a suicide. Most of the time there will be a progression of warning signs that indicate increased risk. The signs will not be limited to any one area such as behavioral, emotional, cognitive, or situational but, rather, will be mixtures in different proportions of problems from each of these areas. The most common emotion observed as a warning sign is a severe depression centered around feelings of not belonging, feelings of inadequacy, failure in school performance, and loss of meaningful personal relationships. Depression increases feelings of alienation and isolation from others, heightening the sense of not belonging. Depression is also expressed in physical symptoms, especially disturbances of sleep and appetite. Other symptoms of depression include apathy, fatigability, loss of interest in usual activities, diminished attention and concentration, cognitive constriction with loss of alternatives, agitation, and a variety of psychosomatic symptoms. Guilt feelings, anxiety, and rage are not infrequent. Heavy use of alcohol and drugs may develop as a means of escape.

Sudden 180-degree changes may appear in personality and appearance, as when the shy person suddenly becomes loud and boisterous, or the usually friendly person becomes withdrawn and uninterested. The young person may seem no longer to care about appearance and cleanliness.

Schoolwork may be neglected, and there may be weight loss, and a lack of interest in the opposite sex. Sudden changes in school behavior may appear, such as erratic class attendance, increasingly poor academic performance, lack of interest and withdrawal, increased irritability and aggressiveness, and preoccupation with death in thoughts and writings. Another important sign occurs in making final arrangements by giving away prized possessions and personal belongings.

Helping the suicidal teenager to overcome the suicidal crisis involves essentially listening honestly, attentively and nonjudgmentally, sharing feelings openly, and providing hope through an action plan that finds help in the use of family, school, community, and personal resources. Professional treatment is often not required if others express sufficient interest, care, and concern to help the at-risk youth through the difficult period. However, professional treatment is needed in those cases where the problems are more difficult, and deep-seated conflicts may need to be addressed.

See also Adolescence and Death; Suicide.

—NORMAN L. FARBEROW

References

Farberow, N.L., Litman, R.E., & Nelson, F.K. (1986). "Survey of youth suicide in California." Paper presented at joint annual meeting of the American Association of Suicidology, and Congress of the International Association for Suicide Prevention. San Francisco, May 1987.

Peck, M.L., Farberow, N.L., & Litman, R.E. (Eds.) (1985). *Youth suicide.* New York: Springer.

U.S. National Center for Health Statistics (1950–1983). *Vital statistics of the United States, Vol. 2. Mortality, Part A.* Washington, DC: U.S. Government Printing Office.

World Health Organization (1965–1982). *World health statistics annual.* Vol. 1. Geneva: World Health Organization.

Youth suicide in the United States, 1970–1980. (1986). Atlanta: Centers for Disease Control.

SUICIDE AND LIFE-THREATENING BEHAVIOR (JOURNAL)

This quarterly journal is an official publication of the American Association of Suicidology. It was established in 1971 with psychologist Edwin S. Shneidman as founding editor. The current editor is sociologist Ronald Maris.

Suicide and Life-Threatening Behavior is devoted to "emerging approaches in theory and practice related to self-destruction, other-destructive, and life-threatening behaviors." Specific topics include suicide, life-threatening actions that resemble suicide in some way, suicide prevention, death, and varied threats to life from both within the person and from the external world. Contributions are welcome from all the research and clinical disciplines that bear on suicide and other life-threatening behaviors.

Types of articles published can be illustrated by the contents of a recent issue (1987, Vol. 17, No. 3): "Cohort, Age, and Period Effects in the Analysis of U.S. Suicide Patterns: 1933–1978"; "Female Suicide and Wife Abuse: A Cross-Cultural Perspective"; "Suicide in Texas: A Cohort Analysis of Trends in Suicide Rates, 1945–1980"; "Suicide Among American Indian Adolescents: An Overview"; "An Empirical Investigation of Shneidman's Formulations Regarding Suicide: Age and Sex"; and "Cognitive Rigidity in Suicide Attempters." Book reviews are featured.

The journal is indexed in numerous resource publications, such as *Index Medicus, Abstracts on Criminology and Penology, Community Mental Health Review, Human Sources Abstracts,* and *Safety Science Abstracts.*

Manuscripts are reviewed by an international board of experts. Submissions should be made in quadruplicate, with a 100-word abstract. The entire manuscript should be double-spaced, typed on one side on regular bond paper. The American Psychological Association standard style should be used, and length should not be over twenty pages except for unusual circumstances.

Manuscripts should be submitted to:

Dr. Ronald Maris
Center for the Study of Suicide
University of South Carolina
228 Callcott Building
Columbia, SC 29208

Subcription information can be obtained from:

The Guilford Press
72 Spring Street
New York, NY 10012

See also American Association of Suicidology; Suicide.

—ROBERT KASTENBAUM

SURVIVAL BELIEFS AND PRACTICES: BAHA'I

The Baha'i faith is a revealed world religion, not a cult or sect, not an offshoot of Islam, although its beginnings are rooted in Islamic culture just as Christianity begins in the context of Jewish culture. Founded in 1844 in Persia (Iran), the Baha'i faith has spread throughout the world and presently has an estimated 4.5 million adherents as well as 140 national administrative institutions (known as National Spiritual Assemblies). Its international center is in Haifa, Israel, where the elected members of the Universal House of Justice govern the affairs of the religion.

Progressive Stages of Enlightenment

Basing their beliefs on the hundreds of revealed writings of the founder, Baha'u'llah (Mirza Husayn Ali, 1817–1892), Baha'is believe in the essential unity of all world religions. God continually guides humankind toward enlightenment and fulfillment through a succession of teachers, called Manifestations. Baha'is believe that Baha'u'llah ("The Glory of God") is the most recent of these Divine Teachers, and the appellation "Baha'i" signifies "a follower of the Glory of God."

Baha'is do not believe that Baha'u'llah has a greater spiritual station than those prophets who preceded or will appear after him. All Manifestations alike have innate knowledge, live exemplary lives, and are uniquely specialized by God to reveal the next stage in the education of humankind. However, the teachings of Baha'u'llah are especially designed by God to meet the exigencies of the present period in history. Baha'u'llah teaches that this period will witness the fulfillment of human spiritual destiny, the establishment of a world civilization. This is the time that all the previous prophets longed to witness: "The time fore-ordained unto the peoples and kindreds of the earth is now come. The promises of God, as recorded in the holy Scriptures, have all been fulfilled" (Baha'u'llah, *Gleanings*, 12–13).

The Manifestations have thus been fully coordinated in their purpose to assist humanity in bringing forth "an ever-advancing civilization" (*Gleanings*, 15). Likewise, they one and all attribute the power of their utterance to the authority of God speaking through them, not to their own invention or genius. From the Baha'i view, then, the world religions are one continuous religion revealed in progressive stages of enlightenment.

Because each new revelation is designed to respond to the requirements of the age in which the prophet appears, the teachings of Baha'u'llah are necessarily vast in scope and various in theme but revolve around the imperative of recognizing and implementing the unity of the family of man: "It is not for him to pride himself who loveth his own country, but rather for him who loveth the whole world. The earth is but one country, and mankind its citizens" (*Gleanings*, 259).

At the heart of these teachings is the notion that the physical world is but a shadowy reflection of the world of the spirit: "Know thou that the Kingdom is the real world, and this nether place is only its shadow stretching out" ('Abdu'l-Baha, *Selections*, 178). Likewise, the essential reality of each individual is the spirit or soul. In fact, the Baha'i writings describe the spiritual education of human souls as the purpose of physical creation itself: "If there were no man, the perfections of the spirit would not appear, and the light of the mind would not be resplendent in this world. This world would be like a body without a soul"

('Abdu'l-Baha, *Some Answered Questions*, 201).

Physical Death as a Beginning

The nature of the soul and its continuation after its association with the physical world is described with great care in the Baha'i scriptures. The soul has a beginning, when it associates with the body at conception, but it endures eternally. Thus, the physical stage of existence is a carefully designed learning experience wherein spiritual attributes are perceived and acquired by means of physical metaphors and analogues.

The progress of the soul is not impaired when one does not seem fully to benefit from the rewards of this arrangement, whether because of physical or mental illness, retardation, or other reasons. Like light reflected through the mirror of the body, the soul's effulgence is sometimes hidden from others in the physical world, but spiritual progress is equally available to all, especially since the process of spiritual development continues most forcefully after the dissociation of the soul from the body at death: "Know thou of a truth that the soul, after its separation from the body, will continue to progress until it attaineth the presence of God, in a state and condition which neither the revolution of ages and centuries nor the changes and chances of this world, can alter" (Baha'u'llah, *Gleanings*, 155).

For the Baha'i, then, physical life, though occurring only once, is a vital foundation for further development, and is only the beginning stage in an eternal process of learning and growth. From such a view, physical demise is not an end, but a birth into a vastly different and more expansive stage of spiritual education. Physical life functions like the gestation of a child in the womb of its mother—it is a period of preparation for a birth into an environment more befitting the gradually developed attributes and faculties of the soul.

In general, then, the Baha'i writings portray death as a time of joyous release and fulfillment: "I have made death a messenger of joy to thee. Wherefore dost thou grieve?" (Baha'u'llah, *The Hidden Words*, 11). But while one's spiritual ascent is destined for completion beyond physical existence, the Baha'i writings also place great emphasis on utilizing the special opportunities of this life to promote spiritual development. For unlike the next life where truth is unveiled and apparent, in the physical stage of existence humanity is tested, sifted, and trained, much as is a student in a classroom.

In short, one is not automatically assured of success—the Baha'i Writings state that one enters the next world in essentially the same condition in which one departs this life. A willful negligence of one's spiritual development might result in the entrance into a spiritual world without developed spiritual faculties. Furthermore, there is a sort of judgment or evaluation of one's physical performance at the point of transition to the next life: "It is clear and evident that all men shall, after their physical death, estimate the worth of their deeds, and realize all that their hands have wrought" (*Gleanings*, 171). In addition, the Baha'i Writings imply that participation in the benefits of a spiritual existence will be dependent on our having attended to our spiritual education in the embryonic stage of our existence. For while all souls are created equal, the progress of each soul is dependent on its efforts: "the souls of the believers, at the time when they first become manifest in the world of the body, are equal, and each is sanctified and pure. In this world, however, they will begin to differ one from another, some achieving the highest station, some a middle one, others remaining at the lowest stage of being" ('Abdu'l-Baha, *Selections*, 171).

Principles of Existence in the Afterlife

Baha'u'llah withholds any complete portrait of the afterlife, stating that it is wise to concentrate instead on utilizing the earthly classroom: "If any man be told that which hath been ordained for such a soul . . . his whole being will instantly blaze out in his great longing to attain that most exalted, that sanctified and resplendent station. . . ." (*Gleanings*, 156). Nevertheless, a number of major principles about that existence are made clear:

1. This life is neither arbitrary nor capricious. Physical experience has as its animating purpose the development of such human judgment and insight as will be applicable to the continued progress of the soul in the world beyond.

2. We will retain the self-same identity and consciousness in the afterlife because "the mind is the power of the human spirit" ('Abdu'l-Baha, *Some Answered Questions*, 209), and "the personality of the rational soul is from its beginning; it is not due to the instrumentality of the body" (*Some Answered Questions*, 239–40).

3. In the world beyond we will be aware of our physical lives and we will recognize and communicate with other souls in that realm.

4. Because the continued purpose of our existence will be spiritual growth, we will have access to knowledge that may have been veiled to us in the physical world: "Once he hath departed this life, he will behold, in that world whatsoever was hidden from him here" ('Abdu'l-Baha, *Selections*, 171).

5. Further growth will be possible through a variety of means: the prayers of others, the works done in our names, the mercy of God, and our own prayers and efforts (Hatcher, 1987, p. 141–54).

6. Though experiencing the afterlife is not dependent on being a Baha'i, the nature of that experience, at least in its initial stages, is conditioned by how one has performed in the physical world: "They that are the followers of the one true God shall, the moment they depart out of this life, experience such joy and gladness as would be impossible to describe, while they that live in error shall be seized with such fear and trembling, and shall be filled with such consternation, as nothing can exceed" (*Gleanings*, 171).

7. The Baha'i Writings do not portray the afterlife in terms of merely two categories of experience (a heaven for those who succeed and a hell for those who fail). Spiritual success or failure is always relative, whether in this life or the next. Baha'u'llah thus describes terms like "heaven" and "hell" as metaphorical expressions of spiritual realities, not as physical abodes or permanent states of existence. Heaven is proximity to God; hell is remoteness. And since we cannot remain static, we are always approaching one or the other of these conditions.

Salvation: A Motion Toward Endless Possibilities

This observation brings us to possibly the most significant distinction between Baha'i belief and many other theologies: salvation is not a single point of faith, belief, or achievement. Rather, salvation is a motion toward endless possibilities. For while the human soul will ever remain a human soul, it is capable of infinite development. However spiritually refined one may become, one can always acquire more virtues or understand and express a single virtue with ever greater perfection. The process of human spiritual development is never a finished thing, and, at least in this life, one is never unfailingly secure from waywardness and decline, since free will is always operant.

According to the Baha'i scriptures, there is no regression in the afterlife, only progress. At the same time, in the next life "to cease to progress is the same as to decline" ('Abdu'l-Baha, *Some Answered Questions*, 233). Thus, a soul who is "deprived of these divine favors, although he continues after death is considered as dead by the people of truth" (*Some Answered Questions*, 225). Therefore, the Baha'i Writings repeatedly admonish that two things are incumbent upon everyone in this life: to discover the teachings of the Manifestation (recognize the Prophet), and follow His ordinances. It is not sufficient merely to accept and acknowledge His station. Indeed, one definition of "faith" is "first, conscious knowledge, and second, the practice of good deeds" ('Abdu'l-Baha, *Selections*, 383).

For the Baha'i, deeds not words are the signs and fruit of spiritual development in this life. So it is that the Baha'i community worldwide is dedicated to establishing the foundations of world unity and accord, not merely to promulgating a theology or a set of social principles. Toward this end, Baha'u'llah revealed a blueprint for world peace which Baha'is are attempting to implement.

—JOHN S. HATCHER

References

I. Baha'i Writings

'Abdu'l-Baha (1978). *Selections from the writings of 'Abdu'l-Baha.* Compiled by the Research Department of the Universal House of Justice. Translated by a Committee at the Baha'i World Centre and M. Gail. Haifa, Israel: Baha'i World Centre.

'Abdu'l-Baha (1981). *Some answered questions.* Compiled and translated by L.C. Barney. 5th ed. Wilmette, IL: Baha'i Publishing Trust.

Baha'u'llah (1939). *The hidden words of Baha'u'llah.* Translated by S. Effendi. Wilmette, IL: Baha'i Publishing Trust.

Baha'u'llah (1950). *Kitab-i-Iqan: The book of certitude.* 2nd ed. Translated by S. Effendi. Wilmette, IL: Baha'i Publishing Trust.

Baha'u'llah (1976). *Gleanings from the Writings of Baha'u'llah.* 2nd ed. Translated by S. Effendi. Wilmette, IL: Baha'i Publishing Trust.

Baha'u'llah & 'Abdu'l-Baha (1976). *Baha'i World Faith: Selected writings of Baha'u'llah and 'Abdu'l-Baha.* 2nd ed. Wilmette, IL: Baha'i Publishing Trust.

Motlagh, H. (1985). *Unto him shall we return: Selections from the Baha'i Writings on the reality and immortality of the human soul.* Wilmette, IL: Baha'i Publishing Trust.

II. History and Commentary

Esselemont, J.E. (1980). *Baha'u'llah and the New Era: An introduction to the Baha'i Faith.* 4th ed. Wilmette, IL: Baha'i Publishing Trust.

Hatcher, J.S. (1986). "Baha'i Faith." In C.J. Johnson & M.G. McGee (Eds.) *Encounters with eternity: Religious views of death and life after death.* New York: Philosophical Library, pp. 37–60.

Hatcher, J.S. (1987). *The purpose of physical reality: The kingdom of names.* Wilmette, IL: Baha'i Publishing Trust.

Hatcher, J.S. & Martin, J.D. (1984). *The Baha'i Faith: The emerging global religion.* San Francisco: Harper & Row.

SURVIVAL BELIEFS AND PRACTICES: BAPTIST

Baptists, following the doctrine of the priesthood of all believers, differ widely in their theology. Nevertheless, the majority of Baptists would adhere to basic biblical insights about death as those have been expressed in classical Christianity and conservative Protestant thought.

Theologically speaking, death is regarded as an intrusion into what God desires for human beings. Death is a result of sin (Genesis 3; Romans 3:23). Death entered the world because of one man's sin, but each person encounters death because all, like Adam, have sinned (Romans 5:12–21). Yet it is life, not death, which is the Creator's final word for humankind. The way in which life triumphs over death is through the resurrection of Jesus Christ. In His resurrection, Jesus Christ has conquered humanity's final enemy, death (I Corinthians 15). God gives life to all of the created existence except to those persons and rebellious angels who reject God. Cosmic redemption is an affirmation that God will ultimately bring all orders of life, except those who reject God, to fulfill their intended purpose. The whole of creation is awaiting redemption from the ravages of human wrongdoing (Romans 8:28ff). Christ will restore all things as they were intended to be (Colossians 1:13–23).

Finally God will restore and reconstitute the cosmos (Revelation 21:5). The destiny of humankind is settled through the individual's relationship to Jesus Christ. Therefore, the gospel of Jesus Christ must be proclaimed through all the world (Matthew 28:19–20). People are held accountable for whatever witness God grants them (Romans 1). To be confronted with the Gospel about Jesus Christ, and consciously to reject it is to place oneself in dire peril (Matthew 10:15). It is the obligation of people to accept the good news of God. By so doing, they are saved (Ephesians 2:8–9). To be saved means to be sustained in a godly life on earth and to live with God, in God's presence, after death.

Those who deny Jesus Christ are judged by that denial (John 16:5–15). People are cast out of the presence of Christ if they fail to do the things Christ commands (Matthew 25). Salvation is by faith and it leads into good works. Unbelief and wickedness will be punished by God. The state and place of punishment is likened to a trash heap of undying fire, a place of shadow where one cannot see God or worship God, a place of darkness.

Most Baptists believe that the destiny of the individual is decided in the one historical life each person is granted. Baptists tend to deny reincarnation, transmigration of souls, and universalism (the doctrine that all persons must be saved, even if after death). Hell is the absence of the fellowship of God. Dying is the door to one's eternal destiny.

—WILLIAM L. HENDRICKS

References

Hendricks, W.L. (1986). "A Baptist perspective." In C.J. Johnson & M.G. McGee (Eds.) *Encounters with eternity.* New York: Philosophical Library, 81–84.
Old Testament: Genesis.
New Testament: Colossians, I Corinthians, Ephesians, John, Revelations, Romans.

SURVIVAL BELIEFS AND PRACTICES: BUDDHIST

The Buddha

The historical Buddha was renowned as a great teacher who by his life as well as his words promulgated the ideals of goodwill, love, and tolerance for differences. He was also a master of an innovative form of the dialectic method of instruction and established a method that is still employed by Buddhists today. Son of a prince in northern India, Siddhartha Gautama (or Siddhattha Gotama) chose his own path as teacher rather than entering the career that was awaiting him as a raja, or presiding officer. He acquired an exceptional understanding of life, attaining enlightenment *(bodhi)* at the age of 35. Central to his enlightenment were meditations on birth, illness, and death, in short, on the mysteries of human existence and suffering. According to tradition, there had been several other buddhas before his time, but most of their teachings had been lost prior to Gautama's birth.

Soon after his death at the age of 80 (486 BC is the date most often cited by Western scholars; Buddhist tradition proposed 543 or 544 BC), Buddha had become the basis for a cult. At first his followers celebrated the life and personality of Gautama, especially his compassion *(Karuna)* for all mankind. Many anecdotes drawn from the life of Buddha remain a heritage from this early cult, whose original beliefs and practices are most closely perpetuated today by the Theravada sect. Gradually, Buddha the historical figure became interwoven into a philosophy and way of life that was expressed in a rich and poetic literature. Although there are a variety of forms through which the Buddha has been venerated, the many followers of this influential religion share the core ideal of emulating his enlightened way of life.

Buddhist Thought and Principles

All that exists moves through cycles of creation and destruction. Changes, transitions, appearances, and disappearances do not represent a temporary state of affairs, nor an imperfect view of reality. Unlike Platonic and Christian thought, Buddhism sees the here-and-now as real and authentic, and perpetual process rather than an end-point perfection or catastrophe as the law of the universe. Buddhist thought has also long held the belief that planet Earth is but one of a great many worlds—billions, or any large number one would like to imagine. Human life on earth is valuable in itself but does not necessarily occupy a special place in the cosmic scheme. Earth and all its life forms are but part of a vast system in which birth, abiding, destruction, and rebirth have always and will always be the rule.

Buddhism emphasizes the nature of existence in the here-and-now. The quality of this existence can be imperfect and have the experiential accompaniment of suffering and anguish, or it can approach "right being." It all depends on the individual.

How one fares at the moment and through all future lives is contingent upon the virtues that one has developed and exercised. Knowledge is of critical importance in this endeavor. To achieve a sense of harmony with the universal forces one must be aware of the conditions under which life exists, including what it means to be here right now. The kind of knowledge that is necessary also requires a masterful discipline of the self. It is not by amassing a mountain of external facts that one learns the essential truths; rather, the pathway is that of arduous spiritual discovery. Failure to make these discoveries and develop virtues does not lead to damnation and everlasting hell. There is no wrathful god to deal out such punishment, nor is any condition permanent—even the enlightened and virtuous person will again be reborn into suffering. Instead, the individual achieves little or much spiritual development and either develops or fails to develop a sense of right being.

Dying, Death, and After Lives

Death is followed by rebirth. Although Buddhists secure in their faith do not fear death, they are concerned about the form in which they will appear in their next incarnation. It is a great blessing to have had a life in human form; one may have had to accumulate virtue in hundreds of previous existences in order to have attained this favored status. The individual who achieves enlightenment is able to break free of the otherwise perpetual cycle of births, deaths, and rebirths. Adhering to the Buddhist way of life does not guarantee that one will attain this state of enlightenment, nor is it limited to Buddhists. Any person can attain wisdom and compassion through a personal journey of spiritual discovery. One learns to overcome the common human error of assuming that one has or is a solid, independent self, what might be called a "self-thing." We deceive ourselves in supposing that we have a continuous and autonomous self. It is closer to the mark to realize that "I" and "me" are but somewhat clumsy ways of referring to consciousness, awareness, or a kind of mental process whose nature it is to undergo transformation. Consistent with this view, Buddhists do not believe in

bodily resurrection. It is consciousness or awareness that survives physical death.

Understanding the Buddhist conception of existence requires a sensitivity to metaphor and multiple levels of thought. As Klein (1986, p. 103) observes: "The mind is deeper than its ordinary uses lead us to suspect. . . . When its capacity is realized, mind is transformed. In this way, descriptions of death and rebirth are meant to reveal the processes by which ordinary persons achieve full enlightenment." Buddhism, then, expresses faith in human potential—not to endure punishment or seek redemption, but rather to cultivate one's mental and spiritual qualities in affinity with and on behalf of all living beings.

This view of life is also expressed in Buddhist interpretrations of dying and death. There is no escapism regarding the inevitability of death. Great accomplishments and profound understanding do not exempt one from death—the galaxies themselves undergo cycles of destruction. Furthermore, one dies alone even if in the company of loving family and companions. In this departure from the life one has known, it is not possible to take any possessions, any keepsakes across the border. Recognizing how the end must come, the Buddhist also recognizes how little time there is in a life to develop wisdom, insight, and compassion. Spiritual development is therefore an urgent matter and one that requires constant attention. The contemplation of death is a glowing reminder to Buddhists that they should avail themselves of their precious and limited opportunities for attaining enlightenment.

The dying person experiences a gradual withdrawal of consciousness or the mental principle from the sense organs. (This process bears some resemblance to Freud's much later conception of "decathexis" in which "libidinal investments" return from the world to the psyche.) Buddhist literature also offers a stage theory of dying that preceded the well-known Kubler-Ross (1969) version by more than a millenium. The Buddhists distinguish eight stages of dying, each of which is marked by an internal vision or mental state as well as by external signs. Sudden death, as through a highway accident, compresses the stages and does not give the individual the opportunity to imbue dying with his or her own unique spirituality. How a person moves through these stages depends much upon the previous state of spiritual development that has been attained. It is here, as life edges into death, that all one's virtues, wisdom, and self-discipline become especially significant. Death in confusion and despair will have its impact upon the person's next rebirth. Those whose last hours are calm, filled with love and compassion for others, and who are aware of the reality of impermanence will take some of these qualities into their next lives. Prayers and other offerings by family, friends, and spiritual advisors can be helpful in this process.

During the first three stages, the dying person becomes thinner and more frail, drier, and cooler, each of these physical changes having its accompaniment in mental imagery. The breath ceases during the fourth stage. His Holiness Tenzin Gyatso, the fourteenth Dalai Lama, writes that at this time, "If a doctor came, he would say you were already dead; however, from our point of view, you are still in the process of dying. . . . Your sense consciousnesses has disappeared, but the mental consciousness remains. However, this does not mean that you could revive" (Gyatso, 1985, p. 175).

The imagery of light becomes especially important during the second set of stages, when one is in effect dead to the world yet still imbued with an inner awareness. Visions suffused with white moonlight are followed by red sunlight, and then by darkness. In a sense, this is where the passage known as dying really occurs, the loss of light and consciousness. But then one is finally granted the vision of dawn spread across a clear and infinite sky. This is known as the clear light of death. An enlightened and fortunate person may continue in this stage for an extended period of time. According to some reports over the centuries and into the present day, a dying person may remain for weeks in a condition resembling sleep, the body showing no further signs of deterioration, while presumably continuing to experience the clear light of death. According to the Dalai Lama, a person who dies from natural causes and without much physical deterioration is likely to remain in

this rare and subtle state of mind (the clear light of death) for about three days.

When consciousness leaves the body there are natural physical signs that can be recognized by others, but the deceased person may not immediately realize his or her new transitional status ("I'm talking to people: why do they not answer?"). During this intermediary state one may have a number of dream adventures and travel freely and instantaneously. (There are obvious parallels with the phenomena of near-death experiences and encounters with phantoms or ghosts.) After a period of time (49 days is the number usually held by tradition), one is reborn, and the "drop of subtle consciousness" becomes the core of a new body.

It is difficult for Westerners to follow Buddhist techniques such as those described in the Tibetan Book of the Dead. Generally, one must have tutors and guides and have become very familiar with both the general philosophy and its many details. Nevertheless, some Buddhist principles may be accessible to Westerners, for example, exploring and gaining control over one's mind while in good health (see also Jeremy Taylor in the references to **Ars Moriendi**), and helping the dying person to leave this life in a calm and peaceful manner. A distinctive tenet of Buddhism is that because all of us have had many previous incarnations, we have also had a great many previous relationships with each other and, therefore, excellent reason to treat each other with compassion and goodwill.

See also Ars Moriendi; Life After Death?; Near-Death Experiences; Stages of Dying.

—ROBERT KASTENBAUM

References

Evans-Wentz, W.Y. (Ed.) (1960). *The Tibetan Book of the dead.* New York: Oxford University Press.

Gyatso, T., XIV Dalai Lama (1984). *Kindness, clarity, and insight.* Ithaca, NY: Snow Lion Publications.

Hopkins, J. (1983). *Meditation on emptiness.* London: Wisdom Publications.

Klein, A.C. (1986). "Buddhism." In C.J. Johnson & M.G. McGee (Eds.) *Encounters with eternity.* New York: Philosophical Library, pp. 85–108.

Kubler-Ross, E. (1969). *On death and dying.*
New York: Macmillan.

Rinbochay, V.D.L. & Hopkins, J. (1979).
Death, the intermediate state and rebirth.
Ithaca, NY: Snow Lion Publications.

Robinson, S. (1970). *The Buddhist religion.*
Belmont, CA: Dickenson.

SURVIVAL BELIEFS AND PRACTICES: CHURCH OF THE LATTER-DAY SAINTS

Members of The Church of Jesus Christ of Latter-Day Saints are also known as Mormons, taking this name from a document held sacred by the church, The Book of Mormon. Generally, members prefer the term Latter-Day Saints (LDS), as this more adequately describes their distinctive articles of faith. There are approximately six million LDS members in the United States; the Church has long had a presence in England and is also active in many other parts of the world.

A well established part of the religious establishment today, the LDS, as a formal faith, have a relatively short but very eventful history and hold some beliefs that differ markedly from other Christian-oriented churches. The founder of the Latter Day Saints Church was Joseph Smith, who was born in Sharon, Vermont, in 1805, and later moved with his family to upstate New York. During Smith's youth, this part of the nation was the scene of intense competition among various Protestant denominations as well as cults that usually had exciting, but short-lived influences. In his authoritative *Articles of Faith* (first edition, 1899), James E. Talmage quotes the young Smith's response to the religious ferment and controversy he saw taking place around him:

> At length I came to the conclusion that I must either remain in darkness and confusion, or else I must do as (The Epistle of) James directs, that is, ask of God. . . . I retired to the woods to make the attempt. It was on the morning of a beautiful, clear day, early in the spring of eighteen hundred and twenty. . . . I kneeled down and began to offer up the desire of my heart to God. I had scarce-

ly done so, when immediately I was seized upon by some power which entirely overcame me. . . (Talmage, 1974, p. 10).

The young man saw "a pillar of light exactly over my head, above the brightness of the sun, which descended gradually until it fell upon me." Two personages then appeared, standing above him in the air, "whose brightness and glory defy all description." Smith was told by the personages that the religious creeds of his time were corrupt. He had a second angelic visitation on the night of September 21, 1823, again accompanied by a brilliant light. This personage revealed that his name was Moroni and he had been sent as a divine messenger. Moroni spoke several prophecies that were variants of Bible passages, and told the young man of a book that had been written upon gold plates. Smith later went to a hill described to him in this angelic vision and located a stone box that contained the book and other objects described by Moroni.

These experiences laid the foundation for what was to become in 1830 the formal organization (at Fayette, New York) of the Church of Jesus Christ of Latter-Day Saints. The Book of Mormon was produced by Smith as his translation of the previously unknown ancient history of the Americas. This history included a visitation from Jesus Christ who descended from Heaven after crucifixion and resurrection. The LDS faith, then, is based upon scripture and beliefs held in common with other Christian-oriented denominations, but also draws upon rediscoveries and revelations that introduce other concepts and practices.

Survival Beliefs and Practices

The LDS conception of life after death is intimately related to the belief that a regeneration of nature will be attained when the Millennium has "run its blessed course." God will then "wipe away all tears from their eyes," as John has said, "and there shall be no more death, neither sorrow, nor crying, neither shall there be any more pain. . ." The earth itself, as Talmage (p. 378) writes, must "undergo a change analogous to death, and is to be regenerated in a way comparable to a resurrection."

In essentially the same way as the "ordained rejuvenation of earth," there will be a resurrection of the bodies of all beings who have had an existence upon it. The doctrine is one of "a literal resurrection; an actual reunion of the spirits of the dead and the tabernacles with which they were clothed during mortal probation; and transition from mortality to immortality in the case of some who will be in the flesh at the time of the Lord's advent, and who, because of individual righteousness, are to be spared the sleep of the grave" (Talmage, p. 381).

There will actually be two resurrections. The first resurrection will be limited to those who were righteous and just during their lives on earth. As Paul has asserted in his epistles to the saints, "For as in Adam all die, even so in Christ shall all be made alive. But every man in his own order: Christ the firstfruits; afterward they that are Christ's at his coming." Latter-day relevation confirms the priority for resurrection of the just, which will also include the gathering unto the Lord of saints who are alive on the earth at the time of the coming. "And they who have slept in their graves shall come forth, for their graves shall be opened; and they also shall be caught up to meet him in the midst of the pillar of heaven—They are Christ's, the first fruits. . . " This company of the righteous will include all who have lived faithfully according to the laws of God as made known to them. Children who have died in their innocence and heathens who groped for spiritual light but died in ignorance will be counted among the righteous company to be quickened at the first resurrection.

The second and final resurrection will encompass the dead who were not eligible for the first resurrection. The LDS articles of faith emphasize that the resurrection is to be universal: "While it is true that the dead shall be brought forth in order, each as he is prepared for the first or a later stage, yet everyone who has tabernacled in the flesh shall again assume his body and, with spirit and body reunited, he shall be judged" (Talmage, p. 391). This restoration includes everyone, regardless of age, sex, virtue, or wickedness, "and even there shall not be so much as a hair of their heads be lost; but every thing shall be restored to its perfect frame. . . " All will then be subjected to the final judgment and found either worthy or unworthy.

One tenet of LDS faith and practice may seem particularly unusual to outsiders, but is regarded as entirely appropriate and indispensable by members. Baptism of the dead should be understood within the church's conception of baptism in general. Baptism is regarded as symbolic of burial, followed by resurrection. The form of baptism (including immersion) favored by the LDS is the result of latter-day revelation and is required of all who would seek salvation. The dead as well as the living must be exposed to the gospel, as the Lord rules and judges both the quick and the dead. Realizing that many have lived and died without knowing the true gospel during the long periods of spiritual darkness, the LDS conducts baptism for the dead so they, too, can benefit from the saving ordinances of the kingdom. Although eternal punishment will be the lot of the wicked when they are judged as such on the final resurrection, those who were not informed of the true gospel during their lives will not be condemned on this basis if they are provided with a latter-day baptism.

—ROBERT KASTENBAUM

References

Eyre, R.M. (1986). "The Church of the Latter-Day Saints." In C.J. Johnson & M.G. McGee (Eds.) *Encounters with eternity.* New York: Philosophical Library, 129–56.

Mullen, R. (1966). *The Latter-Day Saints: The Mormons yesterday and today.* New York: Doubleday & Co.

Smith, J. (1981). *The Book of Mormon.* Salt Lake City: The Church of Jesus Christ of Latter-Day Saints.

Talmage, J.E. (1899/Reprint 1974). *Articles of faith.* Salt Lake City, UT: The Church of Jesus Christ of Latter-Day Saints.

SURVIVAL BELIEFS AND PRACTICES: CHURCHES OF CHRIST

The message for life and death proclaimed in the Churches of Christ is that life is the singular opportunity to declare for God. One does this through believing in his son Jesus Christ, repenting of sin, confessing faith in Christ and being baptized (immersed) in the name of the Father, Son, and Holy Spirit. The person who accepts Christ is charged by him to live a full, fruitful, rewarding life here-and-now. At death such a person will go to an intermediate place of blessing. She or he will be conscious, awaiting the judgment day. At the judgment she or he will be welcomed by God to live with him eternally in heaven. This is a message of great hope, comfort, and joy.

The person who refuses to accept Christ, or who never hears the gospel, or who accepts but is unfaithful, is one who lives a shallow, confused, and troubled life. After death he or she will go to a place of torment, awaiting the final judgment. At the final judgment he will be pronounced guilty by God and punished eternally. Despite the fact that the steps to avoid eternal punishment are found in the Scriptures, the majority of persons succumb to the temptations of Satan, and in the end are consigned to eternal punishment.

Death is an anxious moment because by it one faces many unknowns. The one who has received Christ and remained faithful to his calling is encouraged to believe that death is a time of peace, a passageway to the joys of eternal life. The one, however, who rejects the gracious salvation offered by God should of necessity greatly fear death. For him it is a passageway to separation, torture, and eternal destruction. Likewise, the one who has accepted Christ but who has only in a borderline way dedicated his life to discipleship, and who with some frequency has committed overt sin, will be condemned at the final judgment.

The sources for these views among Churches of Christ members are the Scriptures, especially the New Testament. These views are essentially those of mainstream traditional Protestantism as represented by such documents as the Westminster Confession of Faith.

—THOMAS H. OLBRICHT

References

Hill, D. (1982). *Death and dying.* Abilene, TX: Quality Publications.

Kyker, R. (1982). *God's man in time of death. A ministry of comfort.* Abilene, TX: Abilene Christian Bookstore.

Olbricht, T.H. (1986). "The Churches of Christ." In C.J. Johnson & M.G. McGee (Eds.) *Encounters with eternity.* New York: Philosophical Library, 109–28.

Turner, J.J. (1975). *Life, death, and beyond.* Shreveport, LA: Lambert Book House.

SURVIVAL BELIEFS AND PRACTICES: HINDU

The Faith and Its Origins

The Hindu faith was originally known as Sanatana Dharma—eternal religion. It is, in fact, the most ancient of the religions that continue to have numerous adherents. An estimated 500 million people practice Hinduism today, both in its homeland of India and throughout the world (Adiswarananda, 1986). The term *Hindu* itself is a Persian mispronunciation of *Sindhu*, the Sanskrit word for the Indus river, which, in turn, gave its name to the land of India.

The origins of the Hindu faith predate what is usually considered to be the historical era. The Vedic religion, which gradually evolved into contemporary Hinduism, was already an ancient system of belief and practice 500 years before the birth of Christ. It involved the worship of many gods who had rather vivid and distinct personalities. These included Soma, god of liquor and agriculture, Agni, god of fire, and Indra, the demon-slayer who delivered the human race from darkness.

In the Rig-Veda, Vedic Hinduism possesses a document that was nearly as old in Biblical times as the Judeo-Christian scriptures are today. Written in an archaic form of Sanskrit, the Rig-Veda offers a story of creation and hymns to the gods. The theme of sacrifice that is found in the Rig-Veda is amplified in other ancient texts, such as the Atharva-veda with its magical incantations and ceremonies:

> Sacrifice was at the center of the Vedic religion: a succession of oblations and prayers, fixed according to strict liturgy, in which the culmination was reached when the offering was placed in the fire. The objective of the ritual was to enter into communication with the divine world and thence to acquire certain advantages which profane initiatives could not enjoy. Sometimes vegetable, sometimes animal, the offering consisted predominately of the Soma plant, from which is extracted a liquor which possesses intoxicating qualities (Renou, 1962, p. 23).

Hindu religion has many variant schools or sects. Much attention is given to the performance of rituals, but there are also social, moral, and philosophical aspects. The rule, "Do unto others as thou wouldst be done to" has long been a tenet of Hinduism; people are to behave kindly and generously and thereby encourage others to do the same.

During that remarkable period of cultural development throughout the ancient world—approximately the fifth century BC—significant new texts marked the beginnings of modern Hinduism. Collectively these are known as the Upanishads ("The Equivalences"). It is in these writings that the concept is introduced of an individual soul (*atman*) that is at one with the universal soul (*brahman*). In some contrast to Vedic polytheism, the Upanishads speak of a single reality and a single god who, nevertheless, has numerous aspects or godheads (Brahma, Shiva, Vishnu). Gradually, the ideas offered in the Upanishads provided the basis for a Hindu faith that proved more accessible and attractive to a broader constituency. The popularity of Hinduism further increased with the appearance of Mahabharata (The Great Epics), one of which has become widely read by Westerners as well: Bhagavad-gita (Celestial Song). Among later texts, the Tantras (Sacred Books) have been influential. As a living tradition, Hinduism has continued to foster articulate thinkers with the capacity to act on their beliefs, such as Rabindranath Tagore and Mahatma Gandhi.

Death and Afterlife in Hinduism

Through death, Hindus believe, one hopes to achieve liberation (*modsha*). This is an ecstatic union with *Brahman,* the universal soul: "That which is without beginning and ending . . . and unchanging—one is freed from the jaws of death." To be liberated both from earthly life and from the terror of death, one must experience a searing self-transformation, become, in effect, a burnt sacrifice. It is in this way that the type of incandescent self-knowledge necessary for the passage through death can be achieved. One does not attain this self-knowledge through long study and discipline, nor is it a supernatural or miraculous event. Reason, always subject to doubt, does not suffice, nor does blind faith. One must experience Brahman directly; one must become Brahman through knowing Brahman. Put in a different way—one must taste of immortality before death, and this can occur only through a transforming sense of self-knowledge that is like no other form of knowledge.

The lives we lead on earth are crucial for determining the nature of our afterlives. Hinduism, therefore, tends to emphasize ways of living rather than the details or attractions of the hereafter. As Swami Adiswarananda (1986, p. 182) phrases it, "One who has had no 'here' will have no hereafter." However, Hinduism does hold that rebirth follows death. Our lives are not snuffed out forever; therefore, one should not be slave to the terror of annihilation. Nevertheless, it would be foolish to expect that our physical bodies will join us in the next cycle; the continuity is of a spiritual nature. Immortality is an inherent potential of all human souls, regardless of race or creed (notwithstanding the traditional Hindu caste system; note also that there is no clear scriptural support for the practice of *Sati* or suttee).

The thoughtful person will not try to hide from the reality of death by tricks of thought or elusive actions. Death is as fundamental as life, indeed together they are part of a single reality. When assailed by fearful thoughts, one can bear in mind that we have all passed successfully through other separations, beginning with the moment of birth. Tagore writes, "I was not aware of the moment when I first crossed the threshold of this life. . . . When in the morning I looked upon the light I felt in a moment that I was no stranger in this world, that the inscrutable without name and form had taken . . . the form of my mother. Even so, in death the same unknown will appear as ever known to me. And because I love this life, I know I shall love death as well" (cited by Rao, 1974, p. 165).

Hinduism also has a place for a more activist orientation, as in Gandhi's resolve to set all metaphysical speculation and all personal sorrow aside and see to his duty on earth. Since one need not fear death and should not give in to incapacitating grief, it is good to use one's time and energies in the service of those who suffer in this life.

See also Suttee (*Sati*).

—ROBERT KASTENBAUM

References

Adiswarananda, Swami (1986). "Hinduism." In C.J. Johnson & M.G. McGee (Eds.) *Encounters with eternity.* New York: Philosophical Library, pp. 157–84.

Holck, F.H. (Ed.) (974). *Death and Eastern thought.* Nashville: Abingdon Press.

Macnicol, N. (Ed.) (1938). *Hindu scriptures.* London: J.M. Dent.

Radhakrishnan, S. (1948). *The Bhagavadgita.* London: Allen & Unwin.

Radhakrishnan, S. (1953). *The principal Upanishads.* London: Allen & Unwin.

Rao, K.L.S. (1974). "Modern Hindu thought." In F.H. Holck (Ed.) *Death and Eastern thought.* Nashville: Abingdon Press, pp. 164–97.

Renou, L. (Ed.) (1952). *Hinduism.* New York: George Braziller.

SURVIVAL BELIEFS AND PRACTICES: ISLAMIC

Beliefs about life after death in Islam are a blending of scriptural narrative, the elaboration of tradition, the conclusions of theologians, and the hopes and fears expressed by popular piety. Although there is occasional disagreement about detail, on the whole the picture is quite clear and the expectation commonly shared.

Essential to the understanding of the Islamic view of resurrection and continuing life after death is the recognition of the absolute power and authority of God over the events of human life and the flow of time and history. Each life is ordained by God to last a certain number of days and years and no human act or will can change that. Likewise the span of history from the creation to the end of time is set and sure, its extent known to God alone.

The two earliest messages of the Qur'an (Koran), believed to be God's word revealed through the Prophet Muhammad to his community in seventh century Arabia, are of God's oneness and the reality of the day of resurrection. For the Muslim, to acknowledge the oneness or integratedness of the divine is to devote oneself to living a life of integrity, of moral and ethical responsibility. And it is strictly in terms of the way one lives and the degree to which God's commandments for human behavior are heeded, says the Qur'an, that individual judgment will be accorded on the day of resurrection. Thus human behavior is linked to the recognition of the being of God, and the deeds of this life bear fruit specifically and directly in the next.

The afterlife in Islamic understanding has two points of reference: the time immediately after individual death until the events of the day of resurrection, and the final passing away of time after the resurrection, final judgment, and consignment to abodes of reward or punishment. The first of these, called the time of waiting or **barzakh** (referring to the barrier separating the living from the dead), is not discussed in any detail in the Qur'an. It has, however, engaged the imagination of the Muslims over the centuries, and many traditions have circulated that describe the pleasures and torments of those waiting in their graves. With graphic and sometimes startling detail these narratives serve to underscore the basic point that the one who has lived a good and moral life on earth will enjoy pleasant circumstances in the interim before the resurrection, while the lapsed or sinful individual will experience anything from unpleasantness to severe tribulation in the grave. Descriptive in effect, the function of this material has been didactic and homiletic.

The Qur'an has much more to say about the events that comprise the narrative of the coming of the eschaton than about the waiting period. These events can be organized into a logical sequence, although the Qur'an itself does not present them in quite that way. First is that series of earthly phenomena that will signal the beginning of the end of time. The natural order will be disrupted by the occurrence of such cataclysmic happenings as the heavens splitting apart, the earth being rent, the mountains set moving and the seas boiling. Preceding these natural disasters will be a parallel disruption of the moral order. This ethical and cosmic upheaval is the first act of the drama of the final day and the signal that resurrection is at hand.

At this point, the souls of all persons who have ever lived are reunited with their bodies in the graves and are brought to life again by God. This resurrection, which is both physical and spiritual, begins the process by which human beings are called to an accounting of their earthly deeds. It is generally believed that the first mortal to be raised will be the Prophet Muhammad. After the resurrection, say the medieval manuals of eschatology, individuals will wait in terror for the execution of judgment. In one of the most graphic descriptions of the Qur'anic narrative the righteous are given the records of their earthly deeds in their right hands and the ungodly are given their records in their left hands. The consequences of this distinction are clear, and after an elaboration of the judgment process through which such modalities as the balance scale (*mizan*) on which deeds are weighed and the bridge (*sirat*) over which only the righteous can walk with ease, the final consignment is made.

Descriptions of the two eternal abodes—the garden (*jannah*) of paradise and the fire (*nar*) of punishment—are frequent and graphic in the Qur'an. Sometimes presented as single realms and sometimes as multiple and graduated, these habitations are clearly intended to reward or punish in very specific and uncompromising ways. The flames of the fire crackle

and roar; its fierce boiling waters, scorching wind and smoke burn and stifle. By contrast, the inhabitants of the garden enjoy fruits and cool drink, pleasant shade and gentle speech, and wear robes of the finest silk. All desires are provided for, and the ultimate promise is that one will be in the presence of God.

This fairly straightforward narrative of the events of the last day has engendered a number of questions from members of the Islamic community. Are the joys and punishments of the respective abodes physical or spiritual in nature, or both? The consensus is that they are both, and that resurrection of the bodies is meant in a literal sense. Is there anyone to intercede for those who were misled in life into false behavior? This issue is complex, and while the Qur'an seems to say no, the traditions are full of references to the Prophet Muhammad interceding on behalf of his community, and even to God himself acting as intercessor for those on whom he has mercy.

The very question of the relationship of God's mercy to his justice has ramifications for the understanding of the final determination of one's station in eternity. Is the fire an eternal habitation, as the Qur'an seems to suggest, or will it pass away when souls (and bodies) have been properly punished? Many have concluded that after a period of purgation, God, in his infinite mercy, will extinguish the fires of damnation and will draw back all of his community, the faithful and the faithless alike, to remain eternally in his presence.

The overall picture of life after death in the Islamic understanding thus serves both as a comfort to the bereaved and as a challenge to the community to live lives of integrity and responsibility, with the sure knowledge that the fruits of today's labor will be enjoyed in the hereafter and that both justice and mercy will prevail in the life to come.

See also Barzakh.

—JANE I. SMITH

References

Ecklund, R. (1941). *Life between death and resurrection according to Islam.* Uppsala: Wiksells Boytryckeri-A.B.

El-Saleh, S. (1971). *La vie future selon le Coran.* Paris: Librarie Philosophique J. Vrin.

Evrin, M.S. (1960). *Eschatology in Islam.* Istanbul: Institute of Advanced Islamic Studies.

Gardet, L. (1967). *Dieu et la destinee de l'homme.* Paris: Librarie Philosophique J. Vrin.

Makino, S. (1970). *Creation and termination.* Tokyo: Keio Institute of Cultural and Linguistic Studies.

O'Shaughnessy, T. (1969). *Muhammad's thoughts on death.* Leiden: E.J. Brill.

Smith, J.I. & Haddad, Y.Y. (1981). *The Islamic understanding of death and resurrection.* Albany, NY: State University of New York Press.

Watts, W.M. (1948). *Free will and predestination in early Islam.* London: Luzac.

SURVIVAL BELIEFS AND PRACTICES: JEWISH

There is no fixed definition of the terms most closely associated with survival beliefs and practices that has been totally acceptable to all Jewish thinkers in any given historical era. These include the two key concepts of the Messiah and resurrection as well as a wide variety of other terms that have been used to denote life after death, such as a world to come, the end of days, and the days of Messiah. Often the terms are vague or abstruse; at times they flow into one another. Although the teachings of the talmudic sages are linked to verses in the Pentateuch (especially the Book of Daniel), they are interpreted in divergent ways by rabbis. The differences of opinion—some very fundamental—often reach wholly antiethical conclusions that imply the complete negation of one doctrine by another. Even the medieval sages who articulated their beliefs in a highly systematic manner did not reach accord among themselves. The debate has become even more vehement since the Jewish enlightenment of the eighteenth century.

In this regard, the advice of George Foote Moore (1954, p. 389) is appropriate: "Any attempt to systematize the Jewish notions of the hereafter imposes upon them an order and consistency which does not exist in them . . . . their religious significance lies in the definitive establishment of the doctrine of retribution after death, not in the ways in which men imagined it."

An apt illustration of the murkiness of some of the concepts is *She'ol.* In Genesis (38:35 and 44:31) She'ol denotes the final abode of the dead. Eventually it came to mean the final abode of all humankind. It is difficult to pin down exactly what is meant by *She'ol,* but it generally implies only a place where the dead lead a shadowy existence, a netherworld.

Remarkably, however, despite the lack of clarity of these concepts, Jews for centuries held them to be incontrovertible, fundamental, even undeniable as an article of faith. Maimonides, in the thirteenth century, held that the twin concepts of Messiah and physical resurrection were among the thirteen basic beliefs. In the fourteenth century, Hasdai Crescas revised Maimonides' formulation of the basic truths but still kept immortality as one of them. Resurrection remained a cardinal belief in the fifteenth century when Simon ben Zemah Duran reduced the basic number to three. Still later, philosopher Joseph Albo revised the basic concepts again but also retained immortality as fundamental to the faith.

In Nazi Germany, hundreds of thousands of Jews, packed in cattle-cars headed for the crematoria, sang the old hymn, "I Believe in the Coming of the Messiah." Philosopher Hermann Cohen has observed that "If the Jewish religion had done nothing more for mankind than proclaim the Messianic idea of the Old Testament prophets, it could have claimed to be the bedrock of all the world's ethical culture" (cited by Levinthal, 1935). Even those who in contemporary times reject the after-death beliefs still retain a faith in the immortality of the soul.

Despite the unwavering stability of these ideas, the preponderance of Jews today do not understand these concepts, let alone appreciate their history. This may be a lingering effect of the efforts made by postemancipation rationalist Jewish philosophers in their rebellion against ancient and medieval thinking. They convinced many that the sole emphasis of Judaism is on this-worldliness, not sullied or compromised by metaphysical ruminations of a hereafter in any form.

Surveying the major thinkers, however, one can say with confidence that the vast majority of Jews in every age have believed in survival, in some form of life after death, whether this be the Messiah, the resurrection of the physical body, or only the immortality of the soul.

The Messiah

The generic term *Messiah* means "anointed one." Kings and priests were anointed in ancient times to set them apart from the common person. This specialness was also applied to the spiritual leadership of a descendant of the house of David, and anointed by God. The anointed one will bring redemption to this world. It will then be a time of true bliss, unparalleled in our own existence. It will not be a new world, a qualitatively different world—rather, it will be this world brought to perfection. Universal peace, tranquility, lawfulness, and goodness will prevail, and all will acknowledge the unity and lordship of God.

The traditional outlook of Judaism is that the Messiah will be the dominating figure of an age of universal peace and plenty. Through a restored Israel, he will bring about the spiritual regeneration of humanity, when all will blend into one brotherhood to perform righteousness with a perfect heart: "On that day the Lord shall be One, and his name One" (Zechariah 14:9). Jewish prayers are replete with references to the messianic hopes and aspirations. There is hardly a prophet of note who does not mention the Messiah and the messianic age.

Will the Messiah be a specific person, or will he only represent an era of perfection—*yemot ha'Mashiach,* the "days of the Messiah?" Traditional Judaism believes in the coming of a flesh-and-blood mortal sent expressly by God to complete the mission of His people. The traditional belief is that people must strive to better the world and by these efforts help bring on the Messiah. The personal Messiah, supernaturally introduced to humanity, will not be a divine personality as in Christianity. He will herald a redemption granted by God, but Messiah will have no ability to fabricate that redemption himself. He will have no miraculous powers; he will not be able to atone for the sins of others; he will have no superhuman relationship to God. Instead, he will be an exalted personality of incomparable ability who will begin the rehabilitation of the Jewish people and the subsequent regeneration of all humanity.

Some theologians have disputed the idea of a supernatural introduction of the Messiah and the whole idea of a personal Messiah. However, there does stand a two-millenia tradition that affirms this position—despite the rational analyses, let alone the metaphysical misgivings of sophisticated contemporary theologians.

Resurrection

The doctrine of Israel's messianic redemption is integrally entwined with that of resurrection. The belief that God "will open your graves and bring you out of the graves" (Ezekiel 37:12) is presumed throughout the Bible, expressing itself through figures of speech and metaphors that imply the power of God and even the power of the prophets to revive the dead. It is most eloquently expressed by Ezekiel in his vision of the Valley of the Dry Boncs.

During the second commonwealth, the belief in the resurrection, the body, in contradistinction to the immortality of the soul, became a fundamental of Pharisee belief. By the time of its redaction, the Mishnah records: "He who says there is no resurrection of the dead will have no share in the world to come" (Sanhedrim 10:1). Maimonides codified this as a never-to-be-denied component of the faith.

There is a clear difference between the doctrines of resurrection and immortality of the soul. Resurrection refers to the return of the soul to the resuscitated body. It is based on the idea of the unity of body and soul. However, the doctrine of the soul's immortality is based on the Hellenistic antithesis between body and soul. The body shrivels, but the soul is liberated from its imprisonment in the flesh and remains immortal.

A cluster of uniquely Jewish concepts emerge from this understanding of resurrection. A human being's ultimate destiny is not in his or her hands alone, by virtue of his or her immortal soul. It is an act of God's mercy to revive humans after they have slept in the dust. Judaism does not address a disembodied soul, but a whole person; salvation is not a private enterprise, but a corporate redemption of all humans. The body has value as a creation of God, and not only as a housing for the spirit: life on earth has value.

Conclusion

Jews have long had an abiding faith in a world beyond the grave (Lamm, 1969). The conviction in a life after death—unprovable but unshakable—has been cherished since the beginning of thinking humanity's life on earth. It makes its appearance in religious literature not as commanded irrevocably by an absolute god, but as though it has been growing and developing naturally in the soul. The belief then sprouts forth through prayer and hymn. Only later does it become extrapolated in complicated metaphysical speculation.

The afterlife has not been "thought up." It is not a rational construction of a religious philosophy that has been imposed on believers. It has sprung from within the hearts of masses of men and women, a sort of *consensus genium*, inside out, a hope beyond and above the rational, a longing for the warm sun of eternity. On this view, the afterlife is not a theory to be proven logically or demonstrated by rational analysis. It is axiomatic. It is to the soul what oxygen is to the lungs.

See also Kaddish; National Institute for Jewish Hospice.

—MAURICE LAMM

References

Birnbaum, P. (1964). *A book of Jewish concepts.* New York: Hebrew Publishing.
Jacobs, L. (1964). *Principles of the Jewish faith.* New York: Basic Books.
Lamm, M. (1969). *The Jewish way in death and mourning.* New York: Jonathan David.
Levinthal, I.H. (1935). *Judaism, an analysis and an interpretation.* New York: Funk & Wagnalls.
Moore, G.F. (1954). *Judaism.* Vol. 2. Cambridge, MA: Harvard University Press.
Urbach, E.E. (1979). *The sages: Their concepts and beliefs.* Jerusalem: Magnes Press.
Weiss-Rosmarin, T. (1972). *Judaism and Christianity: The differences.* New York: The Jewish Book Club.

SURVIVAL BELIEFS AND PRACTICES: ROMAN CATHOLIC

Historical Perspective

The first Christians comprised "a small group in the midst of what it regarded as a largely hostile world" (Best, 1985, p. 169). Set apart from other religions by a number of their beliefs and practices, the early Christians were often subjected to suspicion and ridicule. The Roman Empire did not engage in systematic persecution, but it did disapprove of the new cult's rejection of existing religious and civic practices and sporadically investigated alleged improper activities (Wilken, 1984). This small "fringe" group not only survived, but became the foundation for one of the world's most influential and enduring religions. Beliefs regarding death and the afterlife were significant aspects of the Christian outlook on life from the very beginning.

Death and the Afterlife: Basic Conception

As the first codification of the Christian view of death and the afterlife, the Roman Catholic doctrine has provided a model followed more or less closely by other denominations. There are some differences to be noted, but the similarities deserve first consideration.

The Old Testament most often touches upon death as the inevitable end of life. Examples include:

> He cometh forth like a flower, and is cut down: he fleeth also as a shadow, and continueth not. . . . As the waters fail from the sea, and the flood decayeth

and drieth up: So shall man lieth down and riseth not. . . . the grave is mine house: I have made my bed in the darkness. I have said to corruption, Thou art my father: to the worm, Thou art my mother and my sister... (Job 14:2; 17:13).

What man is he that liveth, and shall not see death?

. . . . As for man, his days are as grass: as a flower of the field, so he flourisheth. For the wind passeth over it, and it is gone; and the place thereof shall know it no more (Psalms 89; 103).

Those seeking a doctrine of future life in the Old Testament can point to a few statements such as:

The King of the universe will raise us up to an everlasting renewal of life, because we have died for his laws (Macc. 7:11).

And many of them that sleep in the dust of the earth shall awake, some to everlasting life, and some to shame and ever-lasting contempt (Dan. 12:2).

Relying largely upon the Old Testament, those of the Jewish faith have not expressed the widespread affirmation of afterlife that became characteristic of Christianity. The New Testament provides a richer source of scriptural authority for belief in survival after death. Some examples include:

And this is the will of him that sent me, that every one which seeth the Son, and believeth on him, may have everlasting life: and I will raise him up at the last day (John 5:39).

But now being made free from sin, and become servants to God, ye have your fruit unto holiness, and the end everlasting life. For the wages of sin is death; but through the gift of God is eternal life through Jesus Christ our Lord (Rom. 6:22).

For he that soweth to his flesh shall of the flesh reap corruption; but he that soweth to the Spirit shall of the Spirit reap life everlasting (Gal. 6:8).

The underlying philosophy is dualistic, e.g., there is both a physical and a spiritual reality. The body must surely die, being subject to the limitations of its physical nature. But the soul is immortal and can survive the death of its body. This concept had been in the air for some time, and was quite familiar to the Persians and Greeks. Nevertheless, the new Christian version had a character and appeal of its own. Christ raising the dead, Christ on the cross, and Christ arisen from the tomb were among the powerful images that brought a passion and immediacy not to be found in abstract philosophical discourse. Along with its vision of God the Father (no longer but one of many deities as worshipped, for example, by the Romans), there was the compelling account of the Son of God and his sacrifice on behalf of all humanity. Teaching love, kindness, and understanding, Christ had undergone a terrible ordeal at the hands of other men. His triumph over death demonstrated the mercy and power of a supreme God who cared about the human condition.

The life and death of Christ provides a sublime model for all Christians. In the Catholic view, eternal life is a gift from a merciful God, but faith in Christ and triumph over sin and temptation are also indispensable. The joyful prospect of eternal life is tempered by realization that eternal punishment is also a possibility. The impenitent sinner will not escape punishment. "It is clear that there is a strong body of New Testament evidence pointing in the direction of a continuing punishment . . . (although) God does all that can be done for man's salvation. . . . That there is a dread reality Scripture leaves us in no doubt" (Morris, 1967, pp. 196–97).

Punishment and Purgatory

It is in connection with the punishment doctrine that the Roman Catholic Church specifies a condition that has not been accepted by most other branches of the Christian faith. Purgatory (bearing some resemblance to the older conception of Hades) is an intermediate place or condition between Heaven and Hell. Literally, it is where the soul that has succumbed to temptation must be cleansed (purged) of its sins. Purgatorial fire was vividly discussed by Augustine in the fifth century AD, but did not become an established Catholic doctrine until the thirteenth century. Over the years there were numerous specific versions of Purgatory that can be correlated with other beliefs and cultural-political developments of the time (Le Goff, 1984).

Political circumstances contributed to the new salience given to the Purgatory doctrine in the sixteenth century. The Renaissance popes had made Rome a glittering center for the renewal of the arts. Many of the world's enduring artistic treasures were created through papal commissions. In this and in other ways, the Church spent itself into serious difficulties. Hard-pressed for money, Pope Leo X chose to sell indulgences on an unprecedented scale. This practice was criticized by many within the Church, but without effect. For many Catholics, the most objectionable aspect of Pope Leo X's marketing of indulgences was his revival of a practice introduced by Pope Sixtus IV in 1476: souls held captive in Purgatory could have their terms of suffering reduced if their relatives purchased indulgences and commissioned prayers and masses (Tuchman, 1984). Purgatory had become an instrument of fundraising. The common people as well as many aristocrats and priests were enraged by this maneuver. At the height of this fundraising campaign (1517), Martin Luther nailed his 95 theses on the church door at Wittenberg, and soon the Protestant movement had become a major rival to the Roman Catholic establishment. Trying to raise money by releasing the dead from Purgatory was not the fundamental cause of the great schism, but it was one of the "last straws" that fell upon a populace already distressed by a Church establishment that seemed to have elevated temporal priorities over the spiritual. Reform did gather strength within the Church, but not until the Protestant alternative had risen to its feet.

The Purgatory doctrine has had a number of significant effects. As Purgatory became a more accepted and influential doctrine, it provided "the function of a prison for suffering souls" (Le Goff, p. 293), thereby keeping such spirits from disturbing the living. Another effect was the intensification of interest in making use of the confessional. By sincere confession and repentance, one might reduce the likelihood of consignment to Purgatory. The fear of Purgatory might also enable the devout to overcome the temptation of

committing sins in the first place. Still another effect was the heightened interest in precisely how one's life comes to an end. The deathbed scene and the dying process in general became of particular importance from the moral standpoint (See also **Deathbed Scenes; Memento Mori, Tame Death**).

Among other distinctive facets of Roman Catholic belief and practice is the utilization of saints for consolation and intermediation. Prayers to a particular saint may take many forms and have many objectives which include but are not limited to supplications regarding one's own death and afterlife and the status of deceased loved ones.

Many have found consolation and inspiration from the Roman Catholic approach to death and the afterlife. Even those who do not share the faith have been moved by the beauty of sacred music, cathedrals, and other works of art inspired by Catholicism, as well as by the examples of piety, charity, and courage demonstrated by many believers.

The emphasis here upon death and afterlife should not lead us to neglect the relevance of Catholic teachings for the living of daily life (e.g., Newman, 1949; Smith, 1949). The devout Catholic has available a rich tradition that invites one to look beyond the tribulations and limitations of everyday life and to find meaning, consolation, and challenge in his or her living heritage.

See also Deathbed Scenes; Extreme Unction; *Memento Mori*; Survival Beliefs and Practices: Jewish; Tame Death.

—ROBERT KASTENBAUM

References

Best, E. (1985). "Church". In P.J. Achtemeier (Ed.) *Harper's bible dictionary.* New York: Harper & Row, pp. 168–70.

Le Goff, J. (1984). *The birth of purgatory.* Chicago: University of Chicago Press.

Morris, L. (1967). "Eternal punishment". In E.F. Harrison, G.W. Bromiley, & C.F.H. Henry (Eds.) *Baker's dictionary of theology.* Grand Rapids: Baker Book House, pp. 196–97.

Newman, J.H., Cardinal (1949). *Sermons and discourses (1825–39).* New York: Longmans, Green.

Nickelsburg, G.W.E. (1972). *Resurrection, immortality, and eternal life in intertestamental Judaism.* Cambridge, MA: Harvard University Press.

Rahner, K. (1966). *Theological investigations. Vol. IV: More recent writings.* Baltimore: Helicon Press.

Smith, G.D. (1949). *The teaching of the Catholic Church.* Vols. I & II. New York: Macmillan.

Stendahl, K. (1965). *Immortality and resurrection.* New York: Macmillan.

Tuchman, B.W. (1984). *The march of folly.* New York: Alfred A. Knopf.

Wilken, R.L. (1984). *The Christians as the Romans saw them.* New Haven and London: Yale University Press.

SURVIVAL BELIEFS AND PRACTICES: SEVENTH-DAY ADVENTIST

The Protestant Seventh-Day Adventists denomination, which had its beginnings in the northeastern United States in 1844, has since grown to an international movement with a worldwide membership of nearly five million. Throughout their history Seventh-Day Adventists have maintained distinctive beliefs concerning the state of the dead. These beliefs are inseparable from their doctrine concerning the nature of man, which they believe is the teaching of the Bible.

Humans are composed of a physical body and a mysterious life force from God, who created them (Genesis 2:7), but as conscious individuals they are unitary entities. They are said not to *have* souls but to *be* living souls. The spirit that animates humans must be regarded as an impersonal force, for the individual human being does not preexist his or her creation and birth. When the spirit is withdrawn the human being dies and ceases to be "a living soul." There is no intrinsic conscious entity that survives death, and death is a condition of total unconsciousness in the grave. "For the living know that they will die, but the dead know nothing, and they have no more reward; for the memory of them is lost" (Ecclesiastes 9:5).

Seventh-Day Adventists do not place their hope of survival after death upon any inherent immortality in humans, but, in accordance with their understanding of the Bible, their hope is placed upon a gracious act of God, namely, the resurrection of the dead at the eschaton. The final resurrection will be of the whole person, i.e., corporeal, but the resurrected bodies of believers will be glorified (I Corinthians 15). The resurrection will occur in two phases: a first resurrection of the righteous to eternal life, and a second resurrection of the impenitent wicked to judgment (Daniel 12:2; John 5:28–29). The first resurrection accompanies the second coming of Christ, which inaugurates the millennium. The second resurrection occurs at the end of the millennium (I Thessalonians 4:13–17; Revelation 20). The wicked are raised only to undergo judgment, after which they are annihilated in Gehenna, the "lake of fire." This means that "Hell" will not be an unending torment, but, rather, a final, cleansing destruction in which evil will perish. "Heaven" as the place where God and the righteous dwell will ultimately move to this earth, after it has been purified in the cleansing fire (2 Peter 3:10–13; Revelation 20, 21).

An individual's ultimate fate depends upon his or her relationship with God and His Christ. A saving relationship is one of faith, manifest in loving obedience to God's will made known, producing a character pleasing in His sight. The infinite mind of God marks well and remembers all such righteous people, and plans that they shall rise to be with Him eternally.

Seventh-Day Adventists have no distinctive funeral practice but adapt those of any culture to their theology. They do not, however, favor funerary extravagance.

—ROBERT M. JOHNSTON

References

Bible readings for the home (1949). Mountain View, CA: Pacific Press, pp. 491–528.

Johnston, R.M. (1986). "Seventh-day Adventist Church." In C.J. Johnson & M. G. McGee (Eds.) *Encounters with eternity.* New York: Philosophical Library, 277–92.

Provonsha, J. (1981). *Is death for real? An examination of reported near-death experiences in the light of the resurrection.* Mountain View, CA: Pacific Press.

Seventh-Day Adventists answer questions on doctrine (1957). Washington, DC: Review and Herald.

SURVIVAL BELIEFS AND PRACTICES: UNITED METHODIST

United Methodist beliefs about death and life after death are similar to those of most mainline Protestants, and the central practice which expresses such beliefs is the Christian funeral. In addition to this service, the sacraments of Baptism and Holy Communion, pastoral care, and Christian proclamation are used to symbolize and teach the Christian faith regarding death and life after death, to prepare believers for the reality of death, and to comfort the bereaved.

Bases of Beliefs

The belief in life after death is based upon the scriptural witness to the resurrection of Jesus Christ and upon Christ's promise of eternal life to those who follow him. It is also supported by tradition, personal experience, and reason. The Apostles' Creed, the Nicene Creed, and the Korean Creed affirm, respectively: "(I believe) . . . in the resurrection of the body and the life everlasting." "And I look for the resurrection of the dead, and the life of the world to come." "We believe in the eternal triumph of righteousness, and in the life everlasting" (*Methodist Hymnal*, 1964, pp. 738, 739, 741). Eternal life begins and can be experienced when it is received by the believer, and it is symbolized by baptism (where the believer is buried with Christ, dies to sin, and rises to life abundant). Reason is used by United Methodists not to prove the reality of life after death but to point to its validity and to express its importance.

The Funeral Service

United Methodist beliefs and practices regarding death and life after death come together in the funeral service. Here death is acknowledged as real. The use of euphemisms such as "sleeping" is discouraged, grief and loss are addressed, and the distinction between resurrection and immortality is emphasized. Human existence is not seen to be immortal by nature. Rather, the Christian funeral service proclaims that Jesus Christ triumphs over death, that Jesus defeats the enemy, death. This basic teaching both comforts the bereaved at the service and confronts all present with their own finitude. The funeral service concludes with a committal of the body to the ground, sea, or crematorium, reminding the mourners of the transience of temporal life. The committing of the soul to God proclaims God's everlasting love and care. A memorial service differs from a funeral service in that at a memorial service the body is not usually present.

A significant part of both services is that of naming. The services rightly center on the proclamation of God's gifts of earthly and eternal life, but it is quite appropriate to name the deceased, to recall the goodness of the deceased as an example to those present, and to commend the soul of the deceased to God's eternal love.

The funeral or memorial service reinforces the communal nature of Christian faith. It normally takes place amid the community of faith, preferably in a church building where Christian symbols and associations with religious experiences are present. Just as at Baptism when the believer became a part of the church on earth, so after death he or she becomes a part of the church in heaven, according to Methodist faith.

> One family we dwell in him,
> One Church above, beneath,
> Though now divided by the stream,
> The narrow stream of death;
> One army of the living God,
> To his command we bow;
> Part of his host have crossed the flood,
> And part are crossing now.
> (*Methodist Hymnal,* p. 302).

Resurrection of the Body

The essential Methodist belief regarding life after death (expressed in creeds, hymns, the "Articles of Religion," and the "Confession of Faith") is located in the phrase, "resurrection of the body." This belief affirms that just as the whole, real person (body, mind, spirit) dies, so does the whole person rise to eternal life. The risen body is, to be sure, a "spiritual body" and will differ from one's earthly body, but it is the same, recognizable person who is resurrected. There is continuity between one's earthly life and one's life after death, and the deepest relationships on earth (between the believer and God and between the believer and others) will not be negated but fulfilled in the life everlasting.

Generally speaking, United Methodists reject the ideas of purgatory and transmigration of souls. These are seen to be in conflict on the one hand with reality and importance of human response in earthly life, and on the other hand with acknowledging the transience and finitude of earthly life. United Methodists are not dogmatic about details regarding the nature of heaven and the times of judgment (in this life, immediately after death, a last day judgment), and a wide diversity of expression is found among them. However, the core belief in the resurrection of the body and in the reality of life after death (in a recognizable, meaningful way) is a central affirmation of the United Methodist Church.

See also Funerals.

—JAMES I. WARREN, JR.

References

The book of discipline of the United Methodist Church. (1984). Nashville: The Methodist Publishing House.
Colaw, E. (1987). *Beliefs of a United Methodist Christian.* Nashville: Discipleship Resources.
Harrell, C.J. (1961). *Christian affirmations.* Nashville: Abingdon Press.
Johnson, C.J. & McGee, M.G. (Eds.) (1986). *Encounters with eternity.* New York: Philosophical Library.
The Methodist hymnal. (1964). Nashville: The Methodist Publishing House.
A service of death and resurrection (1979). Nashville: Abingdon Press.
Stokes, M.B. (1956). *Major Methodist beliefs.* Nashville: Abingdon Press.

SUTTEE *(SATI)*

Suttee is the English corruption of the Sanskrit term *Sati.* In the evolution of Hindu society in India and in the use of the term outside of India, distinctions between the origins and corruptions of terms, meanings, and practices are important.

The term *Sati* denotes a virtuous woman or a faithful, devoted wife. Timeless and selfless devotion was the classical expectation of the Hindu wife. The term Sati did not originally mean the forced cremation or self-immolation of widows. Early accretion of additional meaning occurred because Sati was also the name of the wife of the god Mahadeva. Mahadeva was another name of Shiva, just as Sati was another name for Durga or Devi in the evolution of Hindu mythology. In the ideals represented in the Hindu pantheon, Sati was the ideal wife. Sati's father was critical of Mahadeva because of his wild appearance and his meditations in strange places, including at cremations and funerals. Sati was utterly embarrassed by her father when he was publicly critical of Mahadeva at a gathering of the gods to which Mahadeva was not invited. Sati committed suicide at her father's place in defense of her husband's honor. This act provided a historic standard of devotion. Incidentally, when Mahadeva found out about Sati's death, he carried her body in mourning until it crumbled to earth.

Heroic Suicide in Hindu Culture

Heroic suicide was not a sin in the ideals of Hindu culture. There is not only Sati but also the epic Mahabharata in which the hero Bhisma selected the place and manner of his own death rather than defend in war against someone who had been a woman in a previous life. Aspects of this non-Christian conception of selfless suicide can be seen in the fasts of Mahatma Gandhi and the actions of various Hindu and Buddhist saints and heroes.

Hinduism is a broad umbrella that shades many different value systems. The *advaita vedanta* (nondualistic vedanta) philosophy would frown on inequality of caste, race, or sex. The best of the philosophical books, the Upanishads, implies the unity of all existence. A different tradition of inequality of caste and sex comes out of the Hindu law books including the Code of Manu. Exaggerations or corruptions of Manu can create further inequalities. However, neither Manu nor any other Hindu scripture calls for anything resembling what is called "Suttee"—the involuntary or quasi-voluntary death or self-immolation of a widow. Even the Rig Veda's early solitary reference to a widow's duty is hardly a clear order for immolation; it simply admonishes a widow to rise from beside her dead husband's body. Vedantic philosophy and reform has continued to be an antidote to the inequalities defined by Manu.

It is clear, then, that voluntary suicide out of devotion or principle was not a sin. However, voluntary and involuntary suicide of widows and other inequalities occurred in early India, increased in medieval times, declined after the work of Hindu reform movements and English legislation in the nineteenth century, and occasionally occurs in parts of contemporary India.

Early Greek accounts following Alexander's invasion of northern India refer to the suicides of the widows of tribal chieftains. In India, as well as elsewhere in the world, many early tribal groups believed in the timeless bonding of families—including their animals. Voluntary suicide was admired by some. But the corruption of the ideal also occurred in the nexus of the forces of sexism, greed, and the economic realities of widowhood. The plight of the widow remains unsolved even today in many societies. Members of ruling clans and castes provided moral support for Sati at varying times in India, including the sixth and seventh centuries AD. Brahmins were known to provide their blessings in the fifteenth and sixteenth centuries in the southern empire of Vijaynagar. Heroic voluntary versions of Sati exist in Indian history. When in 1301 the Moslem conqueror Alauddin successfully stormed the fortress of Chitor defended by Rajput leaders Gora and Badal, the widows burned themselves in an enclosure before the conquerors entered.

Corruptions of Sati continued to develop. The line between voluntary and involuntary immolation was crossed in many cases. Crowd behavior, expectations of inheritance, anger over a modest dowry or contributions of a wife's family to the marriage, dislike of a widow, and unwillingness to care for a widow were some of the forces at work. In some isolated cases even

Muslim widows influenced by dominant Hindu customs were subjected to Sati. This tradition was not without opposition. Islamic emperors often condemned Sati. Aurangzeb in 1663 proclaimed his opposition to Sati. However, there was minimal enforcement during Islamic rule.

Under English Rule

The coming of English rule in the eighteenth century did little to stop the corruptions of Sati. English rule initially meant a generally benevolent neutrality in religious and social matters—the English preferred to concentrate on economics and geopolitics. Then in the 1820s a reform movement began, particularly in the eastern province of Bengal where about 500 cases of Sati occurred per year. On the Indian side the reform movement was led by Raja Ram Mohan Roy who not only opposed Sati but also later started the Brahmo Sanraj movement as an antidote to the dualistic caste aspects of Hinduism. On the English side there was support from Lord William Bentinck, the governor general. Early English reforms began with legislation against infanticide (1802) and the Sati of minors and pregnant women (1812, 1817). Some orthodox Hindu leaders opposed reform. Roy's life was threatened by some of the supporters of Raja Radha Kanta Deb. Roy persisted with his own reform efforts, however, and also endorsed those of Lord Bentinck.

In 1829 England instituted a statute against involuntary Sati and any aid for voluntary Sati. Bentinck's work was followed by continued support from the subsequent governor general, the first Lord Hardinge. Domestic support continued to be provided by Hindu reform groups. In addition to the abolition of Sati, reform groups expanded their commitment to include the remarriage of widows.

England ruled India through a dual system. Much of India received direct English rule while the governance of at least a third of the nation was delegated to Indian princes. The decline of Sati clearly occurred in areas of direct English rule such as Bengal. It remained tenuous in the princely states. Interestingly, some of the flareups of the practice of Sati in the late twentieth century have occurred in the princely states with martial traditions. However, what centuries ago was an elitist tradition has in its later versions known no boundaries of caste.

Strengthening the Rights of Women

In a still largely patriarchal and patrilineal society, brutality against women does occur in spite of the march of rights. But not all is Sati. Cruelty against wives over dowry or inheritance is different from Sati. Nondualistic vedanta traditions and reform movements continue to work on strengthening the rights of women.

Involuntary or voluntary Sati is the rare exception today, rather than the rule. But the true Sati—the heroic devotion and voluntary death for principle—remains as a trapped ideal in some orthodox circles of Hindu society.

See also Survival Beliefs and Practices: Hindu.

—JOYOTPAUL CHAUDHURI

References

Basham, A.L. (Ed.) (1975). *A cultural history of India.* Oxford: Clarendon Press.
Majundar, R.C., Raychaudhuri, H.C., & Daiita, K. (1967). *An advanced history of India.* New York: St. Martin's Press.

T

TAME DEATH

In *The Hour of Our Death* (1981), historian Philippe Aries offers an illuminating description and analysis of attitudes toward death over a period of approximately a thousand years. He draws upon rich and varied source materials: diaries, letters, wills and testaments, novels, poems, paintings, tomb sculpture, municipal reports. Most of his sources are European, although some attention is also given to the United States.

Aries proposes "tame death" as one of his major organizing concepts. In his view, for much of human history people met their death in a way that is difficult for us to imagine today because of our own emphasis on individual identity.

> The ancient attitude in which death is close and familiar yet diminished and desensitized is too different from our own view, in which it is so terrifying that we no longer dare say its name. Thus, when we call this familiar death the tame death, we do not mean that it was once wild and that it was later domesticated. On the contrary, we mean that is has become wild today when it used to be tame. The tame death is the oldest death there is. (Aries, p. 28)

In the traditional or tame death, the dying person knows that he or she is soon to die. The attitude is generally one of resignation to the inevitable. Whether death is to come as the result of illness, injury, or execution, the person conveys the impression of accepting this fate. There is no extravagant emotional scene, no protest. Often, if death does not come quickly after saying the last prayer or giving the last instructions, the person simply waits in silence for the end. In fact, "familiar simplicity" is seen by Aries as one of the essential characteristics of the tame death. The other major aspect was its public nature. From ancient times until the rise of self-conscious individuality, dying people were not avoided or isolated. The public side of the tame or familiar death was still manifest on some occasions through the late eighteenth and early nineteenth centuries despite complaints by "hygienically minded doctors" who complained about the number of people who "invaded the bedrooms of the dying" (Aries, p. 19). One can still find some modern survivals of the tame death tradition, but the increasingly individualistic orientation of Western society has made it ever more likely that a person will die alone in a hospital bed.

Some Implications

Aries' numerous examples do suggest that for many centuries people were more likely to end their lives in a death that was accepted as a natural and familiar part of the human experience. The phenomena of intense death anxiety, denial, and struggle can then be seen as a fairly recent development, as can the rejection of the dying person as somehow "dirty," "failed," or "frightening." This knowledge might raise some new questions about why death has become so anxiety-arousing and avoidant in modern times. Research on death anxiety and related topics might become more productive if lessons and hypotheses were drawn from the historical dimension as presented by Aries and others (Choron, 1963, 1964; Kastenbaum, 1988; Spencer,

1960). The neglected study of deathbed scenes in our own society might also be stimulated.

The hospice philosophy of care (not encompassed by Aries) embodies some of the earlier beliefs that the dying person is still part of the human community and that the last days of life can be natural, simple, and appropriate. It does not seem reasonable to expect that hospice or any other contemporary agency can recreate past attitudes that were intimately related to a very different social, philosophical, and technological world, but it might be possible to turn the tide against increasing the emotional suffering and isolation of the dying person.

See also Appropriate Death; Death Anxiety: Measures; Deathbed Scenes; Hospice: Philosophy and Practice; Tombs.

—ROBERT KASTENBAUM

References

Aries, P. (1981). *The hour of our death.* New York: Alfred A. Knopf.

Choron, J. (1963). *Death and Western thought.* New York: Collier Books.

Choron, J. (1964). *Modern man and mortality.* New York: Macmillan.

Kastenbaum, R. (1988). "Safe death in the postmodern world." In G. Gilmore (Ed.) *Safer death.* New York: Plenum, pp. 1–13.

Spencer, T. (1960). *Death and Elizabethan tragedy.* New York: Pageant Books.

THANATOLOGY

The study of death-related behaviors, thoughts, feelings, and phenomena is sometimes known as thanatology. The term was introduced by Elie Metchnikoff (1903), a distinguished life scientist and disciple of Louis Pasteur. One of the first eminent researchers to envision the development of gerontology and thanatology, Metchnikoff also provided the names for both new disciplines. Thanatology was derived from the Greek *Thanatos,* in mythology the twin of *Hypnos* (sleep). Roswell Park (1912) may have been the first to employ this term in the United States. Although gerontology has won almost universal acceptance as designation for the study of aging and the aged, thanatology has not been applied as consistently to death-related phenomena. Some researchers believe that the term *thanatology* has been too closely associated with theological and other nonempirical approaches; others have objected to the word itself as sounding too pretentious. There is no competitor as such to the term *thanatology.* The alternative has been to use the word *death* (as in death studies), or to specify the topic under consideration (e.g., funeral rituals, mortality rates, terminal care).

The topics encompassed by thanatology have come to the fore since the end of World War II. Existential philosophy provided one important current of stimulation and contributed to renewed interest in the problem of suicide. A suicide prevention movement of international scope was soon joined by studies of individual and cultural attitudes toward death. Important empirical investigations of grief and bereavement were conducted. New books and journals (See **Death Studies** and **Omega, Journal of Death and Dying**) provided the foundations for death education and further studies. A clinical and research literature that could be encompassed under the name of thanatology was well established by the end of the 1970s, and continues to grow. Legal and ethical problems now claim increasing attention, along with studies of hospice care and other supportive programs.

See also Death Studies; *Omega, Journal of Death and Dying.*

—ROBERT KASTENBAUM

References

Choron, J. (1963). *Death and Western thought.* New York: Colliers.

Metchnikoff, M.E. (1903). *The nature of man.* New York: G.P. Putnam & Sons.

Park, R. (1912). "Thanatology: A questionnaire and a plea for a neglected study." *Journal of the American Medical Association, 58:* 1243–46.

Pine, V.R. (1977) "A socio-historical portrait of death education." *Death Education, 1:* 57–84.

Pine, V.R. (1986) "The age of maturity for death education: A sociohistorical portrait of the era 1976–1985." *Death Education, 10:* 209–32.

"THANATOPSIS"

In 1817 *The North American Review* published a long poem that brought instant fame to its author and soon became one of the best known meditations on death and immortality in the English language. William Cullen Bryant (1794–1878) was only 17 when he wrote "Thanatopsis" (from the Greek: "a view of death"), and had become a man of letters by the time it appeared in print. Popular during his full and productive life, Bryant is still most closely associated with "Thanatopsis" in the minds of many readers.

Although it might be considered remarkable for a youth to write an impressive and enduring poem on the subject of death, in fact, young people often do think intensely on this subject and those with expressive gifts may create striking works of art. Among the other claims this poem may continue to exert on our interest is its masterfully wrought expression of concerns that a great many other young people have felt when sensing their mortality.

The opening lines establish a serene mood and a leisurely, reflective pace that suggest an unhurried stroll through a place of natural beauty:

> To him who in the love of nature holds
> Communion with her visible forms, she speaks
> A various language; for his gayer hours
> She has a voice of gladness, and a smile
> And eloquence of beauty; and she glides
> Into his darker musings, with a mild
> And healing sympathy that steals away
> Their sharpness ere he is aware.

This introduction establishes the tone of communion with nature and very gently touches upon the central question by acknowledging "darker musings." The poet then utters a more anguished cry:

> When thoughts
> Of the last bitter hour come like a blight
> Over thy spirit, and sad images
> Of the stern agony, and shroud, and pall,
> And breathless darkness, and the narrow house,
> Make thee to shudder, and grow sick at heart—

What *is* one to do—especially the young man already haunted by intimations of his eventual fate? Distancing himself from his conservative religious upbringing, Bryant sought the comforting answer less in scripture and theological doctrines than in nature:

> Go forth, under the open sky, and list
> To Nature's teachings, while from all around—
> Earth and her waters, and the depths of air—
> Comes a still voice. . . .

He reveals his Deistic philosophy in the acceptance of the inevitable loss of one's prized individuality, for:

> Earth, that nourished thee, shall claim
> Thy growth, to be resolved to earth again,
> And, lost each human trace, surrendering up
> Thine individual being. . . . a brother to the insensible rock. . . .

Bryant suggests there is comfort to be found in the knowledge:

> All that breathe
> Will share thy destiny . . .

And that:

> The youth in life's fresh spring, and he who goes
> In the full strength of years, matron and maid,
> The speechless babe, and the gray-headed man—
> Shall one by one be gathered to thy side,
> By those who, in their turn shall follow them.

It is the final stanza, however, that most captured the imagination of Bryant's readers and offered a vision perhaps as reassuring for its secure and elegant expression as for its substantive message:

> So live, that when thy summons comes to join
> The innumerable caravan, which moves
> To that mysterious realm, where each shall take
> His chamber in the silent halls of death,
> Thou go not, like the quarry-slave at night,
> Scourged to his dungeon, but, sustained and soothed
> By an unfaltering trust, approach thy grave

Like one who wraps the drapery of his
  couch
About him, and lies down to pleasant
  dreams.

As Lafcadio Hearn (1917) has observed, Bryant's message is "If you live well, you need not be afraid to die." Hearn wryly adds, "The lesson is good, and consoling, but it is not particularly original; and the greatest merit of the composition is the well-sounding blank verse . . . sonorous, correct, and cold. Perhaps classic verse ought to be in such cases a little cold. One must not show too much emotion, especially, in treating any vast and solemn subject" (Hearn, p. 309).

Bryant's most celebrated poem has perhaps already edged toward obscurity for a contemporary generation that, by most reports, reads few poems (especially ones that go on a bit) and that may be impatient with the classic style. Nevertheless, there yet may be readers who will find comfort in both the view of death and the stately words with which it is expressed. For death educators and counselors, "Thanatopsis" might still serve as a conversation-opener to explore death-related thoughts. And, regardless of our own particular beliefs, we might all find something to admire in the way one young person confronted the topic of death and thereby became more responsive to the perhaps less articulate expressions of those who hazard this topic today.

See also "Crossing the Bar."

—ROBERT KASTENBAUM

References

Bryant, W.C. "Thanatopsis" (1817); still reprinted in many poetry anthologies.
Hearn, L. (1917). *Life and literature.* New York: Dodd, Mead.

THANATOS (MAGAZINE)

Thanatos, founded in 1975, offers a humanistic approach to the issues of death and dying. Written with insight and compassion, the articles relate triumph and pain, provide understanding, and promote growth and healing. Created by professionals and private individuals, the magazine represents no one philosophical viewpoint. Listings of resources and workshops from across the country, as well as reviews of new publications and audiovisual materials are featured regularly. Subscribers to *Thanatos* include counselors, volunteers, nurses, teachers, clergy, students, thanatologists, libraries, funeral directors, support groups, bereaved persons, and everyday people.

Manuscripts submitted for possible publication should be typed, double spaced, with margins at least one inch all around. Two copies of the manuscript are appreciated, but there is no need to send the original. More detailed requirements are available upon request. Preference is given to material 750 to 1,500 words in length.

Thanatos prefers to publish nonfiction. Books and film reviews are welcome. Review of material can take up to two months, and publication can take as long as four months after acceptance. *Thanatos* is unable to pay authors' fees but does provide copies of the issue in which an individual's work appears.

Subscription and business correspondence should be directed to:

Thanatos
P.O. Box 6009
Tallahassee, FL 32314

—BETH P. POPPELL

TOMBS

The creation of tombs for ceremonial disposal of the dead is one of the very early marks of concerted human activity, for the awareness of death is one of the factors that distinguishes our species from animals. In one of the earliest identifiable tombs, a Paleolithic example from Western Europe, the body had been sprinkled with red ochre. Since red ochre is the color of blood, it is thought that the act was a symbolic attempt to maintain the semblance of life, perhaps in another world. The word itself derives from the Latin *tumba,* a place of burial, an excavation in earth or rock for the reception of a dead

Transi of Peter Niderwirt (died 1522), Eggenfelden, Germany. "The snakes and frogs on the later German transis, often joined by other loathsome creatures . . . served to further enhance the horror felt in the presence of death and decay, thus making the spectator more vulnerable to the moralist's admonition to good behavior." Reprinted, by permission, from Kathleen Cohen, *Metamorphosis of a Death Symbol: The Transi Tomb in the Late Middle Ages and the Renaissance,* University of California Press, #43. © 1973 by The Regents of the University of California.

body. A mound raised over the body was known as a tumulus.

Ancient Tombs and Their Significance

Tombs from ages past not only tell us much about the physical lives of a people, but they also offer important clues about their metaphysical beliefs. The all-powerful rulers of many early societies created tombs that would ensure a continuation in the next world of the activities and support they had enjoyed in this life. Skeletons of wives, concubines and attendants, even horses, were found in ancient tombs in China and Sumeria, apparently all ritually killed to accompany their lord into the next world. Such sacrifices normally accompanied the emperors of the Shang period, and even continued into later times. Yi, the Chinese Marquis of Zeng who died in 433 BC, was accompanied by a vast treasure and by the bodies of twenty-one women.

This practice was replaced by the more humane procedure of making figures of wood or clay which served as surrogates for their human and animal counterparts. The most impressive collection of such figures was prepared for the tomb of Qin Shihuangdi, the First Emperor or Qin, who died in 210 BC. A veritable army of over 7,000 life-sized ceramic figures have so far been excavated from his tomb in the Lishan necropolis near Xian. This ceramic army included warriors and horses as well as female attendants. Such elaborate concern for the dead emperor was based upon the belief that the emperor, now an attendant of the gods, would intercede for his people.

Tomb of Marguerite of Austria (died 1530). The double imagery of the deceased person as both living and dead is augmented here by angels that welcome the departed soul into heaven. Reprinted, by permission, from Kathleen Cohen, *Metamorphosis of a Death Symbol: The Transi Tomb in the Late Middle Ages and the Renaissance,* University of California Press, #75. © 1973 by The Regents of the University of California.

Tombstone of Johannes Permetter (died 1505), Ingolstadt, Germany. Reprinted, by permission, from Kathleen Cohen, *Metamorphosis of a Death Symbol: The Transi Tomb in the Late Middle Ages and the Renaissance*, University of California Press, #40. © 1973 by The Regents of the University of California.

Perhaps the most famous of the tombs of ancient rulers are the great pyramids erected at Giza by Egyptian pharaohs of the Old Kingdom. These tombs contained all that was needed to ensure the continued existence and comfort of the pharoahs in the shadowy underworld. The pharoah's survival is thought to have guaranteed the collective survival of his people, a fact that explained the elaborate procedures used to mummify his body as well as the enormous expense of creating and equipping his tomb. Although the tombs of the great pharoahs were ransacked in antiquity, we can appreciate some of the magnificence they must have contained from the objects found in the long undisturbed tomb of the minor New Kingdom pharoah, Tutankhamen.

By the time of the New Kingdom, the Egyptian practice of building elaborate tombs had spread to members of the minor nobility, who decorated their tombs with colorfully detailed frescoes. From these paintings we are able to learn much about the life of the ancient Egyptians. We see peasants at work planting and harvesting, other workers following various trades necessary to provide goods and services, and household servants performing their chores. Entertainment was not neglected either, for musicians and dancing girls were included to help while away the long hours of eternity. Chinese tombs of the Han and Tang periods contained similar paintings, and Egyptian as well as Chinese tombs often contained small ceramic figures of animals, workers, musicians, and dancers.

Tombs from many less sophisticated cultures contained food and objects such as weapons, jewelry, and ceramic vessels that could be used in the next life. These tombs ranged in shape from simple holes dug in the ground, large vases that contained the bodies, and stone cairns, to huge circular beehive tombs like those of the ancient Mycenaeans in Bronze Age Greece. Beautiful objects of gold were found in all types of tombs, from the simple graves of the ancient Celtic and Germanic peoples to those of the Peruvians and Mexicans of ancient Mesoamerica.

Greek tomb monuments of the classical period shifted from providing material objects for survival in the next life to elegiac memorials of the present life. In beautiful stone reliefs or vase paintings, men bid their wives fond farewells, mothers take leave of their children, or a family simply stands quietly together.

Different types of tombs in the same society often indicate an amalgamation of culture groups within that society, for our rituals of death are extremely conservative. The mysterious Etruscans continued to use the cremation urns utilized by many Indo-European groups, but they also used sarcophagi which entombed the entire body, a practice popular in Asia Minor from whence they are thought to have emigrated to Italy.

The tombs of the Romans reflected an even greater diversity as they amalgamated growing numbers of cultural groups into the Roman Empire. Beautifully carved funerary urns were maintained in columberia or "dove cottes," while elaborate sarcophagi were enclosed in mausoleums or buried in cemeteries that by law were outside the city walls. The sarcophagi were carved with images reflecting the variety of religions that enfolded into the Roman belief system. One victorious Roman general even had an Egyptian type pyramid constructed to mark his resting place.

Early Christian Tombs

Early Christians followed the Jewish custom of burial rather than cremation, and the earliest Christian tombs are found in the catacombs outside Rome. Holes were cut in the soft tufa of the underground passages; the body was placed inside, and the tomb was either bricked up or closed with a marble slab. Symbols expressing the Christian hope of resurrection—anchors, dolphins, fish—were carved or painted on the slabs, and small chapels were included in the catacombs where services for the dead and the agape feast, a funeral meal, could be held.

When Christianity was recognized as the official religion of the Roman Empire, Christian tombs became more elaborate. The sarcophagi created for the Emperor Constantine and his family were carved of porphyry, the royal purple stone from Egypt, and were decorated with representations of grapes and their harvesting and crushing. These images combined the old Dionysiac beliefs of renewal through the death and dismemberment of the god of wine with Christian beliefs in the redeeming blood and body of Christ made manifest in the wine and bread of the Eucharist.

Christian sarcophagi of the fourth and fifth centuries contained images which gave hope of salvation: Daniel in the lion's den, Jonah and the whale, Suzanna and the elders, the three children in the fiery frunace, and images that echoed the popular prayer: "Oh Lord, deliver us as you delivered Daniel from the lion's den, Jonah from the belly of the whale . . ." etc.

The quality of tombs produced in Europe from the fifth through the eleventh centuries declined as society was rocked by the upheavals of the early Medieval period. By the twelfth century, however, greater polical stability and growing wealth produced more elaborate tombs. The most popular type, known as the gisant, was to dominate sepulchral imagery into the Renaissance. A gisant is a recumbant figure of the deceased that has been dressed in everyday or sacerdotal garments and represented as being alive, whether awake or asleep. Some writers use this term to refer to any recumbent sepulchral figure. On these tombs the deceased was depicted recumbent on top of his or her sacophagus, calm, hands folded in prayer, and eyes open, existing in hope and certainty of salvation. Often kneeling angels beside the pillow served both as pages and to welcome the deceased into heaven. Heraldic animals lay at the feet: often a lion for man, symbolizing strength, and a small dog for a woman, symbolizing fidelity. The deceased were most often portrayed at the age of 33, for since this was the age of Christ's death, it was considered to be the appropriate age for all Christian souls to be resurrected.

The Transi Image

In the later Middle Ages a very different type of image appeared, in which the deceased was depicted as a naked corpse, often rotting and devoured by worms. Many of these images reflected the memento mori theme that had become popular after the images of the Black Death. These tombs contain inscriptions warning the spectator to think on death: "I was like you, and you will be like me, food for worms." The inscriptions went on to implore the spectator to "pray for me," for it was believed that the prayers of the living could help the dead through their fearful ordeal, and even help to get them into paradise.

Several of these so-called transi images seem to come to life and to stand up, taking all their rotting flesh and worms with them. A transi is a representation of the deceased as a corpse, whether nude or wrapped in a shroud. The most outstanding is the sixteenth-century tomb of Rene of Chalons in Bar-le-Duc, France. The key to the meaning of this striking and macabre image lies in the upraised arm of the figurine, which originally held a representation of Rene's heart. Rene's corpse holds his heart aloft, offering it to God with a gesture of devotion, and expressing his confidence in the resurrection of the dead: "And though after my skin, worms destroy this body, yet in my flesh shall I see God" (Job 19:26). The gestures of the figure have been interpreted as symbolizing the three theological virtues: faith, hope, and charity. The eyes turned upward toward heaven mean "I believe"; the right hand on the breast signifies "I hope"; and the heart elevated toward God means "I love."

Tombs of Beauty and Magnificence

Although "transi" tombs were somewhat popular in England and northern Europe, they did not find favor with the Italians, who preferred idealized images. The most famous Italian tomb is the one constructed in the early sixteenth century by Michelangelo in San Lorenzo, Florence, for Giuliano and Lorenzo de'Medici. In this magnificent funerary chapel the two brothers are depicted in classical armour, seated on either side of the chapel and flanked by allegorical figures. The personalities of the two men—Giuliano an active doer and Lorenzo a passive thinker—are depicted in their respective poses. The evocation of classical heroes and the emphasis on human personality rather than the expression of hope for salvation demonstrates the spiritual shift from the Middle Ages to the Renaissance. The older tradition was not totally lost, however, for a beautiful representation of the favored intercessor, the Virgin Mary, is enthroned with her divine child at the end of the chapel that contains the tombs.

One of the most beautiful funerary foundations in the world is the Taj Mahal, which was built in Agra, India, by the Mogul Emperor Shah Jehan to commemorate his beloved wife, Muntaz. Her tomb is the focal point of an exquisite group of white marble buildings which include a magnificent entrance gate and a mosque in addition to the building that houses the tomb itself. This impressive structure is complemented by extensive gardens and reflecting pools. Inlaid with delicate floral patterns in semiprecious stones, the exquisitely proportioned buildings along with their gardens embody the Islamic image of paradise as a garden.

The exuberant Baroque spirit of Europe's seventeenth century Counter Reformation is best illustrated by Bernini's magnificent tomb of Pope Alexander VII in St. Peter's Cathedral. Placed above a doorway, the figures were designed to emphasize both spatial illusionism and emotional power. Pope Alexander is flanked by allegorical figures who symbolize the virtues of his pontificate. However, the figure of a skeleton creeps out from under a magnificent drapery, holding his hourglass aloft, symbolizing the fact that time brings death, even to the most powerful.

Changing Images in More Recent Times

The figure of fleeting time, symbolized by the skeleton with his hourglass or sickle, became a popular addition to sepulchral imagery in the eighteenth century, a motif often reduced to a skull with wings. As such, it was engraved on many early American tombstones, as well as others found all over Europe.

People of the nineteenth century preferred more sentimental images for their tombs, often a mourning or weeping angel. The same idea was expressed in more restrained form by Canova and other neoclassic sculptors. The nineteenth century also saw the proliferation of commemorative sepulchral monuments, which praised actions of famous warriors, statesmen, and artists.

Twentieth-century tombs are, for the most part, marked by simple plaques or crosses, but a few have risen to the symbolic importance of earlier monuments. Tombs dedicated to unknown soldiers, often marked by eternal flames, embody the gratitude of modern nations to the men and women who have given their lives in twentieth-century wars. Lenin's tomb perhaps comes the closest of any modern monument to the symbolic power of tombs of early rulers. The great stone structure in Red Square is the goal of pilgrimage for millions of Russians who stand long hours in line to solemnly file past his body. Lenin's carefully embalmed corpse, like those of the pharaohs of ancient Egypt, seems to represent the collective life of his people.

See also (The) Black Death; Cemeteries; Dance of Death (*Danse Macabre*); Epitaph; Funerals; *Memento Mori*; Psychopomp; Survival Beliefs and Practices: Islamic.

—KATHLEEN COHEN

References

Carter, H. (1972). *The tomb of Tutankhamen.* New York: E.P. Dutton.

Cohen, K. (1973). *Metamorphosis of a death symbol.* Berkeley, CA: University of California Press.

Hearn, M.K. (1979). "An ancient Chinese army rises from underground sentinel duty." *Smithsonian,* November: 38–51.

Jacob, H. (1954). *Idealism and realism: A study of sepulchral symbolism.* Leiden: E.J. Brill.

Los Angeles County Museum of Art (1987). *The quest for eternity: Chinese ceramic sculptures from the People's Republic of China.*

Panofsky, E. (n.d., c.1970). *Tomb sculpture: Its changing aspects from ancient Egypt to Bernini.* New York: Harry Abrams.

TRAJECTORIES OF DYING

Dying occurs over a period of time. This obvious fact has many significant implications for dying people, their family, friends, and caregivers. Although the time course of dying has been observed and discussed by numerous clinicians and researchers, it remained for Barney G. Glaser and Anselm L. Strauss (1968) to develop a systematic framework for analysis and interpretation. These sociologists, also notable for their contribution to the study of awareness of dying (1965; See **Awareness of Dying**), observed patient, family, and staff behavior in a variety of institutional settings. Their primary fieldwork was conducted in six hospitals of various types in the San Francisco Bay area, as well as by behavior samplings in Italy, Greece, and Scotland. As Glaser and Strauss (1968, p. xi) describe their methodology:

> the reader who is unacquainted with this style of field need only imagine the sociologist moving rather freely within each medical service, having announced to the personnel his intention of "studying terminal patients and what happens around them." He trails personnel around the service, watching them at work, sometimes questioning them about details. He sits at the nursing station. He listens to conversations. Occa-

sionally he queries the staff members, either about events he has seen or about events someone has described to him. Sometimes he interviews personnel at considerable length, announcing an "interview," perhaps even using a tape recorder. He sits in on staff meetings. He follows, day by day, the progress of various patients, observing staff interactions with them and conversation about them. He talks with patients, telling them only that he is "studying the hospital." His field work takes place during the day, evening, and night; it may last from ten minutes to many hours.

They found that degree of certainty as well as time were keys to understanding the events and interactions that occur throughout the dying process. A patient may be viewed as certain to die, very likely to die, or unlikely to die. Hospital staff tend to think, feel, and act differently, depending upon how they have classified each patient with respect to their possible death. Basically, the doctors and nurses responsible for a patient's care do not like surprises; they want to prepare themselves mentally and emotionally for the most probable course of events. This means that in a particular instance the hospital staff will either have its expectations confirmed or invalidated by what happens. The certainty dimension is closely interwoven with the particular time course or "trajectory" followed by a dying patient. A particular patient will be regarded as fitting into one of the following categories:

1. Certain death at a known time
2. Certain death at an unknown time
3. Uncertain death but a known time when the certainty will be established
4. Uncertain death and an unknown time when the question will be resolved

Types of Terminal Trajectory

Among the several types of terminal or dying trajectories observed by Glaser and Strauss, the following two are of particular importance.

The Lingering Trajectory. A patient's life is fading slowly, gradually, and inevitably. The staff is most likely to provide custodial services rather than aggressive, all-out treatment. Dramatic attempted "deathbed rescue" scenes are rare. Physicians and nurses are apt to believe that such efforts would not be successful in prolonging what might be called "quality life." Often involved is the further belief that the dying person is ready for the end, having suffered through a long, progressive loss of function and no longer finds much satisfaction in life. This type of trajectory is often observed in geriatric units. Wherever it takes place, the patient dying with a lingering trajectory usually has little control over what happens. Having become accustomed to the downhill process, family members are likely to leave everything to the discretion of the medical staff. The relatively long time involved can give the dying person ample opportunity to settle his or her own state of mind and to make whatever decisions that remain (revising a will, contacting a distant relative). It is also common for emotional bonds to form between the person dying on a lingering trajectory and those who have been providing care. A nurse in a geriatric facility, for example, may feel a personal loss and sorrow because she has come to know and like a person who is now on his deathbed; on the other hand, she has known of his terminal trajectory for a long time and never expected any other kind of ending. Lingering trajectories are becoming ever more common in the United States and other nations where an increasing number of people are living to advanced ages where death will result from deteriorative conditions acting over a period of time.

The Expected Quick Trajectory. This is the acute or emergency situation in which life or death hang in the immediate balance. Time is of the essence in responding to life-threatening conditions. All the human and technological resources of a modern medical center may be called upon in a rescue effort (even if the odds are much against success). There are marked differences in the kinds of situation that can arise in the expected quick trajectory. It might be judged, for example, that the patient will certainly die in a matter of minutes unless effective treatment begins at once. However, if treatment is successful, the person might return to normal life. By contrast, another patient may seem to be in stable condition at the moment, but the staff realizes that a crisis could develop at any time. There must be constant vigilance

which, of course, contributes to tension and strain. In still other circumstances, the staff may be convinced that there is nothing effective that can be done; this patient will die soon, no matter what.

There is also an unexpected quick trajectory. One of the major problems that can be encountered in this type of situation is the unpleasant task of informing family members that a person who may have been in good health a few hours before is now close to death. Personnel coping with accident victims in an emergency room or trauma center often find themselves with this difficult challenge.

Cautions and Guidelines

The trajectories of dying described by Glaser and Strauss deserve serious consideration by all who work in medical settings, as well as by those who befriend, assist, and counsel family members. Their work is perhaps most useful in making us more sensitive to the expectations made by professional caregivers and family members regarding the probability of death and the length of the dying process. Strauss and Glaser (1970) have also offered a detailed case history of a person experiencing a dying trajectory that might be found useful in understanding this process. Other examples of people trying to cope with uncertainty, time course, and other aspects of the dying process are provided by Munley (1983), and Paulay (1980). Nash (1977) reveals how the sense of dignity of dying patients might be preserved through their ordeal if health care personnel are more sensitive to their needs.

Hospital personnel form self-protective tactics in relating to the dying person. In some situations it may appear that they are acting more to protect their own emotions than to provide optimal comfort for and communication with the patient. One might remember, however, that some of these problems arise not so much from the individual problems of the staff members as from pressures generated in the complex bureaucratic structures of our overall health care system. Staff as well as patients can fall victim to a highly regulated, cost-sensitive bureaucracy. As Glaser and Strauss have observed, both staff and patients may be caught up in an ill-advised "crisis" treatment onslaught, and each may inadvertently cause the other emotional anguish because of unrealistic expectations regarding certainty, time course, and other matters.

A special caution is often appropriate where geriatric patients are involved. There is a strong bias in our society to the effect that elderly men and women are ready for death and that their lives no longer mean very much to them. Flaws in this assumption have been pointed out by a number of observers (e.g., Gadow, 1987; Kastenbaum, 1987), yet there is still an inclination to accept the lingering trajectory of a geriatric patient as a phenomenon that cannot and should not be disturbed by therapeutic interventions. If our health care system is sometimes too aggressive and frantic in attempting to rescue those in imminent danger of death, it is also sometimes too passive and "philosophical" in withholding effective care from the older patient.

See also Awareness of Dying; Deathbed Scenes; Dying.

—ROBERT KASTENBAUM

References

Gadow, S.A. (1987). "Death and age: A natural connection?" *Generations,* Spring: 15–18.

Glaser, B.G. & Strauss, A.L. (1965). *Awareness of dying.* Chicago: Aldine.

Glaser, B.G. & Strauss, A.L. (1968). *Time for dying.* Chicago: Aldine.

Kastenbaum, R. (1987). "When a long life ends: The search for meaning." *Generations,* Spring: 9–13.

Munley, A. (1983). *The hospice alternative.* New York: Basic Books

Nash, M.L. (1977). "Dignity of person in the final phase of life—an exploratory study." *Omega, Journal of Death and Dying, 8:* 71–80.

Paulay, D. (1980). "Slow death: One survivor's experience." In R.A. Kalish (Ed.) *Death, dying, transcendence.* Farmingdale, NY: Baywood, pp. 37–42.

Strauss, A.L. & Glaser, B.G. (1970). *Anguish.* Mill Valley, CA: The Sociology Press.

TUONELA

In the ancient Finnish folklore known as the Kalevala, Tuonela was the Domain of Death. The Kalevala includes a variety of images of beliefs from different historical periods. Originally, the Finnish word "Tuonela" presumably meant only the resting place of a single dead person, a covered grave. This concept is illustrated by the expression, "'house of Tuoni'' (Death) in the song, "Rock the Child to Tuonela." Here as in other lullabies that feature the same theme, the grave is described as a cosy and gentle place in which a small child can rest comfortably. The ancient origins of the song are reflected in the building materials of the grave which are featured in different versions of the lyrics. The roof of the house is often described as made of turf, the floor of sand, the back wall of deer bones, the side walls of the bones of crickets, and the front wall of apple tree wood. This original concept of the house of Tuoni later expanded to encompass the whole graveyard as the dwelling place of the dead.

In the Kalevala these concepts are related to the name Pohjola, or North Farm. The abode of the dead (Manala), or Death's Domain, has received features from Christianity, particularly the emphasis that in death people have to suffer for the bad deeds they committed during their lives.

Death's Domain is surrounded by Death's River. The dead are transported across the river by Death's Maiden at the darkest moment of the night. It was believed that the edge of the earth, facing a steep precipice, was situated at the remotest corner of North Farm, Death's River flowing below. This concept of a river separating the living from the dead may have been borrowed from Graeco-Roman mythology which, in turn, had found the concept in Egyptian and Babylonian beliefs. The journey to Death's Domain was long and frightening. Finnish laments include several descriptions of the difficult road to Death's Domain, from which remote abode "few have returned."

Death's Domain has inspired numerous Finnish artists. In his illustrations for the Kalevala, Akseli Gallen-Kallela, a well-known Finnish painter, included works representing Death's Domain, such as "Lemminkainen's Mother." Lemminkainen was a warrior whose shattered body was found in the River of Death by his mother, who reassembled the fragments and restored him to life. The composer Jean Sibelius and the writer Aleksis Kivi are among other Finnish artists who have described Death's Domain in their works.

See also Charon; Hades; Lullabies of Death; Styx.

—KALLE ACHTÉ

References

Haavio, M. (1952). *Vainamoinen—eternal sage.* Helsinki: FF Communications, No. 144.

Kemppinen, K. (1967). *Haudantakainen elama karjalaisen muinaisuson ja vertailevan uskontotieteen valossa.* Helsinki: Karjalan tutkimusseuran Julkasuja 1.

Kuusi, A-L. (1976). "Finnish mythology." In P. Hajdu (Ed.) *Ancient cultures of the Uralian peoples.* Budapest: Corvina Press, pp. 243–63.

U

UNIFORM ANATOMICAL ACT

This Act provides the basis for decisions and procedures involved in bequeathing bodies or body parts upon death. The Uniform Anatomical Gift Act (UAGA) was approved by the National Conference of Commissioners on Uniform State Laws in 1968. This Act is now in effect in every state of the United States and in Puerto Rico, although slight variations exist. The Canadian provinces of Alberta, British Columbia, Newfoundland, Nova Scotia, and Quebec adopted a similar measure known as the Model Human Tissue Act in 1976. Comparable laws are also in effect in a number of other nations as well.

Those who wish to make an anatomical donation upon their own death can do so by completing a Uniform Donor Card or specifying this intention in a will or other suitable document. The Uniform Donor Card is made available in some states as an option to all licensed drivers, and can be obtained from other sources as well, such as health departments.

The most important features of the UAGA are the following:

1. The Act authorizes the gift of all or part of a human body after death for specified purposes. The gift takes effect upon death.
2. The donor must be a person 18 years of age or older and of sound mind.
3. Close relatives may give all or part of the decedent's body for specified purposes if the decedent did not authorize an anatomical gift but also did not express disapproval of such a gift

being made. The Act establishes a priority of kinship for decision-making, with a surviving spouse having the first rights, followed by adult child, parent, adult sibling, and guardian.
4. Authorization to make an anatomical gift includes the right of medical specialists to determine if the gift is suitable for the intended purposes.
5. The Act specifies the classes of organizations and persons who may accept anatomical gifts, and the purposes for which these may be used. Accredited medical and dental schools, for example, may be donees, and purposes can include therapy, transplantion, education, or research. The will, donor card, or other document can either specify the donee or leave this decision open.
6. The person who has completed a donor card or other document can revoke or amend this agreement at any time. In the case of a donor card, this can be done simply by destroying it, since there usually is no other copy.
7. The donee has the right to accept or reject the gift.
8. The state continues to exercise its rights and regulations with respect to autopsies.

There are a number of sensitive issues associated with the Uniform Anatomical Gift Act. The timing of death, for example, may be a critical factor in determining whether or not an acceptable anatomical gift can be made. In turn, the timing of death may depend on both the nature of the life support systems that are being utilized, the definition and criteria of death, and the availability of medical personnel to determine and certify death. There are also many emotional facets. Family members may differ among themselves in their attitudes toward anatomical gifts, some preferring traditional funeral and burial procedures, others favoring organ donations. Clear and open communication regarding dying, death, and final arrangements can help to reduce anxieties and confusion when a crisis situation arises.

For more information contact:

National Transplant Information Center
135 Flower Hill Road
Huntington, NY 11743

See also Death Certificate; Funerals.

—ROBERT KASTENBAUM

References

National Conference of Commissioners on Uniform State Laws (1968). *Uniform Anatomical Gift Act.*

Rosenfeld, A. (1969). *The second genesis: The coming control of life.* Englewood Cliffs, NJ: Prentice-Hall.

V

VAMPIRE

The most infamous of vampires—Count Dracula—first saw the light of day (not an altogether pleasant prospect for his species) in 1897. Bram Stoker's novel (and play) has contributed a compelling and enduring image to the public imagination. Stoker, described by one of his biographers as "a genial, red-bearded giant" (Ludlam, 1962, p. 8), wrote a number of other works of fiction, including some with enterprising and novel elements (such as a nineteenth-century prophesy of an aerial bombing attack, and a deadly snake lady). As Wolf (1975) notes in his introduction to his invaluable annotated version of *Dracula*, these productions were rather astonishing, coming from the pen of a man whose first book was entitled *The Duties of Clerks of Petty Sessions in Ireland.*

Count Dracula

The origin of Count Dracula in Stoker's mind owed something to stories his mother had told him about a cholera epidemic that had exposed many to the sight of corpses, but also to his fascination with Sheridan Le Fanu's story, "Carmilla," which featured a female vampire. Another inspiration came from conversations with a professor of oriental languages from the University of Budapest (Glut, 1975). Arminius Vambery regaled Stoker with accounts of "the un-dead." According to folk belief in Transylvania and other parts of the world, there were mysterious and merciless creatures, neither alive nor dead,

who preyed on the blood of human victims. (Vambery became the original for the vampire expert in *Dracula,* Dr. Van Helsing.) Finally (but not surprisingly, considering his readings and conversations), Stoker had a nightmare in which he encountered not an ordinary vampire, but a veritable lord of the undead. He now had his own special monster to offer a public fond of chilling horrors, and enriched this creation by touring Transylvania and evoking the more desolate and mysterious reaches of its landscape.

As a book, *Dracula* is a prime example of the Gothic romance and displays ample characteristics of the genre. The unique and horrifying nature of Count Dracula makes its effect against the background of proper Victorian types: a virginal young lady, her "brave lad," a rational detective in the guise of a professor, etc. It is probable that many later representatives of the literary vampire tradition often do not inspire the same ecstasy of terror because they lack the context of purity and naivete against which Dracula's evil so tellingly reveals itself.

By now, the habits of Dracula are very well known and have been adopted by almost all subsequent vampires. He has superhuman physical and mental powers, including extraordinary strength, the ability to transform himself into an airborne bat, and the mind-influencing talent of a master hypnotist. A mere human cannot match Dracula when he is in possession of such powers. The vampire's most shocking behavior, of course, is his predatory habit. Ruled by blood-lust, Count Dracula can assuage his hunger only by feeding upon the blood of live prey, preferably humans, and, most preferably, beautiful young women. These infamous attacks produce a horror that goes well beyond the moment—the victims may themselves turn into vampires who, in turn, will also seek human prey. However, even the lord of the undead has his own limits and perils. He dare not remain abroad when daylight breaks but must lodge himself securely in his coffin. There he is a weak and helpless creature until the dark of night again renews his strength and his terrible hunger.

But the vampire's claim on our fantasy life goes well beyond these obvious characteristics. Count Dracula also embodies a potent erotic force. There is no question but that a thinly disguised (and therefore even more powerful) sexual agenda is expressed by this tall, dark (and, when he chooses, handsome) stranger. To a Victorian audience unused to explicit sexual scenes in books and plays, Dracula and his maiden victims presented highly charged sensuous encounters.

The intimate connection between sexuality and death is perhaps the most distinctive feature of the stories told of Count Dracula and other vampires. The sharp distinction that Western societies usually make between "alive" and "dead" is challenged by the vampire's special status. Eroticism is also treated as a phenomenon that goes well beyond the traditional act of sexual relations. With their marauding undead and passionate violence, the vampire stories challenge the comforting assumption that sex and death can be kept in separate, airtight compartments. The unique mixture of Victorian moral sentiment and growing awareness of science helped to create this borderline image of a deadly sensuality and a sensuous death.

Blood became the most significant link among life/sex/death phenomena ("Blood is the life": Deuteronomy 12:33). In a sense, the attack of the vampire was "sexier than sex" at the same time that it represented an unnatural claim of the Undead upon the living. It is worth recalling that this was an era during which blood transfusions were being developed, autopsies pursued with renewed interest, and the sciences displayed an alarming interest in matters of life, death, sexuality, and reproduction that had formerly been essentially the province of custom and reli-

gion. (Dr. Frankenstein and his monster were another literary product of this era.)

Dracula and his works presented an especially unsettling dilemma that seems to prefigure an ethical and emotional problem of the present day. What are we to do if one of our own loved ones has entered that twilight zone between life and death? A scene from Dracula:

> "Brave lad! A moment's courage, and it's done. This stake must be driven through her. . . . Take this stake in your left hand, ready to place the point over the heart, and the hammer in your right. Then when we begin our prayer for the dead . . . strike in God's name, that so all may be well with the dead that we love, and that the Un-Dead pass away. . . . " The Thing in the coffin writhed; and a hideous, blood-curdling screech came from the opened red lips. The body shook and quivered and twisted in wild contortions. . . . Finally it lay still . . . There, in the coffin lay no longer the foul Thing that we had so dreaded. . . . but Lucy as we had seen her in her life, with her face of unequalled sweetness and purity (Stoker, in Wolf, 1975, p. 194).

The Vampire Tradition

Vampirelike creatures were already well established in folktales and mythology long before Count Dracula stalked his first victim. The salience of blood has accompanied vampire stories since ancient times. "The notion behind vampirism traces way back in time—to man the hunter, who discovered that when blood flowed out of the wounded beast or a fellow human, life, too, drained away. Blood was the source of vitality! Thus men sometimes smeared themselves with blood and sometimes drank it. The idea of drinking blood to renew vitality became transferred from the living to the dead, and thereupon the vampire entered history" (McNally & Florescu, 1972, p. 144). Ancient tales from many cultures have described creatures of the vampire type whose basic characteristics are similar to those of the modern era (Summers, 1928). Although there is an obvious connection between the vampire of mythology and the vampire bat (*Desmodus rotundus*), this does not provide an adequate explanatory source, as tales of the blood-lusting Undead have often developed in cultures that did not have experience with the humble *D. rotundus*.

Attention has been given to vampire lore in the history of the Slavic peoples (Perkowski, 1976). Not only is there a rich historical tradition of vampire tales, but some still believe in the reality of the vampire menace today. Belief in vampires tends to be embedded in an overall world view in which creatures can transform themselves from one shape to another (the werewolf being another example). Vampires usually are recruited from those who in their earthly life had been sorcerers, murderers, or otherwise unpleasant people and whose bodies now were possessed by an unclean spirit. There are also accidental ways of becoming a vampire, as when an unclean shadow falls upon somebody, or even if a dog or cat leaps over a person. The Slavic vampire is perhaps even more difficult to guard against than the specifically Dracula type, since it can "assume every sort of shape" (Machal, 1976, p. 25). Dr. Van Helsing would approve of the Slavic custom for destroying vampires, which is essentially the staking-through-the-heart-of-corpse technique he recommended in *Dracula*.

Medieval religion did much to strengthen the vampire's reputation. As Eaves (1976, p. 146) notes, "The incubi and succubi of mediavealists, and going still further back, the entities under different names, differ very little from the Vampire. . . ." Yeomans (1986) goes even further in concluding that the vampire gained its place in our imagination largely through the Church's insistence that good and evil be strictly separated, with a strong tendency to personify both. In Yeomans's psychohistorical interpretation, the vampire has become a creature who dwells in our imagination because we can neither dismiss the unacceptable or "evil" side of our nature nor confront and integrate it as part of our total personality.

One of the most interesting reexaminations of the vampire tradition has been provided by scholars Raymond T. McNally and Radu Florescu (1972). They offer an actual historical personage as the figure from whom Count Dracula was derived (it is possible that Stoker knew of this man). Vlad Tepes (1431–1476) was a nobleman of the Transylvania region who richly earned his nickname, "Dracul" or "Dracula," which mean both "devil" and "dragon." He is also known to history as "Vlad the Impaler" for his favorite way of torturing and killing those who stood in his way or aroused his volatile rage. It is obvious that Vlad Tepes was a notably violent man in an age that was filled with strife, ambition, and treachery. He differed from other warlike princes in the extent of his depradations, his cunning, and his sheer enjoyment of killing. However, the historical Dracula was never reported to have had those characteristics that are peculiar to the vampire—but he did live in a real castle and rule a superstitious peasantry in just the kind of landscape that we would expect to find in a vampire film.

The Vampire Today (or Tonight)

The vampire has proven to be a popular and profitable "star" in films. Glut (1975) discusses many of these films, but even more have appeared in recent years and the genre does not seem to have quite exhausted itself yet. There is often a parody aspect about the vampire character today (as, for example, in the comedy film, *Love at First Bite*). Occasional attempts are still made to present the essence of the vampire in a serious light but with a contemporary sensitivity and style (as in the David Bowie film, *The Hunger*). Some films, like *The Hunger* draw upon ancient mythology and traditions in an innovative way, while many others are no more than routine copies of earlier versions.

Among recent books, attention should be given to the vampire trilogy by A. Rice. *Interview with the Vampire* (1976), *The Vampire Lestat* (1985), and *Queen of the Damned* (1988) are highly readable and absorbing stories that are connected with our own times. They are perhaps unique in offering the vampire's own perspective, including his sorrows, joys, fears, and regrets. Furthermore, there is a persistent philosophical dimension that will interest many who have a serious interest in the meaning of life and death. There is, for example, the question of what "life" (or, at least, existence) can mean when one does not have one's own death to fear or welcome. One of the most interesting psychosociological aspects (especially in *The Vampire Lestat*) is the observation that the vampire may be losing its status as completely evil and alien. As a reawakened vampire learns about life in the 1980s, he discovers that the decline of sexual repression and other forces that made Evil so fascinating in the past has resulted in the vampire becoming not quite so alien and alarming in the modern day.

Another possible contemporary link with the vampire tradition is the fact that the worldwide AIDS epidemic may be reviving many old unconscious fears, especially those involving blood and "unsafe" ways of dying (Kastenbaum, 1988). In other words, the vampire image may now have taken the all too palpable form of an unholy, sex-related, blood-stealing catastrophe.

See also Acquired Immune Deficiency Syndrome (AIDS); Autopsy; Personifications of Death.

—ROBERT KASTENBAUM

References

Eaves, O.A. (1976). "Modern vampirism: Its dangers, and how to avoid them." In J.L. Perkowski (Ed.) *Vampires of the Slavs.* Cambridge, MA: Slavica Publishers, pp. 140–55.

Glut, D.F. (1975). *The Dracula book.* Metuchen, NJ: Scarecrow Press.

Kastenbaum, R. (1988). "Safe death in the postmodern world." In G. Gilmore (Ed.) *Safer death.* New York: Plenum.

Ludlam, H. (1962). *The Life Study of Bram Stoker.* London: H. Foulsham & Co.

Machal, J. (1976). "Slavic mythology." In J.L. Perkowski (Ed.) *Vampires of the Slavs.* Cambridge, MA: Slavica Publishers, pp. 19–75.

McNally, R.T. & Florescu, R. (1972). *In search of Dracula.* Greenwich, CT: New York Graphic Society.

Perkowski, J.L. (Ed.) (1976). *Vampires of the Slavs.* Cambridge, MA: Slavica Publishers.

Rice, A. (1976). *Interview with the vampire.* New York: Random House.

Rice, A. (1985). *The vampire Lestat.* New York: Alfred A. Knopf.

Rice. A. (1988). *Queen of the damned.* New York: Alfred A. Knopf.

Summers. M. (1928). *The vampire and his kith and kin.* New York: E.P. Dutton.

Wolf, L. (1975). *The annotated Dracula.* New York: Carlson N. Potter.

Yeomans, P.A. (1986). "The vampire as a psychological metaphor." Unpublished Master's Thesis, Antioch University, Antioch, OH.

Z

ZOMBIE

The zombie has become such a stock figure of late-late night horror movies that both its ancient roots and its real-life contemporary manifestations have been somewhat neglected. The typical Hollywood version is an entranced, heavy-footed, walking corpse who has risen from the grave to behave rather nastily, often at a master's bidding. The makeup department has often provided the zombie with a grotesque combination of features signifying decomposition and decay as well as remnants of human character.

A Symbol of Renewal

Perhaps the zombie deserves more dignity. He, she, or it is, after all, an embodiment of one of the most ancient human aspirations—rejuvenation. The zombie is connected with the rejuvenation fantasy through the symbol of the serpent.

The snake as a symbol of rebirth following death is an ancient, yet ever-present conception which can be traced through endless patterns of sculpture, painting, verse, and the mythos of gods, demigods, or heroic mortals. This is so because during its yearly period of hibernation the snake sheds its skin and reappears as if renewed. The wisdom of the serpent, which is suggested by its watchful lidless eye, lies essentially in mankind's having projected into this lowly creature his own secret wish to obtain from the earth a knowledge he cannot find in waking daylight con-

sciousness alone (Henderson & Oakes, 1963, pp. 39–40).

This symbolism has been widespread, if not universal, through the centuries. Some commentators have even suggested that the serpent in the Garden of Eden was not really the personification of evil, but, rather, a long-recognized representation of fertility and renewal whose reputation was later impugned by moralistic interpretations of Genesis. As one particular expression of this common symbolism, the zombie was associated with a West African python cult. The term itself apparently referred primarily to the process by which the dead could become reanimated through a secret power. Later, the word was also applied to the person who received this power. The zombie tradition spread to other parts of the world, notably Haiti, where it has remained part of voodoo ritual.

It is obvious that the now-familiar image of the zombie as a dismal and perhaps menacing creature has little relationship to the conception of life reconstituting itself from death and having a new opportunity for joyous, vigorous, and spontaneous expression. How the exciting prospect of renewed life turned into the sodden and fearful zombie is a question to which no adequate answers have been proposed.

The Making of a Zombie

Not surprisingly, there has been considerable skepticism regarding the existence of "real zombies"—dead people restored to life through some process unknown to all but the masters of voodoo. However, an unusual recent investigation by an American scientist has led to important new information. In *The Serpent and the Rainbow* (1985), Wade Davis reports not only on his ethnobotanical inquiry into the process of making a zombie, but also his personal experiences with what he calls the voudon society. His book will fascinate many readers for its story of personal adventuring as well as for the discoveries that finally came his way. Davis (1988) has since published a more scholarly report on his work.

Although there was a specific "secret" to be found, Davis emphasizes repeatedly that the meaning and making of a zombie cannot be understood without appreciating the entire culture of the voudon society. Belief systems and expectations play a very significant role in the creation of a zombie and its closely related phenomenon, "voodoo death" (the difficult-to-explain death of a person who expects to die because of certain rituals and suggestions). Davis also points out that, although the details differ, suggestibility and belief systems have affected health, illness, and vulnerability to death in mainstream Western societies as well as the (to us) exotic world of voodoo/voudon.

One almost spoils Davis's absorbing story by simply reporting his main findings. His books will still be instructive and interesting, however, after one learns that he discovered the specific pharmacological agents involved in creating the zombie effect. The chemical known as tetrodotoxin is one of the most powerful known poisons. This lethal substance can also be employed to produce a state of profound numbing and paralysis if it is administered by a very knowledgeable voodoo practitioner in just the right way. The tetrodotoxin used in the making of zombies is derived from the skin of two species of the puffer fish, although it can come from other sources as well. Tetrodotoxin would never be given by mouth, for this would produce certain death within a few minutes. Instead, powder containing this chemical would be very lightly applied to the skin. The resultant state would be one that closely resembles death, what has been called thanatomimesis (Kastenbaum & Aisenberg, 1972). Critics have pointed out that Davis

himself never saw a zombie, nor have his findings conclusively proven that tetrodoxin is the specific chemical agent that produces the zombie condition (Kemp, 1988). Davis acknowledges these limitations, but holds that the tetrodoxin hypothesis is consistent with the available information.

The zombie, then, seems to be a person who has been placed into a thanatomimetic state in which there is no apparent responsiveness to stimulation. The victim may then be treated as though a corpse, given a funeral service, and buried. Within a short time, if all goes according to plan, the numbed victim will be removed from the grave and restored to functioning through a combination of physical and social-religious procedures. Both the establishment of the zombie state and its subsequent reversal are hazardous procedures that can go awry. For religious as well as pragmatic reasons, the process of creating a zombie is taken very seriously and is far from an everyday occurrence.

This brief account does not do justice to the intricacies of the process, especially the social, religious, and even political factors involved. Although current research indicates that the making of a zombie does not involve the reanimation of a corpse (but rather the restoration of a person in the grips of an inhibitory toxic drug), it is also clear that the zombie is not entirely the creation of scriptwriters.

See also Personifications of Death; Necromancy; Vampire.

—ROBERT KASTENBAUM

References

Davis, W. (1985). *The serpent and the rainbow.* New York: Warner Books.

Davis, W. (1988). *Passage of darkness: The ethnobiology of the Haitian Zombie.* Durham, NC: University of North Carolina Press.

Henderson, J.L. & Oakes, M. (1963). *The wisdom of the serpent.* New York: Collier Books.

Kastenbaum, R. & Aisenberg, R.B. (1972). *The psychology of death.* New York: Springer.

Kemp, M. (1988). "Chemistry of voodoo." *Discover,* January: 26–28.

Index

ROBERT KASTENBAUM, Ph.D.

Robert Kastenbaum is Professor of Gerontology at Arizona State University. He has served as president of the American Association of Suicidology and chair of the Behavioral and Social Sciences Section of the Gerontological Society of America. Founder-editor of *Omega, Journal of Death and Dying,* and the *International Journal of Aging and Human Development,* Dr. Kastenbaum has also served as director of a geriatric hospital, consultant to the National Hospice Study, and clinical psychologist. His books include *Death, Society, and Human Experience; The Psychology of Death* (with Ruth B. Aisenberg); and *Alcohol and Old Age* (with Brian L. Mishara). He has published many scientific papers on such topics as time perspective, creativity, lifespan development, aging, dying, death, grief, and suicide. Current research interests include deathbed scenes and creativity throughout the lifespan. His four-part docudrama, *Youth's the Tune, Age the Song,* has been produced for National Public Radio.

BEATRICE KASTENBAUM, M.S.N., R.N.

Beatrice Kastenbaum is Faculty Associate in the College of Nursing at Arizona State University. She was co-founder of Hospice at Home in Wayland, Massachusetts. In addition to spending much of her career teaching nursing students, she was the first clinical coordinator of the oncology unit at Boston University Hospital. Her current interests include the nursing care of dying patients, with special emphasis on the needs of people with cancer and AIDS.